Mastering Perl for Bioinformatics

Other resources from O'Reilly

Related titles

Beginning Perl for Bioinformatics

Developing Bioinformatics Computer Skills

Sequence Analysis in a Nutshell

BLAST

oreilly.com

oreilly.com is more than a complete catalog of O'Reilly books. You'll also find links to news, events, articles, weblogs, sample chapters, and code examples.

oreillynet.com is the essential portal for developers interested in open and emerging technologies, including new platforms, programming languages, and operating systems.

Conferences

O'Reilly & Associates brings diverse innovators together to nurture the ideas that spark revolutionary industries. We specialize in documenting the latest tools and systems, translating the innovator's knowledge into useful skills for those in the trenches. Visit *conferences.oreilly.com* for our upcoming events.

Safari Bookshelf (*safari.oreilly.com*) is the premier online reference library for programmers and IT professionals. Conduct searches across more than 1,000 books. Subscribers can zero in on answers to time-critical questions in a matter of seconds. Read the books on your Bookshelf from cover to cover or simply flip to the page you need. Try it today with a free trial.

Mastering Perl for Bioinformatics

James D. Tisdall

O'REILLY®

Beijing · Cambridge · Farnham · Köln · Paris · Sebastopol · Taipei · Tokyo

Mastering Perl for Bioinformatics
by James D. Tisdall

Published by O'Reilly & Associates, Inc., 1005 Gravenstein Highway North, Sebastopol, CA 95472.

O'Reilly & Associates books may be purchased for educational, business, or sales promotional use. Online editions are also available for most titles (*safari.oreilly.com*). For more information, contact our corporate/institutional sales department: (800) 998-9938 or *corporate@oreilly.com*.

Editor:	Lorrie LeJeune
Production Editor:	Mary Anne Weeks Mayo
Cover Designer:	Ellie Volckhausen
Interior Designer:	David Futato

Printing History:

September 2003:   First Edition.

ISBN: 0-596-00307-2
[M]

Table of Contents

Part II.   Perl and Bioinformatics

Part III. Appendixes

Foreword

If you can't do bioinformatics, you can't do biology, and Perl is the biologist's favorite language for doing bioinformatics. The genomics revolution has so altered the landscape of biology that almost anyone who works at the bench now spends much of his time at the computer as well, browsing through the large online databases of genes, proteins, interactions and published papers. For example, the availability of an (almost) complete catalog of all the genes in human has fundamentally changed how anyone involved in genetic research works. Traditionally, a biologist would spend days thinking out the strategy for identifying a gene and months working in the lab cloning and screening to get his hands on it. Now he spends days thinking out the appropriate strategy for mining the gene from a genome database, seconds executing the query, and another few minutes ordering the appropriate clone from the resource center. The availability of genomes from many species and phyla makes it possible to apply comparative genomics techniques to the problems of identifying functionally significant portions of proteins or finding the genes responsible for a species' or strains distinguishing traits.

Parallel revolutions are occurring in neurobiology, in which new imaging techniques allow functional changes in the nervous systems of higher organisms to be observed in situ; in clinical research, where the computer database is rapidly replacing the paper chart; and even in botany, where herbaria are being digitized and cataloged for online access.

Biology is undergoing a sea change, evolving into an information-driven science in which the acquisition of large-scale data sets followed by pattern recognition and data mining plays just as prominent a role as traditional hypothesis testing. The two approaches are complementary: the patterns discovered in large-scale data sets suggest hypotheses to test, while hypotheses can be tested directly on the data sets stored in online databases.

To take advantage of the new biology, biologists must be as comfortable with the computer as they now are with thermocyclers and electrophoresis units. Web-based access to biological databases and the various collections of prepackaged data analysis tools are wonderful, but often they are not quite enough. To really make the most of the information revolution in biology, biologists must be able to manage and analyze large amounts of data obtained from many different sources. This means writing software. The ability to create a Perl script to automate information management is a great advantage: whether the task is as simple as checking a remote web page for updates or as complex as knitting together a large number of third-party software packages into an analytic pipeline.

In his first bioinformatics book, *Beginning Perl for Bioinformatics*, Jim introduced the fundamentals of programming in the language most widely used in the field. This book goes the next step, showing how Perl can be used to create large software projects that are scalable and reusable. If you are programming in Perl now and have experienced that wave of panic when you go back to some code you wrote six months ago and can't understand how the code works, then you know why you need this book. If you are an accomplished programmer who has heard about bioinformatics and wants to learn more, this book is also for you. Finally, if you are a biologist who wants to ride the crest of the information wave rather than being washed underneath it, then buy both this book along with *Beginning Perl for Bioinformatics*. I promise you won't be disappointed.

—Lincoln Stein
Cold Spring Harbor, NY
September 2003

Preface

The history of biological research is filled with examples of new laboratory techniques which, at first, are suitable topics for doctoral theses but eventually become so widely useful and standard that they are learned by most undergraduates. The use of computer programming in biology research is such an increasingly standard skill for many biologists. Bioinformatics is one of the most rapidly growing areas of biological science. Fundamentally, it's a cross-disciplinary study, combining the questions of computer science and programming with those of biological research.

As active sciences evolve, unifying principles and techniques developed in one field are often found to be useful in other areas. As a result, the established boundaries between disciplines are sometimes blurred, and the new principles and techniques may result in new ways of seeing the science as a whole. For instance, molecular biology has developed a set of techniques over the past 50 years that has also proved useful throughout much of biology in general. Similarly, the methods of bioinformatics are finding fertile ground in such fields as genetics, biochemistry, molecular biology, evolutionary science, development, cell studies, clinical research, and field biology.

In my view, *bioinformatics*, which I define broadly as the use of computers in biological research, is becoming a foundational science for a broad range of biological studies. Just as it's now commonplace to find a geneticist or a field biologist using the techniques of molecular biology as a routine part of her research, so can you frequently find that same researcher applying the techniques of bioinformatics. Molecular biology and bioinformatics may not be the researcher's main areas of interest, but the tools from molecular biology and bioinformatics have become standard in searching for the answers to the questions of interest. The Perl programming language plays no small part in that search for answers.

About This Book

This book is a continuation of my previous book, *Beginning Perl for Bioinformatics* (also by O'Reilly & Associates). As the title implies, *Mastering Perl for Bioinformatics* moves you to a more advanced level of Perl programming in bioinformatics. In this volume, I cover such topics as advanced data structures, object-oriented programming, modules, relational databases, web programming, and more advanced algorithms. The main goal of this book is to help you learn to write Perl programs that support your research in biology and enable you to adapt and use programs written by others.

In the process of honing your programming skills, you will also learn the fundamentals of bioinformatics. For many readers, the material presented in these two books will be sufficient to support their goals in the laboratory. However, this book is not a comprehensive survey of bioinformatics techniques. Both *Mastering Perl for Bioinformatics* and *Beginning Perl for Bioinformatics* emphasize the computer programming aspects of bioinformatics. As a serious student, you should expect to follow this groundwork with further study in the bioinformatics literature. Even the Perl programming language has more complexity than can fit in this cross-disciplinary text.

Readers already familiar with basic Perl and the elements of DNA and proteins can use *Mastering Perl for Bioinformatics* without reference to *Beginning Perl for Bioinformatics*. However, the two books together make a complete course suitable for undergraduates, graduate students, and professional biologists who need to learn programming for biology research.

A companion web site at *http://www.oreilly.com/catalog/mperlbio* includes all the program code in the book.

What You Need to Know to Use This Book

This book assumes that you have some experience with Perl, including a working knowledge of writing, saving, and running programs; basic Perl syntax; control structures such as loops and conditional tests; the most common operators such as addition, subtraction, and string concatenation; input and output from the user, files, and other programs; subroutines; the basic data types of scalar, array, and hash; and regular expressions for searching and for altering strings. In other words, you should be able to program Perl well enough to extract data from sources such as GenBank and the Protein Data Bank using pattern matching and regular expressions.

If you are new to Perl but feel you can forge ahead using a language summary and examples of programs, Appendix A provides a summary of the important parts of the Perl language. Previous programming experience in a high-level language such as C, Java, or FORTRAN (or any similar language); some experience at using subroutines to break a large problem into smaller, appropriately interrelated parts; and a tinkerer's delight in taking things apart and seeing what makes them tick may be all the computer-science prerequisites you need.

This book is primarily written for biologists, so it assumes you know the elementary facts about DNA, proteins, and restriction enzymes; how to represent DNA and protein data in a Perl program; how to search for motifs; and the structure and use of the databases GenBank, PDB, and Rebase. Because the book assumes you are a biologist, biology concepts are not explained in detail in order to concentrate on programming skills.

Biological data appears in many forms. The most important sources of biological data include the repository of public genetic data called GenBank (Genetic Data Bank) and the repository of public protein structure data called PDB (Protein Data Bank). Many other similar sources of biological data such as Rebase (Restriction Enzyme Database) are in wide use. All the databases just mentioned are most commonly distributed as text files, which makes Perl a good programming tool to find and extract information from the databases.

Organization of This Book

Here's a quick summary of what the book covers. If you're still relatively new to Perl you may want to work through the chapters in order. If you have some programming experience and are looking for ways to approach problems in bioinformatics with Perl, feel free to skip around.

Part I, *Object-Oriented Programming Perl*

Chapter 1, *Modular Programming with Perl*
> Modules are the standard Perl way of "packaging" useful programs so that other programmers can easily use previous work. Such standard modules as CGI, for instance, put the power of interactive web site programming within reach of a programmer who knows basic Perl. Also discussed in later chapters are Bioperl, for manipulating biological data, and DBI, for gaining access to relational databases. Modules are sometimes considered the most important part of Perl because that's where a lot of the functionality of Perl has been placed. In this chapter I show how to write your own modules, as well as how to find useful modules and use them in your programs.

Chapter 2, *Data Structures and String Algorithms*
> Complex data structures and references are fundamentally important to Perl. The basic Perl data structures of scalar, array, and hash go a long way toward solving many (perhaps most) Perl programming problems. However, many commonly used data structures such as multidimensional arrays, for instance, require more sophisticated Perl data structures to handle them. Perl enables you to define quite complex data structures, and we'll see how all that works.
>
> String algorithms are standard techniques used in bioinformatics for finding important data in biological sequences; with them, you can compare two sequences, align two or more sequences, assemble a collection of sequence fragments, and so forth. String algorithms underlie many of the most commonly used programs in biology research, such as BLAST. In this chapter, a string

matching algorithm that finds the closest match to a motif, based on the technique of dynamic programming, is presented in the form of a working Perl program.

Chapter 3, *Object-Oriented Programming in Perl*

Object-oriented programming is a standard approach to designing programs. I assume, as a prerequisite, that you are familiar with the programming style called declarative programming. (For example, C and FORTRAN are declarative; C++ and Java are object-oriented; Perl can be either.) It's important for the Perl programmer to be familiar with the object-oriented approach. For instance, modules are usually defined in an object-oriented manner.

This chapter presents, step by step, the concepts and techniques of object-oriented Perl programming, in the context of a module that defines a simple class for keeping track of genes.

Chapter 4, *Sequence Formats and Inheritance*

In this chapter, object-oriented programming is further explored in the context of developing software to convert sequence files to alternate formats (FASTA, GCG, etc.). The concept of class inheritance is introduced and implemented.

Chapter 5, *A Class for Restriction Enzymes*

This chapter further develops object-oriented programming by writing a class that handles Rebase restriction enzyme data, a class that calculates restriction maps, and a class that draws restriction maps.

Part II, *Perl and Bioinformatics*

Chapter 6, *Perl and Relational Databases*

Relational databases are important in programming because they save, organize, and retrieve data sets. This chapter introduces relational databases and the SQL language and includes information on designing and administering databases. I take a close look at how one such relational database management system, the popular MySQL, is used from the Perl language.

Chapter 7, *Perl and the Web*

Web programming is one of Perl's areas of strength. In this chapter, I start an example that puts a laboratory up on the Web using Perl and the CGI module. The software developed in previous chapters for restriction mapping is made accessible from the Web.

Chapter 8, *Perl and Graphics*

Using computer graphics to display data is one of the most important programming skills in bioinformatics. In this chapter, graphics programs are used to dynamically display the output of restriction maps and data presented as graphs on the Web. The Perl module GD is discussed and used to generate maps on the fly from web page queries.

Chapter 9, *Introduction to Bioperl*

Bioperl is a set of modules used by Perl programmers to write bioinformatics applications. In this chapter you'll see an introduction of the Bioperl project. Bioperl is open source (free under a very nonrestrictive copyright) and developed by a group of volunteers, many based in supportive research organizations. In recent years it has achieved critical mass and is now adequately documented and fairly broad in scope. If you do Perl bioinformatics programming, you should certainly be aware of what Bioperl has to offer, to avoid reinventing the wheel.

Part III, *Appendixes*

Appendix A, *Perl Summary*

This appendix summarizes the parts of Perl we've covered.

Appendix B, *Installing Perl*

This appendix outlines how to install Perl.

Conventions Used in This Book

The following conventions are used in this book:

Constant width

Used for arrays, classes, code examples, loops, modules, namespaces, objects, packages, statements, and to show the output of commands.

Italics

Used for commands, directory names, filenames, URLs, variables, and for new terms where they are defined.

 This icon designates a note, which is an important aside to the nearby text.

 This icon designates a warning relating to the nearby text.

Comments and Questions

Please address comments and questions concerning this book to the publisher:

O'Reilly & Associates, Inc.
1005 Gravenstein Highway North
Sebastopol, CA 95472

(800) 998-9938 (in the United States or Canada)
(707) 829-0515 (international or local)
(707) 829-0104 (fax)

There is a web page for this book, which lists errata, examples, or any additional information. You can access this page at:

http://www.oreilly.com/catalog/mperlbio

To comment or ask technical questions about this book, send email to:

bookquestions@oreilly.com

For more information about books, conferences, Resource Centers, and the O'Reilly Network, see the O'Reilly web site at:

http://www.oreilly.com

Acknowledgments

My editor, Lorrie LeJeune, deserves special thanks for her work in developing the bioinformatics titles at O'Reilly. Her level of expertise is rare in any field. I thank Lorrie, Tim O'Reilly, and their colleagues for making it possible to bring these books to the public. I thank my technical reviewers for their invaluable expert help: Joel Greshock, Joe Johnston, Andrew Martin, and Sean Quinlan. I also thank Dr. Michael Caudy for his helpful suggestions in Chapter 3. I thank again those individuals mentioned in the first volume, especially those friends who have supported me during the writing of this book. I am also grateful to all those readers of the first volume who took the time and trouble to point out errors and weaknesses; their comments have substantially improved this volume as well. I thank Eamon Grennan and Jay Parini for their patient help with my writing. And I especially thank my much-loved children Rose, Eamon, and Joe, who are my most sincere teachers.

## PART I

Object-Oriented Programming in Perl

## CHAPTER 1

Modular Programming with Perl

Perl modules are essential to any Perl programmer. They are a great way to organize code into logical collections of interacting parts. They collect useful Perl subroutines and provide them to other programs (and programmers) in an organized and convenient fashion.

This chapter begins with a discussion of the reasons for organizing Perl code into modules. Modules are comparable to subroutines: both organize Perl code in convenient, reusable "chunks."

Later in this chapter, I'll introduce a small module, GeneticCode.pm. This example shows how to create simple modules, and I'll give examples of programs that use this module.

I'll also demonstrate how to find, install, and use modules taken from the all-important CPAN collection. A familiarity with searching and using CPAN is an essential skill for Perl programmers; it will help you avoid lots of unnecessary work. With CPAN, you can easily find and use code written by excellent programmers and road-tested by the Perl community. Using proven code and writing less of your own, you'll save time, money, and headaches.

What Is a Module?

A Perl *module* is a library file that uses package declarations to create its own namespace. Perl modules provide an extra level of protection from name collisions beyond that provided by my and use strict. They also serve as the basic mechanism for defining object-oriented classes.

Why Perl Modules?

Building a medium- to large-sized program usually requires you to divide tasks into several smaller, more manageable, and more interactive pieces. (A rule of thumb is that each "piece" should be about one or two printed pages in length, but this is just a general guideline.) An analogy can be made to building a microarray machine, which requires that you construct separate interacting pieces such as housing, temperature sensors and controls, robot arms to position the pipettes, hydraulic injection devices, and computer guidance for all these systems.

Subroutines and Software Engineering

Subroutines divide a large programming job into more manageable pieces. Modern programming languages all provide subroutines, which are also called functions, coroutines, or macros in other programming languages.

A subroutine lets you write a piece of code that performs some part of a desired computation (e.g., determining the length of DNA sequence). This code is written once and then can be called frequently throughout the main program. Using subroutines speeds the time it takes to write the main program, makes it more reliable by avoiding duplicated sections (which can get out of sync and make the program longer), and makes the entire program easier to test. A useful subroutine can be used by other programs as well, saving you development time in the future. As long as the inputs and outputs to the subroutine remain the same, its internal workings can be altered and improved without worrying about how the changes will affect the rest of the program. This is known as *encapsulation*.

The benefits of subroutines that I've just outlined also apply to other approaches in software engineering. Perl modules are a technique within a larger umbrella of techniques known as *software encapsulation and reuse*. Software encapsulation and reuse are fundamental to object-oriented programming.

A related design principle is *abstraction*, which involves writing code that is usable in many different situations. Let's say you write a subroutine that adds the fragment TTTTT to the end of a string of DNA. If you then want to add the fragment AAAAA to the end of a string of DNA, you have to write another subroutine. To avoid writing two subroutines, you can write one that's more abstract and adds to the end of a string of DNA whatever fragment you give it as an argument. Using the principle of abstraction, you've saved yourself half the work.

Here is an example of a Perl subroutine that takes two strings of DNA as inputs and returns the second one appended to the end of the first:

```
sub DNAappend {
        my ($dna, $tail) = @_;

        return($dna . $tail);
}
```

This subroutine can be used as follows:

```
my $dna = 'ACCGGAGTTGACTCTCCGAATA';
my $polyT = 'TTTTTTTT';

print DNAappend($dna, $polyT);
```

If you wish, you can also define subroutines polyT and polyA like so:

```
sub polyT {
    my ($dna) = @_;

    return DNAappend($dna, 'TTTTTTTT');
}
sub polyA {
    my ($dna) = @_;

    return DNAappend($dna, 'AAAAAAAA');
}
```

At this point, you should think about how to divide a problem into interacting parts; that is, an optimal (or at least good) way to define a set of subroutines that can cooperate to solve a particular problem.

Modules and Libraries

In my projects, I gather subroutine definitions into separate files called *libraries*,[*] or *modules*, which let me collect subroutine definitions for use in other programs. Then, instead of copying the subroutine definitions into the new program (and introducing the potential for inaccurate copies or for alternate versions proliferating), I can just insert the name of the library or module into a program, and all the subroutines are available in their original unaltered form. This is an example of software reuse in action.

To fully understand and use modules, you need to understand the simple concepts of namespaces and packages. From here on, think of a Perl *module* as any Perl library file that uses package declarations to create its own namespace. These simple concepts are examined in the next sections.

Namespaces

A *namespace* is implemented as a table containing the names of the variables and subroutines in a program. The table itself is called a *symbol table* and is used by the running program to keep track of variable values and subroutine definitions as the

---

[*] Perl *libraries* were traditionally put in files ending with *.pl*, which stands for *perl library*; the term *library* is also used to refer to a collection of Perl modules. The common denominator is that a library is a collection of reusable subroutines.

program evolves. A namespace and a symbol table are essentially the same thing. A namespace exists under the hood for many programs, especially those in which only one default namespace is used.

Large programs often accidentally use the same variable name for different variables in different parts of the program. These identically named variables may unintentionally interact with each other and cause serious, hard-to-find errors. This situation is called *namespace collision*. Separate namespaces are one way to avoid namespace collision.

The package declaration described in the next section is one way to assign separate namespaces to different parts of your code. It gives strong protection against accidentally using a variable name that's used in another part of the program and having the two identically-named variables interact in unwanted ways.

Namespaces Compared with Scoping: my and use strict

The unintentional interaction between variables with the same name is enough of a problem that Perl provides more than one way to avoid it. You are probably already familiar with the use of my to restrict the scope of a variable to its enclosing block (between matching curly braces {}) and should be accustomed to using the directive use strict to require the use of my for all variables. use strict and my are a great way to protect your program from unintentional reuse of variable names. Make a habit of using my and working under use strict.

Packages

Packages are a different way to protect a program's variables from interacting unintentionally. In Perl, you can easily assign separate namespaces to entire sections of your code, which helps prevent namespace collisions and lets you create modules.

Packages are very easy to use. A one-line package declaration puts a new namespace in effect. Here's a simple example:

```
$dna = 'AAAAAAAAAA';
package Mouse;
$dna = 'CCCCCCCCCC';
package Celegans;
$dna = 'GGGGGGGGGG';
```

In this snippet, there are three variables, each with the same name, $dna. However, they are in three different packages, so they appear in three different symbol tables and are managed separately by the running Perl program.

The first line of the code is an assignment of a poly-A DNA fragment to a variable $dna. Because no package is explicitly named, this $dna variable appears in the default namespace main.

The second line of code introduces a new namespace for variable and subroutine definitions by declaring package Mouse;. At this point, the main namespace is no longer active, and the Mouse namespace is brought into play. Note that the name of the namespace is capitalized; it's a well-established convention you should follow. The only noncapitalized namespace you should use is the default main.

Now that the Mouse namespace is in effect, the third line of code, which declares a variable, $dna, is actually declaring a separate variable unrelated to the first. It contains a poly-C fragment of DNA.

Finally, the last two lines of code declare a new package called Celegans and a new variable, also called $dna, that stores a poly-G DNA fragment.

To use these three $dna variables, you need to explicitly state which packages you want the variables from, as the following code fragment demonstrates:

```
print "The DNA from the main package:\n\n";
print $main::dna, "\n\n";

print "The DNA from the Mouse package:\n\n";
print $Mouse::dna, "\n\n";

print "The DNA from the Celegans package:\n\n";
print $Celegans::dna, "\n\n";
```

This gives the following output:

```
The DNA from the main package:

AAAAAAAAAA

The DNA from the Mouse package:

CCCCCCCCCC

The DNA from the Celegans package:

GGGGGGGGGG
```

As you can see, the variable name can be specified as to a particular package by putting the package name and two colons before the variable name (but after the $, @, or % that specifies the type of variable). If you don't specify a package in this way, Perl assumes you want the current package, which may not necessarily be the main package, as the following example shows:

```
#
# Define the variables in the packages
#

$dna = 'AAAAAAAAAA';

package Mouse;
```

```
$dna = 'CCCCCCCCCC';

#
# Print the values of the variables
#

print "The DNA from the current package:\n\n";
print $dna, "\n\n";

print "The DNA from the Mouse package:\n\n";
print $Mouse::dna, "\n\n";
```

This produces the following output:

```
The DNA from the current package:
CCCCCCCCCC

The DNA from the Mouse package:
CCCCCCCCCC
```

Both print $dna and print $Mouse::dna reference the same variable. This is because the last package declaration was package Mouse;, so the print $dna statement prints the value of the variable $dna as defined in the current package, which is Mouse.

The rule is, once a package has been declared, it becomes the current package until the next package declaration or until the end of the file. (You can also declare packages within blocks, evals, or subroutine definitions, in which case the package stays in effect until the end of the block, eval, or subroutine definition.)

By far the most common use of package is to call it once near the top of a file and have it stay in effect for all the code in the file. This is how *modules* are defined, as the next section shows.

Defining Modules

To begin, take a file of subroutine definitions and call it something like Newmodule.pm. Now, edit the file and give it a new first line:

```
package Newmodule;
```

and a new last line 1;. You've now created a Perl module.

To make a Celegans module, place subroutines in a file called Celegans.pm, and add a first line:

```
package Celegans;
```

Add a last line 1;, and you've defined a Celegans module. This last line just ensures that the library returns a true value when it's read in. It's annoying, but necessary.

Storing Modules

Where you store your .pm module files on your computer affects the name of the module, so let's take a moment to sort out the most important points. For all the details, consult the perlmod and the perlmodlib parts of the Perl documentation at *http://www.perldoc.org*. You can also type perldoc perlmod or perldoc perlmodlib at a shell prompt or in a command window.

Once you start using multiple files for your program code, which happens if you're defining and using modules, Perl needs to be able to find these various files; it provides a few different ways to do so.

The simplest method is to put all your program files, including your modules, in the same directory and run your programs from that directory. Here's how the module file Celegans.pm is loaded from another program:

```perl
use Celegans;
```

However, it's often not so simple. Perl uses modules extensively; many are built-in when you install Perl, and many more are available from CPAN, as you'll see later. Some modules are used frequently, some rarely; many modules call other modules, which in turn call still other modules.

To organize the many modules a Perl program might need, you should place them in certain standard directories or in your own development directories. Perl needs to know where these directories are so that when a module is called in a program, it can search the directories, find the file that contains the module, and load it in.

When Perl was installed on your computer, a list of directories in which to find modules was configured. Every time a Perl program on your computer refers to a module, Perl looks in those directories. To see those directories, you only need to run a Perl program and examine the built-in array @INC, like so:

```perl
print join("\n", @INC), "\n";
```

On my Linux computer, I get the following output from that statement:

```
/usr/local/lib/perl5/5.8.0/i686-linux
/usr/local/lib/perl5/5.8.0
/usr/local/lib/perl5/site_perl/5.8.0/i686-linux
/usr/local/lib/perl5/site_perl/5.8.0
/usr/local/lib/perl5/site_perl/5.6.1
/usr/local/lib/perl5/site_perl/5.6.0
/usr/local/lib/perl5/site_perl
.
```

These are all locations in which the standard Perl modules live on my Linux computer. @INC is simply an array whose entries are directories on your computer. The way it looks depends on how your computer is configured and your operating system (for instance, Unix computers handle directories a bit differently than Windows).

Note that the last line of that list of directories is a solitary period. This is shorthand for "the current directory," that is, whatever directory you happen to be in when you run your Perl program. If this directory is on the list, and you run your program from that directory as well, Perl will find the .pm files.

When you develop Perl software that uses modules, you should put all the modules together in a certain directory. In order for Perl to find this directory, and load the modules, you need to add a line before the use MODULE directives, telling Perl to additionally search your own module directory for any modules requested in your program. For instance, if I put a module I'm developing for my program into a file named Celegans.pm, and put the Celegans.pm file into my Linux directory */home/tisdall/MasteringPerlBio/development/lib*, I need to add a use lib directive to my program, like so:

```
use lib "/home/tisdall/MasteringPerlBio/development/lib";

use Celegans;
```

Perl then adds my development module directory to the @INC array and searches there for the Celegans.pm module file. The following code demonstrates this:

```
use lib "/home/tisdall/MasteringPerlBio/development/lib";

print join("\n", @INC), "\n";
```

This produces the output:

```
/home/tisdall/MasteringPerlBio/development/lib
/usr/local/lib/perl5/5.8.0/i686-linux
/usr/local/lib/perl5/5.8.0
/usr/local/lib/perl5/site_perl/5.8.0/i686-linux
/usr/local/lib/perl5/site_perl/5.8.0
/usr/local/lib/perl5/site_perl/5.6.1
/usr/local/lib/perl5/site_perl/5.6.0
/usr/local/lib/perl5/site_perl
.
```

Thanks to the use lib directive, Perl can now find the Celegans.pm file in the @INC list of directories.

A problem with this approach to finding libraries is that the directory pathnames are hardcoded into each program. If you then want to move your own library directory somewhere else or move the programs to another computer where different pathnames are used, you need to change the pathnames in all the program files where they occur.

If, for instance, you download several programs from this book's web site, and you don't want to edit each one to change pathnames, you can use the PERL5LIB environmental variable. To do so, put all the modules under the directory */my/perl/ modules* (for example). Now set the PERL5LIB variable:

```
PERL5LIB=$PERL5LIB:/my/perl/modules
```

You can also set it this way:

```
setenv PERL5LIB /my/perl/modules
```

If you have "taint" security checks enabled in your version of Perl, you still have to hardcode the pathname into the program. This, of course, behaves differently on different operating systems.

You can also specify an additional directory on the command line:

```
perl -I/my/perl/modules myprogram.pl
```

There's one other detail about modules that's important. You'll sometimes see modules in Perl programs with names such as `Genomes::Modelorganisms::Celegans`, in which the name is two or more words separated by two colons. This is how Perl looks into subdirectories of directories named in the `@INC` built-in array. In the example, Perl looks for a subdirectory named `Genomes` in one of the `@INC` directories; then for a subdirectory named `Modelorganisms` within the `Genomes` subdirectory; finally, for a file named `Celegans.pm` within the `Modelorganisms` subdirectory. That is, my module is in the file:

```
/home/tisdall/MasteringPerlBio/development/lib/Genomes/Modelorganisms/Celegans.pm
```

and it's called in my Perl program like so:

```
use lib "/home/tisdall/MasteringPerlBio/development/lib";

use Genomes::Modelorganisms::Celegans;
```

There are more details you can learn about storing and finding modules on your computer, but these are the most useful facts. See the `perlmod`, `perlrun`, and `perlmodlib` sections of the Perl manual for more details if and when you need them.

Writing Your First Perl Module

Now that you've been introduced to the basic ideas of modules, it's time to actually examine a working example of a module.

In this section, we'll write a module called `Geneticcode.pm`, which implements the genetic code that maps DNA codons to amino acids and then translates a string of DNA sequence data to a protein fragment.

An Example: Geneticcode.pm

Let's start by creating a file called `Geneticcode.pm` and using it to define the mapping of codons to amino acids in a hash variable called `%genetic_code`. We'll also discuss a subroutine called `codon2aa` that uses the hash to translate its codon arguments into amino acid return values.

Here are the contents of the first module file Geneticcode.pm:

```perl
package Geneticcode;

use strict;
use warnings;

my(%genetic_code) = (

    'TCA' => 'S',      # Serine
    'TCC' => 'S',      # Serine
    'TCG' => 'S',      # Serine
    'TCT' => 'S',      # Serine
    'TTC' => 'F',      # Phenylalanine
    'TTT' => 'F',      # Phenylalanine
    'TTA' => 'L',      # Leucine
    'TTG' => 'L',      # Leucine
    'TAC' => 'Y',      # Tyrosine
    'TAT' => 'Y',      # Tyrosine
    'TAA' => '_',      # Stop
    'TAG' => '_',      # Stop
    'TGC' => 'C',      # Cysteine
    'TGT' => 'C',      # Cysteine
    'TGA' => '_',      # Stop
    'TGG' => 'W',      # Tryptophan
    'CTA' => 'L',      # Leucine
    'CTC' => 'L',      # Leucine
    'CTG' => 'L',      # Leucine
    'CTT' => 'L',      # Leucine
    'CCA' => 'P',      # Proline
    'CCC' => 'P',      # Proline
    'CCG' => 'P',      # Proline
    'CCT' => 'P',      # Proline
    'CAC' => 'H',      # Histidine
    'CAT' => 'H',      # Histidine
    'CAA' => 'Q',      # Glutamine
    'CAG' => 'Q',      # Glutamine
    'CGA' => 'R',      # Arginine
    'CGC' => 'R',      # Arginine
    'CGG' => 'R',      # Arginine
    'CGT' => 'R',      # Arginine
    'ATA' => 'I',      # Isoleucine
    'ATC' => 'I',      # Isoleucine
    'ATT' => 'I',      # Isoleucine
    'ATG' => 'M',      # Methionine
    'ACA' => 'T',      # Threonine
    'ACC' => 'T',      # Threonine
    'ACG' => 'T',      # Threonine
    'ACT' => 'T',      # Threonine
    'AAC' => 'N',      # Asparagine
    'AAT' => 'N',      # Asparagine
    'AAA' => 'K',      # Lysine
    'AAG' => 'K',      # Lysine
    'AGC' => 'S',      # Serine
```

```
      'AGT' => 'S',    # Serine
      'AGA' => 'R',    # Arginine
      'AGG' => 'R',    # Arginine
      'GTA' => 'V',    # Valine
      'GTC' => 'V',    # Valine
      'GTG' => 'V',    # Valine
      'GTT' => 'V',    # Valine
      'GCA' => 'A',    # Alanine
      'GCC' => 'A',    # Alanine
      'GCG' => 'A',    # Alanine
      'GCT' => 'A',    # Alanine
      'GAC' => 'D',    # Aspartic Acid
      'GAT' => 'D',    # Aspartic Acid
      'GAA' => 'E',    # Glutamic Acid
      'GAG' => 'E',    # Glutamic Acid
      'GGA' => 'G',    # Glycine
      'GGC' => 'G',    # Glycine
      'GGG' => 'G',    # Glycine
      'GGT' => 'G',    # Glycine
);


#
# codon2aa
#
# A subroutine to translate a DNA 3-character codon to an amino acid
#   Version 3, using hash lookup

sub codon2aa {
      my($codon) = @_;

      $codon = uc $codon;

      if(exists $genetic_code{$codon}) {
            return $genetic_code{$codon};
      }else{
            die "Bad codon '$codon'!!\n";
      }
}

1;
```

Now, let's examine the code. First, the module declares its package with a name (Geneticcode) that is the same as the file it is in (Geneticcode.pm), but minus the file extension .pm.

The directives:

```
use strict;
use warnings;
```

will appear in all the code. The use strict directive enforces the use of the my directive for all variables. The use warnings directive produces useful messages about potential problems in your code. (It is possible to turn both directives off when required—to avoid annoying warnings in your program output, for instance. See the perldiag, perllexwarn, and perlmodlib sections of the Perl manual.)

Finally, there is a subroutine definition for codon2aa. As an argument, this subroutine takes a codon represented as a string of three DNA bases and returns the amino acid code corresponding to the codon. It accomplishes this by a simple lookup in the hash %genetic_code and returns the result from the subroutine using the return built-in function.

The codon2aa subroutine calls die and exits the program when it encounters an undefined codon. See the exercises at the end of this chapter for a discussion of the pros and cons of this behavior.

In my earlier book, I defined the hash %genetic_code within the subroutine codon2aa. That meant that every time the subroutine was called, the hash would have to be initialized, which took a bit of time. In this version, the hash only has to be initialized once, when the program is first called, which results in a significant speedup. The definition of the hash is outside of the subroutine definition, but in the namespace of the Geneticcode package. The hash is initialized when the Geneticcode.pm module is loaded by this statement:

```
use Geneticcode;
```

Every subsequent call to the codon2aa subroutine simply accesses the hash without having to initialize it each time.

Here's an example that uses the new Geneticcode module, which is saved in a file called testGeneticcode and run by typing perl testGeneticcode:

```perl
use strict;
use warnings;

use lib "/home/tisdall/MasteringPerlBio/development/lib";

use Geneticcode;

my $dna = 'AACCTTCCTTCCGGAAGAGAG';

# Initialize variables
my $protein = '';

# Translate each three-base codon to an amino acid, and append to a protein
for(my $i=0; $i < (length($dna) - 2) ; $i += 3) {
        $protein .= Geneticcode::codon2aa( substr($dna,$i,3) );
}

print $protein, "\n";
```

Recall that the Perl built-in function substr can extract a portion of a string. In this case, substr extracts from $dna the three characters beginning at the position given in the counter variable $i; this three-character codon is then passed as the argument to the subroutine codon2aa. This program produces the output:

```
NLPSGRE
```

Expanding Geneticcode.pm

Now, let's expand our `Geneticcode` module example. This new version of the module includes a few short helper subroutines. The interest here lies in how the subroutines interact with each other in the module's namespace, and how to access the code within the module from a Perl program that uses the module.

Modules are a great way to organize code into logical collections of interacting parts. When you create modules, you need to decide how to organize your code into the appropriate collection of modules. Here, we have some subroutines that translate codons into amino acids; others read sequence data from files and print it to the screen. This is a fairly obvious division of functionality, so let's create two modules for this code. We'll expand the `Geneticcode` module; let's also create a `SequenceIO` module. Of course, the new module will be created in a file called `SequenceIO.pm`, and that file will be placed in a directory that Perl can find—in this case, the same directory in which we've placed the `Geneticcode` module.

Here's the code for `Geneticcode.pm`:

```perl
package Geneticcode;

use strict;
use warnings;

my(%genetic_code) = (

    'TCA' => 'S',       # Serine
    'TCC' => 'S',       # Serine
    'TCG' => 'S',       # Serine
    'TCT' => 'S',       # Serine
    'TTC' => 'F',       # Phenylalanine

    ... as before ...

    'GAG' => 'E',       # Glutamic Acid
    'GGA' => 'G',       # Glycine
    'GGC' => 'G',       # Glycine
    'GGG' => 'G',       # Glycine
    'GGT' => 'G',       # Glycine
);


#
# codon2aa
#
```

```perl
# A subroutine to translate a DNA 3-character codon to an amino acid
#    Version 3, using hash lookup

sub codon2aa {
    my($codon) = @_;

    $codon = uc $codon;

    if(exists $genetic_code{$codon}) {
        return $genetic_code{$codon};
    }else{

            die "Bad codon '$codon'!!\n";
    }
}


#
# dna2peptide
#
# A subroutine to translate DNA sequence into a peptide

sub dna2peptide {

    my($dna) = @_;

    # Initialize variables
    my $protein = '';

    # Translate each three-base codon to an amino acid, and append to a protein
    for(my $i=0; $i < (length($dna) - 2) ; $i += 3) {
        $protein .= codon2aa( substr($dna,$i,3) );
    }

    return $protein;
}

# translate_frame
#
# A subroutine to translate a frame of DNA

sub translate_frame {

    my($seq, $start, $end) = @_;
    my $protein;

    # To make the subroutine easier to use, you won't need to specify
    #   the end point-it will just go to the end of the sequence
    #   by default.
    unless($end) {
        $end = length($seq);
    }
```

```
    # Finally, calculate and return the translation
        return dna2peptide ( substr ( $seq, $start - 1, $end -$start + 1) );
}

1;
```

Now, we have in one module the code that accomplishes a translation from the genetic code. However, we also need to read sequence in from FASTA sequence files, and print out sequence (the translated protein) to the screen. Because these needs are likely to recur in many programs, it makes sense to make a separate module for just the file reading, sequence extraction, and sequence printing operations. (This may even be too much in one module; maybe there should be separate modules for each need? See the exercises at the end of the chapter.)

Here's the code for the second module SequenceIO.pm, which handles reading from a file, extracting FASTA sequence data, and printing sequence data:

```
package SequenceIO;

use strict;
use warnings;

# get_file_data
#
# A subroutine to get data from a file given its filename

sub get_file_data {

    my($filename) = @_;

    # Initialize variables
    my @filedata = (  );

    open(GET_FILE_DATA, $filename) or die "Cannot open file '$filename':$!\n\n";

    @filedata = <GET_FILE_DATA>;

    close GET_FILE_DATA;

    return @filedata;
}

# extract_sequence_from_fasta_data
#
# A subroutine to extract FASTA sequence data from an array

sub extract_sequence_from_fasta_data {

    my(@fasta_file_data) = @_;

    # Declare and initialize variables
    my $sequence = '';
```

```perl
    foreach my $line (@fasta_file_data) {

        # discard blank line
        if ($line =~ /^\s*$/) {
            next;

        # discard comment line
        } elsif($line =~ /^\s*#/) {
            next;

        # discard fasta header line
        } elsif($line =~ /^>/) {
            next;

        # keep line, add to sequence string
        } else {
            $sequence .= $line;
        }
    }

    # remove non-sequence data (in this case, whitespace) from $sequence string
    $sequence =~ s/\s//g;

    return $sequence;
}

# print_sequence
#
# A subroutine to format and print sequence data

sub print_sequence {

    my($sequence, $length) = @_;

    # Print sequence in lines of $length
    for ( my $pos = 0 ; $pos < length($sequence) ; $pos += $length ) {
        print substr($sequence, $pos, $length), "\n";
    }
}

1;
```

Before we discuss the code, let's see a small program that uses it:

```perl
# Translate a DNA sequence into one of the six reading frames

use strict;
use warnings;

use lib "/home/tisdall/MasteringPerlBio/development/lib";
use Geneticcode;
use SequenceIO;

# Initialize variables
my @file_data = (  );
my $dna = '';
```

```perl
    my $revcom = '';
    my $protein = '';

    # Read in the contents of the file "sample.dna"
    @file_data = SequenceIO::get_file_data("sample.dna");

    # Extract the sequence data from the contents of the file "sample.dna"
    $dna = SequenceIO::extract_sequence_from_fasta_data(@file_data);

    # Translate the DNA to protein in one of the six reading frames
    #    and print the protein in lines 70 characters long

    print "\n -------Reading Frame 1--------\n\n";

    $protein = Geneticcode::translate_frame($dna, 1);

    SequenceIO::print_sequence($protein, 70);

    exit;
```

Here's the input file:

```
> sample dna   (This is a typical fasta header.)
agatggcggcgctgaggggtcttgggggctctaggccggccacctactgg
tttgcagcggagacgacgcatggggcctgcgcaataggagtacgctgcct
gggaggcgtgactagaagcggaagtagttgtgggcgcctttgcaaccgcc
tgggacgccgccgagtggtctgtgcaggttcgcgggtcgctggcggggt
cgtgagggagtgcgccgggagcggagatatggagggagatggttcagacc
cagagcctccagatgccggggaggacagcaagtccgagaatggggagaat
gcgcccatctactgcatctgccgcaaaccggacatcaactgcttcatgat
cgggtgtgacaactgcaatgagtggttccatggggactgcatccggatca
ctgagaagatggccaaggccatccgggagtggtactgtcgggagtgcaga
gagaaagaccccaagctagagattcgctatcggcacaagaagtcacggga
gcgggatggcaatgagcgggacagcagtgagccccgggatgagggtggag
ggcgcaagaggcctgtccctgatccagacctgcagcgccgggcagggtca
gggacaggggttggggccatgcttgctcggggctctgcttcgccccacaa
atcctctccgcagcccttggtggccacacccagccagcatcaccagcagc
agcagcagcagatcaaacggtcagcccgcatgtgtggtgagtgtgaggca
tgtcggcgcactgaggactgtggtcactgtgatttctgtcgggacatgaa
gaagttcgggggccccaacaagatccggcagaagtgccggctgcgccagt
gccagctgcgggcccgggaatcgtacaagtacttcccttcctcgctctca
ccagtgacgccctcagagtccctgccaaggccccgccggccactgcccac
ccaacagcagccacagccatcacagaagttagggcgcatccgtgaagatg
aggggcgcagtggcgtcatcaacagtcaaggagcctcctgaggctacagcc
acacctgagccactctcagatgaggaccta
```

Here's the output of the program:

```
-------Reading Frame 1--------

RWRR_GVLGALGRPPTGLQRRRRMGPAQ_EYAAWEA_LEAEVVVGAFATAWDAAEWSVQVRGSLAGVVRE
CAGSGDMEGDGSDPEPPDAGEDSKSENGENAPIYCICRKPDINCFMIGCDNCNEWFHGDCIRITEKMAKA
IREWYCRECREKDPKLEIRYRHKKSRERDGNERDSSEPRDEGGGRKRPVPDPDLQRRAGSGTGVGAMLAR
GSASPHKSSPQPLVATPSQHHQQQQQQIKRSARMCGECEACRRTEDCGHCDFCRDMKKFGGPNKIRQKCR
LRQCQLRARESYKYFPSSLSPVTPSESLPRPRRPLPTQQQPQPSQKLGRIREDEGAVASSTVKEPPEATA
TPEPLSDEDL
```

A few comments are in order. First, the subroutines for translating codons are in the Geneticcode module. They include the hash %genetic_code and the subroutines codon2aa, dna2peptide, and translate_frame, which are involved with translating DNA data to peptides. The subroutines for reading sequence data in from files, and for formatting and printing it to the screen, are in the SequenceIO module. They are the subroutines get_file_data, extract_sequence_from_fasta_data, and print_sequence.

Now, we have two modules and code that exercises them; let's look at some more facets of using modules.

Using Modules

So far, the benefit of modules may seem questionable. You may be wondering what the advantage is over simple libraries (without package declarations), since the main result seems to be the necessity to refer to subroutines in the modules with longer names!

Exporting Names

There's a way to avoid lengthy module names and still use the short ones if you place a call to the special Exporter module in the module code and modify the use MODULE declaration in the calling code.

Going back to the first example Geneticcode.pm module, recall it began with this line:

```
package Geneticcode;
```

and included the definition for the hash genetic_code and the subroutine codon2aa.

If you add these lines to the beginning of the file, you can export the symbol names of variables or subroutines in the module into the namespace of the calling program. You can then use the convenient short names for things (e.g., codon2aa instead of Geneticcode::codon2aa). Here's a short example of how it works (try typing perldoc Exporter to see the whole story):

```
package Geneticcode;

require Exporter;
@ISA = qw(Exporter);

@EXPORT_OK = qw(...);        # symbols to export on request
```

Here's how to export the name codon2aa from the module only when explicitly requested:

```
@EXPORT_OK = qw(codon2aa);    # symbols to export on request
```

The calling program then has to explicitly request the codon2aa symbol like so:

```
use Geneticcode qw(codon2aa);
```

If you use this approach, the calling program can just say:

```
codon2aa($codon);
```

instead of:

```
Geneticcode::codon2aa($codon);
```

The Exporter module that's included in the standard Perl distribution has several other optional behaviors, but the way just shown is the safest and most useful. As you'll see, the object-oriented programming style of using modules doesn't use the Export facility, but it is a useful thing to have in your bag of tricks. For more information about exporting (such as why exporting is also known as "polluting your namespace"), see the Perl documentation for the Exporter module (by typing perldoc Exporter at a command line or by going to the *http://www.perldoc.com* web page).

CPAN Modules

The Comprehensive Perl Archive Network (CPAN, http://*www.cpan.org)* is an impressively large collection of Perl code (mostly Perl modules). CPAN is easily accessible and searchable on the Web, and you can use its modules for a variety of programming tasks.

By now you should have the basic idea of how modules are defined and used, so let's take some time to explore CPAN to see what goodies are available.

There are two important points about CPAN. First, a large number of the things you might want your programs to do have already been programmed and are easily obtained in downloadable modules. You just have to go find them at CPAN, install them on your computer, and call them from your program. We'll take a look at an example of exactly that in this section.

Second, all code on CPAN is free of charge and available for use by a very unrestrictive copyright declaration. Sound good? Keep reading.

CPAN includes convenient ways to search for useful modules, and there's a CPAN.pm module built-in with Perl that makes downloading and installing modules quite easy (when things work well, which they usually do). If you can't find CPAN.pm, you should consider updating your current version.

You can find more information by typing the following at the command line:

```
perldoc CPAN
```

You can also check the Frequently Asked Questions (FAQ) available at the CPAN web site.

What's Available at CPAN?

The CPAN web site offers several "views" of the CPAN collection of modules and several alternate ways of searching (by module name, category, full text search of the module documentation, etc.). Here is the top-level organization of the modules by overall category:

```
Development Support
Operating System Interfaces
Networking Devices IPC
Data Type Utilities
Database Interfaces
User Interfaces
Language Interfaces
File Names Systems Locking
String Lang Text Proc
Opt Arg Param Proc
Internationalization Locale
Security and Encryption
World Wide Web HTML HTTP CGI
Server and Daemon Utilities
Archiving and Compression
Images Pixmaps Bitmaps
Mail and Usenet News
Control Flow Utilities
File Handle Input Output
Microsoft Windows Modules
Miscellaneous Modules
Commercial Software Interfaces
Not In Modulelist
```

Searching CPAN

CPAN's main web page has a few ways to search the contents. Let's say you need to perform some statistics and are looking for code that's already available. We'll go through the steps necessary to search for the code, download and install it, and use the module in a program.

At the main CPAN page, look for "searching" and click on *search.cpan.org*. If you search for "statistics" in all locations, you'll get over 300 hits, so you should restrict your search to modules with the pull-down menu. You'll get 25 hits (more by the time you read this); here's what you'll see:

```
1.  Statistics::Candidates
Statistics-MaxEntropy-0.9 - 26 Nov 1998 - Hugo WL ter Doest

2. Statistics::ChiSquare
How random is your data?
Statistics-ChiSquare-0.3 - 23 Nov 2001 - Jon Orwant
```

3. Statistics::Contingency
Calculate precision, recall, F1, accuracy, etc.
Statistics-Contingency-0.03 - 09 Aug 2002 - Ken Williams

4. Statistics::DEA
Discontiguous Exponential Averaging
Statistics-DEA-0.04 - 17 Aug 2002 - Jarkko Hietaniemi

5. Statistics::Descriptive
Module of basic descriptive statistical functions.
Statistics-Descriptive-2.4 - 26 Apr 1999 - Colin Kuskie

6. Statistics::Distributions
Perl module for calculating critical values of common statistical distributions
Statistics-Distributions-0.07 - 22 Jun 2001 - Michael Kospach

7. Statistics::Frequency
simple counting of elements
Statistics-Frequency-0.02 - 24 Apr 2002 - Jarkko Hietaniemi

8. Statistics::GaussHelmert
General weighted least squares estimation
Statistics-GaussHelmert-0.05 - 18 Apr 2002 - Stephan Heuel

9. Statistics::LTU
An implementation of Linear Threshold Units
Statistics-LTU-2.8 - 27 Feb 1997 - Tom Fawcett

10. Statistics::Lite
Small stats stuff.
Statistics-Lite-1.02 - 15 Apr 2002 - Brian Lalonde

11. Statistics::MaxEntropy
Statistics-MaxEntropy-0.9 - 26 Nov 1998 - Hugo WL ter Doest

12. Statistics::OLS
perform ordinary least squares and associated statistics, v 0.07.
Statistics-OLS-0.07 - 13 Oct 2000 - Sanford Morton

13. Statistics::ROC
receiver-operator-characteristic (ROC) curves with nonparametric confidence bounds
Statistics-ROC-0.01 - 22 Jul 1998 - Hans A. Kestler

14. Statistics::Regression
weighted linear regression package (line+plane fitting)
StatisticsRegression - 26 May 2001 - ivo welch

15. Statistics::SparseVector
Perl5 extension for manipulating sparse bitvectors
Statistics-MaxEntropy-0.9 - 26 Nov 1998 - Hugo WL ter Doest

16. Statistics::Descriptive::Discrete
Compute descriptive statistics for discrete data sets.
Statistics-Descriptive-Discrete-0.07 - 13 Jun 2002 - Rhet Turnbull

```
17. Bio::Tree::Statistics
Calculate certain statistics for a Tree
bioperl-1.0.2 - 16 Jul 2002 - Ewan Birney

18. Device::ISDN::OCLM::Statistics
OCLM statistics superclass
Device-ISDN-OCLM-0.40 - 02 Jan 2000 - Merlin Hughes

19. Device::ISDN::OCLM::CurrentStatistics
OCLM current call statistics
Device-ISDN-OCLM-0.40 - 02 Jan 2000 - Merlin Hughes

20. Device::ISDN::OCLM::ISDNStatistics
OCLM ISDN statistics
Device-ISDN-OCLM-0.40 - 02 Jan 2000 - Merlin Hughes

21. Device::ISDN::OCLM::Last10Statistics
OCLM Last10 call statistics
Device-ISDN-OCLM-0.40 - 02 Jan 2000 - Merlin Hughes

22. Device::ISDN::OCLM::LastStatistics
OCLM last call statistics
Device-ISDN-OCLM-0.40 - 02 Jan 2000 - Merlin Hughes

23. Device::ISDN::OCLM::ManualStatistics
OCLM manual call statistics
Device-ISDN-OCLM-0.40 - 02 Jan 2000 - Merlin Hughes

24. Device::ISDN::OCLM::SPStatistics
OCLM service provider statistics
Device-ISDN-OCLM-0.40 - 02 Jan 2000 - Merlin Hughes

25. Device::ISDN::OCLM::SystemStatistics
OCLM system statistics
Device-ISDN-OCLM-0.40 - 02 Jan 2000 - Merlin Hughes
```

Let's check out the Statistics::ChiSquare module.

First, click on the link to Statistics::ChiSquare; you'll see a summary of the module, complete with a description, overview, discussion of the method, examples of use, and information about the author.

One of the modules looks interesting; let's download and install it. How big is the source code? If you click on the source link, you'll find that the module is really just one short subroutine with the documentation defined right in the module. Here's the subroutine definition part of the module:

```
package Statistics::ChiSquare;

# ChiSquare.pm
#
# Jon Orwant, orwant@media.mit.edu
#
```

```
# 31 Oct 95, revised Mon Oct 18 12:16:47 1999, and again November 2001
# to fix an off-by-one error
#
# Copyright 1995, 1999, 2001 Jon Orwant.  All rights reserved.
# This program is free software; you can redistribute it and/or
# modify it under the same terms as Perl itself.
#
# Version 0.3.  Module list status is "Rdpf"

use strict;
use vars qw($VERSION @ISA @EXPORT);

require Exporter;
require AutoLoader;

@ISA = qw(Exporter AutoLoader);
# Items to export into callers namespace by default. Note: do not export
# names by default without a very good reason. Use EXPORT_OK instead.
# Do not simply export all your public functions/methods/constants.
@EXPORT = qw(chisquare);

$VERSION = '0.3';

my @chilevels = (100, 99, 95, 90, 70, 50, 30, 10, 5, 1);
my %chitable = ();

# assume the expected probability distribution is uniform
sub chisquare {
    my @data = @_;
    @data = @{$data[0]} if @data == 1 and ref($data[0]);
    my $degrees_of_freedom = scalar(@data) - 1;
    my ($chisquare, $num_samples, $expected, $i) = (0, 0, 0, 0);
    if (! exists($chitable{$degrees_of_freedom})) {
        return "I can't handle ", scalar(@data),
          " choices without a better table.";
    }
    foreach (@data) { $num_samples += $_ }
    $expected = $num_samples / scalar(@data);
    return "There's no data!" unless $expected;
    foreach (@data) {
        $chisquare += (($_ - $expected) ** 2) / $expected;
    }
    foreach (@{$chitable{$degrees_of_freedom}}) {
        if ($chisquare < $_) {
            return
              "There's a <$chilevels[$i+1]% and <$chilevels[$i]% chance that this data
                  is random.";
        }
        $i++;
    }
    return "There's a <$chilevels[$#chilevels]% chance that this data is random.";
}
```

```
Suppose you roll a die 100 times, and it shows 30 sixes.
Is the die loaded?
In statistics, the chi-square test calculates "how random"
a series of numbers is.  But it doesn't simply say "yes"
or "no".  Instead, it gives you a confidence interval,
which sets upper and lower bounds on the likelihood that
the variation in your data is due to chance.  See the
examples below.
  ...
```

The documentation continues with more discussion and some concrete examples that use the module and interpret the results.

Very often, the SYNOPSIS part of the documentation is all you need to look at. It shows you specific examples of how to call the code in the module. In this case, because it's a very simple module, there is just one subroutine that can be used. As you see from the documentation excerpt, you just need to pass the chisquare subroutine an array of numbers and print out the return value to use the code. Let's try it. We'll take as our input an array of numbers that corresponds to the stops of the Broadway-7th Avenue local subway train on the west side of Manhattan, from 14th Street up to 137th Street in Harlem. (We'll assume you didn't run fast enough and missed the A train.) Let's see how random these stops really are:

```
use strict;
use warnings;

use Statistics::ChiSquare;

my(@subwaystops) = (14, 18, 23, 28, 34, 42, 50, 59, 66, 72, 79, 86, 96, 103, 110,
116, 125, 137);

print chisquare(@subwaystops);
```

This produces the output:

```
There's a <1% chance that this data is random.
```

(Knowing firsthand the feelings of long-suffering New York City Subway riders, I predict that this result might provoke some spirited discussion. Nevertheless, we seem to have working code.)

Problems with CPAN Modules

Actually, the sharp-eyed reader may have noticed a problem in our mad dash uptown. In the first line of the SYNOPSIS section, there's the following:

```
use Statistics::Chisquare;
```

The name of the module is spelled Chisquare, whereas in all other places in the documentation the module is spelled ChiSquare with a capital S. In Perl, the case of a letter, uppercase or lowercase, is important, and this looks suspiciously like a typographical error in the documentation. If you try use Statistics::Chisquare, you'll

discover that the module can't be found, whereas if you try use Statistics::
ChiSquare, the module is there. This is a minor bug, but some modules have poor
documentation, and it can be a time-consuming problem, especially if you are forced
to wade into the module code or try various tests, to figure out how the module
works.

Apart from bugs, I've also mentioned the problem that some modules are not tested,
or designed, for all operating systems. In addition, many modules require other modules to be present. It's possible to configure CPAN to automatically install all the
required modules a requested module uses, as described in the CPAN documentation, but you may need to intervene personally. It's useful to remember that if you
have a program that uses a certain module running on one computer, and you move
the program to another computer, you may have to install the required modules on
the new computer as well.

Saving the worst for last, it's also important to remember that contributing to CPAN
is open to one and all, and not all the code there is well-written or well-tested. The
heavily used modules are, but counterexamples can be found. So, don't bet the farm
on your code just because it uses a CPAN module; you should still carefully read the
documentation for the module and test your program.

The CPAN FAQ explains in detail the way to be a good citizen when it comes to testing and reporting bugs that you discover in CPAN code.

Exercises

Exercise 1.1
> What are the problems that might arise when dividing program code into sepa-
> rate module files?

Exercise 1.2
> What are the differences between libraries, modules, packages, and namespaces?

Exercise 1.3
> Write a module that finds modules on your computer.

Exercise 1.4
> Where do the standard Perl distribution modules live on your computer?

Exercise 1.5
> Research how Perl manages its namespaces.

Exercise 1.6
> When might it be necessary to export names from a module? When might it be
> useful? When might it be convenient? When might it be a very bad idea?

Exercise 1.7

The program `testGeneticcode` contains the following loop:

```
# Translate each three-base codon to an amino acid, and append to a protein
for(my $i=0; $i < (length($dna) - 2) ; $i += 3) {
        $protein .= Geneticcode::codon2aa( substr($dna,$i,3) );
}
```

Here's another way to accomplish that loop:

```
# Translate each three-base codon to an amino acid, and append to a protein
my $i=0;
while (my $codon = substr($dna, $i += 3, 3) ) {
        $protein .= Geneticcode::codon2aa( $codon );
}
```

Compare the two methods. Which is easier to understand? Which is easier to maintain? Which is faster? Why?

Exercise 1.8

The subroutine `codon2aa` causes the entire program to halt when it encounters a "bad" codon in the data. Often (usually) it is best for a subroutine to return some indication that it encountered a problem and let the calling program decide how to handle it. It makes the subroutine more generally useful if it isn't always halting the program (although that is what you want to do sometimes).

Rewrite `codon2aa` and the calling program `testGeneticcode` so that the subroutine returns some error—perhaps the value `undef`—and the calling program checks for that error and performs some action.

Exercise 1.9

Write a separate module for each of the following: reading a file, extracting FASTA sequence data, and printing sequence data to the screen.

Exercise 1.10

Download, install, and use a module from CPAN.

## CHAPTER 2

Data Structures and String Algorithms

So far in this book, I've used the standard Perl data structures of scalars, arrays, and hashes. However, it is often necessary to handle data with a more complex structure than what those basics allow. For instance, it is frequently useful to have a two-dimensional array.

In this chapter, you'll learn how to define and use *references* and *complex data structures*. After you learn the fundamentals, you'll apply the new techniques to implement a biologically important algorithm. These techniques are also fundamental to the implementation of object-oriented programming, as you'll see in Chapter 3.

The algorithm we'll study is called *approximate string matching*. It lets you find the closest match for a peptide fragment in a protein, for instance. It uses an algorithmic technique called *dynamic programming*, an essential tool for many similar biological tasks, such as aligning biological sequences. In this chapter, you'll see how Perl references can be used to write programs for data problems with more complex relationships. References are also used for the objects of object-oriented programming.

Basic Perl Data Types

Before tackling references, let's review the basic Perl data types:

Scalar
> A scalar value is a string or any one of several kinds of numbers such as integers, floating-point (decimal) numbers, or numbers in scientific notation such as 2. 3E23. A scalar variable begins with the dollar sign $, as in $dna.

Array
> An array is an ordered collection of scalar values. An array variable begins with an at sign @, as in @peptides. An array can be initialized by a list such as @peptides = ('zeroth', 'first', 'second'). Individual scalar elements of an array are referred to by first preceding the array name with a dollar sign (an individual element of an array is a scalar value) and then following the array name

with the position of the desired element in square brackets. Thus the first element of the @peptides array is referenced by $peptides[0] and has the value 'zeroth'. (Note that array elements are given the positions 0, 1, 2, ..., *n*-1, where *n* is the number of elements in the array.)

Recall that printing an array within double quotes causes the elements to be separated by spaces; without the double quotes, the elements are printed one after the other without separations. This snippet:

```
@pentamers = ('cggca', 'tgatc', 'ttggc');

print "@pentamers", "\n";
print @pentamers, "\n";
```

produces the output:

```
cggca tgatc ttggc
cggcatgatcttggc
```

Hash

A hash is an unordered collection of key value pairs of scalar values. Each scalar *key* is associated with a scalar value. A hash variable begins with the percent sign %, as in %geneticmarkers. A hash can be initialized like an array, except that each pair of scalars are taken as a key with its value, as in:

The => symbol is just a synonym for a comma that makes it easier to see the key/value pairs in such lists.* An individual scalar value is retrieved by preceding the hash name with a dollar sign (an individual value is a scalar value) and following the hash name with the key in curly braces, as in $geneticmarkers{'hairless'}, which, because of how it's initialized, has the value 'no'.

References

Many computer languages provide variables that allow you to refer to, or point at, other values. So, instead of a variable containing data such as a string or number of interest, the variable contains the *location* of the data; it tells you where to go to get the value you want. In Perl, the use of a scalar variable to refer to another value is called a *reference*, and the value being pointed at is called a *referent*.

References allow you to do many useful things in Perl; you can define multidimensional arrays and other more complex data structures and avoid copying large amounts of data (for instance, when passing arguments into subroutines). Using references can make your programs faster, more efficient, and shorter. References have a number of uses, as you'll see in the next sections.

---

* It also forces the left side to be interpreted as a string.

References to Scalars

Here's an example of a reference:

```
$peptide = 'EIQADEVRL';

$peptideref = \$peptide;

print "Here is what's in the reference:\n";
print $peptideref, "\n";

print "Here is what the reference is pointing to:\n";
print ${$peptideref}, "\n";
print $$peptideref, "\n";
```

This Perl code produces the following output:

```
Here is what's in the reference:
SCALAR(0x80fe4ac)
Here is what the reference is pointing to:
EIQADEVRL
EIQADEVRL
```

What's going on here?

First, a string value of EIQADEVRL is assigned to the scalar variable $peptide. Next, a backslash operator is used before the $peptide variable to return a reference to the variable. This reference is saved in the scalar variable $peptideref.

The next lines of code show what this example really does. When you print out the (actual) value of the reference variable $peptideref, you get the value:

```
SCALAR(0x80fe4ac)
```

This says that the reference variable $peptideref is pointing to a scalar value (which is the value of the scalar variable $peptide). It also gives a hexadecimal number that specifies where in the computer memory the value for that variable resides.

The 0x at the beginning of the number says that it is a hexadecimal number.[*] Hexadecimal (base 16) numbers are a way to specify locations in computer memory. The exact location in the computer memory where this $peptide value resides is almost never of practical importance to you. However, it can help when debugging code that uses references, and so it is displayed when you print the value of a reference as we've just done or when you use the Perl ref command (which we'll use later).

---

[*] Recall that hexadecimal numbers use 16 digits, from 0 to f, and that the decimal (base 10) numbers:

0, 1, 2, 3, 4, 5, 6, 7, 8, 9, 10, 11, 12, 13, 14, 15, 16

correspond to the hexadecimal (base 16) numbers:

0, 1, 2, 3, 4, 5, 6, 7, 8, 9, a, b, c, d, e, f, 10

Dereferencing

Finally, our code fragment performs the essential task of *dereferencing* a reference. In Perl a reference to a scalar variable can be dereferenced by surrounding it with curly braces {} and prepending another dollar sign to it. ${$peptideref} returns the value the reference variable is pointing at. The value being pointed at is the same as the value of the $peptide variable, which has the value 'EIQADEVRL', so ${$peptideref} also has the value 'EIQADEVRL'.

Surrounding a reference with curly braces before prepending the appropriate symbol ($ for scalar, @ for array, % for hash) is generally the best way to dereference reference variables. As you start using more intricate references, you'll find that it's often the only way to dereference properly. However, for simple reference variables, it is possible to omit the additional curly braces. So, our example shows both ways of dereferencing our scalar reference:

```
${$peptideref}
$$peptideref
```

In Perl, every reference must be dereferenced properly in the program (in other words, by the programmer) to be useful. Perl doesn't automatically dereference for you, nor can it figure out when you want a reference or when you want the value that the reference is pointing to. So, it's up to you to specify that you want the value of a reference by prepending a %, @, or $ to hash, array, or scalar references, respectively. (And, as just pointed out, you often need to surround the reference with curly braces, although for simple references, they can be omitted.)

Anonymous data

A scalar constant can also be referenced, as in the following code:

```
$peptideref = \'EIQADEVRL';

print "Here is what's in the reference:\n";
print $peptideref, "\n";

print "Here is what the reference is pointing to:\n";
print ${$peptideref}, "\n";
```

This produces the output:

```
Here is what's in the reference:
SCALAR(0x80fe4a0)
Here is what the reference is pointing to:
EIQADEVRL
```

In this case the reference points directly to a location in memory in which the string value EIQADEVRL is being stored.

Compare this code with the previous example. The reference was to an existing variable that held a scalar value. Think of it as a scalar value with a "name" that is the already existing variable. Now, the reference is to a scalar value alone. This scalar value isn't contained in any variable; it has no name. Thus, it's called an *anonymous referent*, which can only be used via the reference to it.

You may well ask, "Why bother?" Anonymous scalars are, for most practical purposes, not any more desirable than simple scalar variables. However, anonymous data structures, and references to them, are frequently useful, as you shall see.

References of References

It is sometimes useful to have references of references. Since a reference is just a variable containing a scalar value, it's possible to make a reference to a reference:

```
$value = 'ACGAAGCT';
$refvalue = \$value;
$refrefvalue = \$refvalue;

print $value, "\n";
print $$refvalue, "\n";
print $$$refrefvalue, "\n";
```

This prints out:

```
ACGAAGCT
ACGAAGCT
ACGAAGCT
```

(Notice that here I've omitted the surrounding curly braces from around the references.) You can also apply several levels of reference at one go:

```
$value = 'ACGAAGCT';
$refrefrefvalue = \\\$value;

print $value, "\n";
print $$$$refrefrefvalue, "\n";
```

This prints out:

```
ACGAAGCT
ACGAAGCT
```

References to Arrays

References to arrays obey pretty much the same syntax as references to scalars. You make a reference to an array by prepending a backslash to the @ sign; you dereference the array by surrounding the reference variable with curly braces and prepending an @ sign, as in the following example:

```
@pentamers = ('cggca', 'tgatc', 'ttggc');

$arrayref = \@pentamers;

print "Here is what's in the reference:\n";
print $arrayref, "\n";
```

```
print "Here is what the reference is pointing to:\n";
print "@{$arrayref}\n";

print "Here is the second value in the array:\n";
print ${$arrayref}[1], "\n";
```

This Perl code produces the following output:

```
Here is what's in the reference:
ARRAY(0x80fe4c4)
Here is what the reference is pointing to:
cggca tgatc ttggc
Here is the second value in the array:
tgatc
```

An important point to remember here is that Perl doesn't automatically know if you want the data a reference is pointing to or the reference variable itself. If it's pointing to a scalar value, it's up to you to prepend the $ sign to the reference in order to dereference the value. Similarly, as in this example, if a reference is pointing to an array value, it's up to you to prepend the @ sign to the reference to dereference the value; @{$arrayref} is correct; @$arrayref is also okay.

On the other hand, if you want the value of one element of the referenced array, you prepend a dollar sign because the value will be a scalar value. Recall that to get the scalar value of one element of an array you use a dollar sign; for example, $array[0]. Similarly, to get the scalar value of one element from an array with a reference, you prepend a dollar sign; for example, ${$arrayref}[0] or $$arrayref[0].

The arrow operator

References to arrays (and references to hashes and subroutines) can be *dereferenced* using another syntax that's popular and important to learn. If $arrayref is a reference to an array, then to dereference the second element (for instance) of that array, you can say either:

```
$$arrayref[1]
```

or, equivalently:

```
$arrayref->[1]
```

The following code fragment shows this:

```
@pentamers = ('cggca', 'tgatc', 'ttggc');

$arrayref = \@pentamers;

print "Here is the second element of the pentamers array:\n";
print $$arrayref[1], "\n";

print "And here it is again:\n";
print $arrayref->[1], "\n";
```

This code prints out:

```
Here is the second element of the pentamers array:
tgatc
And here it is again:
tgatc
```

The *arrow operator* appears between the name of the reference to an array and the square brackets and subscript. It works similarly with hashes and with subroutines, as you'll see later.

As a convenient shortcut, it is sometimes possible to drop multiple arrow operators in a reference. Thus, if:

```
$array = [ [ 'Dennis', 'Drayna' ], [ 'Callum', 'Bell' ] ];
```

the following are synonymous:

```
print $$array[1][2];
print $array->[1][2];
print $array->[1]->[2];
```

Here's the output:

```
BellBellBell
```

I'll show more examples of this shortcut later in this chapter.

Anonymous arrays

You can create an anonymous array by surrounding a list with square brackets. (A mnemonic device to remember this bit of syntax is that square brackets are also used with arrays to refer to a particular element, as in $arr[4].) You can then create a reference to the anonymous array like so:

```
$pentamers = ['cggca', 'tgatc', 'ttggc'];

print "The third and last element of the array is ", $pentamers->[2], "\n";
```

This gives the output:

```
The third and last element of the array is ttggc
```

In this case, $pentamers is a reference to an (anonymous) array. The third element can equally well be printed using $$pentamers[2]. The entire array is named by prepending an @ sign:

```
$pentamers = ['cggca', 'tgatc', 'ttggc'];

print "The third and last element of the array is $$pentamers[2]\n";
print "The entire array is: @$pentamers\n";
```

This produces the output:

```
The third and last element of the array is ttggc
The entire array is: cggca tgatc ttggc
```

References to Hashes

References to hashes also follow the same rules as references to scalars and arrays. You make a reference to a hash by prepending a backslash to the % sign; you dereference by prepending the percent sign to the dollar sign on the reference variable:

```
%geneticmarkers = ('curly' => 'yes', 'hairy' => 'no', 'topiary' => 'yes');

$hashref = \%geneticmarkers;

print "Here is what's in the reference:\n";
print $hashref, "\n";

print "Here is what the reference is pointing to:\n";
foreach $k (keys %$hashref) {
    print "key\t$k\t\tvalue\t$$hashref{$k}\n";
}

print "Dereferencing using the arrow operator:\n";
foreach $k (keys %$hashref) {
    print "key\t$k\t\tvalue\t$hashref->{$k}\n";
}
```

This Perl code produces the following output:

```
Here is what's in the reference:
HASH(0x80fe4c4)
Here is what the reference is pointing to:
key        topiary              value       yes
key        curly                value       yes
key        hairy                value       no
Dereferencing using the arrow operator:
key        topiary              value       yes
key        curly                value       yes
key        hairy                value       no
```

Notice that the keys are printed in a different order than they were specified: hashes do not preserve the order of their keys. (Also recall that, in a double quoted string, \t prints a tab space.)

If you want one value of the referenced hash, you prepend a dollar sign because the value will be a scalar value. To get one value of a hash, you use a dollar sign, e.g., $geneticmarkers{'curly'}; to get one value from a reference to a hash, you also use a dollar sign, e.g., $$hashref{'curly'}.

The arrow operator -> works with hashes the way it works with arrays. With hashes, the arrow operator is placed between the name of the hash and the curly braces. To illustrate:

```
%geneticmarkers = ('curly' => 'yes', 'hairy' => 'no', 'topiary' => 'yes');

$hashref = \%geneticmarkers;
```

```
print "For key 'curly' the value is '", $$hashref{'curly'}, "'\n";
print "For key 'curly' the value is '", $hashref->{'curly'}, "'\n";
```

This prints:

```
For key 'curly' the value is 'yes'
For key 'curly' the value is 'yes'
```

Anonymous hashes

You can create an anonymous hash by surrounding a list with curly braces. (The mnemonic device to remember this bit of syntax is that curly braces are also used with hashes to refer to a particular key, as in $hash{'curly'}.) You can then create a reference to the anonymous hash like so:

```
$geneticmarkers = {'curly' => 'yes', 'hairy' => 'no', 'topiary' => 'yes'};

print "Here is what is in the anonymous hash:\n";
foreach $k (keys %$geneticmarkers) {
    print "key\t$k\tvalue\t$geneticmarkers->{$k}\n";
}
```

This gives the output:

```
Here is what is in the anonymous hash:
key       topiary      value      yes
key       curly        value      yes
key       hairy        value      no
```

In this case, $geneticmarkers is a reference to an (anonymous) hash. The values can equally well be printed using $$geneticmarkers{$k}or $geneticmarkers->{$k}.

Curly braces can also be used for blocks and for subroutine definitions. The Perl interpreter can occasionally get confused as to which of these constructs is meant, although it's rare. To be clear, you can put a plus sign + in front of an anonymous hash to specify that it is an anonymous hash and not a block:

```
$anonhash = +{ 'one' => 1, 'two' => 2 };
print "The old $$anonhash{'one'} $anonhash->{'two'}\n";
```

This prints:

```
The old 1 2
```

References to Subroutines

References to subroutines are yet another way to reference in Perl. This may seem a little odd. References to scalars, arrays, and hashes are references to data structures. But references to subroutines? A subroutine isn't a data structure, so how did this come about?

There are two reasons why references to subroutines make sense the same way that references to data structures make sense. The first reason is that just as variables are managed with Perl's symbol tables, so also are subroutine definitions managed by the symbol table. In Chapter 3, you'll see the deliberate manipulation of a symbol table to make subroutine definitions on the fly. In this sense, subroutines, hashes, arrays, and scalars all refer to data that has a name.

The second reason is that references to subroutines are sometimes a great tool to use when writing a program. There are times when you might apply one of a number of different subroutines depending on the program logic and the input, and using references to subroutines can make this kind of code easier to write. That's the real justification for just about everything you might find in the toolbox that we call a programming language, right? (I admit it sometimes seems that sheer orneriness was the motivation.)

References to subroutines follow the same rules as references to scalars and arrays. Recall that a subroutine name may optionally be prepended with the ampersand sign & when it is called.* Thus, these two are equivalent:

```
findmotif('ATTAATTTTCCGATC');
&findmotif('ATTAATTTTCCGATC');
```

To make a reference to a subroutine, you prepend a backslash to the ampersand:

```
$subref = \&findmotif;
```

You dereference a subroutine one of two ways: by prepending an ampersand to the subroutine reference, like so:

```
&$subref();
```

or by using the arrow operator, like so:

```
$subref->();
```

This is demonstrated by the following code fragment (which includes a subroutine definition):

```
print "Mark 1:\n";
findmotif('ATTAATTTTCCGATC');

print "Mark 2:\n";
&findmotif('ATTAATTTTCCGATC');

print "Mark 3:\n";
$subref = \&findmotif;
&$subref('ATTAATTTTCCGATC');

print "Mark 4:\n";
$subref = \&findmotif;
$subref->('ATTAATTTTCCGATC');

print "Mark 5:\n";
$subref2 = \findmotif;
&$subref2('ATTAATTTTCCGATC');
```

---

* The ampersand was required in older versions of Perl.

```
sub findmotif {
    my($input) = @_;

    if($input =~ /CCGA/) {
        print "I found CCGA!\n";
    }else{
        print "No motif\n";
    }
}
```

This produces the output:

```
Mark 1:
I found CCGA!
Mark 2:
I found CCGA!
Mark 3:
I found CCGA!
Mark 4:
I found CCGA!
Mark 5:
Not a CODE reference at - line 17.
```

This code defines a little subroutine findmotif that looks for a short motif in DNA sequence data. The first two calls to the subroutine simply demonstrate that you can call subroutines with or without a leading ampersand &. The third calls the subroutine by means of a reference to the subroutine, as just described. The fourth call is by means of a reference to the subroutine using the alternative arrow operator. Finally, the fifth call produces an error; the problem is just a syntactical one; it tries to take a reference to a subroutine by prepending the backslash to the name of the subroutine without including the leading ampersand.

It's useful to remind the gentle reader that the error produced by that fifth call to findmotif occurs only if you don't use the use strict directive (as you are encouraged always to do). Without use strict, the program fails only when it reaches that bad call. With use strict, the program complains and fails immediately. What if that call isn't made until several hours into the running program (which is not an uncommon running time in bioinformatics)? use strict can save a lot of time and effort.

Anonymous subroutines

You can create an anonymous subroutine by giving the keyword sub followed by a subroutine definition within the usual curly braces, followed by a semicolon. An anonymous subroutine definition is just like a normal subroutine definition, except the name of the subroutine is omitted, and you must follow it with a semicolon. (Recall that subroutine definitions normally are not followed by a semicolon, as with the subroutine findmotif in the previous example.)

You can create a reference to the anonymous subroutine like so:

```
$findmotif = sub {
    my($input) = @_;

    if($input =~ /CCGA/) {
        print "I found CCGA!\n";
    }else{
        print "No motif\n";
    }
};

$findmotif->('ATTAATTTTCCGATC');
&$findmotif('ATTAATTTTCCGATC');
```

This gives the output:

```
I found CCGA!
I found CCGA!
```

In this case, $findmotif is a reference to an (anonymous) subroutine. The subroutine reference was dereferenced and called twice to show the use of the two alternative choices of syntax: the prepended ampersand and the arrow operator.

Passing references to subroutines

Perl collapses all arguments to a subroutine as a list of scalars. This makes it impossible to distinguish between, say, two arrays you might try to pass to a subroutine, as the following example illustrates:

```
@aminoacids1 = ('E', 'V', 'L');
@aminoacids2 = ('D', 'T', 'Y');

printacids(@aminoacids1, @aminoacids2);

sub printacids {
    my(@aa1, @aa2) = @_;

    print "Amino acids 1\n";
    print "@aa1\n";
    print "Amino acids 2\n";
    print "@aa2\n";
}
```

This prints out:

```
Amino acids 1
E V L D T Y
Amino acids 2
```

As you can see, the elements of both arrays are passed to the subroutine by means of the special array @_, and Perl assigns this entire array to the first local array @aa1.

In order to pass an arbitrary list of any combination of scalars, arrays, or hashes to a subroutine, it's necessary to pass the values as references. Here's how to fix the previous example:

```
@aminoacids1 = ('E', 'V', 'L');
@aminoacids2 = ('D', 'T', 'Y');

printacids(\@aminoacids1, \@aminoacids2);

sub printacids {
    my($aa1, $aa2) = @_;

    print "Amino acids 1\n";
    print "@$aa1\n";
    print "Amino acids 2\n";
    print "@$aa2\n";
}
```

This prints out:

```
Amino acids 1
E V L
Amino acids 2
D T Y
```

In this version, the subroutine is passed references to the arrays. Inside the subroutine, the references are collected in the variables $aa1 and $aa2 and are dereferenced to print out their contents using the forms @$aa1 and @$aa2.

Even when you're passing just one scalar to a subroutine, you might want to pass a reference. Say you have the DNA sequence of human chromosome 1 in a variable $chrom1. You want to pass this sequence into a subroutine that searches for restriction enzymes. A problem can arise because passing a variable into a subroutine involves making a copy of the data into the subroutine's variables, and you've just used up a significant portion of your computer's memory.

By passing a reference to the DNA sequence data, you avoid making a copy of the data, and your program will use less memory. It will also run much faster because copying large strings is a fairly time-consuming process for a program.

Here's a simple example of how to pass a scalar reference to a subroutine:

```
my $chrom1 = getchrom('1');  # assume we read in human chromosome 1 here

my @enzyme_sites = findrestrictionenzymes(\$chrom1, 'HindIII');

sub findrestrictionenzymes {
  my($seqref, $re) = @_; # $seqref is a reference to a scalar string
                         # $re contains the name of a restriction enzyme

    ... program logic follows, where $$seqref is the sequence data ...
}
```

Writing programs is a type of engineering, and engineering always seems to come back to the idea of tradeoffs. The downside of passing references to subroutines is that anything the subroutine does to the referenced data stays in effect after the subroutine has exited. This "action at a distance" needs to be treated with care, so as not to modify data unintentionally.

Returning references from subroutines

You'll see in Chapter 3 how the subroutine called new returns a reference to an anonymous data structure declared within the subroutine. Until then, I'll defer a detailed discussion of how this works; the bottom line is that a subroutine can return a reference because a reference is "really" just a scalar value.

Symbolic Versus Hard References

There are two kinds of references, hard and symbolic. *Hard references* actually point to locations in computer memory.

For example, a hard reference to a scalar:

```
$name = 'Joel';
```

is defined like so:

```
$nameref = \$name;
```

and the values associated with the hard reference $$nameref are:

```
print '$nameref has the value ', $nameref, ' and points to the referent ',
    $$nameref, "\n";
```

This prints:

```
$nameref has the value SCALAR(0x80fe4ac) and points to the referent Joel
```

Symbolic references refer to a name, not an address. As a brief example, let's say we have four array variables @mark1, @mark2, @mark3, and @mark4. It is possible to have another variable that is set to one of these variable names; let's say the variable is called $arrayname and it's set to the value mark3, and that is the array we want to access.

You can place the $arrayname variable in a block. Because a block returns the value of its last expression, this block returns the string mark3. You can then place the special array symbol @ in front of the block, and Perl will recognize this as meaning the @mark3 array. Here is a demonstration of how this works:

```
@mark1 = ( 'a1', 'a2', 'a3', 'a4' );
@mark2 = ( 'b1', 'b2', 'b3', 'b4' );
@mark3 = ( 'c1', 'c2', 'c3', 'c4' );
@mark4 = ( 'd1', 'd2', 'd3', 'd4' );
```

```
$arrayname = 'mark3';

print "@{$arrayname}\n";
```

This program prints out the result:

```
c1 c2 c3 c4
```

Symbolic references are avoided by some programmers and used frequently by others; you may sometimes come across them, or even find yourself using them. They are used in the AUTOLOAD methods that install methods at runtime, which you'll learn about in the later chapters.

Matrices

Perl matrices are built from simpler data structures using references. Recall that a *matrix* is a set of values that can be uniquely referenced by indexes. If only one index is required, the matrix is one-dimensional (this is exactly how an array works in Perl). If *n* indexes are required, the matrix is *n*-dimensional.

Two-Dimensional Matrices

A two-dimensional matrix is one of the simplest complex data structures. It can be conceptualized as a table of rows and columns, in which each element of the table is uniquely identified by its particular row and column.

There are several ways to build matrices in Perl. We'll look at some of the most useful.

Because there is no built-in matrix data structure, you have to build a matrix from other data structures. The most straightforward way to do this is with an *array of arrays*:

```
@probes = (
    [1, 3, 2, 9],
    [2, 0, 8, 1],
    [5, 4, 6, 7],
    [1, 9, 2, 8]
);

print "The probe at row 1, column 2 has value ", $probes[1][2], "\n";
```

This prints out:

```
The probe at row 1, column 2 has value 8
```

> Recall that in Perl the first element of an array is indexed 0; so row 1 in this program is actually the second row, and column 2 is actually the third column. Sometimes you may want to refer to the 0th row as row 1; you have to adjust your code and your interactions with the user accordingly.

This matrix is implemented as an array (in parentheses), each element of which is a reference to an anonymous array [in square brackets], which itself is a list of integers.

Another good way to build an array is to *declare a reference to an anonymous array*. In the following example, I declare an empty anonymous array and then populate it as desired. This is, in effect, an anonymous array of anonymous arrays:

```
# Declare reference to (empty) anonymous array
$array = [ ];

# Initialize the array
for($i=0; $i < 4 ; ++$i) {
  for($j=0; $j < 4 ; ++$j) {
      $array->[$i][$j] = $i * $j;
  }
}

# Reset one of the elements of the array
$array->[3][2] = 99;

# Print the array
for($i=0; $i < 4 ; ++$i) {
  for($j=0; $j < 4 ; ++$j) {
      printf("%3d ", $array->[$i][$j]);
  }
  print "\n";
}
```

 Note the use of printf to format the output nicely. For a refresher on this Perl function, consult the Perl documentation, by typing:

```
perldoc -f printf
```

and

```
perldoc -f sprintf
```

at a shell prompt or check out *http://www.perldoc.com*.

This program produces the following output:

```
0   0   0   0
0   1   2   3
0   2   4   6
0   3  99   9
```

Alternatively, if the values are known, I can declare this as an anonymous array of anonymous arrays by saying:

```
$array = [
  [0, 0, 0, 0],
  [0, 1, 2, 3],
  [0, 2, 4, 6],
  [0, 3, 99, 9]
];
```

I can also declare an array of anonymous arrays, by saying:

```
@array = (
  [0, 0, 0, 0],
  [0, 1, 2, 3],
  [0, 2, 4, 6],
  [0, 3, 99, 9]
);
```

Notice the slight syntactical difference between an array of anonymous arrays:

```
@array = ( [ ], [ ], ... );
```

and an anonymous array of anonymous arrays:

```
$array = [ [ ], [ ], ... ];
```

Note that Perl also allows you to say:

```
$$array[$i][$j]
```

as a synonym for:

```
$array->[$i][$j]
```

But beware confusing:

```
$array->[$i][$j]
```

with:

```
$array[$i][$j]
```

They are not the same thing and won't refer to the same array if you intermix them!

Very often you read data in from a file that has the elements of a matrix displayed one row per line, and you have to store the data from that file in an array in your Perl program. Say you have the following data:

```
0   0   0   0
0   1   2   3
0   2   4   6
0   3   99  9
```

You can read the data into a Perl array with the following loop:

```
while (<>) {
  @row = split;
  push(@array, [ @row ]);
}
```

This assumes that you've named the file on the command line as an argument to the program. Note that each incoming line is assigned to the special variable $_ on each iteration through the while loop. The split function uses this line stored in $_ by default. Each incoming line is split into an array of its whitespace-separated elements, and then an anonymous array [@row] containing those elements is pushed onto the @array array.

For more details on arrays of arrays, see the perllol manpage; type perldoc perllol at your command prompt or visit the Perl documentation web site at *http://www. perldoc.com*.

Higher-Dimensional Matrices

To use a higher-dimensional matrix, simply add another dimension:

```
# Populate a 3-dimensional array
$array = [ ];

# Initialize the array
for($i=0; $i < 4 ; ++$i) {
  for($j=0; $j < 4 ; ++$j) {
    for($k=0; $k < 4 ; ++$k) {
      $array->[$i][$j][$k] = $i * $j * k;
    }
  }
}
```

The sharp-witted reader may have noticed that we seem to be omitting arrow operators between array subscripts. (After all, these are anonymous arrays of anonymous arrays of anonymous arrays, etc., so shouldn't they be written [$array->[$i]->[$j]-> [$k]?) Perl allows this; only the arrow operator between the variable name and the first array subscript is required. It make things easier on the eyes and helps avoid carpal tunnel syndrome. On the other hand, you may prefer to keep the dereferencing arrows in place, to make it clear you are dealing with references. Your choice.

There's no need to stop at three-dimensional arrays. If higher-dimensional arrays are hard to imagine, just don't think of "dimension" as tied to space. For instance, four-dimensional arrays have points that are uniquely identified by four indices; five-dimensional arrays have points that are uniquely identified by five indices, etc. In fact, subatomic space is thought to contain eleven dimensions.

Sparse Arrays

Some programs need arrays, but only a small number of the array elements are ever used. Such arrays are called *sparse arrays*.

It would be inefficient to declare, for instance, a 1,000-by-1,000 element array, 1 million elements in all, if only 100 elements are ever actually used. For such sparse two-dimensional arrays, it's best to implement the array as a hash of hashes:

```
$array = { };

$array->{4}{83} = 'set';
$array->{34}{9} = 'set';
```

```
print $array->{4}{83}, "\n";
print $array->{34}{9}, "\n";
```

This prints out:

```
set
set
```

Perl creates only the table elements referenced, which makes an efficient implementation for a sparse matrix. However, because merely looking at a location (to see if there's anything there) creates an entry in the hash, you have to use the Perl exists function to keep your hashes sparse when looking at them. exists reports on whether a particular key (or array element) has been created, without actually creating it.* So to explore the sparse matrix just shown, you can say:

```
$array = { };

$array->{4}{83} = 'set';
$array->{34}{9} = 'set';

for(my $i=0 ; $i < 100 ; ++$i) {
    for(my $j=0 ; $j < 100 ; ++$j) {
        if( exists($array->{$i}) and exists($array->{$i}{$j}) ) {
            print "Array element row $i column $j is $array->{$i}{$j}\n";
        }
    }
}
```

This reports, without increasing the size of the array, that:

```
Array element row 4 column 83 is set
Array element row 34 column 9 is set
```

Question: why did you need two exists tests? (Hint: it's a two-dimensional array.) Another question: is $array a hash or a reference to an anonymous hash? Can you implement it the other way? See the exercises for this chapter.

Complex Data Structures

Different algorithms require different data structures. Using references in Perl, it is possible to build very complex data structures.

This section gives a short introduction to some of the possibilities, such as a hash with array values and a two-dimensional array of hashes. See the recommended reading in the "Resources" section of this chapter for books and sections of the Perl manual that are very helpful.

---

* The function defined is related but different; when used on a hash element, it checks if the value is undef, not whether the value exists.

Perl uses the basic data types of scalar, array, and hash, plus the ability to declare scalar references to those basic data types, to build more complex structures. For instance, an array must have scalar elements, but those scalar elements can be references to hashes, in which case you have effectively created an array of hashes.

Hash with Array Values

A common example of a complex data structure is a hash with array values. Using such a data structure, you can associate a list of items with each keyword. The following code shows an example of how to build and manage such a data structure. Assume you have a set of human genes, and for each human gene, you want to manage an array of organisms that are known to have closely related genes. Of course, each such array of related organisms can be a different length:

```perl
use Data::Dumper;

%relatedgenes = ( );

$relatedgenes{'stromelysin'} = [
    'C.elegans',
    'Arabidopsis thaliana'
];
$relatedgenes{'obesity'} = [
    'Drosophila',
    'Mus musculus'
];

# Now add a new related organism to the entry for 'stromelysin'

push( @{$relatedgenes{'stromelysin'}}, 'Canis' );

print Dumper(\%relatedgenes);
```

This program prints out the following (the very useful Data::Dumper module is described in more detail later; try typing perldoc Data::Dumper for the details of this useful way to print out complex data structures):

```perl
$VAR1 = {
        'stromelysin' => [
                        'C.elegans',
                        'Arabidopsis thaliana',
                        'Canis'
                        ],
        'obesity' => [
                        'Drosophila',
                        'Mus musculus'
                        ]
};
```

The tricky part of this short program is the push. The first argument to push must be an array. In the program, this array is @{$relatedgenes{'stromelysin'}}. Examining this array from the inside out, you can see that it refers to the value of the hash with key stromelysin: `$relatedgenes{'stromelysin'}`. You know that the values of this `%relatedgenes` hash are references to anonymous arrays. This hash value is contained within a block of curly braces, which returns the reference to the anonymous array: `{$relatedgenes{'stromelysin'}}`, and the block is preceded by an @ sign that dereferences the anonymous array: `@{$relatedgenes{'stromelysin'}}`.

Two-Dimensional Array of Hashes

As another example, say you have data from a microarray experiment in which each location on a plate can be identified by an x and y location; each location is also associated with a particular gene and has a set of reported measurements. You can implement this particular data as a two-dimensional array, each entry of which is a (reference to a) hash whose keys are gene names and whose values are (references to) arrays of the measurements. Here's how you can initialize one of the entries of that two-dimensional array:

```
$array[3][4]{'stromelysin'} = [3, 4, 5];
```

The position on the plate is represented by an entry in the two-dimensional array such as `$array[3][4]`. The fact that the entry is a hash is shown by the reference to a particular key with `{'stromelysin'}`. That the value for that key is an array is shown by the assignment to that key `$array[3][4]{'stromelysin'}` of the anonymous array `[3, 4, 5]`. To print out the array associated with the key stromelysin, you have to remember to tell Perl that the value for that key is an array by surrounding the expression with curly braces preceded by an @ sign `@{$array[3][4]{'stromelysin'}}`:

```
$array[3][4]{'stromelysin'} = [3, 4, 5];
print "The scores for plate position 3, 4 were @{$array[3][4]{'stromelysin'}}
    \n";
```

This prints:

```
The scores for plate position 3, 4 were 3 4 5
```

A common Perl trick is to dereference a complex data structure by enclosing the whole thing in curly braces and preceding it with the correct symbol: $, @, or %. So, take a moment and reread the last example. Do you see how the following:

```
$array[3][4]{'stromelysin'}
```

is the key for a hash? Do you see how the phrase:

```
@{$array[3][4]{'stromelysin'}}
```

makes it clear that the value for that hash key is an array? Similarly, if the value for that hash key was a scalar, you could say:

```
${$array[3][4]{'stromelysin'}}
```

and if the value for that hash key was a hash, you could say:

```
%{$array[3][4]{'stromelysin'}}
```

Complex Data Structures

References give you a fair amount of flexibility. For example, your data structures can combine references to different types of data. You can have an anonymous array such as in the following short program:

```
$gene = [
    # hash of basic information about the gene name, discoverer,
    #  discovery date and laboratory.
    {
        name       => 'antiaging',
        reference  => [ 'G. Mendel', '1865'],
        laboratory => [ 'Dept. of Genetics', 'Cornell University', 'USA']
    },

    # scalar giving priority
    'high',

    # array of local work history
    ['Jim', 'Rose', 'Eamon', 'Joe']
];

print "Name is ", ${$gene->[0]}{'name'}, "\n";

print "Priority is ", $gene->[1], "\n";

print "Research center is ", ${${$gene->[0]}{'laboratory'}}[1], "\n";

print "These individuals worked on the gene: ", "@{$gene->[2]}", "\n";
```

This program produces the output:

```
Name is antiaging
Priority is high
Research center is Cornell University
These individuals worked on the gene: Jim Rose Eamon Joe
```

Let's examine this code to understand how it works; it contains most of the points made in this chapter.

$gene is a pointer to an anonymous array of three elements. Therefore each element of $gene is referred to by either:

```
$$gene[0]
$$gene[1]
$$gene[2]
```

or equivalently (and our choice in this code) by:

```
$gene->[0]
$gene->[1]
$gene->[2]
```

To be specific, the first element is a reference to an anonymous hash, the second element is a scalar string high, and the third element is a reference to an anonymous workgroup array.

The plot thickens when you examine the anonymous hash that is referenced by the first array element. It has three keys, one of which, name, has a simple scalar value. The other two keys have values that are references to anonymous arrays of scalar strings.

So, this certainly qualifies as a complex data structure!

When you place any of the elements of the $gene anonymous array within a block of curly braces, you have a reference that must be dereferenced appropriately. To refer to the entire hash at the beginning of the array, say:

```
%{$gene->[0]}
```

As done with the program code, the scalar value that is the second element of the array is accessed simply as:

```
$gene->[1]
```

The third part of this data structure is an anonymous array, which we can refer to in total as:

```
@{$gene->[2]}
```

This is also done in the program code.

Now, let's finish by looking into the first element of the $gene anonymous array. This is a reference to an anonymous hash. One of the keys of that hash has a simple scalar string value, which is referenced with:

```
${$gene->[0]}{name}
```

as was done in the program code. To make sure we understand this, let's write it out:

```
${$gene->[0]}{name}
      is
$ hashref      {name}
      is
'antiaging'
```

{$gene->[0]} is a block containing a reference to an anonymous hash. It is then used as is typical for a hash reference: it's preceded by a $ and followed by the key name in curly braces and so resolves to a lookup of the key name in the anonymous hash.

The most intricate dereference in this program is that which digs out the name of the research center:

```
${${$gene->[0]}{laboratory} }[1]
      is
```

```
${$ hashref    {laboratory} }[1]
     is
$  arrayref               [1]
     is
'Cornell University'
```

Here, the {$gene->[0]} is a reference to an anonymous hash. The value for the key laboratory is retrieved from that anonymous hash; the value is an anonymous array. Finally, that anonymous array ${$gene->[0]}{laboratory} is enclosed in a block of curly braces, preceded by a $, and followed by an array index 1 in square brackets, which dereferences the anonymous array and returns the second element Cornell University.

Note that the last expression can also be written as:

```
$gene->[0]->{laboratory}->[1]
```

You see how the use of references within blocks enables you to dereference some rather deep-nested data structures. I urge you to take the time to understand this example and to use the resources listed in the section "Resources."

Printing Complex Data Structures

Sometimes you need to look inside your complex data structures to see what the settings are. One of the most useful ways to examine a data structure is by means of the Data::Dumper module. This module comes standard with all recent versions of Perl.

Here is the summary and part of the synopsis and description as output from the perldoc Data::Dumper command:

```
NAME
        Data::Dumper - stringified perl data structures, suitable
        for both printing and "eval"

SYNOPSIS
        use Data::Dumper;

        # simple procedural interface
        print Dumper($foo, $bar);
(...)

DESCRIPTION
        Given a list of scalars or reference variables, writes out
        their contents in perl syntax. The references can also be
        objects.  The contents of each variable is output in a
        single Perl statement.  Handles self-referential strucTures correctly.

        The return value can be "eval"ed to get back an identical
        copy of the original reference structure.
(...)
```

This output of a two-dimensional array illustrates its use:

```
use Data::Dumper;

$array = [ ];

# Initialize the array
for($i=0; $i < 4 ; ++$i) {
  for($j=0; $j < 4 ; ++$j) {
      $array->[$i][$j] = $i * $j;
  }
}

# Print the array "by hand"
for($i=0; $i < 4 ; ++$i) {
  for($j=0; $j < 4 ; ++$j) {
      printf("%3d ", $array->[$i][$j]);
  }
  print "\n";
}

# Print the array using Data::Dumper
print Dumper($array);
```

This produces the output:

```
0   0   0   0
0   1   2   3
0   2   4   6
0   3   6   9
$VAR1 = [
        [
          0,
          0,
          0,
          0
        ],
        [
          0,
          1,
          2,
          3
        ],
        [
          0,
          2,
          4,
          6
        ],
        [
          0,
          3,
          6,
```

```
            9
        ]
    ];
```

You can make a nicer display by knowing exactly what the data is and in what form to write it out. Data::Dumper can also display the data in a fairly readable format (and there are several options as to how the data is displayed). In addition, Data::Dumper allows you to dump a data structure out to a file and then read it in to another program. See the perldoc Data::Dumper manpage for more details.

You can also print out an array of arrays @array by printing each row one at a time. Remember that each row is an anonymous array, so each entry of the @array array is a reference to an anonymous array:

```
@array = (
  [0, 0, 0, 0],
  [0, 1, 2, 3],
  [0, 2, 4, 6],
  [0, 3, 99, 9]
);

for $anon (@array) {
  print "@$anon\n";
}
```

See the Perl perllol reference page for more information on initializing and printing arrays of arrays.

Data Structures in Action

The previous sections introduced a fair amount of new Perl syntax and capabilities. Now, let's see some of these new capabilities in action.

The Problem of String Matching

It is frequently important in biology to find the best possible match for a short sequence in a longer sequence; for example, between an oligonucleotide and the sequence of DNA that has been cloned in a YAC or BAC. This match need not always be perfect; frequently, what is important is to find the closest match available. This problem is known in computer science as approximate string matching, and dynamic programming is a popular technique used to compute the solution.

The problem of string matching is to find a pattern, such as a nucleotide or peptide fragment, in a longer text such as a chromosome or protein.

The problem of approximate string matching is to find a pattern in a text in which the match might not be perfect. Perhaps a few of the characters are different or missing; the problem is to find the best match possible.

Genetic Variability and String Matching

Biologically, approximate matches are of commanding importance. Evolutionary changes between species can make genes with essentially the same function collect a fair number of individual base changes; they may even have acquired differences in exon structure. Even within a species, individual base changes among groups in the population (single nucleotide polymorphisms) are important causes of disease and important clues in the discovery of disease-causing genes.

Mutations tend to accumulate over time in noncoding regions of DNA; mutations in coding regions tend to avoid altering critical regions essential for the functioning of the gene (where mutations may be fatal to the organism). Even a noncoding region may be critical to the regulation of a gene and thus tend to resist mutations. As a result, studying where mutations are not accumulating is often an important clue to discerning the function and control of a gene and its associated protein.

Due to the redundancy of the genetic code, mutations in DNA may not affect the coding of the associated protein. Other mutations may make a change in a coded amino acid, but it may be an amino acid with similar properties to the original amino acid; for instance, both amino acids may be hydrophilic. Tracing these kinds of mutations is another source of important information about the process of mutation. It can give vital clues to the conservation of critical coding regions and to the folding of proteins.

Biologists will have no difficulty expanding upon the preceding brief motivation for studying approximate string matching and other techniques that find similarities between biological molecules. Many standard laboratory techniques rely on the annealing of a molecule to another molecule with similar, but not necessarily exact, structure.

In the discussion that follows, you'll use your new knowledge of complex data structures in Perl to implement an algorithm that finds approximate matches of patterns in text, such as DNA fragments in chromosomes or peptide fragments in proteins.

The algorithm I present is an example of dynamic programming; it relies on computing the entries to a matrix.

Dynamic Programming

Dynamic programming computes the values for small subproblems and stores those values in a matrix. The stored values are then used to solve larger subproblems (without incurring the cost of recomputing the smaller subproblems) and so on until the solution to the overall problem is found. The term "dynamic programming" is a bit of a misnomer since it doesn't involve changing values over time as the word "dynamic" suggests.

This approach relies on having a data structure available to store the intermediate values as the algorithm proceeds. The data structure may require a fair amount of computer memory, but the overall speed of the algorithm often makes the memory cost worthwhile. In this section, we'll use a Perl multidimensional array, namely a simple two-dimensional matrix, to solve an approximate string matching problem.

Our algorithm will find a (shorter) pattern in a (longer) text. We'll start with a two-dimensional array, or matrix. The columns of the matrix will be associated with the (shorter) pattern, and the rows of the matrix will be associated with the (longer) text. The zeroth row and the zeroth column will be initialized to the appropriate starting values. We'll then calculate each value in the matrix by examining adjacent, already calculated values in conjunction with the characters of the pattern and the text. After the entire matrix has been filled in, we'll have the answer to our problem. That is, we'll find the position(s) in the text that most closely match the pattern, and we'll do so by simply examining the values in the last row of the matrix.

Approximate String Matching

You've most likely learned how to use regular expressions to find any of a set of possible patterns in a string. Approximate string matching is similar: an approximate string matching algorithm finds any of a set of possible patterns in a string. However, the two approaches are quite different in their capabilities and their ease of use. Simply stated, approximate string matching can find many close matches to a pattern that would be very tedious to specify using regular expressions.

Edit Distance

There are several ways to measure the distance between two strings, and our algorithm will use one such measure. Some variants of this measure are considered in the exercises at the end of the chapter.

Our algorithm uses the idea of *edit distance* to measure the similarity between two strings. The idea is quite simple. Assume that there are three things you can do to alter a string:

Substitution
    Change any character to a different character

Deletion
    Delete any character

Insertion
    Insert a new character at any position

Now, let's say that every time you make any of these three edits, you incur an edit cost of 1. Now, call the edit distance between two strings as the minimum edit cost needed to change one string into the other.

For instance, let's say there are two strings portend and profound. You can apply the following edits to portend:

```
portend
        (delete o)
prtend
        (insert o)
protend
        (change t to f)
profend
        (change e to o)
profond
        (insert u)
profound
```

You can see that five edits were applied. Assuming you can't find a quicker way to change one string into the other, the edit distance between the two strings is 5.

Clearly, you can also start from the other string and apply the same edits in reverse (just interchanging the deletions and insertions, and reversing the substitutions). So, starting from profound, delete u, change o to e, change f to t, delete o, and finally insert o, to arrive at portend.

The relevance of this concept of edit distance to sequence alignment is simply: the smaller the edit distance, the better the alignment.

We'll ignore for the moment whether these are the most biologically relevant types of edits. However, you may want to start thinking of "edits" as "mutations," and consider whether the problem is perhaps formulated too simplistically to model the actual process of mutation. What about the differences between DNA and proteins in this regard? Should we permit switching the order of two adjacent characters as an edit? How about reversing a substring of the string, as in the known biological process of inversion? Does our assignment of an equal cost to each "edit" make biological sense? Keep these questions in mind; we may eventually want to improve the algorithm by incorporating some of the modifications suggested by these ideas.

In approximate string matching, the problem is to find a (short) pattern in a (usually much longer) text. Of the many possible variants of this problem, let's find the location(s) in the text with the smallest possible edit distance from the pattern. We'll do so in the next section.

A string matching program

Now that you've got an idea of the nature of the problem, its importance to biology, and the basic definitions that we'll use in approaching the problem, let's take a look at a Perl program that solves our problem using dynamic programming. This program uses the references and multidimensional arrays introduced earlier in this chapter.

As usual, my approach is to proceed as quickly as possible to practical matters, not dwelling on the theoretical aspects of the computer science involved. I urge the interested reader to consult the references at the end of the chapter for more satisfying details on the techniques of dynamic programming and on the many different approaches that have been developed to solve the approximate string matching problem.

The following is a Perl program for approximate string matching, followed by a somewhat detailed discussion of how it works. The program proceeds as follows: first, the pattern and text are defined (as peptides in this case). Then the distance matrix, a two-dimensional array, is declared. After initializing the first row and the first column to the appropriate values (to be discussed later), the algorithm proceeds to fill in the matrix. Each matrix location is calculated by examining three adjacent locations, plus the amino acids in the pattern and the text at that spot; the resulting matrix is printed out. Finally, the best match is found by looking for the smallest edit distance entered in the last row of the matrix. The final result is printed out.

```perl
#!/usr/bin/perl

#
# Approximate string matching using dynamic programming
#
#    Find the closest match to the pattern in the text
#

use strict;
use warnings;

my $pattern = 'EIQADEVRL';
print "PATTERN:\n$pattern\n";

my $text = 'SVLQDRSMPHQEILAADEVLQESEMRQQDMISHDE';
print "TEXT:\n$text\n";

my $TLEN = length $text;
my $PLEN = length $pattern;

# D is the Distance matrix, which shows the "edit distance" between
# substrings of the pattern and the text.
# It is implemented as a reference to an anonymous array.
my $D = [ ];

# The rows correspond to the text
# Initialize row 0 of D.
for (my $t=0; $t <= $TLEN ; ++$t) {
    $D->[$t][0] = 0;
}

# The columns correspond to the pattern
# Initialize column 0 of D.
for (my $p=0; $p <= $PLEN ; ++$p) {
    $D->[0][$p] = $p;
}
```

```perl
# Compute the edit distances.
for (my $t=1; $t <= $TLEN ; ++$t) {
    for (my $p=1; $p <= $PLEN ; ++$p) {

        $D->[$t][$p] =

        # Choose whichever of the three alternatives has the least cost
        min3(
            # First alternative
            # The text and pattern may or may not match at this character ...
            substr($text, $t-1, 1) eq substr($pattern, $p-1, 1)
            ? $D->[$t-1][$p-1]  # If they match, no increase in edit distance!
            :  $D->[$t-1][$p-1] + 1,

            # Second alternative
            # If the text is missing a character
            $D->[$t-1][$p] + 1,

            # Third alternative
            # If the pattern is missing a character
            $D->[$t][$p-1] + 1
        )
    }
}

# Print D, the resulting edit distance array
for (my $p=0; $p <= $PLEN ; ++$p) {
    for (my $t=0; $t <= $TLEN ; ++$t) {
        print $D->[$t][$p], " ";
    }
    print "\n";
}

my @matches = ( );
my $bestscore = 10000000;

# Find the best match(es).
# The edit distances appear in the the last row.
for (my $t=1 ; $t <= $TLEN ; ++$t) {
    if( $D->[$t][$PLEN] < $bestscore) {
        $bestscore = $D->[$t][$PLEN];
        @matches = ($t);
    }elsif( $D->[$t][$PLEN] == $bestscore) {
        push(@matches, $t);
    }
}

# Report the best match(es).
print "\nThe best match for the pattern $pattern\n";
print "has an edit distance of $bestscore\n";
print "and appears in the text ending at location";
```

```
    print "s" if ( @matches > 1);
    print " @matches\n";

    sub min3 {
        my($i, $j, $k) = @_;
        my($tmp);

        $tmp = ($i < $j ? $i : $j);
        $tmp < $k ? $tmp : $k;
    }
```

Here is the output:

```
PATTERN:
EIQADEVRL
TEXT:
SVLQDRSMPHQEILAADEVLQESEMRQQDMISHDE
0 0 0 0 0 0 0 0 0 0 0 0 0 0 0 0 0 0 0 0 0 0 0 0 0 0 0 0 0 0 0 0 0 0 0 0
1 1 1 1 1 1 1 1 1 1 1 1 0 1 1 1 1 0 1 1 1 0 1 0 1 1 1 1 1 1 1 1 1 1 0
2 2 2 2 2 2 2 2 2 2 2 1 0 1 2 2 2 1 1 2 2 1 1 1 2 2 2 2 1 2 2 2 1
3 3 3 3 2 3 3 3 3 3 3 2 2 1 1 2 3 3 2 2 2 2 2 2 2 2 2 3 3 2 2 3 3 2
4 4 4 4 3 3 4 4 4 4 4 3 3 2 2 1 2 3 3 3 3 3 3 3 3 3 3 4 3 3 3 4 3
5 5 5 5 4 3 4 5 5 5 5 4 4 3 3 2 2 2 3 4 4 4 4 4 4 4 4 3 4 4 4 3 4
6 6 6 6 5 4 4 5 6 6 6 5 4 4 4 3 3 3 2 3 4 5 4 5 4 5 5 5 4 4 5 5 4 3
7 7 6 7 6 5 5 5 6 7 7 6 5 5 5 4 4 4 3 2 3 4 5 5 5 5 6 6 6 5 5 5 6 6 5 4
8 8 7 7 7 6 5 6 6 7 8 7 6 6 6 5 5 5 4 3 3 4 5 6 6 6 5 6 7 6 6 6 6 7 6 5
9 9 8 7 8 7 6 6 7 7 8 8 7 7 6 6 6 6 5 4 3 4 5 6 7 7 6 6 7 7 7 7 7 7 7 6
```

```
The best match for the pattern EIQADEVRL
has an edit distance of 3
and appears in the text ending at location 20
```

Analysis

Let's examine this program in detail to see how the Perl references and matrices are used and to learn how dynamic programming can solve the approximate string matching problem.

You can see that I specified a short pattern and a fairly short text. The shortness of the text is purely for didactic purposes: I want to show the entire matrix that is computed. To see how it performs, you should try running the program by reading in, say, human chromosome 1, and searching for a 20 basepair oligonucleotide. (You'll probably want to omit the printing of the matrix in this case!)

Because our program needs to refer to the lengths of the pattern and text at several points, we precompute them to save time and to make the code easier to read. ($PLEN is easier to read in those tightly packed loops than length $pattern.)

Next, the array D is declared:

```
    my $D = [ ];
```

$D refers to the anonymous array denoted by [ ]. It is populated as the algorithm progresses, as a two-dimensional array of integers.

The code for the calculation of the edit distance array $D is very short. The 0th row and the 0th column are initialized to start off the computation. The 0th row is initialized to all 0s, and the 0th column is initialized to 0, 1, 2, ... up to PLEN.

Why? Let's talk about how this algorithm is going to work.

Each entry of the TLEN+1 x PLEN+1 matrix contains the edit distance between a prefix of the pattern and a substring of the text. To be more precise: consider the entry of $D at row $t and column $p (we'll call it in actual Perl syntax $D->[$t][$p]). The value of $D at this position represents the edit distance between the prefix of the pattern of length $p, and a substring of the text ending at text position $t.

Let's look at an actual example. Figure 2-1 shows the output of the edit distance matrix again, with the input strings lined up with the rows and columns.

```
  S V L Q D R S M P H Q E I L A A D E V L Q E S E M R Q Q D M I S H D E
  0 0 0 0 0 0 0 0 0 0 0 0 0 0 0 0 0 0 0 0 0 0 0 0 0 0 0 0 0 0 0 0 0 0 0
E 1 1 1 1 1 1 1 1 1 1 1 1 0 1 1 1 1 0 1 1 1 0 1 0 1 1 1 1 1 1 1 1 1 1 0
I 2 2 2 2 2 2 2 2 2 2 2 2 1 0 1 2 2 2 1 1 2 2 1 1 1 2 2 2 2 2 1 2 2 2 1
Q 3 3 3 3 2 3 3 3 3 3 3 2 2 1 1 2 3 3 2 2 2 2 2 2 2 2 2 2 2 3 3 2 2 3 2
A 4 4 4 4 3 3 4 4 4 4 4 3 3 2 2 1 2 3 3 3 3 3 3 3 3 3 3 3 3 4 3 3 3 4 3
D 5 5 5 5 4 3 4 5 5 5 5 4 4 3 3 2 2 2 3 4 4 4 4 4 4 4 4 4 4 3 4 4 4 3 4
E 6 6 6 6 5 4 4 5 6 6 6 5 4 4 4 3 3 2 3 4 5 4 5 4 5 5 5 5 4 4 5 5 5 4 3
V 7 7 6 7 6 5 5 5 6 7 7 6 5 5 5 4 4 4 3 2 3 4 5 5 5 5 6 6 6 5 5 5 6 6 5 4
R 8 8 7 7 7 6 5 6 6 7 8 7 6 6 6 5 5 5 4 3 3 4 5 6 6 6 5 6 7 6 6 6 6 7 6 5
L 9 9 8 7 8 7 6 6 7 7 8 8 7 7 6 6 6 6 5 4 3 4 5 6 7 7 6 6 7 7 7 7 7 7 6
```

Figure 2-1. Edit distance matrix

The entry at row 4 and column 15, that is, $D->[4][15], highlighted in the figure, has the value 1. This means that the first four characters of the pattern, EIQA, are one edit away from a substring that ends at position 15 in the text. Let's check this. The prefix of length 4 of the pattern is EIQA. A substring that ends at position 15 in the text is EILA. (Note that the beginning position of this substring isn't clear; more on that later and in the exercises.) You see that one substitution, of L in the text to Q in the pattern, transforms the one string to the other. By this definition, the edit distance between these two strings is 1. That's what the entry in the matrix says, so that entry is verified.

Take a minute to verify another entry or two.

Because you're looking for a match for the entire pattern, it follows that you merely need to look at the last row of the edit distance matrix $D. Each position in that row shows the edit distance between the entire pattern and a substring of the text that ends at that position.

Take a look at two or three positions in the last row, and satisfy yourself that the value at each of those positions corresponds to the edit distance between the pattern and a substring of the text ending at that position.

Finally, because you're looking for the best match for the pattern in the text, check the position or positions in the last row of the $D matrix that have the minimum value. If there is an exact match for the pattern in the text, there will be a 0 in some position in the last row of the $D matrix.

Make sure you also understand the size of the $D matrix and how the positions correspond to positions in the pattern and text strings.

The border conditions of the computation are given by the 0th row and 0th column. (*Border conditions* are just the starting values of a computation that are initialized before the computation begins.) If you're unfamiliar with border conditions, the initialization may seem a little strange, but it is absolutely typical of many algorithms that they have seemingly trivial border conditions.

Each position in any row, from 1 to TLEN, corresponds to a character of the text, starting from the first character to the last. The 0th row is initialized to all 0s because there is an edit distance of 0 from the prefix of the pattern of length 0 to any position in the text. In other words, the empty string (a pattern of length 0) can be matched at any position of the text, so the edit distance is zero all along the 0th row.

Similarly, the 0th column is initialized to 0, 1, ..., up to PLEN in the last position of the column. These values indicate that at each position in the 0th column, say, at position $p, corresponding to the prefix of the pattern of length $p, it takes $p edits (in particular, $p insertions) to match the substring of the text ending at position 0 (that is, a substring of length 0).

The matrix is now set up, and the 0th column and 0th row are initialized; let's see how the algorithm proceeds.

Figure 2-2 shows the key idea. The value of a position in the matrix, say:

```
$D->[$t][$p]
```

can be computed by checking the values of the three adjacent positions:

```
$D->[$t-1][$p]
$D->[$t][$p-1]
$D->[$t-1][$p-1]
```

and considering whether or not the character at position t of the text is the same as the character at position $p of the pattern.

Let's see how this works. The desired, uncomputed matrix entry at $D->[$t][$p], is represented as ???. The previously computed values at the three adjacent matrix positions are represented by the letters A, B, and C.

Figure 2-2. Computing value for row p and column t

The distance of the match of the pattern prefix of length $p-1 ends at the text at position $t-1, represented in the figure as the integer A. If the next character in the pattern, at position $p, is the same as the next character in the text, at position $t, the edit distance of this longer pattern, which ends at this next position in the text, is still A (because no additional substitution, deletion, or insertion was required).

On the other hand, if the characters are different, you'd get a new value of A+1 for this match of a longer pattern with a later position in the text.

In the code, this first value, which may be one of two different alternatives depending on the characters in the text and the pattern, is programmed using the Perl conditional operator TEST ? Expression1 : Expression2. This operator returns the value of the first expression if the test is true or the value of the second expression if the test is false. Here, the TEST is:

```
substr($text, $t-1, 1) eq substr($pattern, $p-1, 1)
```

the first expression is $D->[$t-1][$p-1], and the second expression is $D->[$t-1][$p-1] + 1.

```
# First alternative
# The text and pattern may or may not match at this character ...
substr($text, $t-1, 1) eq substr($pattern, $p-1, 1)
? $D->[$t-1][$p-1]   # If they match, no increase in edit distance!
: $D->[$t-1][$p-1] + 1,
```

Now, consider the case of the match at the position $D->[$t][$p-1] with value B. This represents the match of the pattern prefix of length $p-1 ending at the text at position $t. If you insert another character of the pattern to match at the same position in the text, that incurs an additional edit distance for the insertion, so the new value is B+1. The code for this value is:

```
# Second alternative
# If the text is missing a character
$D->[$t-1][$p] + 1,
```

Similarly, consider the case of the match at the position $D->[$t-1][$p] with value C. This represents the match of the pattern prefix of length $p ending at the text at position $t-1. If you extend the match to another character of the text to match at the same position in the pattern, that incurs an additional edit distance for the insertion, so the new value is C+1. The following is the code for this value.

```
# Third alternative
# If the pattern is missing a character
$D->[$t][$p-1] + 1
```

These three alternatives are the three arguments to the min3 subroutine, which returns the minimum from among three values.

When considering edit distances, you can start from either string. Inserting a character in one string is the same as deleting a character from the other string, depending on which string you start with.

I assert that this procedure covers all possible ways of extending a match. This assertion can be proved, but in the interests of practicality, we'll skip that essential step of demonstrating program correctness. The interested reader may want to think about how to prove such an assertion or may simply refer to the literature in the "Resources" section.

So, what value do you put in place of the ??? placeholder? Since we're looking for the smallest edit distance, let's choose the minimum of the values that have been examined. If character $t and character $p are the same, you'd choose the minimum of the values A, B+1, and C+1. On the other hand, if character $t and character $p are different, you'd choose the minimum of the values A+1, B+1, and C+1.

That's our algorithm. Take a moment to examine the Perl code, reproduced here, that calculates the matrix, and see how the code reflects our discussion of the algorithm:

```
# Compute the edit distances.
for (my $t=1; $t <= $TLEN ; ++$t) {
    for (my $p=1; $p <= $PLEN ; ++$p) {

        $D->[$t][$p] =

        # Choose whichever of the three alternatives has the least cost
        min3(
            # First alternative
            # The text and pattern may or may not match at this character ...
            substr($text, $t-1, 1) eq substr($pattern, $p-1, 1)
            ? $D->[$t-1][$p-1]   # If they match, no increase in edit distance!
            :  $D->[$t-1][$p-1] + 1,

            # Second alternative
            # If the text is missing a character
            $D->[$t-1][$p] + 1,

            # Third alternative
            # If the pattern is missing a character
            $D->[$t][$p-1] + 1
        )
    }
}
```

Resources

I recommend the following O'Reilly sources for more details on data structures in Perl:

- *Programming Perl,* by Larry Wall, Tom Christiansen, and Jon Orwant. This is the bible of Perl programming. Everything about data structures is explained in detail.
- *Advanced Perl Programming* by Sriram Srinivasan. An excellent book that covers references and data structures.
- *Mastering Algorithms with Perl* by Jon Orwant, Jarkko Hietaniemi, and John Macdonald. A marvelous book, especially if you like this chapter. Many interesting data structures and algorithms are explained and implemented in Perl.
- *The Perl Cookbook* by Tom Christiansen and Nathan Torkington. As the title implies, this book is composed of fairly short recipes that accomplish particular tasks, grouped according to application area.

Here's where to go for Perl documentation:

- The `perlreftut` tutorial page from the Perl documentation gives a short introduction to Perl references (type `perldoc perlreftut` at your command line if Perl is installed, or visit the web page *http://www.perldoc.com*).
- The `perlref` tutorial page from the Perl documentation discusses Perl references in detail.
- The `perldata` tutorial page from the Perl documentation gives an introduction to Perl data structures.
- The `perldsc` tutorial page from the Perl documentation presents a "cookbook" overview of Perl data structures.
- The `perllol` tutorial page from the Perl documentation gives an introduction to arrays of arrays.

The literature on algorithms is vast, including many textbooks as well as advanced monographs and peer reviewed journals. I recommend the following sources as a few entry points for more details on dynamic programming and algorithms:

- *Computer Algorithms* by Sara Baase and Allen VanGelder (Addison Wesley). This book is clearly written for the undergraduate level, and includes a very nice explanation of the algorithm presented in this chapter.
- *Introduction to Algorithms* by Thomas Cormen, Charles Leiserson, and Ron Rivest (MIT Press and McGraw-Hill). An excellent and standard college textbook, well written; can serve as a reference book for the serious programmer.
- *Algorithms on Strings, Trees, and Sequences: Computer Science and Computational Biology* by Dan Gusfield (Cambridge University Press). This book specializes in algorithms for strings, including such topics as sequence alignment. It's

very detailed, but even so, not complete—this is a big field! The best single source on string algorithms, with lots of information about biological sequence similarity.

- *Data Structures and Algorithms* by Alfred Aho, John E. Hopcroft, and Jeffrey Ullman (Addison Wesley). This is the classic book on the science of algorithms.

- *Introduction to Parallel Algorithms and Architectures: Arrays, Trees, Hypercubes* by Frank Thomson Leighton (Morgan Kaufmann). A comprehensive, rigorous text and reference book.

- *Randomized Algorithms* by Rajeev Motwani and Prabhakar Raghavan (Cambridge University Press). A clear, rigorous course.

Exercises

Exercise 2.1

Suggest a programming situation in which it would make sense to have several scalar references to one scalar variable that contains a peptide fragment.

Exercise 2.2

When might you want to use a reference to an (anonymous) scalar constant?

Exercise 2.3

Is $$arr[0] the same as $arr->[0]? Why or why not?

Exercise 2.4

Write a subroutine that returns a reference to a hash. Declare a reference to this subroutine and call it using the reference, then print out the hash whose reference is returned from the subroutine.

Exercise 2.5

Write a subroutine that returns a new anonymous subroutine based on its arguments, which are passed to it as references. Call the subroutine and then call the new subroutine that is returned.

Exercise 2.6

Write a subroutine to multiply two matrices.

Exercise 2.7

Develop a data structure that is a hash at the top level and can be used to record the data from microarray runs.

Exercise 2.8

Write a min subroutine that returns the minimum of two integers. Rewrite min3 using it.

Exercise 2.9

Make a subroutine that prints the distance matrix. Make it handle the display of longer numbers appropriately.

Exercise 2.10

Make the subroutine from Exercise 2.9 also display the pattern and string aligned with the output of the edit distance matrix.

Exercise 2.11

Make a subroutine that returns the edit distance array, the best score, and the locations of the best matches.

Exercise 2.12

Any difference in Exercise 2.11 if you calculate row by row instead of column by column?

Exercise 2.13

In Exercise 2.11, save space by keeping only two rows in memory.

Exercise 2.14

In Exercise 2.11, report on types of edits of matches.

Exercise 2.15

In Exercise 2.14, show the strings aligned, extra spaces for insertions or deletions, and flag mismatches.

Exercise 2.16

In Exercise 2.11, can you speed the program up by skipping computations when it becomes clear that the best score you've already found can't be matched or bettered in that column? Why or why not?

Exercise 2.17

Run the approximate string matching program on large text, such as entire chromosomes. How is the performance?

Exercise 2.18

Make a version of the approximate string matching program that searches for the pattern in libraries of text, and then reports on, say, the top 25 hits. (For example, search for a DNA pattern in all the records of a GenBank library.)

Exercise 2.19

How can you alter the approximate string matching algorithm to give different weights to the three edit possibilities, or to different types of mismatches (e.g., by giving a fairly low weight to mismatches between hydrophobic amino acids or the codons that encode them)?

Exercise 2.20

Write an array that handles eleven dimensions.

Exercise 2.21

Answer the questions at the end of the section "Sparse Arrays": Why do you need two exists tests? Is $array a hash or a reference to an anonymous hash? Can you implement it the other way?

CHAPTER 3

Object-Oriented Programming in Perl

In Chapter 1, you saw how modules are defined and used, and in Chapter 2, how references and data structures work. Now, it's time to introduce the important concepts and techniques of object-oriented programming in Perl that are based on modules and references.

Object-oriented (OO) programming is one of the most important approaches to writing programs, and it is an approach that has been well supported by Perl for quite a while. Other OO languages of interest include Java, C++, and Smalltalk. Many Perl modules are written in an OO style, and their proper use requires some fundamental understanding of the OO approach. Luckily, the key concepts are fairly simple.

Perl easily supports both declarative and OO programming. (Perl was originally a declarative language only; the OO style was added fairly early on.) Declarative programming is characterized by code that declares variables and subroutines, conditional tests, if-else branches, and loops, and various arithmetic, logical, and string operators. It is up to you to manage the definition and use of the variables and subroutines so that they interact in appropriate ways. (You'll see shortly how object-oriented programming imposes additional constraints that help you create well-behaved programs.) Many declarative programming languages are well established, including Perl and such stalwarts as C, FORTRAN, and BASIC, to name just a few. By this point, assuming you have some experience programming in Perl, you should be fairly comfortable with the declarative style.

The first part of this chapter is an overview of OO programming and how OO Perl modules are used. If you're a beginning Perl programmer, you'll find them easy to use because they rarely require you to know how to write OO Perl code. Depending on your needs and goals, this might be all the information you'll require from this chapter.

As a more advanced programmer, you'll sometimes need to write your own OO bioinformatics software. If you're such a programmer, the second part of this chapter will be of greatest interest to you. However, because the material is developed incrementally, you will most likely want to read the chapter in order from beginning to end.

Perl makes clever and simple use of existing mechanisms to support OO programming. Perl packages and modules are used to define OO classes, Perl references define OO objects, and Perl subroutines define OO methods. The definitions of these terms will become clear as you read the chapter, but in brief, OO software is organized into classes that contain data called objects. Subroutines called methods operate on the objects.

Over the course of this chapter, I'll develop a small example object module, Gene.pm, to demonstrate the essentials of OO Perl. Gene.pm is developed in four stages so you can learn the OO style gradually. The final code for Gene.pm serves as a template from which you can begin developing your own OO software.

What Is Object-Oriented Programming?

Object-oriented programming is a way to organize code so it interacts in certain prescribed ways, obeying certain rules about how the data and subroutines are organized. In other words, it imposes a certain programming discipline that can lead to better and more reliable code.

The key idea of OO programming is that all data is stored and modified with special data structures called *objects*, and each kind of object can be accessed only by its defined subroutines called *methods*. The user of an OO class is typically spared the effort of directly manipulating data, and can use class methods for this instead.

The promise of this OO structure of program code is that it makes the resulting programs cleanly designed, more reliable, easier to reuse in other programs, and easier to modify and improve. In essence, the approach imposes certain restrictions on what a programmer can do with the data and subroutines at hand.

Proponents of the OO approach cite the benefits this extra discipline provides. It is certainly true that you can follow good programming practices without using an OO approach. However, OO does provide a well-defined framework for encouraging discipline and good programming practices. In a very flexible language such as Perl, good practices can sometimes be easier to enforce in the framework of OO. We'll see how this comes about in the examples that follow.

Why Object-Oriented Programming?

It is often important and necessary to weigh the costs and benefits of a given system against the alternatives in an applied engineering discipline such as programming. The decision to use OO programming, declarative programming, or some other paradigm, is often subject to religious debates, with some enthusiasts promoting their favorite approach against all comers. This is especially relevant to the Perl programmer, because Perl allows you to write in the declarative or in the OO style. You should know that OO programming isn't always the correct choice for a programming project. Despite the real benefits it can confer upon a software development project, it can also have certain costs; these costs and benefits should be weighed against each other.

For instance, some types of software lend themselves more readily to abstracting with OO techniques than others. Object-oriented software development can sometimes take longer due to the overhead associated with its level of abstraction. OO software sometimes runs slower than other approaches; this has certainly been true in Perl, and although not usually a deal breaker, it is sometimes an important consideration. (Current work on the upcoming Perl 6 is addressing this performance issue.)

In spite of these strictures, OO programming is often an excellent choice; it has become a key approach to writing software in the Perl language.

Terminology

Object

An object is a collection of data that logically belongs together.

For instance, you might have a genome object that would have such *attributes* (or parts) as the name of the organism, the DNA sequence data, the start and end points for each exon, the genes with their associated lists of exons, and so forth. The exact nature of an object is a matter of logic and convenience, and in the end, it depends on the judgment of the programmer as to what collection of attributes makes an object that will accomplish the goals at hand.

A standard term in computer science for a collection of data is a *data structure*. Data structures are often studied in terms of accomplishing certain *algorithms*. It is often the case that the fastest, cleverest way to compute something relies upon putting the data into a special data structure that makes a fast algorithm possible.[*]

In Perl, objects are usually implemented as references to hashes and are marked with their class name. The Perl function bless marks a reference with a class name, as will be explained in this chapter. The Perl function ref can be used to see what class name an object is marked with.

Method

In OO programming, a subroutine called a method is associated with an object. Each type of object has one or more methods that it can call. In this style of programming, the only way to access the data in an object is by the defined methods

---

[*] This point really highlights the importance of spending some time on design at the beginning of your programming, and the importance of using a good efficiency tester such as Benchmark.pm to evaluate alternate solutions.

of the class. This restriction is meant to increase reliability, reusability, and maintainability.

In Perl, methods are implemented as Perl subroutines, although they behave slightly differently from other subroutines. Methods are called from an object, and they know what object they're called on; they don't need to be explicitly imported, and they exist in a hierarchy of classes. If you know how to use Perl subroutines, methods are an easy next step.

Class

Together, the object definitions and the collection of methods for them defines a class. A specific object (say, a genome object for C. elegans) is called an *instance of a class*.

Classes can be related to each other so methods can be inherited into a class from another class. In Perl, classes are implemented as namespaces, by means of the package directive.

Now that you're familiar with the language of OO programming, let's see how it's used.

Using Perl Classes (Without Writing Them)

Before you actually start writing classes, it's helpful to know how to use them. This section shows you how to use OO Perl classes, even if the syntax is new to you and you've never written one yourself.

Thanks to the large and active community of Perl programmers, there are many useful Perl classes already written and freely available to use in your programs. Very often, the class you want already exists. All you need to do is obtain it and use it.

First, you need to find the appropriate module or modules (CPAN is the most common source for modules), install it, and examine the documentation to learn how to use the class. Finding and installing OO modules employs the same process covered in Chapter 1.

What's different about OO modules is how they create data structures and call and pass arguments to subroutines. In short, there's some new syntax to learn that amounts to a slightly different style of programming.

Object-oriented code creates an object by naming the class and calling a special method in the class (usually called new). The newly created object is a reference to a data structure, usually a hash. The object is then used to call methods (or OO subroutines). You're used to subroutines that get their data passed in as arguments; by contrast, OO code has a data structure that calls subroutines to operate on it. My goal in this section is to explain enough of this new terminology and syntax so you can read and understand the documentation for a class, and use it in your own programs.

Let's begin with the documentation for the Carp module, a nonOO module that appears later in this chapter. This is a simple module to use; it defines four subroutines, and the documentation gives brief examples of their use. Because the Carp module comes installed with any recent release of Perl, you don't have to install it. To find out how to use it, type:

```
perldoc Carp
```

(Upper- and lowercase is significant; typing perldoc carp won't work.) Here's the beginning of the output:

```
NAME
        carp    - warn of errors (from perspective of caller)
        cluck   - warn of errors with stack backtrace
                  (not exported by default)
        croak   - die of errors (from perspective of caller)
        confess - die of errors with stack backtrace

SYNOPSIS
        use Carp;
        croak "We're outta here!";

        use Carp qw(cluck);
        cluck "This is how we got here!";
```

It shows what subroutines are available and how to use them in your code. Additional details do appear in the documentation. They are important and sometimes necessary to read carefully, but you usually don't need to delve any further than the SYNOPSIS section that gives examples. To use the croak subroutine, you first load it with the directive use Carp;. You then call croak by providing a string containing a message as an argument; the program prints the message and dies.

The basic Perl documentation is found at *http://www.perldoc.com* and *http://www.perl.com*, and includes standard distribution modules such as Carp. A great many modules such as *ioperl* aren't shipped with the standard Perl distribution. To find the documentation for Bioperl on the web, start at the CPAN web site: *http://www.CPAN.org*. Once you locate Bioperl in CPAN, you'll be directed to the Bioperl home page at *http://www.bioperl.org*. If the modules in question are already installed on your computer system, type at the command line:

```
perldoc bioperl
```

Depending on how up-to-date your version of Bioperl is, you'll get something like:

```
BIOPERL(1)     User Contributed Perl Documentation     BIOPERL(1)

NAME
        Bioperl - Coordinated OOP-Perl Modules for Biology

SYNOPSIS
        Not very appropriate to put a synopsis  - many different
        objects to use. Read on...
```

Bioperl contains a number of Perl objects which are useful in biology. Examples include Sequence objects, Alignment objects and database searching objects. These objects not only do what they are advertised to do in the documenta tion, but they also interact - Alignment objects are made from the Sequence objects and so on. This means that the objects provide a coordinated framework to do computational biology.

If you are new to bioperl, reading biostart.pod will get you aquainted with writing scripts and the main players for the objects.

We now also have a cookbook tutorial in bptutorial.pl which has embedded documentation. Start there if learning-by-example suits you most.

Bioperl development is focused on the objects themselves, and less on the scripts (programs) that put these objects together. There are some example scripts provided in the distribution, but it is not the focus of the objects that are distributed. Of course, as the objects do most of the hardwork for you, all you have to do is combine a number of objects together sensibly.

The intent of the bioperl development effort is to make reusable tools that aid people in creating their own site or job specific applications.

The bioperl.org (http://bioperl.org) website also attempts to maintain links and archives of standalone bio-related perl tools that are not affiliated or related to the core bioperl effort. Check the site for useful code ideas and contribute your own if possible.

The second paragraph of the DESCRIPTION advises you to read biostart.pod if you're new to Bioperl. Type:

```
perldoc biostart
```

and you get the following output (only the first page is reproduced here):

```
BIOSTART(1)    User Contributed Perl Documentation    BIOSTART(1)

NAME
        Bioperl - Getting Started

SYNOPSIS
        #!/usr/local/bin/perl

        use Bio::Seq;
        use Bio::SeqIO;
```

```
$seqin = Bio::SeqIO->new( '-format' => 'EMBL' , -file => 'myfile.dat');
$seqout= Bio::SeqIO->new( '-format' => 'Fasta', -file => '>output.fa');

while((my $seqobj = $seqin->next_seq())) {
     print "Seen sequence ",$seqobj->display_id,", start of seq ",
            substr($seqobj->seq,1,10),"\n";
     if( $seqobj->moltype eq 'dna') {
         $rev = $seqobj->revcom;
         $id  = $seqobj->display_id();
         $id  = "$id.rev";
         $rev->display_id($id);
         $seqout->write_seq($rev);
     }

     foreach $feat ( $seqobj->top_SeqFeatures() ) {
        if( $feat->primary_tag eq 'exon' ) {
           print STDOUT "Location ",$feat->start,":",
                 $feat->end," GFF[",$feat->gff_string,"]\n";
        }
     }
}
```

DESCRIPTION

   Bioperl is a set of Perl modules that represent useful
   biological objects. Some of the key objects represent:
   Sequences, features on sequences, databases of sequences,
   flat file representations of sequences and similarity
   search results.

   Because bioperl is formed from Perl modules, there are no
   actual useable programs in the distribution (this is not
   actually true. In the scripts directory there are a few
   useful programs. But not a great deal...). You have to
   write the programs which use bioperl.

   It is very easy to write programs using the bioperl modules, as a lot of the complex processing happens in the
   modules and not in the part of the program which you have
   to write. The idea is that you can connect up a number of
   the modules to do useful things. The synopsis above gives
   a simple script which uses bioperl. Stepping through this
   script, the lines mean the following things:

   ...

The file gives an example of code that uses Bioperl modules, and the rest of the
biostart documentation explains the example in some detail. Let's take a closer look
at the OO syntax of this example.

After the typical use statements (needed to load the modules), such as:

    use Bio::SeqIO;

the documentation has the following line in the example:

```
$seqin = Bio::SeqIO->new( '-format' => 'EMBL' , -file => 'myfile.dat');
```

This line calls the new method. new is the name typically used in OO Perl for the sub-routine that creates an object. The object that's returned from the method call is saved as a reference in a scalar variable. In this case, the new object in the Bio::SeqIO class is saved in the reference variable $seqin.

The new method is identified by giving the name of the class (Bio::SeqIO), followed by an arrow (->), and finally the method name:

```
Bio::SeqIO->new
```

This is the syntax for calling methods. If you're just interested in using the class, not in understanding the inner mechanisms, you simply have to remember to invoke the new method that creates a class object in this way. The other methods in a class are typically called from a class object that has been previously created (by just such a call to a new method).

Later in the biostart example you see the line:

```
while((my $seqobj = $seqin->next_seq())) {
```

The call to the method next_seq is done as follows:

```
$seqobj = $seqin->next_seq( )
```

Here, the Bio::SeqIO class object $seqin is being used to call the method next_seq in the class Bio::SeqIO. Because $seqin was created as an object in the class Bio::SeqIO, it can be used with arrow notation (->) to call a method in the class, without specifically mentioning the class name. This is how methods other than new are typically called. The result here is saved as $seqobj, a new object.

The important thing to remember about subroutines in OO code is that you create objects by calling the new method in the class. You call other methods by calling them on an object in the class. Both types of calls are accomplished with arrow notation.

Here's a new object being created in a class Myclass:

```
$myobject = Myclass->new( );
```

Here's a method compute being called on that object:

```
$myobject->compute( );
```

One more item in the biostart example that may appear unfamiliar is the way arguments to the methods are specified. Consider this line from the example:

```
$seqin = Bio::SeqIO->new( '-format' => 'EMBL' , -file => 'myfile.dat');
```

The arguments are passed as named arguments, which are pairs with the name of the argument followed by the symbol => followed by a value for the argument. If this looks suspiciously like the notation used to initialize hashes, it's no accident. In this invocation of the new method, you're initializing a new object, which is implemented as a hash, so it makes sense that you'd pass your initial values to the object using hash notation.

The details of how arguments are passed to methods are covered later in the chapter. For now, if you just want to use this class, you'll need to pass your arguments to the new method in the style just shown. Methods in a class usually pass arguments in this hash-like, key => value notation, but not always. If you use the syntax as shown in the documentation, your code will be fine.

One advantage to using a hash for arguments is that the arguments can be given in any order: you don't have to give them in a prescribed order as is often the case when passing a list of scalars as arguments to a subroutine.

I'll return to this biostart example in Chapter 9. For now, know that you should have sufficient syntax information to use a Perl OO module. The next section shows how to start pulling it all together.

Objects, Methods, and Classes in Perl

To the user of a class, the most important piece of information is the interface describing how to use the class. Usually this interface can easily be summarized in a few examples provided by the author of the class. The details of how the class is implemented may change; as long as the interface remains the same, your code needn't change even when the internals of the class you're using change. This provides good modularization, protecting your system from the ripple effects of changes in individual components, thus making your code as a whole more robust and reliable. This is one of the main benefits of OO design.

With OO design, you know that:

- A class is a package.
- An object is a reference to a data structure in the class, that is marked (or "blessed") with the class name.
- A method is a subroutine in the class.

Several other concepts and their associated terminology are also important in object-oriented programming. For instance, *inheritance* enables one class to use the definitions from another class, while adding to or changing the definitions.

At this point you may be wondering: if an object is really just a data structure (usually a reference to a hash), and if a method is really just a subroutine, then why all this new terminology? The answer is that the framework imposed upon these data structures and subroutines, in which each data structure has a defined set of subroutines that alone can access the data structure, is indeed a new level of abstraction—a new set of constraints influencing the programming structure.

These constraints have proved to be so frequently useful that the new terminology of class, object, and method does say something new about the data structures and subroutines involved. Also, there are some new features such as bless and the arrow notation that cause subroutines to behave a little differently, as has been mentioned already, and will be explained in detail. But surprisingly few such additions are needed to transition from a knowledge of Perl's declarative style to Perl's OO style.

When you program using a defined class with its methods and objects, you can gain access to the class data only with the class methods provided by the class designer. The restriction of access to a class's data to the methods alone is called *encapsulation*. From the standpoint of the programmer using the class, exactly how the methods and objects are implemented isn't necessarily a concern. As a programmer using the class, you can regard the class as a black box; you don't have to look inside to see how it is implemented. Usually, it's only the programer writing the code who needs to worry about that.

One final point: in the field of OO programming, different authors define terms in different ways and present differing sets of essential concepts. Be warned that considerable diversity exists in the literature and among the languages that deal with object-orientation. The excellent book *Object Oriented Perl* (see the "Resources" section) includes a table that matches basic concepts with some of the alternate terminologies for those concepts.

Perl Objects Are Usually Hashes

In OO Perl programming, most objects are implemented as hashes and are accessed with blessed references to the hashes.

Each individual component of data in an object—for example, the name of a gene—is called an *attribute* and is assigned a value. The attribute/value nature of the component of an object is well suited to be represented as a key/value pair in a hash data structure.

It is quite possible, and sometimes desirable, to use other data structures such as scalars or arrays as the basis for objects. However, most situations are well handled by the hash data structure. Its benefits include having a name (key) for the data (value), allowing arguments to be specified in any order, and very fast lookup speed.

In this book, all objects are based on the hash data structure.

Arrow Notation (->)

Object-oriented Perl code uses arrow notation (->) to call methods. Understanding how this works is essential to understanding OO Perl. Before you start reading OO

Perl code, let's look more closely at its main features and how arrow notation is used to call methods.*

The arrow notation is used on an object to call a method in a class. Because the object has been blessed (i.e., marked with the class name), Perl can tell from the object what class it's in and so knows to find the method in that same class. With arrow notation, Perl also passes to the method a new argument that automatically appears first in its argument list. The other arguments are shifted over; the first argument is now the second, and so on. *The automatic passing of a new first argument to the method is the key to understanding OO Perl code.*

The method name appears to the right of the arrow. Perl then uses what's immediately to the left of the arrow to identify the class in which to find the method. It also passes information about what's on the left of the arrow to the method, where it appears as the first argument of the method. The left side of the arrow may be in one of two forms:

- The name of the class. Here's an example:

  ```
  TRNA->new( );
  ```

  Here Perl sees that the left side is the name of the TRNA class; therefore it calls the new subroutine in the TRNA package. It also automatically passes the name TRNA to that subroutine as its first argument, shifting any other arguments that may have been explicitly given (you'll see how this feature is used in later examples). You need to save the new object (a blessed reference to a hash) using the assignment operator = as follows:

  ```
  $trna_object = TRNA->new( );
  ```

- An object. Here's an example:

  ```
  $trna_object->findloops( );
  ```

  Perl sees that on the left side of the arrow $trna_object is an object of the TRNA class; it therefore calls the findloops method in the TRNA class. (It can see that $trna_object is a TRNA object because the object was blessed into the TRNA class when it was created by the new method, as I'll explain later.) Perl also passes a reference to the $trna_object object into the findloops method as the first argument to the method, shifting any other arguments that may have been explicitly given.

Why does Perl do it this way? The short answer to that question is that once you understand how it works, your code will become simpler and more usable. You will need to type class names less frequently, and you can use methods written for one class in another class (inheritance).

---

* The arrow (->) also appears in Perl when dealing with complex data structures, as you saw in Chapter 2, where it's used for references to subroutines.

The two new tricks that Perl performs here are:

- Using arrow notation to find the correct method in the correct class
- Passing the method a new first argument

It can find the correct class because objects are blessed with their class name.

Gene1: An Example of a Perl Class

This first example of Perl code defines a very small Perl class. This code does several new things, which I will explain in detail after the code.

This first version of the class is called Gene1, and it demonstrates the essential features needed to implement a simple class. Gene1 looks similar to the last module definition in Chapter 1, but with a few new wrinkles that transform it into OO software. I progress from Gene1.pm to Gene2.pm, then to Gene3.pm, and then to the final version, Gene.pm.

The methods of the Gene1 class will permit creating Gene1 objects and finding out what the values of a Gene1 object's attributes are.

Here's the module that implements a Gene1 class. I put the module into a file called Gene1.pm and place it into a directory on my computer that can be found when Perl needs it. I continue putting my code into my own development library directory, which on my Linux system is the directory */home/tisdall/MasteringPerlBio/ development/lib*. This directory is pointed out to Perl at the beginning of the testGene1 program that appears later as an example of how to use the Gene1.pm module definition. You will probably use a different directory on your computer, in which case you'll have to change this line:

```
use lib "/home/tisdall/MasteringPerlBio/development/lib";
```

You can also put the directory on the command line or set the PERL5LIB environmental variable, as described in Chapter 1. Setting the PERL5LIB variable is the easiest because you don't have to change the use lib lines in the programs.

A Gene1 object consists of a gene name, an organism represented by genus and species, a chromosome, and a reference to a protein structure in the PDB:

```
package Gene1;

use strict;
use warnings;
use Carp;

sub new {
        my ($class, %arg) = @_;
        return bless {
                _name     => $arg{name}     || croak("no name"),
                _organism => $arg{organism} || croak("no organism"),
```

```
                _chromosome => $arg{chromosome}  || "????",
                _pdbref     => $arg{pdbref}      || "????",
            }, $class;
        }

        sub name       { $_[0] -> {_name}      }
        sub organism   { $_[0] -> {_organism}  }
        sub chromosome { $_[0] -> {_chromosome}}
        sub pdbref     { $_[0] -> {_pdbref}     }

        1;
```

That's the whole thing!

> Hash keys that are simple words such as "name," "organism," and so
> on, don't need to have quotes around them when they appear within
> their surrounding curly braces: $arg{name} means the same thing as
> $arg{'name'}.

Here's a small program that uses the Gene1.pm class:

```
use strict;
use warnings;

use lib "/home/tisdall/MasteringPerlBio/development/lib";
use Gene1;

print "Object 1:\n\n";

my $obj1 = Gene1->new(
        name          => "Aging",
        organism      => "Homo sapiens",
        chromosome    => "23",
        pdbref        => "pdb9999.ent"
);

print $obj1->name, "\n";
print $obj1->organism, "\n";
print $obj1->chromosome, "\n";
print $obj1->pdbref, "\n";

print "Object 2:\n\n";

my $obj2 = Gene1->new(
        organism      => "Homo sapiens",
        name          => "Aging",
);

print $obj2->name, "\n";
print $obj2->organism, "\n";
print $obj2->chromosome, "\n";
print $obj2->pdbref, "\n";
```

```
print "Object 3:\n\n";

my $obj3 = Gene1->new(
        organism        => "Homo sapiens",
        chromosome      => "23",
        pdbref          => "pdb9999.ent"
);

print $obj3->name, "\n";
print $obj3->organism, "\n";
print $obj3->chromosome, "\n";
print $obj3->pdbref, "\n";
```

If I put that demonstration program code into file testGene1, I get this output from running that demonstration program with perl testGene1:

```
Object 1:

Aging
Homo sapiens
23
pdb9999.ent


Object 2:

Aging
Homo sapiens
????
????


Object 3:

no name at testGene line 35
```

Now, let's take a look at how this Perl code works.

Details of the Gene1 Class

In this section, I introduce the OO features used to make a class in Perl. First however, I explain the variable naming convention I use, as well as the handy Carp module.

Variable Names and Conventions

Using an underscore in front of a name is a programming convention that usually indicates that the item in question (e.g., a variable or hash key) isn't meant for the outside world but only for internal use.

This is just a convention; Perl doesn't require you to do it. It will, however, make your code easier to read and understand.

I generally follow this convention and put underscores in front of names that I don't want directly accessed by the programmer using the class. (In Perl, unlike some more strict OO languages, you can access data that's internal to a class, which make this naming convention that distinguishes internal variables particularly useful.)

Thus, in my Gene1 class, the attributes _name, _organism, _chromosome, and _pdbref are used internally only as the hash keys for the attributes in the object. When you use the class, as I do in my example program testGene1, you don't even have to know these names exist.

The interface is through arguments that specify the initialization values of these attributes. These arguments are called name, organism, chromosome, and pdbref. I also have methods—the subroutines also called name, organism, chromosome, and pdbref—that return the value of the actual attributes stored in the object.

Carp and croak

The Carp module is called near the top of Gene1.pm with use Carp;.

Carp is a standard Perl module that provides informative error messages in the case of problems. carp prints a warning message; croak prints an error message and dies. They are very much like the Perl functions warn and die; they report the line number in which the problem occured in the error message and report from what subroutine they were called. I use croak in my code; it prints out the error message provided, names the file and the line number and subroutine where it's called from, and then kills the program.

This function is certainly useful during development because it's another way to find errors in a program as it's being created. It also gives program users the ability to report the exact location of a problem, should one occur, to the programming staff (which may be just one programmer, you!).

In my program output, the Carp message is:

```
no name at testGene1 line 35
```

It's produced by the line:

```
_name      => $arg{name}    || croak("no name"),
```

in the Gene1.pm module file. Line 35 of testGene1 is the beginning line of this part of the program:

```
my $obj3 = Gene1->new(
        organism        => "Homo sapiens",
        chromosome      => "23",
        pdbref          => "pdb9999.ent"
);
```

It's the part of the code that tries to do something bad: it's trying to initialize a new object without setting its name. You'll see how this works in more detail in the following sections.

The new Constructor Method

To create objects, I defined a special *constructor method* called new. A call to new returns a new object, properly initialized. The new object is also marked as a member of the class, in this case the class Gene1.

```
sub new {
        my ($class, %arg) = @_;
        return bless {
                _name       => $arg{name}       || croak("no name"),
                _organism   => $arg{organism}   || croak("no organism"),
                _chromosome => $arg{chromosome} || "????",
                _pdbref     => $arg{pdbref}      || "????",
        }, $class;
}
```

Note that each class may have its own requirements for creating a class object, and so each class's constructor method may be different than that for another class.[*] For instance, a constructor may or may not provide default values for its attributes. Still, there's a lot of similarity between the constructor method of most classes.

Let's dissect the code of the constructor new. You'll see how objects are marked as members of a class, and initialized, by their constructor methods. Here are the main novelties:

- The package name Gene1 is automatically passed to the subroutine new as its first argument, even though it isn't included in the argument list.

- The returned hash reference is marked with the name Gene1 (using the bless function) thus making it an object in the Gene1 class.

Everything else here is straightforward Perl subroutine code.

Note that the call to new in the demonstration program testGene1 is made as follows:

```
my $obj = Gene1->new( ... );
```

The scalar variable $obj is a reference that points to the anonymous hash that's returned from the new method. The object is a hash that contains the attributes of the object, namely the key/value pairs of the hash. As usual the reference variable $obj is lexically scoped with my. And, as you see, $obj is marked with the class name Gene1.

The call Gene1->new includes the name of the package Gene1 in which the new subroutine is defined. The package name is the class name; the name of the module file in

---

[*] In particular, a constructor method may have any name in Perl; you could call it constructor, OverTheSun, or anything that you choose. Most programmers just use the very familiar name new.

which the class is defined must be the package name with .pm added. So you have a class Gene1 in a module file Gene1.pm that has the declaration package Gene1;.

The call to new with its arguments is of the form:

```
Gene1->new( key1 => 'value1', key2 => 'value2', ... )
```

This call does two important things:

1. It calls the new subroutine in the Gene1 package.
2. It passes the name Gene1 of the package to the new subroutine as its first argument. Therefore, in the new subroutine, in the line that collects the arguments:

   ```
   my ($class, %arg) = @_;
   ```

   the first argument is automatically the string Gene1 and is assigned to the variable $class.

This first argument Gene1 isn't listed in the usual place in the parentheses after the subroutine name in the call to the subroutine:

```
new( key1 => 'value1', key2 => 'value2', ... )
```

It happens automatically when the package name is used with an arrow (->):

```
Gene1->new( key1 => 'value1', key2 => 'value2', ... )
```

This may seem a bit odd, but it has the desirable advantage of making it unnecessary to type the class name Gene1 twice: once to call the new method in the Gene1 package, and again to pass the class name Gene1 to the new method. Instead of typing:

```
Gene1->new( "Gene1", key1 => 'value1', key2 => 'value2', ... )
```

you can just type:

```
Gene1->new( key1 => 'value1', key2 => 'value2', ... )
```

It's simply a bit of handy syntax the designers of Perl added to save a bit of typing when writing OO code in Perl, nothing more or less.

Now, let's examine the innards of the new constructor method. The new constructor method has the form:

```
sub new {
        my ($class, %arg) = @_;
        return bless {

                ...

        }, $class;
}
```

First, notice that in addition to assigning the first argument, the class name Gene1, to the variable $class, the subroutine captures the rest of the arguments in the hash variable %arg.

Recall, from your previous study of Perl, that initializing a hash by assigning a list to it causes the items in the list to be treated as key/value pairs in the hash. For example, if the arguments are:

```
('Myclass', mykey1 => 'myvalue1', mykey2 => 'myvalue2')
```

the scalar variable $class gets the value Myclass, and the hash variable %arg gets two key/value pairs initialized to the key 'mykey1' with the value 'myvalue1', and the key 'mykey2' with the value 'myvalue2'. Also recall that => is a synonym for a comma.*

Creating an Object with bless

The new constructor then returns the value of:

```
bless { ... }, $class;
```

The built-in Perl function bless does a very simple thing, but it's enough to take a data structure and make it an object in a class. It marks a reference with a class (package) name.

In this code, bless takes two arguments. The first, delimited by a pair of curly braces, is an anonymous hash, which you'll recall is a reference to an unnamed hash. This anonymous hash contains the data of the resulting object. The second argument to bless is just the name of the class, as it was saved in the $class scalar variable.

This call to bless returns a hash that is "marked" with the name of the class. The hash that bless marks is then given to the return function to serve as the returned value of the new method.

The object reference that is returned can now be identified as an object in the class Gene1. The object reference in this example is marked with the name Gene1 and has a hash as its top-level data structure. The new method in the class creates a new object in the class.

Although the first argument to bless in this code is an anonymous hash; in general, it can be any reference to a data structure that serves as an object. It can be a reference to a scalar, an array, a hash, or a more complex data structure. In the example, I am just declaring an anonymous hash in place rather than providing a reference to an existing hash. So, for example, if I declare a hash and a reference to it like so:

```
%hash = ( key1 => 'value1', key2 => 'value2' );
$hashref = \%hash;
```

then I can bless the hash, mark it with the class name HashClass, and save the resulting object:

```
$hashobj = bless $hashref, 'HashClass';
```

---

* It also forces its left side to be interpreted as a string and removes the need to surround the string in quotes, which is exactly what I want here.

Alternatively, the same object $hashobj can be created using an anonymous hash, and one call to bless:

```
$hashobj = bless { key1 => 'value1', key2 => 'value2' }, 'HashClass';
```

Using ref to Report an Object's Class

The Perl function ref reports on the type of element referred to—variable, object, code, etc. If the variable is blessed, ref reports on the class it is marked with.

After the call to new to create the Gene1 object $obj, the line:

```
print ref $obj, "\n";
```

prints out as Gene1.

The Perl function ref returns false if its argument isn't a reference. If it is a reference, it returns one of the following:

```
SCALAR
ARRAY
HASH
CODE
REF
GLOB
LVALUE
```

If the reference has been blessed into a package, that package name is returned from the call to ref.

Initialize an Object with an Anonymous Hash

Here again is the complete definition of the new method in the Gene1 class:

```
sub new {
    my ($class, %arg) = @_;
    return bless {
        _name        => $arg{name}        || croak("no name"),
        _organism    => $arg{organism}    || croak("no organism"),
        _chromosome  => $arg{chromosome}  || "????",
        _pdbref      => $arg{pdbref}      || "????",
    }, $class;
}
```

The first argument to bless is the following anonymous hash:

```
{
        _name        => $arg{name}        || croak("no name"),
        _organism    => $arg{organism}    || croak("no organism"),
        _chromosome  => $arg{chromosome}  || "????",
        _pdbref      => $arg{pdbref}      || "????",
}
```

As should be familiar (if not, see Appendix A for a Perl refresher), the key/value pairs are separated by the "syntactic sugar" symbol =>. The keys are in the first column;

the variable names _name, _organism, _chromosome, and _pdbref are used as the names of the keys.

The desired values are in the second column, following the => symbol. They are given in the form of a Perl logical OR operator. The value has either been passed in, or the default value is used:

```
value || default
```

The values are the values assigned from the argument list to the hash %arg upon entry to the subroutine. If all these arguments are passed to the new method, the hash initializes its four keys (_name, _organism, _chromosome, and _pdbref with those values).

If chromosome or pdbref, is passed to the new method, those values of %arg aren't defined, and the subroutine assigns the default value (the string ????) to the missing keys (_chromosome, _pdbref, or both).

If name or organism aren't passed as arguments to the new method, their values in %arg aren't defined, and by default, the subroutine calls croak and the program exits with an error message.

Let's look closely at a line in the Gene1.pm module that calls croak:

```
_name           => $arg{name}           || croak("no name"),
```

This line is part of a hash initialization. It is initializing an entry with a key _name. The value to be associated with this key is given as:

```
$arg{name}      || croak("no name")
```

This sets the value of the key to the value $arg{name} if that value exists. If $arg{name} doesn't exist, the value croak("no name") is evaluated. The behavior of ||(the or Boolean operator) is that the first argument is evaluated. The second argument is evaluated only if the first argument evaluates to false. In this code, the second argument kills the program and prints an error message when it is evaluated. This is a bit of a trick, but it's a common one that's used in several programming languages that have the Boolean or operator.

Now that you've seen how the new constructor handles its arguments, let's look again at how the test program testGene1 calls the new method, which it does three times:

```
my $obj1 = Gene1->new(
        name            => "Aging",
        organism        => "Homo sapiens",
        chromosome      => "23",
        pdbref          => "pdb9999.ent"
);

my $obj2 = Gene1->new(
        organism        => "Homo sapiens",
        name            => "Aging",
);
```

```
my $obj3 = Gene1->new(
        organism        => "Homo sapiens",
        chromosome      => "23",
        pdbref          => "pdb9999.ent"
);
```

The key/value pairs (the keys are the attributes of the objects) are passed to the new method. Notice that, due to the use of the %arg hash to capture these arguments by new, the order in which the arguments are passed isn't important. This is a nice convenience when creating and initializing objects because there are often many attributes and some may or may not be initialized; being able to ignore the order of the arguments when you call new makes it easier to program. Recall that it's a general property of Perl hashes that the order of the keys isn't important; it has to do with how hashes are implemented, and why they're so fast at retrieving values.

You'll recall that the use of croak in the new method requires the initialization of the name and organism attributes. For instance, $obj3 isn't created with an initial value for the name attribute. The new subroutine was defined to require such an initial value, which makes sense because, at the least, I want every gene in my program to have a name and an originating organism. The output of the testGene1 program shows that this third call to new triggers the croak exit mechanism.

Accessor Methods

Accessor methods are subroutines in the class that return the values of the class attributes. These attributes are usually implemented as keys of the hash that serves as the class object. You can access the attributes of an object, and their values, directly; for example, given an object of the Gene1 class, you can print out its name like so:

```
print $obj->{_name};
```

This gives the value of the key _name in the anonymous hash pointed to by $obj. This works; however, it's not good OO style. It directly accesses the data in the object; good style requires you to access the data through subroutines defined for that purpose. It is preferable to restrict all access of an object's attributes to the use of specific methods.

The actual attribute is called _name. This is initialized from the value of the argument name in the initialization of the arguments, as in this line from new:

```
_name           => $arg{name}      || croak("no name"),
```

That was just a convenient way to pass arguments to new, so you can say:

```
new( name => 'Ecoli' ) instead of new( _name => 'Ecoli' )
```

But you can just define a subroutine called, conveniently, name that returns the value of the attribute $obj->{_name}.

In my program, I have defined a method for each key in the hash. I have method name, which accesses the value of the key _name; I also have a similar method for each other key. Here's how to define a method to access the value of the key _name:

```
sub name        { $_[0] -> {_name}        }
```

This is called by the following line in the testGene1 program:

```
print $obj1->name, "\n";
```

It calls the method name for the object, which then accesses the value of the key _name in the object. In this way the actual implementation of the data that is stored in the object is kept hidden from users of the class methods. If the data is retrieved with a method, and if the author of the class decides at a later date to change the way the object stores its data, the users of the class can still get at the data by making the same method call. Only the internals of the method call will change; the behavior of the method, namely what arguments you give it and what return values you expect from it, stay the same. When the interface remains the same, the code that uses the class can also remain the same, saving everybody time and trouble, even when new versions of the class are developed.

The method name receives the object as its first argument because it is called by:

```
$obj1->name
```

The body of the subroutine uses the Perl built-in @_ array to access its arguments. The first argument to the subroutine is referred to as $_[0]. That first argument is the object, a reference to a hash, so I give it the key _name to retrieve the desired value:

```
$_[0] -> {_name}
```

Finally, since by default a subroutine returns the value of the last statement executed, this subroutine returns the gene name it has retrieved from the object.

Gene2.pm: A Second Example of a Perl Class

Gene1 demonstrated the fundamentals of a Perl class. Now, I'll build a more realistic example, which also includes a few additional standard Perl techniques.

My goal is to present an example that you can imitate in order to begin to develop your own OO software. I'm going to build the example in three more stages, expanding upon the Gene1.pm module. First, I'll add mutators, which are methods that alter the data in an object. I'll also add a method that gives information about the class as a whole, returning the count of how many objects in the class exist in the running program. This depends on the use of *closures*, methods that use variables declared outside the methods. This is the new material in the Gene2.pm module.

After that step, I introduce the AUTOLOAD mechanism, which gives a single class method called AUTOLOAD that can define large numbers of other methods and significantly reduce the amount of coding you need to write to develop a more complex object (among other benefits to be described later). That will be the Gene3.pm module.

We'll end up with a Gene.pm module you can use as a basis for your own Perl module development. It will add a mechanism to specify what properties each attribute has (which can prevent improper data manipulation, for instance). It will show how to initialize an object with class defaults and how to clone an existing object. Finally, Gene.pm will show you how to incorporate the documentation for a class right in the Perl code for the class.

Here is the code for the intermediate Gene2.pm module. Following the Gene2.pm module is an example of the code and output of a small test program that drives the module. Take a minute to look at these two code examples, especially at the comments. The module Gene2.pm contains several new details that will be discussed following the code. The test program should be fairly easy to read and understand.

```perl
package Gene2;

#
# A second version of the Gene.pm module
#

use strict;
use warnings;
use Carp;

# Class data and methods, that refer to the collection of all objects
# in the class, not just one specific object
{
    my $_count = 0;
    sub get_count {
        $_count;
    }
    sub _incr_count {
        ++$_count;
    }
    sub _decr_count {
        --$_count;
    }
}

# The constructor for the class
sub new {
    my ($class, %arg) = @_;
    my $self = bless {
        _name       => $arg{name}       || croak("Error: no name"),
        _organism   => $arg{organism}   || croak("Error: no organism"),
        _chromosome => $arg{chromosome} || "????",
        _pdbref     => $arg{pdbref}      || "????",
    }, $class;
```

```
        $class->_incr_count( );
        return $self;
}


# Accessors, for reading the values of data in an object
sub get_name       { $_[0] -> {_name}       }
sub get_organism   { $_[0] -> {_organism}   }
sub get_chromosome { $_[0] -> {_chromosome} }
sub get_pdbref     { $_[0] -> {_pdbref}     }


# Mutators, for writing the values of object data
sub set_name {
    my ($self, $name) = @_;
    $self -> {_name} = $name if $name;
}
sub set_organism {
    my ($self, $organism) = @_;
    $self -> {_organism} = $organism if $organism;
}
sub set_chromosome {
    my ($self, $chromosome) = @_;
    $self -> {_chromosome} = $chromosome if $chromosome;
}
sub set_pdbref {
    my ($self, $pdbref) = @_;
    $self -> {_pdbref} = $pdbref if $pdbref;
}


1;
```

Here is the small test program `testGene2` that demonstrates how to use the objects and methods in this version `Gene2` of our OO class:

```
#!/usr/bin/perl


#
# Test the second version of the Gene module
#

use strict;
use warnings;

# Change this line to show the folder where you store Gene2.pm
use lib "/home/tisdall/MasteringPerlBio/development/lib";
use Gene2;

#
# Create object, print values
#
print "Object 1:\n\n";

my $obj1 = Gene2->new(
        name           => "Aging",
        organism       => "Homo sapiens",
```

```
            chromosome    => "23",
            pdbref        => "pdb9999.ent"
);

print $obj1->get_name, "\n";
print $obj1->get_organism, "\n";
print $obj1->get_chromosome, "\n";
print $obj1->get_pdbref, "\n";


#
# Create another object, print values ... some will be unset
#
print "\n\nObject 2:\n\n";

my $obj2 = Gene2->new(
            organism    => "Homo sapiens",
            name        => "Aging",
);

print $obj2->get_name, "\n";
print $obj2->get_organism, "\n";
print $obj2->get_chromosome, "\n";
print $obj2->get_pdbref, "\n";


#
# Reset some of the values, print them
#
$obj2->set_name("RapidAging");
$obj2->set_chromosome("22q");
$obj2->set_pdbref("pdf9876.ref");

print "\n\n";

print $obj2->get_name, "\n";
print $obj2->get_organism, "\n";
print $obj2->get_chromosome, "\n";
print $obj2->get_pdbref, "\n";

print "\nCount is ", Gene2->get_count, "\n\n";


#
# Create another object, print values: but this fails
# because the "name" value is required (see the "new"
# constructor in Gene2.pm)
#
print "\n\nObject 3:\n\n";

my $obj3 = Gene2->new(
            organism    => "Homo sapiens",
            chromosome  => "23",
            pdbref      => "pdb9999.ent"
);

print "\nCount is ", Gene2->get_count, "\n\n";
```

Finally, here's the output from the test program `testGene2`:

```
Object 1:

Aging
Homo sapiens
23
pdb9999.ent


Object 2:

Aging
Homo sapiens
????
????

RapidAging
Homo sapiens
22q
pdf9876.ref

Count is 2

Object 3:

Error: no name at testGene2 line 68
```

It's a good idea to take a moment to read through this `Gene2.pm` module, the test program `testGene2`, and the output. Compare this new `Gene2` module with the earlier `Gene1` module. In particular, notice where the methods are defined in the module, and then how they are actually used in the test program. Don't get hung up on the details in this first reading; just look at the overall picture. Notice that the definitions are all in the module `Gene2.pm`, which is then loaded at the beginning of the test program `testGene2`; it is `testGene2` that actually creates the module's objects and uses the module's methods on those objects. In other words, `testGene2` is a program; `Gene2.pm` is a definition of a class that is used in `testGene2`.

Let's begin examining the module code.

Closures

A *closure* keeps track of class data. *Class data* refers not to a particular object, but to several, possibly all, objects of a class that have been created during the running of your program. This is frequently important to do. For instance, say you have a DNA sequencing pipeline that can handle only 20 sequences at any one time. You'd want your controlling program to block any attempt to create more than 20 sequence objects until the pipeline is ready to receive more. To do this, you would keep a count of how many sequence objects your controlling program has created. Closures are a way to program such class data.

A *closure* is a subroutine that uses a variable defined outside the subroutine. By surrounding such a variable and some closures that use that variable within a block, you can use the closures to access the variable from anywhere in the program, and the variable will never go out of scope and lose its value. This section will explain how this works and how to use it in your code.

The following code is new in Gene2.pm:

```perl
# Class data and methods, that refer to the collection of all objects
# in the class, not just one specific object
{
    my $_count = 0;
    sub get_count {
        $_count;
    }
    sub _incr_count {
        ++$_count;
    }
    sub _decr_count {
        --$_count;
    }
}
```

This code creates a variable $_count. $_count is a lexical my variable in a block of curly braces, and therefore is hidden from all parts of the code except within the block. The three methods that are also defined in the same block use the variable $_count. This variable persists throughout the life of the program because the subroutines defined with it are closures. For example, in the code for the class module Gene2.pm, I use $_count to keep a count of how many objects are in existence at any given time. Notice that the method names _incr_count and _decr_count begin with a leading underscore, as does the variable name $_count. They aren't meant to be called by the user of the class but are internal to the module. On the other hand, the remaining method get_count doesn't begin with a leading underscore and is meant to be called whenever the user of the class wants to know what the count is.

The previous section of code implements a closure. It is surrounded by curly braces creating a Perl block. You've seen many blocks associated with loops and conditionals as you learned the fundamentals of Perl. The block here stands on its own without being a part of another programming construct.

Any block, this one included, creates a new *scope* for the variables that occur within it. my variables (also called lexical variables) within a block exist only while the program is executing the statements within that block. When a program leaves a block by passing beyond its closing curly brace, the my variables within it go out of scope. In other words, they cease to exist, and disappear from the program until the program reenters the block, and they are created anew.

The preceding paragraph is correct; however, there is one important "but."

Subroutine definitions don't go out of scope in the way that lexically scoped (my) variables do. It is also possible for a subroutine definition to affect the behavior of a lexically scoped variable. Aha. Read on.

To repeat: subroutine definitions aren't subject to the same constraints as variables in regards to my and blocks. In fact, a subroutine definition is global to the entire package in which it's declared. Perl looks for subroutine definitions at compile-time, before actually running the program, and makes a subroutine definition available to an entire package no matter where the subroutine is declared—even if it's declared in a conditional block that's never reached during runtime—when the program code is actually executed.

As an example, here is a small program with a subroutine definition:

```
#
# A program to demonstrate the global nature of subroutine definitions
#

my $dna = 'ACGT';

if ($dna eq 'ACGT') {
        print "This statement gets executed\n";
        print "Here's the subroutine call:\n";
        isdna($dna);
} else {
        print "This statement does not get executed\n";
        #
        # The following subroutine definition is in a block which is
        # never executed at runtime.
        #
        sub isdna {
                # Print the argument if it is DNA
                if($_[0] =~ /^[ACGT]+$/i) {
                        print $_[0], "\n";
                else {
                        return 0;
                }
        }
}
```

This produces the following output:

```
This statement gets executed
Here's the subroutine call:
ACGT
```

As you see, even though the subroutine definition is buried in a block that's never entered, not even once, it is still available to the program. Perl scans the program at compile-time, reads in any subroutine definition no matter where it is, and the subroutine definition is then available to be called from anywhere in the program at runtime.

Continuing on, in the code from Gene2.pm under consideration, there's the variable definition:

```
my $_count = 0;
```

which occurs outside the following subroutine definitions such as:

```
sub _incr_count {
    ++$_count;
}
```

The variable $_count is declared outside the subroutine _incr_count, but the subroutine uses the variable. Therefore, by definition, the subroutine _incr_count is a closure.

There's just one more piece to the puzzle. Consider again the code fragment from Gene2.pm, which I repeat here:

```
# Class data and methods, that refer to the collection of all objects
# in the class, not just one specific object
{
    my $_count = 0;
    sub get_count {
        $_count;
    }
    sub _incr_count {
        ++$_count;
    }
    sub _decr_count {
        --$_count;
    }
}
```

It seems that when the program leaves the block that encloses this code, the variable $_count should go out of scope and no longer be available to the program. However, in Gene2.pm the $_count variable doesn't cease to exist.

Because the subroutine definitions in this block are global, and because they also reference the variable $_count, Perl knows that at any point in the program you can put in a call to, say, get_count, which in turn needs the variable $_count to execute. Perl doesn't cause the variable $_count to cease to exist because it sees the closures and avoids destroying the variable they reference at runtime. At any point in the program, the value of $_count can be obtained by calling the subroutine. However, the value of $_count can't be accessed in any other way than by get_count or other closure defined within the same block.

To summarize, by defining a variable and a closure that uses that variable within a block, a program can limit access to that variable to calls by the closures. This is exactly what I want to do in setting up class methods that refer to the collection of all objects that are in use.

In Gene2.pm, I want to initialize the count of objects to 0 when the program starts and then increment it by one each time a new object is created. By defining _incr_count as a closure, I can call it from within the new object constructor, ensuring that the variable $_count will keep an accurate count of the number of objects that are created.

Tracking Class Data from the Constructor Method

In this second version of the class, I just have to make a small change to the constructor method, the subroutine new.

Here is the modified new method constructor:

```
# The constructor for the class
sub new {
    my ($class, %arg) = @_;
    my $self = bless {
        _name       => $arg{name}       || croak("Error: no name"),
        _organism   => $arg{organism}   || croak("Error: no organism"),
        _chromosome => $arg{chromosome} || "????",
        _pdbref     => $arg{pdbref}     || "????",
    }, $class;
    $class->_incr_count();
    return $self;
}
```

First, I create the object by blessing (and initializing) an anonymous hash, as before. This time, however, I'll save the object as the local variable $self. This allows me to add a call to the class method _incr_count in order to keep track of the total number of objects created. I'll then return the object $self from the subroutine.

Accessor and Mutator Methods

In the first version of Gene1.pm, I printed the values stored in an object by accessing simple methods such as get_name.

In this new version of Gene2.pm, I have the same specific methods for each attribute for which I may want to see the value. I also include *mutators*, which are subroutines that enable the user of the class to alter the values of attributes of an object.

Here are the accessor and mutator methods for Gene2.pm:

```
# Accessors, for reading the values of data in an object
sub get_name       { $_[0] -> {_name}       }
sub get_organism   { $_[0] -> {_organism}   }
sub get_chromosome { $_[0] -> {_chromosome} }
sub get_pdbref     { $_[0] -> {_pdbref}     }

# Mutators, for writing the values of object data
sub set_name {
```

```
        my ($self, $name) = @_;
        $self -> {_name} = $name if $name;
    }
    sub set_organism {
        my ($self, $organism) = @_;
        $self -> {_organism} = $organism if $organism;
    }
    sub set_chromosome {
        my ($self, $chromosome) = @_;
        $self -> {_chromosome} = $chromosome if $chromosome;
    }
    sub set_pdbref {
        my ($self, $pdbref) = @_;
        $self -> {_pdbref} = $pdbref if $pdbref;
    }
```

The mutators collect two arguments. The first is the reference to the object, which as before, is passed automatically to the method when it is invoked (using the method set_name as an example):

```
$obj->set_name('hairy');
```

The second argument collected is then the first argument given to the call, in this case, setting the gene name to hairy.

The work of the subroutine is accomplished by the line:

```
$self -> {_name} = $name if $name;
```

It simply sets the internal _name attribute to the supplied name (hairy in this example) if the argument $name is supplied. If it's not supplied, the subroutine does nothing.

Again, you see that the internal representation of the attributes of the object are hidden from the class's user. Altering an object's attributes is done with methods; the class author is then free to alter the way in which the attributes are stored, without changing the Application Programming Interface (API), the interface of the class to the outside world. If you use this class, you don't have to change your code when a new version of the class is written.

The test program testGene2 is similar to testGene1, with the addition of examples of the class mutators.

Gene3.pm: A Third Example of a Perl Class

We've gone through two iterations building an OO class with the Gene1.pm and Gene2.pm modules. Now, let's add a few more features and create the Gene3.pm module as a penultimate example for this introduction to OO programming in Perl.

Here is the code for Gene3.pm and for the test program testGene3; also included is the output produced by running testGene3. Following the code will be a discussion of the new features of this third version of our example class. But I'll point out before

---

you read on, that AUTOLOAD is a special name in Perl for a subroutine that will handle a call to any undefined subroutine in a class. (I'll give more details after you look at the code.)

```perl
package Gene3;

#
# A third version of the Gene.pm module
#

use strict;
use warnings;
our $AUTOLOAD; # before Perl 5.6.0 say "use vars '$AUTOLOAD';"
use Carp;

# Class data and methods, that refer to the collection of all objects
# in the class, not just one specific object
{
    my $_count = 0;
    sub get_count {
        $_count;
    }
    sub _incr_count {
        ++$_count;
    }
    sub _decr_count {
        --$_count;
    }
}

# The constructor for the class
sub new {
    my ($class, %arg) = @_;
    my $self = bless {
        _name       => $arg{name}       || croak("Error: no name"),
        _organism   => $arg{organism}   || croak("Error: no organism"),
        _chromosome => $arg{chromosome} || "????",
        _pdbref     => $arg{pdbref}      || "????",
        _author     => $arg{author}      || "????",
        _date       => $arg{date}        || "????",
    }, $class;
    $class->_incr_count();
    return $self;
}

# This takes the place of such accessor definitions as:
#   sub get_attribute { ... }
# and of such mutator definitions as:
#   sub set_attribute { ... }
sub AUTOLOAD {
    my ($self, $newvalue) = @_;
```

```perl
    my ($operation, $attribute) = ($AUTOLOAD =~ /(get|set)(_\w+)$/);

    # Is this a legal method name?
    unless($operation && $attribute) {
        croak "Method name $AUTOLOAD is not in the recognized form (get|set)_
attribute\n";
    }
    unless(exists $self->{$attribute}) {
        croak "No such attribute '$attribute' exists in the class ", ref($self);
    }

    # Turn off strict references to enable "magic" AUTOLOAD speedup
    no strict 'refs';

    # AUTOLOAD accessors
    if($operation eq 'get') {
        # define subroutine
        *{$AUTOLOAD} = sub { shift->{$attribute} };

    # AUTOLOAD mutators
    }elsif($operation eq 'set') {
        # define subroutine
        *{$AUTOLOAD} = sub { shift->{$attribute} = shift; };

        # set the new attribute value
        $self->{$attribute} = $newvalue;
    }

    # Turn strict references back on
    use strict 'refs';

    # return the attribute value
    return $self->{$attribute};
}

# When an object is no longer being used, this will be automatically called
# and will adjust the count of existing objects
sub DESTROY {
    my($self) = @_;
    $self->_decr_count();
}

# Other methods.  They do not fall into the same form as the majority handled by
AUTOLOAD
# This is an example of a method that is both accessor and mutator, depending on the
# number of arguments provided to it.
sub citation {
    my ($self, $author, $date) = @_;
    $self->{_author} = set_author($author) if $author;
    $self->{_date} = set_date($date) if $date;
    return ($self->{_author}, $self->{_date})
}

1;
```

Testing Gene3.pm

Here is the test program testGene3 for the Gene3.pm class:

```perl
#!/usr/bin/perl

#
# Test the third version of the Gene module
#

use strict;
use warnings;

# Change this line to show the folder where you store Gene.pm
use lib "/home/tisdall/MasteringPerlBio/development/lib";
use Gene3;

print "Object 1:\n\n";

# Create first object
my $obj1 = Gene3->new(
        name            => "Aging",
        organism        => "Homo sapiens",
        chromosome      => "23",
        pdbref          => "pdb9999.ent"
);

# Print the attributes of the first object
print $obj1->get_name, "\n";
print $obj1->get_organism, "\n";
print $obj1->get_chromosome, "\n";
print $obj1->get_pdbref, "\n";
# Test AUTOLOAD failure: try uncommenting one or both of these lines
#print $obj1->get_exon, "\n";
#print $obj1->getexon, "\n";

print "\n\nObject 2:\n\n";

# Create second object
my $obj2 = Gene3->new(
        organism        => "Homo sapiens",
        name            => "Aging",
);

# Print the attributes of the second object ... some will be unset
print $obj2->get_name, "\n";
print $obj2->get_organism, "\n";
print $obj2->get_chromosome, "\n";
print $obj2->get_pdbref, "\n";

# Reset some of the attributes of the second object
$obj2->set_name("RapidAging");
$obj2->set_chromosome("22q");
$obj2->set_pdbref("pdf9876.ref");
```

```
$obj2->set_author("D. Enay");
$obj2->set_date("February 9, 1952");

print "\n\n";

# Print the reset attributes of the second object
print $obj2->get_name, "\n";
print $obj2->get_organism, "\n";
print $obj2->get_chromosome, "\n";
print $obj2->get_pdbref, "\n";
print $obj2->citation, "\n";

# Use a class method to report on a statistic about all existing objects
print "\nCount is ", Gene3->get_count, "\n\n";

print "\n\nObject 3:\n\n";

# Create a third object: but this fails
#   because the "name" value is required (see Gene.pm)
my $obj3 = Gene3->new(
        organism        => "Homo sapiens",
        chromosome      => "23",
        pdbref          => "pdb9999.ent"
);

# This line is not reached due to the fatal failure to
#   create the third object
print "\nCount is ", Gene3->get_count, "\n\n";
```

Finally, here is the output from running the test program testGene3:

```
Object 1:

Aging
Homo sapiens
23
pdb9999.ent

Object 2:

Aging
Homo sapiens
????
????

RapidAging
Homo sapiens
22q
pdf9876.ref
D. EnayFebruary 9, 1952

Count is 2

Object 3:

Error: no name at testGene3 line 70
```

How AUTOLOAD Works

The AUTOLOAD mechanism, built into the definition of Perl packages, is simple to use. If a subroutine named AUTOLOAD is declared within a package, it is called whenever an undefined subroutine is called within the package. AUTOLOAD is a special name, and must be capitalized as shown, because Perl is designed that way. Don't use the subroutine name AUTOLOAD (or DESTROY) for any other purpose, or you'll suffer unintended consequences.

Without an AUTOLOAD subroutine defined in a package, an attempt to call some undefined subroutine simply produces an error when the program runs. But if an AUTOLOAD subroutine is defined, it is called instead and is passed the arguments of the undefined subroutine. At the same time, the $AUTOLOAD variable is set to the name of the undefined subroutine.

Here's an example of a short Perl program that tries to call an undefined function:

```perl
#!/usr/bin/perl

use strict;
use warnings;

print "I started the program\n";

report_protein_function("one", "two");

print "I got to the end of the program\n";
```

It gives the following output:

```
I started the program
Undefined subroutine &main::report_protein_function called at jk.pl line 8.
```

Here's what happens when an AUTOLOAD subroutine is defined in the package:

```perl
#!/usr/bin/perl

use strict;
use warnings;
use vars '$AUTOLOAD';

print "I started the program\n";

report_protein_function("one", "two");

print "I got to the end of the program\n";

sub AUTOLOAD {
        print "AUTOLOAD is set to $AUTOLOAD\n";
        print "with arguments ", "@_\n";
}
```

It gives the following output:

```
I started the program
AUTOLOAD is set to main::report_protein_function
with arguments one two
I got to the end of the program
```

Defining Global Variables

Recall that when you start programs with such statements as:

```
use strict;
```

you have to declare all variables as lexically scoped using my. However, there are times when your program needs to use global variables that aren't lexically scoped. To use AUTOLOAD, you need access to the predefined $AUTOLOAD global variable.

To enable access of the package global $AUTOLOAD, you must specifically exempt it from the use strict injunction. This can be accomplished with the use vars statement:

```
use vars '$AUTOLOAD';
```

Other globals can be declared in this way as well, but globals should be used sparingly, and preferably not at all.

Newer versions of Perl (after Version 5.6.0) have a cleaner way to declare global variables even when use strict is in effect:

```
our $AUTOLOAD;
```

This makes the variable $AUTOLOAD a legal global within the scope in which it is declared—in Gene3.pm, the scope is the entire class.

Without our $AUTOLOAD or use vars '$AUTOLOAD', the program won't run; instead, it complains vociferously that:

```
Global symbol "$AUTOLOAD" requires explicit package name
```

AUTOLOAD Simplifies Writing Methods

Having the AUTOLOAD mechanism available can greatly simplify the writing of class methods. Many classes require methods to examine and to change the values of attributes, as have the two previous versions Gene1.pm and Gene2.pm.

If an object has many attributes, you have to write an accessor method and a mutator method for each attribute. This is repetitive; it requires defining more methods every time the list of attributes changes, and, in general, it's hard to maintain such code.

The new version Gene3.pm uses AUTOLOAD to automate the handling of methods for accessors and mutators. All you need do is write the one AUTOLOAD subroutine, and all these similar, basic methods are handled in the same fashion by the one bit of code.

Bypassing use strict

AUTOLOAD starts by fiddling with the use strict statement. Just as it requires the $AUTOLOAD global variable to be exempted from the use strict directive, so does the magic AUTOLOAD speedup (described in the next section) require an exemption from the use strict directive at a specific place within the AUTOLOAD subroutine. Thus, the statement:

```
no strict "refs";
```

turns off the use strict where required. This enables the lines (to be explained later) such as:

```
*{$AUTOLOAD} = sub { return $_[0]->{$attribute} };
```

to bypass the otherwise desirable use strict instruction.

AUTOLOAD arguments

Recall that AUTOLOAD is automatically used when 1) it has been defined, and 2) an undefined subroutine is called. When this happens, AUTOLOAD is simply passed the arguments that would have gone to the undefined subroutine.

For example, say you call an undefined method fold on an object $peptide:

```
$peptide->fold(-style => 'prion')
```

If you define an AUTOLOAD method in the class, it's called and passed the calling object or class name, as usual, plus the arguments -style => 'prion' you were trying to pass to the nonexistent fold method. The global scalar variable $AUTOLOAD is also set to the name of the nonexistent fold method.

The version of AUTOLOAD in Gene3.pm captures one written argument. So, of course, this AUTOLOAD actually captures two arguments: the class object automatically passed into the subroutine by arrow notation, which appears first, and the other arguments, if any. This line in the AUTOLOAD subroutine:

```
my ($self, $newvalue) = @_;
```

assigns the reference to the object to the new variable $self and the value to be set, if any, to the new variable $newvalue.

Using naming conventions to write code: get_ and set_

The various versions of the Gene module have named attributes with beginning underscores, for example, _name for the gene name. The accessors and mutators for attributes have been assigned names that prepend get and set to the beginning of the attribute name, for example, get_name and set_name.

In Gene3.pm, the AUTOLOAD subroutine elevates this convention to an enforced discipline, by recognizing only method names and attribute names that conform to this convention. It first examines the name of the called subroutine as stored in the

$AUTOLOAD global variable, checks if the subroutine name is in the expected form, and if so, extracts the attribute name from the subroutine name with a regular expression. The AUTOLOAD subroutine then checks that the requested attribute exists, and fetches or sets the value of that attribute.

The first part of the AUTOLOAD subroutine does some checking to see if the subroutine name is in the expected form, and if so, it extracts the attribute name, and the requested operation (get or set). This first test:

```
my ($operation, $attribute) = ($AUTOLOAD =~ /(get|set)(_\w+)$/);

# Is this a legal method name?
unless($operation && $attribute) {
    croak "Method name $AUTOLOAD is not in the recognized form (get|set)_attribute\n";
}
unless(exists $self->{$attribute}) {
    croak "No such attribute '$attribute' exists in the class ", ref($self);
    }
```

uses a regular expression to see if the $AUTOLOAD variable is storing a method name that ends with an attribute name (complete with leading underscore) that is defined for objects of this class if it begins with get or set as the desired operation. The regular expression:

```
(get|set)(_\w+)$
```

looks for a name that, after get or set, is composed of an underscore followed by one or more legal word characters (as described in the perlre manpage on regular expressions):

```
_\w+
```

Here, the underscore matches an underscore, and the \w matches any legal word character, and the + matches one or more such word characters. These are remembered and captured in the $operation and $attribute variables by surrounding with parentheses the parts of the regular expression that match the operation and the attribute name:

```
(get|set)(_\w+)
```

This attribute name is assigned to the variable $attribute (for obvious mnemonic reasons) to use in the rest of the subroutine. Similarly, the operation get or set is assigned to the $operation variable.

The second part of the test checks to see if such an attribute name exists in the hash that represents the class object:

```
unless(exists $self->{$attribute}) {
    croak "No such attribute '$attribute' exists in the class ", ref($self);
}
```

The exists Perl command checks to see if a hash key exists; the value for the key may not have been set, but the key must exist. $self is the reference to the class object, so the following:

```
exists $self->{$attribute}
```

checks to see if any such attribute actually exists in the object.

If the method name passed to AUTOLOAD begins with get or set, ends with a name including a leading underscore, and if that name is an existing key in the hash that is the class object, the tests will succeed. If they fail, the program will croak at this point.

AUTOLOAD accessors

The next bit of AUTOLOAD code handles the calls to class accessors:

```
# AUTOLOAD accessors
if($operation eq 'get') {
    # define subroutine
    *{$AUTOLOAD} = sub { shift->{$attribute} };
}
```

The code first determines that a get accessor was wanted. Then the undefined accessor method (whose name has been saved in the variable $AUTOLOAD) is defined. The subroutine definition is placed in the program's symbol table with *{$AUTOLOAD}. The new subroutine gets the object from the arguments by the call to shift. The object is a hash, and the value in the hash for the attribute is returned from the subroutine. So this method is a simple accessor, that, given an attribute name, returns the value. This accessor isn't actually used here; it's just defined in the symbol table.

AUTOLOAD mutators

The next bit of AUTOLOAD code handles the calls to class mutators:

```
# AUTOLOAD mutators
}elsif($operation eq 'set') {
    # define subroutine
    *{$AUTOLOAD} = sub { shift->{$attribute} = shift; };

    # set the new attribute value
    $self->{$attribute} = $newvalue;
}
```

Here, after determining that a set mutator method was called, the undefined mutator method (whose name has been saved in the variable $AUTOLOAD) is defined. The new subroutine gets the object from the arguments by the first call to shift and sets the attribute of the object to the new value, which it gets from the arguments by the second call to shift. After defining the new mutator method, the code actually sets the attribute key to the $newvalue that was passed in as an argument.

Finally, the AUTOLOAD program, after defining the new accessor or mutator method, as the case may be, and setting the new value of the attribute if a mutator method has been defined, returns the value of the attribute:

```
# return the attribute value
return $self->{$attribute};
```

So the AUTOLOAD method both defines the accessor or mutator methods and behaves just like the defined accessor or mutator method by returning the attribute value (if it's a mutator, it first resets the attribute).

AUTOLOAD speedup

The so-called "magic" lines in the accessor and mutator code that I've referred to:

```
*{$AUTOLOAD} = sub { shift->{$attribute} };
```

and:

```
*{$AUTOLOAD} = sub { shift->{$attribute} = shift; };
```

are there purely in order to speed up the code.

AUTOLOAD performs its tasks a bit on the slow side. For a large program that does a lot of getting and setting of attributes, the slowdown is noticeable. What is saved in programming time by having AUTOLOAD handle all these accessors and mutators, is lost in runtime. The slowdown comes from the program having to figure out what is wanted by the undefined methods, the use of regular expressions to parse the names of the methods, etc.

The magic lines actually define the new methods in the symbol table, on the fly, when they don't already exist. (The * gives access to the symbol table, but I'll omit the details of how the symbol table is defined and manipulated and stick to practicalities here.) After they are called once, and the AUTOLOAD overhead is incurred, the methods are thenceforth defined in the symbol table of the running program. So, for instance, the second time that the accessor method get_name is called, the program finds the definition in the symbol table, and AUTOLOAD isn't called. This results in a considerable speedup for the program overall.

I'll not delve too deeply into how this works. Briefly, the $AUTOLOAD variable contains the name of the desired method call, say, get_name. The star * in *{$AUTOLOAD} is a reference to the definition of that method call in the symbol table. This symbol table reference is assigned the part of the expression to the right of the assignment sign (=) that's an (anonymous) subroutine definition.

The symbol table is thus manipulated directly from your program, and the missing accessor and mutator definitions are installed in the symbol table the first time AUTOLOAD is called to handle them. After this first call that invokes AUTOLOAD, the program can find the method definitions in the symbol table and uses those definitions, bypassing AUTOLOAD. For more details, see O'Reilly's *Programming Perl*.

Cleaning Up Unused Objects with DESTROY

When a running program no longer needs a portion of computer memory, what happens to it? How is the program's memory managed? Various possibilities exist, and different languages handle the problem in different ways. For instance, the designer of the language can just leave the memory as it is, unused, and go on and use other memory for other tasks. No clean up is strictly necessary.

However, this might, and does, cause problems with certain kinds of programs. Some programs read in large amounts of data into their memory, perhaps extract some statistics on the data, and then go on to the next large chunk of data to repeat the same operation. A computer's memory is finite; for a program that runs a long time and examines a continuous source of data (say, for instance, the data generated by your sequencing facility), it will at some point use all available main memory.

It is necessary to consider how to clean up memory that is no longer used, so it can be reused by the program. This is sometimes called the *garbage collection* problem. Consideration of this problem has resulted in many approaches and a large amount of literature, which won't be discussed here.

However, sometimes there are practical considerations. In the class module Gene.pm, I'm keeping count of all objects that are created by the running program. In Perl, when a variable is no longer used, its memory is automatically cleaned up. One such instance is when a variable goes out of scope. For instance, in the following code fragment, the variable $i goes out of scope after the if block, and its memory is cleaned up, making it available to the rest of the program:

```
if(1) {
        my $i = 'ACCGGCCGGCCGGTTAATGCATAATC';
        determine_function($i);
}

# $i has gone out of scope here
```

This problem actually affects the Gene.pm module. Say you create a new object, and as the program continues, the object goes out of scope. For instance, if the object was created within a block, and the program leaves the block, the object is then out of scope. Perl will remove the part of memory that held the object, and all will be well... except that the global count of the number of objects will now be off by one!

What is needed is a way to automatically call a bit of code to adjust the global count whenever an object goes out of scope. Perl provides such a mechanism with the DESTROY subroutine. Perl calls the DESTROY method 1) if you've defined a method with that name in your class, and 2) a class object (a reference blessed with the name of the class) goes out of scope. It does so automatically, just as AUTOLOAD is automatically called if you attempt to call a method that doesn't exist on a class object.

In our program, the only thing keeping track of when an object goes out of scope and is garbage collected by Perl is the global count of existing objects. This simple DESTROY subroutine will thus suffice:

```
sub DESTROY {
    my($self) = @_;
    $self->_decr_count();
}
```

Let's see if it works. Here's a test program, testGeneGC (GC for garbage collection):

```
#!/usr/bin/perl

#
# Test the garbage collection of the Gene.pm module
#

use strict;
use warnings;

# Change this line to show the folder where you store Gene.pm
use lib "/home/tisdall/MasteringPerlBio/development/lib";
use Gene;

print "\nCount is ", Gene->get_count, "\n\n";

if(1) {
    # Create first object
    my $obj1 = Gene->new(
            name                => "Gene1",
            organism            => "Homo sapiens",
    );

        print "\nCount is ", Gene->get_count, "\n\n";

    # Create second object
    my $obj2 = Gene->new(
            name                => "Gene2",
            organism            => "Homo sapiens",
    );

    print "\nCount is ", Gene->get_count, "\n\n";

    # Create a third object
    my $obj3 = Gene->new(
            name                => "Gene3",
            organism            => "Homo sapiens",
    );

    print "\nCount is ", Gene->get_count, "\n\n";
}

print "\nCount is ", Gene->get_count, "\n\n";
```

This produces an output that shows that once the three objects created in the scope of the `if` block go out of scope, the count is properly set back to zero:

```
Count is 0
Count is 1
Count is 2
Count is 3
Count is 0
```

As a further test, let's try taking the definition of the DESTROY subroutine out of Gene.pm. Now, try the test program `testGeneGC` to get the following output:

```
Count is 0
Count is 1
Count is 2
Count is 3
Count is 3
```

As you see, the last line still has a count of three Gene objects, when there are in reality none still within scope. To properly keep class-wide data on all objects, the DESTROY subroutine is sometimes a necessity.

For more details on DESTROY, including discussions of how to clean up more complicated data structures, see the "Resources" section.

Gene.pm: A Fourth Example of a Perl Class

We've now come to the fourth and final version of the Gene class, Gene.pm. This final version adds a few more bells and whistles to make the code more reliable and useful. You'll see how to define the class attributes in such a way as to specify the operations that are permitted on them, thus enforcing more discipline in how the class can be used. You'll also see how to initialize an object with class defaults or clone an already existing object. You'll see the standard and simple way in which the documentation for a class can be incorporated into the .pm file. This will conclude my introduction to OO Perl programming (but check out the exercises at the end of the chapter and see later chapters of this book for more ideas).

Building Gene.pm

Here then is the code for Gene.pm. Again, I recommend that you take the time to read this code and compare it to the previous version, Gene3.pm, before continuing with the discussion that follows:

```
package Gene;

#
# A fourth and final version of the Gene.pm class
#
```

```perl
use strict;
use warnings;
our $AUTOLOAD;  # before Perl 5.6.0 say "use vars '$AUTOLOAD';"
use Carp;

# Class data and methods
{
    # A list of all attributes with default values and read/write/required properties
    my %_attribute_properties = (
        _name        => [ '????',      'read.required'],
        _organism    => [ '????',      'read.required'],
        _chromosome  => [ '????',      'read.write'],
        _pdbref      => [ '????',      'read.write'],
        _author      => [ '????',      'read.write'],
        _date        => [ '????',      'read.write'],
    );

    # Global variable to keep count of existing objects
    my $_count = 0;

    # Return a list of all attributes
    sub _all_attributes {
            keys %_attribute_properties;
    }

    # Check if a given property is set for a given attribute
    sub _permissions {
        my($self, $attribute, $permissions) = @_;
        $_attribute_properties{$attribute}[1] =~ /$permissions/;
    }

    # Return the default value for a given attribute
    sub _attribute_default {
            my($self, $attribute) = @_;
        $_attribute_properties{$attribute}[0];
    }

    # Manage the count of existing objects
    sub get_count {
        $_count;
    }
    sub _incr_count {
        ++$_count;
    }
    sub _decr_count {
        --$_count;
    }
}

# The constructor method
# Called from class, e.g. $obj = Gene->new();
sub new {
```

```perl
    my ($class, %arg) = @_;
    # Create a new object
    my $self = bless {}, $class;

    foreach my $attribute ($self->_all_attributes()) {
        # E.g. attribute = "_name",  argument = "name"
        my($argument) = ($attribute =~ /^_(.*)/);
        # If explicitly given
        if (exists $arg{$argument}) {
            $self->{$attribute} = $arg{$argument};
        # If not given, but required
        }elsif($self->_permissions($attribute, 'required')) {
            croak("No $argument attribute as required");
        # Set to the default
        }else{
            $self->{$attribute} = $self->_attribute_default($attribute);
        }
    }
    $class->_incr_count();
    return $self;
}

# The clone method
# All attributes will be copied from the calling object, unless
# specifically overridden
# Called from an exisiting object, e.g. $cloned_obj = $obj1->clone();
sub clone {
    my ($caller, %arg) = @_;
    # Extract the class name from the calling object
    my $class = ref($caller);
    # Create a new object
    my $self = bless {}, $class;

    foreach my $attribute ($self->_all_attributes()) {
        # E.g. attribute = "_name",  argument = "name"
        my($argument) = ($attribute =~ /^_(.*)/);
        # If explicitly given
        if (exists $arg{$argument}) {
            $self->{$attribute} = $arg{$argument};
        # Otherwise copy attribute of new object from the calling object
        }else{
            $self->{$attribute} = $caller->{$attribute};
        }
    }
    $self->_incr_count();
    return $self;
}

# This takes the place of such accessor definitions as:
#  sub get_attribute { ... }
# and of such mutator definitions as:
#  sub set_attribute { ... }
```

```perl
sub AUTOLOAD {
    my ($self, $newvalue) = @_;

    my ($operation, $attribute) = ($AUTOLOAD =~ /(get|set)(_\w+)$/);

    # Is this a legal method name?
    unless($operation && $attribute) {
        croak "Method name $AUTOLOAD is not in the recognized form (get|set)_
attribute\n";
    }
    unless(exists $self->{$attribute}) {
        croak "No such attribute $attribute exists in the class ", ref($self);
    }

    # Turn off strict references to enable "magic" AUTOLOAD speedup
    no strict 'refs';

    # AUTOLOAD accessors
    if($operation eq 'get') {

        # Complain if you can't get the attribute
        unless($self->_permissions($attribute, 'read')) {
            croak "$attribute does not have read permission";
        }

        # Install this accessor definition in the symbol table
        *{$AUTOLOAD} = sub {
            my ($self) = @_;
            unless($self->_permissions($attribute, 'read')) {
                croak "$attribute does not have read permission";
            }
            $self->{$attribute};
        };

    # AUTOLOAD mutators
    }elsif($operation eq 'set') {

        # Complain if you can't set the attribute
        unless($self->_permissions($attribute, 'write')) {
            croak "$attribute does not have write permission";
        }

        # Set the attribute value
        $self->{$attribute} = $newvalue;

        # Install this mutator definition in the symbol table
        *{$AUTOLOAD} = sub {
            my ($self, $newvalue) = @_;
            unless($self->_permissions($attribute, 'write')) {
                croak "$attribute does not have write permission";
            }
            $self->{$attribute} = $newvalue;
        };
    }
```

```perl
    # Turn strict references back on
    use strict 'refs';

    # Return the attribute value
    return $self->{$attribute};
}

# When an object is no longer being used, this will be automatically called
# and will adjust the count of existing objects
sub DESTROY {
    my($self) = @_;
    $self->_decr_count();
}

# Other methods.  They do not fall into the same form as the majority handled by
AUTOLOAD
sub citation {
    my ($self, $author, $date) = @_;
    $self->{_author} = set_author($author) if $author;
    $self->{_date} = set_date($date) if $date;
    return ($self->{_author}, $self->{_date})
}

1;

=head1 Gene

Gene: objects for Genes with a minimum set of attributes

=head1 Synopsis

    use Gene;

    my $gene1 = Gene->new(
        name       => 'biggene',
        organism   => 'Mus musculus',
        chromosome => '2p',
        pdbref     => 'pdb5775.ent',
        author     => 'L.G.Jeho',
        date       => 'August 23, 1989',
    );

    print "Gene name is ", $gene1->get_name();
    print "Gene organism is ", $gene1->get_organism();
    print "Gene chromosome is ", $gene1->get_chromosome();
    print "Gene pdbref is ", $gene1->get_pdbref();
    print "Gene author is ", $gene1->get_author();
    print "Gene date is ", $gene1->get_date();

    $clone = $gene1->clone(name => 'biggeneclone');

    $gene1-> set_chromosome('2q');
    $gene1-> set_pdbref('pdb7557.ent');
```

```
$gene1-> set_author('G.Mendel');
$gene1-> set_date('May 25, 1865');

$clone->citation('T.Morgan', 'October 3, 1912');

print "Clone citation is ", $clone->citation;
```

=head1 AUTHOR

A kind reader

=head1 COPYRIGHT

Copyright (c) 2003, We Own Gene, Inc.

=cut

Defining Attributes and Their Behaviors

This fourth version of Gene.pm does some additional things with the available attributes:

- It collects them in their own hash, %_attribute_properties. This makes it easier to modify the class; you only have to add or delete attributes to this one hash, and the rest of the code will behave accordingly.

- It enables you to specify default values for each attribute. In the Gene.pm class, I just specify the string ???? as the default for each attribute, but any values could be specified.

- This attribute hash specifies, for each attribute, whether it is permitted to read or write it, and if it is required to have a nondefault value provided.

Here is the hash that supports all this:

```
# A list of all attributes with default values and read/write/required properties
    my %_attribute_properties = (
        _name        => [ '????',      'read.required'],
        _organism    => [ '????',      'read.required'],
        _chromosome  => [ '????',      'read.write'],
        _pdbref      => [ '????',      'read.write'],
        _author      => [ '????',      'read.write'],
        _date        => [ '????',      'read.write'],
    );
```

Why have the read/write/required properties been specified? It's because sometimes overwriting an attribute may get you into deep water; for instance, if you have a unique ID number assigned to each object you create, it may be a bad idea to allow the user of the class to overwrite that ID number. Restricting the access to read-only forces the user of the class to destroy an unwanted object and create a new one with a new ID. It depends on the application you're writing, but in general, the ability to enforce read/write discipline on your attributes can help you create safer code.

The required property ensures that the user gives an attribute a value when the object is created. I've already discussed why that is useful in earlier versions of the class; here, I'm just implementing it in a slightly different way.

This way of specifying properties can easily be expanded. For instance, if you want to add a property no_overwrite that prevents overwriting a previously set (nondefault) value, just add such a string to this hash and alter the code of the mutator method accordingly.

Now that we've got a fair amount of information about the attributes collected in a separate data structure, we need a few helper methods to access that information.

First, you need a method that simply returns a list of all the attributes:

```
# Return a list of all attributes
sub _all_attributes {
        keys %_attribute_properties;
}
```

Next, you'll want a way to check, for any given attribute and property, if that property is set for that attribute. The return value is the value of the last statement in the subroutine, which is true or false depending on whether or not the property $permissions is set for the given attribute:

```
# Check if a given property is set for a given attribute
sub _permissions {
    my($self, $attribute, $permissions) = @_;
    $_attribute_properties{$attribute}[1] =~ /$permissions/;
}
```

Finally, to set attribute values, you'll want to report on the default value for any given attribute. This returns the value of the last statement in the subroutine, which is the default value for the given attribute (this is a hash of arrays, and the code is returning the first element of the array stored for that attribute, which contains the default value):

```
# Return the default value for a given attribute
sub _attribute_default {
        my($self, $attribute) = @_;
    $_attribute_properties{$attribute}[0];
}
```

Initializing the Attributes of a New Object

This fourth and final version of Gene.pm has some alterations to the new constructor method. These alterations incorporate tests and actions relating to the new information being specified about the attributes, namely, their default values and their various properties.

I've also added an entirely new constructor method, clone. Recall that the new constructor method is called as a class method (e.g., Gene->new()) and uses default values for every attribute not specified when called. It is often useful to create a new object by copying an old object and just changing some of its values. clone gives this capability. It is called as an object method (e.g., $geneobject->clone()).

Let's examine the changes that were made to the new constructor; then we'll look at the clone constructor.

The newer new constructor

Here is the new version of the code for the new constructor:

```
# The constructor method
# Called from class, e.g. $obj = Gene->new();
sub new {
    my ($class, %arg) = @_;
    # Create a new object
    my $self = bless {}, $class;

    foreach my $attribute ($self->_all_attributes()) {
        # E.g. attribute = "_name",  argument = "name"
        my($argument) = ($attribute =~ /^_(.*)/);
        # If explicitly given
        if (exists $arg{$argument}) {
            $self->{$attribute} = $arg{$argument};
        # If not given, but required
        }elsif($self->_permissions($attribute, 'required')) {
            croak("No $argument attribute as required");
        # Set to the default
        }else{
            $self->{$attribute} = $self->_attribute_default($attribute);
        }
    }
    $class->_incr_count();
    return $self;
}
```

Notice that we start by blessing an empty anonymous hash: bless {}, and then setting the values of the attributes.

These attribute values are set one by one, looping over their list given by the new helper method _all_attributes. Recall that the attribute names start with an underscore, which indicates they are private to the class code and not available to the user of the class. Each attribute is associated with an argument that has the same name without the leading underscore.

The logic of attribute initialization is three part. If an argument and value for an attribute is given, the attribute is set to that value. If no argument/value is given, but a value is required according to the properties specified for that attribute, the program croaks. Finally, if no argument is given and the attribute isn't required, the attribute is set to the default value specified for that attribute.

As before, at the end of the new constructor, the count of objects is increased, and the new object is returned.

The clone constructor

The clone constructor is very similar to the new constructor. In fact, the two subroutines could be combined into one without much trouble. (See the chapter exercises.) However, it makes sense to separate them, especially since it makes it clearer what's happening in the code that uses these subroutines. Besides, you just have to figure that the special ability to clone objects will come in handy in bioinformatics!

Here is the code for the clone constructor:

```perl
# The clone method
# All attributes will be copied from the calling object, unless
# specifically overridden
# Called from an exisiting object, e.g. $cloned_obj = $obj1->clone( );
sub clone {
    my ($caller, %arg) = @_;
    # Extract the class name from the calling object
    my $class = ref($caller);
    # Create a new object
    my $self = bless { }, $class;

    foreach my $attribute ($self->_all_attributes( )) {
        # E.g. attribute = "_name",  argument = "name"
        my($argument) = ($attribute =~ /^_(.*)/);
        # If explicitly given
        if (exists $arg{$argument}) {
            $self->{$attribute} = $arg{$argument};
        # Otherwise copy attribute of new object from the calling object
        }else{
            $self->{$attribute} = $caller->{$attribute};
        }
    }
    $self->_incr_count( );
    return $self;
}
```

Notice, first of all, that this method is called from an object, in contrast to the new constructor, which is called from the class. That is, to create a new object, you say something like:

```perl
$newobject = Myclass->new( );
```

As usual, the class Myclass is named explicitly when calling the new constructor.

On the other hand, to clone an existing object, you say something like:

```perl
$clonedobject = $newobject->clone( );
```

in which the clone constructor is called from an already existing object, in this case, the object $newobject.

Now, in the code for the clone method, the class name must be extracted from the caller by the ref($caller) code because the caller is an object, not a class.

Next, as in the new constructor, an empty anonymous hash is blessed as an object in the class, and then each attribute is considered in turn in a foreach loop.

Now, the argument name associated with the attribute name is extracted. Here, a simpler two-stage test is made. As before, if the argument is specified, the attribute is set as requested. If not, the attribute is set to the value it had in the calling object. Finally, the count of objects is incremented, and the new object is returned.

These two constructors give you some flexibility in how new objects are created and initialized in the Gene class. This flexibility may prove convenient and useful for you.

Permissions

The code to AUTOLOAD has been augmented with checks for appropriate permissions for the various attributes. The part of the code that handles the get_ accessor methods now checks to see if the read flag is set in the attribute hash via the _permissions class method. Notice the code that installs the definition of an accessor into the symbol table has also been modified to accommodate this additional test:

```
# AUTOLOAD accessors
if($AUTOLOAD =~ /.*::get_\w+/) {
    # Install this accessor definition in the symbol table
    *{$AUTOLOAD} = sub {
        my ($self) = @_;
        unless($self->_permissions($attribute, 'read')) {
            croak "$attribute does not have read permission";
        }
        $self->{$attribute};
    };
    # Return the attribute value
    unless($self->_permissions($attribute, 'read')) {
        croak "$attribute does not have read permission";
    }
    return $self->{$attribute};
}
```

Similarly, the part of AUTOLOAD that defines mutator methods for setting attribute values now checks for write permissions in a similar fashion.

Gene.pm Test Program and Output

Here is a test program testGene that exercises some of the new features of Gene.pm, followed by its output. It's worthwhile to take the time to read the testGene program, looking back at the class module Gene.pm for the definitions of the objects and methods and seeing what kind of output the test program creates. Also, see the exercises for suggestions on how to further modify and extend the capabilities of Gene.pm.

```perl
#!/usr/bin/perl

#
# Test the fourth and final version of the Gene module
#

use strict;
use warnings;

# Change this line to show the folder where you store Gene.pm
use lib "/home/tisdall/MasteringPerlBio/development/lib";
use Gene;

print "Object 1:\n\n";

# Create first object
my $obj1 = Gene->new(
        name            => "Aging",
        organism        => "Homo sapiens",
        chromosome      => "23",
        pdbref          => "pdb9999.ent"
);

# Print the attributes of the first object
print $obj1->get_name, "\n";
print $obj1->get_organism, "\n";
print $obj1->get_chromosome, "\n";
print $obj1->get_pdbref, "\n";
# Test AUTOLOAD failure: try uncommenting one or both of these lines
#print $obj1->get_exon, "\n";
#print $obj1->getexon, "\n";

print "\n\nObject 2:\n\n";

# Create second object
my $obj2 = Gene->new(
        organism        => "Homo sapiens",
        name            => "Aging",
);

# Print the attributes of the second object ... some will be unset
print $obj2->get_name, "\n";
print $obj2->get_organism, "\n";
print $obj2->get_chromosome, "\n";
print $obj2->get_pdbref, "\n";

# Reset some of the attributes of the second object
# set_name will cause an error
#$obj2->set_name("RapidAging");
$obj2->set_chromosome("22q");
$obj2->set_pdbref("pdf9876.ref");
$obj2->set_author("D. Enay");
$obj2->set_date("February 9, 1952");
```

```
    print "\n\n";

    # Print the reset attributes of the second object
    print $obj2->get_name, "\n";
    print $obj2->get_organism, "\n";
    print $obj2->get_chromosome, "\n";
    print $obj2->get_pdbref, "\n";
    print $obj2->citation, "\n";

    # Use a class method to report on a statistic about all existing objects
    print "\nCount is ", Gene->get_count, "\n\n";

    print "Object 3: a clone of object 2\n\n";

    # Clone an object
    my $obj3 = $obj2->clone(
            name            => "screw",
            organism        => "C.elegans",
            author          => "I.Turn",
    );

    # Print the attributes of the cloned object
    print $obj3->get_name, "\n";
    print $obj3->get_organism, "\n";
    print $obj3->get_chromosome, "\n";
    print $obj3->get_pdbref, "\n";
    print $obj3->citation, "\n";

    print "\nCount is ", Gene->get_count, "\n\n";

    print "\n\nObject 4:\n\n";

    # Create a fourth object: but this fails
    #   because the "name" value is required (see Gene.pm)
    my $obj4 = Gene->new(
            organism        => "Homo sapiens",
            chromosome      => "23",
            pdbref          => "pdb9999.ent"
    );

    # This line is not reached due to the fatal failure to
    #   create the fourth object
    print "\nCount is ", Gene->get_count, "\n\n";
```

Here is the output from running the preceding program:

```
Object 1:

Aging
Homo sapiens
23
pdb9999.ent

Object 2:
```

```
Aging
Homo sapiens
????
????

Aging
Homo sapiens
22q
pdf9876.ref
D. EnayFebruary 9, 1952

Count is 2

Object 3: a clone of object 2

screw
C.elegans
22q
pdf9876.ref
I.TurnFebruary 9, 1952

Count is 3


Object 4:

No name attribute as required at testGene line 89
```

How to Document a Perl Class with POD

An essential part of programming is documentation. Comments in the code are an important part of documenting code for those who have to read it or modify it in the future.

Equally as important is documentation for those who have to use the code. A short, accurate, practical guide to using a Perl class is absolutely necessary in order for the class to be generally useful.

Perl uses a language called POD (plain old documentation) to put documentation right in the code. The fourth and final version of Gene.pm has POD documentation embedded in it.

To gain access to the documentation, you merely have to type:

```
perldoc Gene.pm
```

in the same directory in which the Gene.pm lives. (For other options, see the perlpod manpage on the Web, or type perldoc perlpod.)

Given that this book contains copious amounts of explanation of the code, I've kept the POD documentation to a minimum. The POD language is simple; the best way to use it to write good documentation is to copy and modify the documentation style that's used by some other well-written module. You will almost always want to give a bit more information than the example shown here; try examining the documentation for some Perl modules on your computer, for example, perldoc CGI or, if it's installed, perldoc Bioperl.

The Perl interpreter will ignore everything from a line beginning:

```
=head1
```

up to a line beginning:

```
=cut
```

so you can embed your POD documentation in with your Perl code without difficulty.

It's also worth pointing out that many filters exist that will take your .pm file with its embedded POD documentation and produce versions of the documentation in HTML, LaTEX, plain text, *nroff*, or other formats.

Here's the output you get from typing perldoc Gene.pm:

```
Gene(3)          User Contributed Perl Documentation          Gene(3)

Gene
        Gene: objects for Genes with a minimum set of attributes

Synopsis
        use Gene;

        my $gene1 = Gene->new(
            name        => 'biggene',
            organism    => 'Mus musculus',
            chromosome  => '2p',
            pdbref      => 'pdb5775.ent',
            author      => 'L.G.Jeho',
            date        => 'August 23, 1989',
        );

        print "Gene name is ",        $gene1->get_name( );
        print "Gene organism is ",    $gene1->get_organism( );
        print "Gene chromosome is ",  $gene1->get_chromosome( );
        print "Gene pdbref is ",      $gene1->get_pdbref( );
        print "Gene author is ",      $gene1->get_author( );
        print "Gene date is ",        $gene1->get_date( );

        $clone = $gene1->clone(name => 'biggeneclone');

        $gene1-> set_chromosome('2q');
        $gene1-> set_pdbref('pdb7557.ent');
        $gene1-> set_author('G.Mendel');
        $gene1-> set_date('May 25, 1865');

        $clone->citation('T.Morgan', 'October 3, 1912');

        print "Clone citation is ", $clone->citation;
```

AUTHOR
       A kind reader

COPYRIGHT
       Copyright (c) 2003, We Own Gene, Inc.

Additional Topics

Included in this section are a few more topics you may find useful.

Using Class::Struct to Define Classes

The kind of simple OO class that I've developed in this chapter has proved so useful that some clever folks have written a Perl module Class::Struct that automates the construction of classes of this type.

It's worth examining Class::Struct because it can be a great timesaver for some situations. It's been used to create classes for many widely used modules. Type:

```
perldoc Class::Struct
```

to get the whole story.

Class Inheritance

An important part of OO programming deals with the use of one class to help define another. For instance, you may have a class Protein that defines attributes common to all proteins. You can then use the Protein class to define a new class ZincFingers, which perhaps would have all the attributes of the Protein class plus some additional attributes relevant to the study of zinc fingers.

You'll see the use of class inheritance in the next chapter.

Bioperl

Bioperl is a collection of modules of intense interest to the Perl bioinformatics programmer, written mostly in OO style. I'll take a look at the Bioperl software in Chapter 9.

Resources

A vast number of techniques are used in OO software development in Perl; many more than I have space to explore in this book. For more details than can fit into this book, I recommend these sources for more details on OO programming in Perl.

- *Object Oriented Perl* by Damian Conway (Manning Publishers). This is an excellent book and is useful for beginners to advanced. It even includes a few bioinformatics examples! My introduction to OO Perl has drawn gratefully on Conway's book. I urge readers who will be doing further OO Perl programming to get a copy. Some material is slightly dated; for example, the material on pseudohashes should be skipped.
- The `perlobj` page from the Perl documentation.
- The `perlboot` tutorial page from the Perl documentation is a beginning introduction to Perl objects.
- The `perltoot` tutorial page from the Perl documentation is a more detailed introduction to Perl objects.
- The `perltootc` tutorial page from the Perl documentation also includes more information on class methods.
- The `perlbot` tutorial page from the Perl documentation is a bag of tricks for Perl OO programming.
- Some books already mentioned in earlier chapters have extensive information about Perl OO programming, such as *Programming Perl*, *Perl Cookbook*, and *Advanced Perl Programming*.

Exercises

Exercise 3.1

Write brief descriptions of the main features of declarative programming, OO programming, logic programming, and functional programming. (See the "Resources" section.)

Exercise 3.2

Give an example of a programming job that would be better with OO programming than with declarative programming.

Exercise 3.3

Give an example of a programming job that would be better with declarative programming than with OO programming.

Exercise 3.4

What bioinformatics problem might be best addressed with logic programming?

Exercise 3.5

Download and use a Perl class from CPAN.

Exercise 3.6

Write a Perl class that manages laboratory supplies.

Exercise 3.7

When would you want a separate initialization method for a class; when would you want the initialization to be part of the new constructor?

Exercise 3.8

Modify Gene.pm to keep count of how many objects refer to given organisms, chromosomes, authors, pdb references, and names.

Exercise 3.9

Add a DESTROY method to a class so an object can self-destruct.

Exercise 3.10

Beginning in the code for Gene3.pm you'll find the following regular expression:

```
if($AUTOLOAD =~ /.*(_\w+)/) {
    $attribute = $1;
```

This only catches the last part of a name that has an underscore. What if you want to allow names such as get_other_var? Write a regular expression that would extract such names as other_var from get_other_var.

Exercise 3.11

In the code for Gene2.pm you'll find the following regular mutator method:

```
sub set_name {
    my ($self, $name) = @_;
    $self->{_name} = $name if $name;
}
```

This breaks if $name has certain values such as "", 0, or 0E0. How can you catch these cases?

Sequence Formats and Inheritance

This chapter applies concepts and techniques from previous chapters to a concrete project: handling sequence files. The chapter also introduces a few new techniques including a very important one called class inheritance. The code developed in this chapter will also be incorporated into later chapters.

Class inheritance allows you to define a new class by *inheriting* from other classes—altering or making additions as needed. It's a style of software reuse that is particular to object-oriented design.

The first class developed in this chapter is a simple one: reading and writing files. Using inheritance, you can extend that class to a new one that can recognize, read, and write data in several different biological sequence datafile formats.

The goal is, as always, to learn enough about Perl to develop software for your own needs. The code in this chapter is designed with this goal in mind. In particular, the exercises at the end of the chapter will ask you to extend and improve the code in various ways.

Inheritance

You've seen the use of modules and how a Perl program can use all the code in a module by simply loading it with the use command. This is a simple and powerful method of *software reuse*, by which software can be written once but used many times by different programs.

You've also seen how object-oriented Perl defines classes in terms of modules, and how the use of classes, methods, and objects provides a more structured way to reuse Perl software.

There's another way to reuse Perl classes. It's possible for a class to *inherit* all the code and definitions of another *base class*. (This base class is sometimes called a *superclass* or a *parent class*.) The new *derived class* (a.k.a. *subclass*) can add more definitions or redefine certain definitions. Perl then automatically uses the definitions of everything in the old class (but treats them as if they were defined in this new derived class), unless it finds them first in the derived class.

In this chapter, I'll first develop a class FileIO.pm, and then use the technique of inheritance to develop another class SeqFileIO.pm that inherits from FileIO.pm. This way of reusing software by inheritance is extremely convenient when writing object-oriented software. For instance, I make SeqFileIO do a lot of its work simply by inheriting the base class FileIO and then adding methods that handle sequence file formats. I could use the same base class FileIO to write a new class that specializes in handling HTML files, microarray datafiles, SNP database files, and so on. (See the exercises at the end of the chapter.)

When inheriting a class, it is sometimes necessary to do a bit more than just add new methods. In the SeqFileIO class, I add some attributes to the object, and as a result the hash %_attribute_properties also has to be changed. So in the new class I define a new hash with that name, and as a result the old definition from the base class is forgotten and the new, redefined hash is used. As you read the new class, compare it with the base class FileIO. Make note of what is new in the class (e.g., the various put methods), what is being redefined from the base class (e.g., the hash just mentioned), and what is being inherited from the base class (e.g., the new constructor.) This can help prepare you to write your own class that uses inheritance.

Occasionally, you want to invoke a method from a base class that has been overridden. You can use the special SUPER class for that purpose. I don't use that in the code for this chapter, but you should be aware that it is possible to do.

FileIO.pm: A Class to Read and Write Files

Even though you can easily obtain excellent modules for reading and writing files, this chapter shows you how to build a simple one from scratch. One reason for doing this is to better understand the issues every bioinformatics programmer needs to face, such as how to organize files and keep track of their contents. Another reason is so you can see how to extend the class to deal with the multiple file format problem that is peculiar to bioinformatics.

It's not uncommon for a biologist to use several different types of formats of files containing DNA or protein sequence data and translate from one format to another. Doing these translations by hand is very tedious. It's also tedious to save alternate forms of the same sequence data in differently formatted files. You'll see how to alleviate some of this pain by automating some of these tasks in a new class called SeqFileIO.pm.

Class inheritance is one of the main reasons why object-oriented software is so reusable. In order to see clearly how it works, let's start with the simple class FileIO.pm and later use it to define a more complex class, SeqFileIO.pm.

FileIO is a simple class that reads and writes files, and stores simple information such as the file contents, date, and write permissions.

You know that it's often possible to modify existing code to create your own program. When I wrote FileIO.pm, I simply made a copy of the Gene.pm module from Chapter 3 and modified it.

On my Linux system, I started by copying FileIO.pm from Gene.pm and giving it a new name:

```
cp Gene.pm FileIO.pm
```

I then edited the new file FileIO.pm changing the line near the top that says:

```
package Gene;
```

to:

```
package FileIO;
```

The filename must be the same as the class name, with an additional .pm.

Though I now needed to modify the module to do what I want, a surprising amount of the overall framework of the code—its constructor, accessor and mutator methods, and its basic data structures—remains the same. Gene.pm already contained such useful parts as a new constructor, a hash-based object data structure, accessor methods to retrieve values of the attributes of the object, and mutator methods to alter attribute values. These are likely to be needed by most classes that you'll write in your own software projects.

Analysis of FileIO

Following is the code for FileIO, with commentary interspersed:

```
package FileIO;

#
# A simple IO class for sequence data files
#

use strict;
use warnings;
our $AUTOLOAD; # before Perl 5.6.0 say "use vars '$AUTOLOAD';"
use Carp;

# Class data and methods
{
    # A list of all attributes with defaults and read/write/required/noinit
properties
    my %_attribute_properties = (
        _filename    => [ '',        'read.write.required'],
        _filedata    => [ [ ],       'read.write.noinit'],
```

```perl
        _date        => [ '',        'read.write.noinit'],
        _writemode   => [ '>',       'read.write.noinit'],
    );

    # Global variable to keep count of existing objects
    my $_count = 0;

    # Return a list of all attributes
    sub _all_attributes {
            keys %_attribute_properties;
    }

    # Check if a given property is set for a given attribute
    sub _permissions {
        my($self, $attribute, $permissions) = @_;
        $_attribute_properties{$attribute}[1] =~ /$permissions/;
    }

    # Return the default value for a given attribute
    sub _attribute_default {
            my($self, $attribute) = @_;
        $_attribute_properties{$attribute}[0];
    }

    # Manage the count of existing objects
    sub get_count {
        $_count;
    }
    sub _incr_count {
        ++$_count;
    }
    sub _decr_count {
        --$_count;
    }
}
```

In this first part of FileIO.pm file, the headers are exactly the same as in Gene.pm.

The opening block, which contains the class data and methods, also remains the same except for the hash %_attribute_properties. This new version of the hash has different attributes (the filename, the file data, the last modification date of the file, and the mode to use in writing a file) tailored to the needs of reading and writing files.

In addition to the read, write, and required properties, there is also a new "no initialization" (or noinit) property. An attribute with the noinit property may not be given an initial value when an object is created with a call to the new constructor. In this module, attributes such as data from the file, or the date on the file, are set only when the file is read or written. You may also have noticed that the default value for the filedata attribute is an anonymous array.

Note that each attribute has both read and write properties. This being the case, you can simply omit the listing of the properties. However, in the interest of future modification, when I may want to add some attribute that won't have both properties, I've left in the specification of the two read and write properties. (Note that one method name, get_count, doesn't start with an underscore; this encourages you to call this method to get a count of how many objects currently exist.)

The constructor method

You'll notice in the following code that I have cut the new constructor down to the bare bones.

```
# The constructor method
# Called from class, e.g. $obj = FileIO->new( );
sub new {
    my ($class, %arg) = @_;

    # Create a new object
    my $self = bless {}, $class;

    $class->_incr_count( );
    return $self;
}
```

Why did I do so? Read on.

The read method

The code continues with the read method:

```
# Called from object, e.g. $obj->read( );
sub read {
    my ($self, %arg) = @_;

    # Set attributes
    foreach my $attribute ($self->_all_attributes( )) {
        # E.g. attribute = "_filename",  argument = "filename"
        my($argument) = ($attribute =~ /^_(.*)/);

        # If explicitly given
        if (exists $arg{$argument}) {
            # If initialization is not allowed
            if($self->_permissions($attribute, 'noinit')) {
                croak("Cannot set $argument from read: use set_$argument");
            }
            $self->{$attribute} = $arg{$argument};
        # If not given, but required
        }elsif($self->_permissions($attribute, 'required')) {
            croak("No $argument attribute as required");
        # Set to the default
        }else{
            $self->{$attribute} = $self->_attribute_default($attribute);
        }
    }
}
```

```
    # Read file data
    unless( open( FileIOFH, $self->{_filename} ) ) {
        croak("Cannot open file " . $self->{_filename} );
    }
    $self->{'_filedata'} = [ <FileIOFH> ];
    $self->{'_date'} = localtime((stat FileIOFH)[9]);
    close(FileIOFH);

}
```

This new read method has two parts. The first includes the initialization of the object's attributes from the arguments and the defaults as specified in the %_attribute_properties hash. The second includes the reading of the file and the setting of the _filedata and _date attributes from the file's contents and its last modification time.

The first loop in the program initializes the attributes. If an attribute is specified as an argument, the first test is to see if the noinit property is set. This forbids initializing the attribute, in which case the program croaks. Otherwise, the attribute is set.

If the attribute isn't passed as an argument but has a required property (only the _filename attribute has the required property), the program croaks.

Finally, if the argument isn't given and not required, the attribute is set to the default value.

After performing those initializations, the read method reads in the specified file. If it can't open the file, the program croaks. (See the exercises for a discussion of this use of croak.)

The file is read by the line:

```
    $self->{'_filedata'} = [ <FileIOFH> ];
```

In list context, the input operator on the opened filehandle, which is given by <FileIOFH> reads in the entire file. This is done within an anonymous array, as determined by the square brackets around the input operator angle brackets. A reference to this anonymous array containing the file's contents is then assigned to the _filedata attribute.

stat and localtime functions

Finally, the Perl stat and localtime functions are called to generate a string with the file's last modification time, which is assigned to the object attribute _date.

This method of reading a file makes many choices. For instance, the stat command returns an array with many more items of interest about a file, such as its size, owner, access permission modes, and so on (the tenth item of which is the modification time). As you develop your programs, you should be paying attention to details such as whether you need to save some of these additional attributes of a file, the last modification date, or notes about the kind of data in the file.

The next line of code in the program:

```
#
# N.B. no "clone" method is necessary
#
```

is yet another choice to think about. Are there occasions when cloning a file object makes sense? Maybe I'd like to clone a file object, make some small change to the data, give it a new filename, and write it out. Why have I left this out?

The write method

The code continues:

```
# Write files
# Called from object, e.g. $obj->write( );
sub write {
    my ($self, %arg) = @_;

    foreach my $attribute ($self->_all_attributes( )) {
        # E.g. attribute = "_filename",  argument = "filename"
        my($argument) = ($attribute =~ /^_(.*)/);

        # If explicitly given
        if (exists $arg{$argument}) {
            $self->{$attribute} = $arg{$argument};
        }
    }

    unless( open( FileIOFH, $self->get_writemode . $self->get_filename ) ) {
        croak("Cannot write to file " .  $self->get_filename);
    }
    unless( print FileIOFH $self->get_filedata ) {
        croak("Cannot write to file " .  $self->get_filename);
    }
    $self->set_date(scalar localtime((stat FileIOFH)[9]));
    close(FileIOFH);

    return 1;
}
```

The write method handles writing a file object out to an actual file. First, all arguments corresponding to attributes are set as requested. The file is then opened for writing, using the _writemode attribute to specify; for example, > for truncating the file before writing or >> for appending to the file. The print FileIOFH statement actually does the writing to the opened FileIOFH filehandle, retrieving the file data from the object with the get_filedata method defined by means of AUTOLOAD. Finally, the object's _date attribute is reset to the new modification time.

AUTOLOAD

The next section of code is the AUTOLOAD method itself:

```perl
# This takes the place of such accessor definitions as:
#   sub get_attribute { ... }
# and of such mutator definitions as:
#   sub set_attribute { ... }
sub AUTOLOAD {
    my ($self, $newvalue) = @_;

    my ($operation, $attribute) = ($AUTOLOAD =~ /(get|set)(_\w+)$/);

    # Is this a legal method name?
    unless($operation && $attribute) {
        croak "Method name '$AUTOLOAD' is not in the recognized form\n";
    }
    unless(exists $self->{$attribute}) {
        croak "No such attribute '$attribute' exists in the class ", ref($self);
    }

    # AUTOLOAD accessors
    if($operation eq 'get') {
        unless($self->_permissions($attribute, 'read')) {
            croak "$attribute does not have read permission";
        }

        # Turn off strict references to enable symbol table manipulation
        no strict "refs";
        # Install this accessor definition in the symbol table
        *{$AUTOLOAD} = sub {
            my ($self) = @_;
            unless($self->_permissions($attribute, 'read')) {
                croak "$attribute does not have read permission";
            }
            if(ref($self->{$attribute}) eq 'ARRAY') {
                return @{$self->{$attribute}};
            }else{
                return $self->{$attribute};
            }
        };
        # Turn strict references back on
        no strict "refs";

        # Return the attribute value
        # The attribute could be a scalar or a reference to an array
        if(ref($self->{$attribute}) eq 'ARRAY') {
            return @{$self->{$attribute}};
        }else{
            return $self->{$attribute};
        }
```

```
    # AUTOLOAD mutators
    }elsif($operation eq 'set') {
        unless($self->_permissions($attribute, 'write')) {
            croak "$attribute does not have write permission";
        }

        # Turn off strict references to enable symbol table manipulation
        no strict "refs";
        # Install this mutator definition in the symbol table
        *{$AUTOLOAD} = sub {
                my ($self, $newvalue) = @_;
            unless($self->_permissions($attribute, 'write')) {
                croak "$attribute does not have write permission";
            }
            $self->{$attribute} = $newvalue;
        };
        # Turn strict references back on
        no strict "refs";

        # Set and return the attribute value
        $self->{$attribute} = $newvalue;
        return $self->{$attribute};
    }
}
```

This AUTOLOAD method has grown! There's only one difference, however, between this
code and the AUTOLOAD code for the Gene.pm class. The new set of attributes for
FileIO.pm don't all take simple scalar values, as was the case with Gene.pm. Another
attribute, _filedata, is a reference to an anonymous array. In order for the accessors
to return the correct data, they must check to see if an attribute is a scalar or a reference to an array; the accessors can then dereference and return the data from the
method call.

So the accessors, and the definitions of them installed into the symbol table, test for
an array reference and dereference it accordingly. Other than that, this AUTOLOAD
method is exactly the same as that defined for Gene.pm.

You may also have noticed that sections of code in the AUTOLOAD method are almost
identical to each other. Recall that AUTOLOAD is invoked when a method with no subroutine defining it is called. AUTOLOAD must do two things. First, it performs whatever
method is requested; for example, if an accessor method is requested, it returns the
appropriate value. Second, it defines the subroutine that implements the requested
method and installs it in the symbol table so the next time the method is called,
AUTOLOAD and its considerable overhead won't be necessary. Because of these parameters, the code AUTOLOAD executes to handle the requested method is nearly identical
with the method that AUTOLOAD also defines.

Finally, here are the last sections of the FileIO.pm program:

```
    # When an object is no longer being used, this will be automatically called
    # and will adjust the count of existing objects
```

```
sub DESTROY {
    my($self) = @_;
    $self->_decr_count( );
}

# Other methods. They do not fall into the same form as the majority handled by
AUTOLOAD
#

1;
```

The only change here is that there are no other methods (Gene.pm had a citation method).

Finishing FileIO

To finish FileIO.pm, here's some very terse (too terse for anything but a textbook) POD documentation:

```
=head1 FileIO

FileIO: read and write file data

=head1 Synopsis

    use FileIO;

    my $obj = RawfileIO->read(
        filename => 'jkl'
    );

    print $obj->get_filename, "\n";
    print $obj->get_filedata;

    $obj->set_date('today');
    print $obj->get_date, "\n";

    print $obj->get_writemode, "\n";

    my @newdata = ("line1\n", "line2\n");
    $obj->set_filedata( \@newdata );

    $obj->write(filename => 'lkj');
    $obj->write(filename => 'lkj', writemode => '>>');

    my $o = RawfileIO->read(filename => 'lkj');
    print $o->get_filename, "\n";
    print $o->get_filedata;

    my $gene1 = Gene->new(
        name => 'biggene',
        organism => 'Mus musculus',
        chromosome => '2p',
```

```
        pdbref => 'pdb5775.ent',
        author => 'L.G.Jeho',
        date => 'August 23, 1989',
    );

    print "Gene name is ", $gene1->get_name( );
    print "Gene organism is ", $gene1->_get_organism( );
    print "Gene chromosome is ", $gene1->_get_chromosome( );
    print "Gene pdbref is ", $gene1->_get_pdbref( );
    print "Gene author is ", $gene1->_get_author( );
    print "Gene date is ", $gene1->_get_date( );

    $clone = $gene1->clone(name => 'biggeneclone');

    $gene1-> set_chromosome('2q');
    $gene1-> set_pdbref('pdb7557.ent');
    $gene1-> set_author('G.Mendel');
    $gene1-> set_date('May 25, 1865');

    $clone->citation('T. Morgan', 'October 3, 1912');

    print "Clone citation is ", $clone->citation;

=head1 AUTHOR

James Tisdall

=head1 COPYRIGHT

Copyright (c) 2003, James Tisdall

=cut
```

Testing the FileIO Class Module

Now that we've got a class module, complete with examples of its use, let's write a small test program and see how it works. Since the examples in the documentation are, in effect, a small test program, let's try running it. We'll use the file `file1.txt` I created with my text editor that contains:

```
> sample dna   (This is a typical fasta header.)
agatggcggcgctgaggggtcttggggggctctaggccggccacctactgg
tttgcagcggagacgacgcatggggcctgcgcaataggagtacgctgcct
gggaggcgtgactagaagcggaagtagttgtgggcgcctttgcaaccgcc
tgggacgccgccgagtggtctgtgcaggttcgcgggtcgctggcgggggt
cgtgagggagtgcgccggggagcggagatatggagggagatggttcagacc
cagagcctccagatgccggggaggacagcaagtccgagaatggggagaat
acacctgagccactctcagatgaggaccta
```

I'll take the code from the documentation pretty much as is, just adding strict and warnings. I'll also include a use lib directive that adds my development library directory to the list of directories in @INC, which tells my computer's Perl where to look for

---

modules. (Recall that you can either edit this line, override it with the *PERL5LIB* environmental variable, or give your own directory on the command line.) I also add a few print statements to make the output easier to read:

```perl
#!/usr/bin/perl

use strict;
use warnings;
use lib "/home/tisdall/MasteringPerlBio/development/lib";

use FileIO;

my $obj = FileIO->new( );

$obj->read(
  filename => 'file1.txt'
);

print "The file name is ", $obj->get_filename, "\n";
print "The contents of the file are:\n", $obj->get_filedata;
print "\nThe date of the file is ", $obj->get_date, "\n";

$obj->set_date('today');
print "The reset date of the file is ", $obj->get_date, "\n";

print "The write mode of the file is ", $obj->get_writemode, "\n";

print "\nResetting the data and filename\n";
my @newdata = ("line1\n", "line2\n");
$obj->set_filedata( \@newdata );

print "Writing a new file \"file2\"\n";
$obj->write(filename => 'file2');

print "Appending to the new file \"file2\"\n";
$obj->write(filename => 'file2', writemode => '>>');

print "Reading and printing the data from \"file2\":\n";

my $file2 = FileIO->new( );

$file2->read(
  filename => 'file2'
);

print "The file name is ", $file2->get_filename, "\n";
print "The contents of the file are:\n", $file2->get_filedata;
```

I finally run the test program to get the following output:

```
The file name is file1.txt
The contents of the file are:
> sample dna  (This is a typical fasta header.)
```

```
agatggcggcgctgaggggtcttgggggctctaggccggccacctactgg
tttgcagcggagacgacgcatggggcctgcgcaataggagtacgctgcct
gggaggcgtgactagaagcggaagtagttgtgggcgcctttgcaaccgcc
tgggacgccgccgagtggtctgtgcaggttcgcgggtcgctggcggggt
cgtgagggagtgcgccgggagcggagatatggagggagatggttcagacc
cagagcctccagatgccggggaggacagcaagtccgagaatggggagaat
acacctgagccactctcagatgaggaccta

The date of the file is Thu Dec  5 11:22:56 2002
The reset date of the file is today
The write mode of the file is >

Resetting the data and filename
Writing a new file "file2"
Appending to the new file "file2"
Reading and printing the data from "file2":
The file name is file2
The contents of the file are:
line1
line2
line1
line2
```

The module seems to be performing as hoped. So, now we have a simple module that reads and writes files and provides a few options for the write mode.

But, frankly, this isn't too impressive. You've already been reading and writing files in Perl without the overhead of this FileIO module. The interface to the code is nice, and it's good to have objects that contain the file data, but what has really been accomplished?

The real power of this approach is coming up next. Using class inheritance, this simple module can be extended relatively easily in a very useful direction.

It's another case of the basic software engineering approach of making small, simple, generally useful tools, and then combining them into more powerful and specific applications. So, next, I'll take my simple FileIO class and use it as a *base class* for a bioinformatics-specific class.

SeqFileIO.pm: Sequence File Formats

Our primary interest is bioinformatics.Can we extend the FileIO class to handle biological sequence datafiles? For example, can a class be written that takes a GenBank file and writes the sequence out in FASTA format?

Using the technique of inheritance, in this section I present a module for a new class SeqFileIO that performs several basic functions on sequence files of various formats. When you call this module's read method, in addition to reading the file's contents and setting the name, date, and write mode of the file, it automatically determines the format of the sequence file, extracts the sequence, and when available, extracts the annotation, ID, and accession number. In addition, a set of put methods makes it easy to present the sequence and annotation in other formats.*

Analysis of SeqFileIO.pm

The first part of the module SeqFileIO.pm contains the block with definitions of the new, or revised, class data and methods.

The first thing you should notice is the use command:

```
use base ( "FileIO" );
```

This Perl command tells the current package SeqFileIO it's inheriting from the base class FileIO. Here's another statement that's often used for this purpose:

```
@ISA = ( "FileIO" );
```

The @ISA predefined variable tells a package that it "is a" version of some base class; it then can inherit methods from that base class. The use base directive sets the @ISA array to the base class(es), plus a little else besides. (Check perldoc base for the whole story.) Without getting bogged down in details use base works a little more robustly than just setting the @ISA array, so that's what I'll use here:

```
package SeqFileIO;

use base ( "FileIO" );

use strict;
use warnings;
#use vars '$AUTOLOAD';
use Carp;

# Class data and methods
{
    # A list of all attributes with defaults and read/write/required/noinit
properties
    my %_attribute_properties = (
        _filename    => [ '',    'read.write.required'],
        _filedata    => [ [ ],   'read.write.noinit'],
        _date        => [ '',    'read.write.noinit'],
        _writemode   => [ '>',   'read.write.noinit'],
        _format      => [ '',    'read.write'],
        _sequence    => [ '',    'read.write'],
        _header      => [ '',    'read.write'],
        _id          => [ '',    'read.write'],
        _accession   => [ '',    'read.write'],
    );
```

---

* Don Gilbert's readseq package (see *http://iobio.bio.indiana.edu/soft/molbio/readseq* and *ftp://ftp.bio.indiana.edu/molbio/readseq/classic/src*) is the classic program (written in C) for reading and writing multiple sequence file formats.

```perl
# Return a list of all attributes
sub _all_attributes {
        keys %_attribute_properties;
}

# Check if a given property is set for a given attribute
sub _permissions {
    my($self, $attribute, $permissions) = @_;
    $_attribute_properties{$attribute}[1] =~ /$permissions/;
}

# Return the default value for a given attribute
sub _attribute_default {
        my($self, $attribute) = @_;
    $_attribute_properties{$attribute}[0];
}

my @_seqfileformats = qw(
    _raw
    _embl
    _fasta
    _gcg
    _genbank
    _pir
    _staden
);
sub isformat {
    my($self) = @_;

    for my $format (@_seqfileformats) {
        my $is_format = "is$format";

        if($self->$is_format) {
            return $format;
        }
    }
    return 'unknown';
}

}
```

The power of inheritance

A comparison with the opening block in the base class FileIO is instructive. You'll
see that I'm redefining the %_attribute_properties hash and the methods in the
block that access the hash as closures. This is necessary to extend the new class to
handle new attributes that relate specifically to sequence datafiles:

_format
    The format of the sequence datafile, such as FASTA or GenBank
_sequence
    The sequence data extracted from the sequence datafile as a scalar string

_header

The header part of the annotation; defined somewhat loosely in this module

_id

The ID of the sequence datafile, such as a gene name or other identifier

_accession

The accession number of the sequence datafile, when provided

You'll notice, in comparing this opening block with the opening block of the base class `FileIO`, that the methods and variables relating to counting the number of objects has been omitted in this new class.

Here's where you see the power of inheritance for the first time. When the code in the new `SeqFileIO.pm` module tries to call, say, the get_count method, and Perl sees that it's not defined in the module, it will go on a hunt for the method in the base class and use the definition it finds there. On the other hand, if it finds the method in `SeqFileIO.pm`, it just uses that; if the get_count method appeared in the base class but is redefined in `SeqFileIO.pm`, it uses that redefinition and ignores the older definition in the base class.

So, you don't have to rewrite methods in the base class(es); you can just call them. Perl not only finds them, it also calls them as if they were defined in the new class. For example, ref($self) returns SeqFileIO, not FileIO, without regard to whether the method is defined in the new class or inherited from the old class.

Finally, there are some new definitions in this new version of the opening block. An array @_seqfileformats lists the sequence file formats the module knows about, and a method isformat calls the methods associated with each format (such as is_fasta defined later in the module) until it either finds what format the file is in or returns unknown.

The @_seqfileformats array uses the qw operator. This splits the words on whitespace (including newlines) and returns a list of quoted words. It's a convenience for giving lists of words without having to quote each one or separate them by commas. (Check the perlop manpage for the section on "RegExp Quote-Like Operators" for all the variations and alternative quoting operators.)

Following the opening block, notice that there is no new method defined in this class. The simple, bare-bones new method from the FileIO class serves just as well for this new class; thanks to the inheritance mechanism, there's no need to write a new one. A program that calls SeqFileIO->new will use the same method from the FileIO class, but the class name will be properly set to SeqFileIO for the new object created.

A new read method

The next part of the program has a rewrite of the read method. As a result, the read method from the parent FileIO class is being overridden:

```
# Called from object, e.g. $obj->read( );
sub read {
    my ($self, %arg) = @_;

    # Set attributes
    foreach my $attribute ($self->_all_attributes( )) {
        # E.g. attribute = "_filename",  argument = "filename"
        my($argument) = ($attribute =~ /^_(.*)/);

        # If explicitly given
        if (exists $arg{$argument}) {
            # If initialization is not allowed
            if($self->_permissions($attribute, 'noinit')) {
                croak("Cannot set $argument from read: use set_$argument");
            }
            $self->{$attribute} = $arg{$argument};
        # If not given, but required
        }elsif($self->_permissions($attribute, 'required')) {
            croak("No $argument attribute as required");
        # Set to the default
        }else{
            $self->{$attribute} = $self->_attribute_default($attribute);
        }
    }

    # Read file data
    unless( open( FileIOFH, $self->{_filename} ) ) {
        croak("Cannot open file " .  $self->{_filename} );
    }
    $self->{'_filedata'} = [ <FileIOFH> ];
    $self->{'_date'} = localtime((stat FileIOFH)[9]);
    $self->{'_format'} = $self->isformat;
    my $parsemethod = 'parse' . $self->{'_format'};
    $self->$parsemethod;

    close(FileIOFH);
}
```

The new read method just shown is almost exactly the same as the read function in the FileIO class. There are only three new lines of code, just before the end of the subroutine, preceding the call to the close function:

```
$self->{'_format'} = $self->isformat;
my $parsemethod = 'parse' . $self->{'_format'};
$self->$parsemethod;
```

These three new lines initialize the new attributes that were defined for this class. First, a call to isformat determines the format of the file and sets the _format attribute appropriately. The appropriate parse_ method name is then constructed, and finally, a call to that method is made. As you're about to see, the parse_ methods extract the sequence, header, ID, and accession number (or as many of these as possible) from the file data and set the object's attributes accordingly.

So, by the end of the read method, the file data has been read into the object, the format determined, and the interesting parts of the data (such as the sequence data) parsed out.

New Methods: is, parse, and put

The rest of the module consists of three groups of methods that handle the different sequence file formats. These methods didn't appear in the more simple and generic FileIO module and must be defined here:

is_

> Tests to see if data is in a particular sequence file format

parse_

> Parses out the sequence, and when possible the header, ID, and accession number

put_

> Takes the sequence attribute, and when available the header, ID, and accession number attributes, and writes them in the sequence file format named in the format attribute

is_ methods

The first group of methods tests an object's file data to see if it conforms to a particular sequence file format:

```
sub is_raw {
  my($self) = @_;

  my $seq = join('', @{$self->{_filedata}} );
  ($seq =~ /^[ACGNT\s]+$/) ? return 'raw' : 0;
}

sub is_embl {
  my($self) = @_;

  my($begin,$seq,$end) = (0,0,0);

  foreach( @{$self->{_filedata}} ) {
    /^ID\s/ && $begin++;
    /^SQ\s/ && $seq++;
    /^\/\// && $end++;
    (($begin == 1) && ($seq == 1) && ($end == 1)) && return 'embl';
  }
  return;
}
```

```perl
sub is_fasta {
  my($self) = @_;

  my($flag) = 0;

  for(@{$self->{_filedata}}) {
    #This to avoid confusion with Primer, which can have input beginning ">"
    /^\*seq.*:/i && ($flag = 0) && last;
    if( /^>/ && $flag == 1) {
      last;
    }elsif( /^>/ && $flag == 0) {
      $flag = 1;
    }elsif( (! /^>/) && $flag == 0) { #first line must start with ">"
      last;
    }
  }
  $flag ? return 'fasta' : return;
}

sub is_gcg {
  my($self) = @_;

  my($i,$j) = (0,0);

  for(@{$self->{_filedata}}) {
    /^\s*$/ && next;
    /Length:.*Check:/ && ($i += 1);
    /^\s*\d+\s*[a-zA-Z\s]+/ && ($j += 1);
    ($i == 1) && ($j == 1) && return('gcg');
  }
  return;
}


sub is_genbank {
  my($self) = @_;

  my $Features = 0;

  for(@{$self->{_filedata}}) {
    /^LOCUS/ && ($Features += 1);
    /^DEFINITION/ && ($Features += 2);
    /^ACCESSION/ && ($Features += 4);
    /^ORIGIN/ &&  ($Features += 8);
    /^\/\// && ($Features += 16);
    ($Features == 31) && return 'genbank';
  }
  return;
}

sub is_pir {
  my($self) = @_;
```

```perl
    my($ent,$ti,$date,$org,$ref,$sum,$seq,$end) = (0,0,0,0,0,0,0,0);

    for(@{$self->{_filedata}}) {
      /ENTRY/ && $ent++;
      /TITLE/ && $ti++;
      /DATE/ && $date++;
      /ORGANISM/ && $org++;
      /REFERENCE/ && $ref++;
      /SUMMARY/ && $sum++;
      /SEQUENCE/ && $seq++;
      /\/\/\// && $end++;
      $ent == 1 && $ti == 1 && $date >= 1 && $org >= 1
        && $ref >= 1 && $sum == 1 && $seq == 1 && $end == 1
        && return 'pir';
    }
    return;
  }

  sub is_staden {
    my($self) = @_;
    for(@{$self->{_filedata}}) {
      /<-+([^-]*)-+>/ && return 'staden';
    }
    0;
  }
```

is_ methods are designed to be fast. They don't check to see if the file conforms to the official file format in every detail. Instead, they look to see if, given that the file is supposed to be a sequence file, there is a good indication that it is a particular file format. In other words, these methods perform heuristic, not rigorous, tests. If they are well conceived, these methods correctly identify the different formats without confusion and with a minimum of code and computation. However, they don't ensure that a format is conforming in every respect to the official format definition. (See the exercises for other approaches to file format recognition.)

Also, note that these are fairly simple tests; for example, the is_raw method doesn't check for the IUB ambiguity codes but only the four bases A, C, G, T, plus N for an undetermined base. Furthermore, some software systems have more than one format, for which only one format is shown here, such as PIR and GCG. The bottom line is that this code does what it is intended to do, but not more. It is, however, fairly short and easy to modify and extend, and I encourage you to try your hand at doing so in the exercises.

An interesting Perl note: the "leaning toothpick" regular expression notation for three forward slashes /// is a bit forbidding because each forward slash needs a backslash escape in front of it:

```perl
    /\/\/\// && $end++;
```

An alternative would be to use m and a separator other than /, which leads to more readable code:

```
m!///! && $end++;
```

One more interesting Perl note: in this code, I return a false value from a subroutine like so:

```
return;
```

This is a bit confusing because unless you already know or check in the documentation for return, it's not clear what's happening. In a scalar context, return; returns the undefined value undef; in a list context, return; returns an empty list. So, no matter what context the subroutine is called from, a valid value is returned.

put_ methods

The next group of put_ methods returns an object's sequence and annotation data in a particular sequence file format:

```perl
sub put_raw {
  my($self) = @_;

  my($out);
  ($out = $self->{_sequence}) =~ tr/a-z/A-Z/;
  return($out);
}

sub put_embl {
  my($self) = @_;

  my(@out,$tmp,$len,$i,$j,$a,$c,$g,$t,$o);

  $len = length($self->{_sequence});
  $a=($self->{_sequence} =~ tr/Aa//);
  $c=($self->{_sequence} =~ tr/Cc//);
  $g=($self->{_sequence} =~ tr/Gg//);
  $t=($self->{_sequence} =~ tr/Tt//);
  $o=($len - $a - $c - $g - $t);
  $i=0;
  $out[$i++] = sprintf("ID    %s %s\n",$self->{_header}, $self->{_id} );
  $out[$i++] = "XX\n";
  $out[$i++] = sprintf("SQ    sequence %d BP; %d A; %d C; %d G; %d T; %d other;\n",
              $len, $a, $c, $g, $t, $o);
  for($j = 0 ; $j < $len ; ) {
      $out[$i] .= sprintf("%s",substr($self->{_sequence},$j,10));
      $j += 10;
      if( $j < $len && $j % 60 != 0 ) {
        $out[$i] .= " ";
      }elsif ($j % 60 == 0 ) {
        $out[$i++] .= "\n";
      }
  }
}
```

```perl
    if($j % 60 != 0 ) {
      $out[$i++] .= "\n";
    }
    $out[$i] = "//\n";
    return @out;
}

sub put_fasta {
  my($self) = @_;

  my(@out,$len,$i,$j);

  $len = length($self->{_sequence});
  $i = 0;
  $out[$i++] = "> " . $self->{_header} . "\n";
  for($j=0; $j<$len ; $j += 50) {
    $out[$i++]=sprintf("%.50s\n",substr($self->{_sequence},$j,50));
  }
  return @out;
}

sub put_gcg {
  my($self) = @_;

  my(@out,$len,$i,$j,$cnt,$sum);
  $len = length($self->{_sequence});

  #calculate Checksum
  for($i=0; $i<$len ;$i++) {
    $cnt++;
    $sum += $cnt * ord(substr($self->{_sequence},$i,1));
    ($cnt == 57)&& ($cnt=0);
  }
  $sum %= 10000;

  $i = 0;
  $out[$i++] = sprintf("%s\n",$self->{_header});
  $out[$i++] = sprintf("     %s Length: %d (today)  Check: %d  ..\n", $self->{_id},
                    $len, $sum);
  for($j = 0 ; $j < $len ; ) {
      if( $j % 50 == 0) {
        $out[$i] = sprintf("%8d  ",$j+1);
      }
      $out[$i] .= sprintf("%s",substr($self->{_sequence},$j,10));
      $j += 10;
      if( $j < $len && $j % 50 != 0 ) {
        $out[$i] .= " ";
      }elsif ($j % 50 == 0 ) {
        $out[$i++] .= "\n";
      }
  }
  if($j % 50 != 0 ) {
    $out[$i] .= "\n";
  }
```

```perl
    return @out;
}

sub put_genbank {
  my($self) = @_;

  my(@out,$len,$i,$j,$cnt,$sum);
  my($seq) = $self->{_sequence};

  $seq =~ tr/A-Z/a-z/;
  $len = length($seq);
  for($i=0; $i<$len ;$i++) {
    $cnt++;
    $sum += $cnt * ord(substr($seq,$i,1));
    ($cnt == 57) && ($cnt=0);
  }
  $sum %= 10000;
  $i = 0;
  $out[$i++] = sprintf("LOCUS       %s       %d bp\n",$self->{_id}, $len);
  $out[$i++] = sprintf("DEFINITION  %s , %d bases, %d sum.\n", $self->{_header},
                       $len, $sum);
  $out[$i++] = sprintf("ACCESSION  %s\n", $self->{_accession}, );
  $out[$i++] = sprintf("ORIGIN\n");
  for($j = 0 ; $j < $len ; ) {
      if( $j % 60 == 0 ) {
        $out[$i] = sprintf("%8d  ",$j+1);
      }
      $out[$i] .= sprintf("%s",substr($seq,$j,10));
      $j += 10;
      if( $j < $len && $j % 60 != 0 ) {
        $out[$i] .= " ";
      }elsif($j % 60 == 0 ) {
        $out[$i++] .= "\n";
      }
  }
  if($j % 60 != 0 ) {
    $out[$i] .= "\n";
    ++i;
  }
  $out[$i] = "//\n";
  return @out;
}

sub put_pir {
  my($self) = @_;

  my($seq) = $self->{_sequence};
  my(@out,$len,$i,$j,$cnt,$sum);
  $len = length($seq);
  for($i=0; $i<$len ;$i++) {
    $cnt++;
    $sum += $cnt * ord(substr($seq,$i,1));
    ($cnt==57) && ($cnt=0);
  }
```

```
$sum %= 10000;
$i = 0;
$out[$i++] = sprintf("ENTRY            %s\n",$self->{_id});
$out[$i++] = sprintf("TITLE            %s\n",$self->{_header});
#JDT ACCESSION out if defined
$out[$i++] = sprintf("DATE             %s\n",'');
$out[$i++] = sprintf("REFERENCE        %s\n",'');
$out[$i++] = sprintf("SUMMARY #Molecular-weight %d  #Length %d  #Checksum %d\
                n",0,$len,$sum);
$out[$i++] = sprintf("SEQUENCE\n");
$out[$i++] = sprintf("            5        10        15        20        25        30\n");
for($j=1; $seq && $j < $len ; $j += 30) {
  $out[$i++] = sprintf("%7d ",$j);
  $out[$i++] = sprintf("%s\n", join(' ',split(//,substr($seq, $j - 1,length($seq)
                < 30 ? length($seq) : 30))) );
}
$out[$i++] = sprintf("///\n");
return @out;
}


sub put_staden {
  my($self) = @_;

  my($seq) = $self->{_sequence};
  my($i,$j,$len,@out);

  $i = 0;
  $len = length($self->{_sequence});
  $out[$i] = ";\<------------------\>\n";
  substr($out[$i],int((20-length($self->{_id}))/2),length($self->{_id})) = $self->
                        {_id};
  $i++;
  for($j=0; $j<$len ; $j+=60) {
    $out[$i++]=sprintf("%s\n",substr($self->{_sequence},$j,60));
  }
  return @out;
}
```

The put_ methods are, by necessity, more cognizant of the detailed rules of a particular file format.

Note the Perl function ord in put_gcg. This built-in function gives the numeric value of a character. Other Perl functions such as sprintf and substr can be reviewed as necessary by typing perldoc -f substr (for example) or by visiting the *http://www. perdoc.com* web page.

parse_ methods

parse_, the third and final group of methods, parses the contents of a file in a particular format, extracting the sequence and, if possible, some additional header information.

```perl
sub parse_raw {
  my($self) = @_;

## Header and ID should be set in calling program after this
  my($seq);

  $seq = join('',@{$self->{_filedata}});
  if( ($seq =~ /^([acgntACGNT\-\s]+)$/)) {
    ($self->{_sequence} = $seq) =~ s/\s//g;
  }else{
    carp("parse_raw failed");
  }
}


sub parse_embl {
  my($self) = @_;

  my($begin,$seq,$end,$count) = (0,0,0,0);
  my($sequence,$head,$acc,$id);

  for(@{$self->{_filedata}}) {
    ++$count;
    if(/^ID/) {
      $begin++;
      /^ID\s*(.*\S)\s*/ && ($id = ($head = $1)) =~ s/\s.*//;
    }elsif(/^SQ\s/){
      $seq++;
    }elsif(/^\/\/\//){
      $end++;
    }elsif($seq == 1){
      $sequence .= $_;
    }elsif(/^AC\s*(.*(;|\S)).*/){ #put this here - AC could be sequence
      $acc .= $1;
    }
    if($begin == 1 && $seq == 1 && $end == 1) {
      $sequence =~ tr/a-zA-Z//cd;
      $sequence =~ tr/a-z/A-Z/;
      $self->{_sequence} = $sequence;
      $self->{_header} = $head;
      $self->{_id} = $id;
      $self->{_accession} = $acc;
      return 1;
    }
  }
  return;
}

sub parse_fasta {
  my($self) = @_;

  my($flag,$count) = (0,0);
  my($seq,$head,$id);
```

```perl
  for(@{$self->{_filedata}}) {
    #avoid confusion with Primer, which can have input beginning ">"
    /^\*seq.*:/i && ($flag == 0) && last;

    if(/^>/ && $flag == 1) {
      last;
    }elsif(/^>/ && $flag == 0){
      /^>\s*(.*\S)\s*/ && ($id=($head=$1)) =~ s/\s.*//;
      $flag=1;
    }elsif( (! /^>/) && $flag == 1) {
      $seq .= $_;
    }elsif( (! /^>/) && $flag == 0) {
       last;
    }
    ++$count;
  }
  if($flag) {
    $seq =~ tr/a-zA-Z-//cd;
    $seq =~ tr/a-z/A-Z/;

    $self->{_sequence} = $seq;
    $self->{_header} = $head;
    $self->{_id} = $id;
  }
}

sub parse_gcg {
  my($self) = @_;

  my($seq,$head,$id);
  my($count,$flag) = (0,0);

  for(@{$self->{_filedata}}) {
    if(/^\s*$/) {
      ;
    }elsif($flag == 0 && /Length:.*Check:/){
      /^\s*(\S+).*Length:.*Check:/;
      $flag=1;
      ($id=$1) =~ s/\s.*//;
    }elsif($flag == 0 && /^\S/) {
      ($head = $_) =~ s/\n//;
    }elsif($flag == 1 && /^\s*[^\d\s]/) {
      last;
    }elsif($flag == 1 && /^\s*\d+\s*[a-zA-Z \t]+$/) {
       $seq .= $_;
    }
    $count++;
  }
  $seq =~ tr/a-zA-Z//cd;
  $seq =~ tr/a-z/A-Z/;
  $head = $id unless $head;
```

```perl
      $self->{_sequence} = $seq;
      $self->{_header} = $head;
      $self->{_id} = $id;

      return 1;
}
#
#
sub parse_genbank {
  my($self) = @_;

  my($count,$features,$flag,$seqflag) = (0,0,0,0);
  my($seq,$head,$id,$acc);

  for(@{$self->{_filedata}}) {
    if( /^LOCUS/ && $flag == 0 ) {
      /^LOCUS\s*(.*\S)\s*$/;
      ($id=($head=$1)) =~ s/\s.*//;
      $features += 1;
      $flag = 1;
    }elsif( /^DEFINITION\s*(.*)/ && $flag == 1) {
      $head .= " $1";
      $features += 2;
    }elsif( /^ACCESSION/ && $flag == 1 ) {
      /^ACCESSION\s*(.*\S)\s*$/;
      $head .= " ".($acc=$1);
      $features += 4;
    }elsif( /^ORIGIN/ ) {
      $seqflag = 1;
      $features += 8;
    }elsif( /^\/\// ) {
      $features += 16;
    }elsif( $seqflag == 0 ) {
      ;
    }elsif($seqflag == 1) {
      $seq .= $_;
    }
    ++$count;
    if($features == 31) {
      $seq =~ tr/a-zA-Z//cd;
      $seq =~ tr/a-z/A-Z/;

      $self->{_sequence} = $seq;
      $self->{_header} = $head;
      $self->{_id} = $id;
      $self->{_accession} = $acc;

      return 1;
    }
  }
  return;
}
```

```perl
sub parse_pir {
  my($self) = @_;

  my($begin,$tit,$date,$organism,$ref,$summary,$seq,$end,$count) =
                  (0,0,0,0,0,0,0,0,0);
  my($flag,$seqflag) = (0,0);
  my($sequence,$header,$id,$acc);

  for(@{$self->{_filedata}}) {
    ++$count;
    if( /^ENTRY\s*(.*\S)\s*$/ && $flag == 0 ) {
      $header=$1;
      $flag=1;
      $begin++;
    }elsif( /^TITLE\s*(.*\S)\s*$/ && $flag == 1 ) {
      $header .= $1;
      $tit++;
    }elsif( /ORGANISM/ ) {
      $organism++;
    }elsif( /^ACCESSIONS\s*(.*\S)\s*$/ && $flag == 1 ) {
      ($id=($acc=$1)) =~ s/\s*//;
    }elsif( /DATE/ ) {
      $date++;
    }elsif( /REFERENCE/ ) {
      $ref++;
    }elsif( /SUMMARY/ ) {
      $summary++;
    }elsif( /^SEQUENCE/ ) {
      $seqflag = 1;
      $seq++;
    }elsif( /^\/\/\/\// && $flag == 1 ) {
      $end++;
    }elsif( $seqflag == 0 ) {
      next;
    }elsif( $seqflag == 1 && $flag == 1) {
      $sequence .= $_;
    }
    if( $begin == 1 && $tit == 1 && $date >= 1 && $organism >= 1
        && $ref >= 1 && $summary == 1 && $seq == 1 && $end == 1
      ) {
      $sequence =~ tr/a-zA-Z//cd;
      $sequence =~ tr/a-z/A-Z/;

      $self->{_sequence} = $seq;
      $self->{_header} = $header;
      $self->{_id} = $id;
      $self->{_accession} = $acc;

      return 1;
    }
  }
  return;
}
```

```
sub parse_staden {
  my($self) = @_;

  my($flag,$count) = (0,0);
  my($seq,$head,$id);
  for(@{$self->{_filedata}}) {
    if( /<---*\s*(.*[^-\s])\s*-*--->(.*)/ && $flag == 0 ) {
      $id = $head = $1;
      $seq .= $2;
      $flag = 1;
    }elsif( /<---*(.*)-*--->/ && $flag == 1 ) {
      $count--;
      last;
    }elsif( $flag == 1 ) {
      $seq .= $_;
    }
    ++$count;
  }
  if( $flag ) {
    $seq =~ s/-/N/g;
    $seq =~ tr/a-zA-Z-//cd;
    $seq =~ tr/a-z/A-Z/;

    $self->{_sequence} = $seq;
    $self->{_header} = $head;
    $self->{_id} = $id;

    return 1;
  }
  return;
}

1;
```

That's the end of the SeqFileIO.pm module that defines the SeqFileIO class.

You can see that to add the capability to handle a new sequence file format, you simply have to write new is_, put_, and parse_ methods, and add the name of the new format to the @_seqfiletypes array. So, extending this software to handle more sequence file formats is relatively easy. (See the exercises.)

To end this chapter, here is a small test program testSeqFileIO that exercises the main parts of the SeqFileIO.pm module, followed by its output. See the exercises for a discussion of ways to improve this test.

Testing SeqFileIO.pm

Here is the program testSeqFileIO to test the SeqFileIO module:

```perl
#!/usr/bin/perl

use strict;
use warnings;
use lib "/home/tisdall/MasteringPerlBio/development/lib";

use SeqFileIO;

#
# First test basic FileIO operations
#   (plus filetype attribute)
#

my $obj = SeqFileIO->new( );

$obj->read(
  filename => 'file1.txt'
);

print "The file name is ", $obj->get_filename, "\n";
print "The contents of the file are:\n", $obj->get_filedata;
print "\nThe date of the file is ", $obj->get_date, "\n";
print "The filetype of the file is ", $obj->get_filetype, "\n";

$obj->set_date('today');
print "The reset date of the file is ", $obj->get_date, "\n";

print "The write mode of the file is ", $obj->get_writemode, "\n";

print "\nResetting the data and filename\n";
my @newdata = ("line1\n", "line2\n");
$obj->set_filedata( \@newdata );

print "Writing a new file \"file2.txt\"\n";
$obj->write(filename => 'file2.txt');

print "Appending to the new file \"file2.txt\"\n";
$obj->write(filename => 'file2.txt', writemode => '>>');

print "Reading and printing the data from \"file2.txt\":\n";

my $file2 = SeqFileIO->new( );

$file2->read(
  filename => 'file2.txt'
);

print "The file name is ", $file2->get_filename, "\n";
print "The contents of the file are:\n", $file2->get_filedata;
print "The filetype of the file is ", $file2->get_filetype, "\n";
```

```perl
print <<'HEADER';

########################################
#
# Test file format recognizing and reading
#
########################################

HEADER

my $genbank = SeqFileIO->new();
$genbank->read(
  filename => 'record.gb'
);
print "The file name is ", $genbank->get_filename, "\n";
print "\nThe date of the file is ", $genbank->get_date, "\n";
print "The filetype of the file is ", $genbank->get_filetype, "\n";
print "The contents of the file are:\n", $genbank->get_filedata;

print "\n##################\n##################\n##################\n";

my $raw = SeqFileIO->new();
$raw->read(
  filename => 'record.raw'
);
print "The file name is ", $raw->get_filename, "\n";
print "\nThe date of the file is ", $raw->get_date, "\n";
print "The filetype of the file is ", $raw->get_filetype, "\n";
print "The contents of the file are:\n", $raw->get_filedata;

print "\n##################\n##################\n##################\n";

my $embl = SeqFileIO->new();
$embl->read(
  filename => 'record.embl'
);
print "The file name is ", $embl->get_filename, "\n";
print "\nThe date of the file is ", $embl->get_date, "\n";
print "The filetype of the file is ", $embl->get_filetype, "\n";
print "The contents of the file are:\n", $embl->get_filedata;

print "\n##################\n##################\n##################\n";

my $fasta = SeqFileIO->new();
$fasta->read(
  filename => 'record.fasta'
);
print "The file name is ", $fasta->get_filename, "\n";
print "\nThe date of the file is ", $fasta->get_date, "\n";
print "The filetype of the file is ", $fasta->get_filetype, "\n";
print "The contents of the file are:\n", $fasta->get_filedata;

print "\n##################\n##################\n##################\n";
```

```perl
my $gcg = SeqFileIO->new( );
$gcg->read(
  filename => 'record.gcg'
);
print "The file name is ", $gcg->get_filename, "\n";
print "\nThe date of the file is ", $gcg->get_date, "\n";
print "The filetype of the file is ", $gcg->get_filetype, "\n";
print "The contents of the file are:\n", $gcg->get_filedata;

print "\n##################\n##################\n#################\n";

my $staden = SeqFileIO->new( );
$staden->read(
  filename => 'record.staden'
);
print "The file name is ", $staden->get_filename, "\n";
print "\nThe date of the file is ", $staden->get_date, "\n";
print "The filetype of the file is ", $staden->get_filetype, "\n";
print "The contents of the file are:\n", $staden->get_filedata;

print "\n##################\n##################\n#################\n";

print <<'REFORMAT';

#########################################
#
# Test file format reformatting and writing
#
#########################################

REFORMAT

print "At this point there are ", $staden->get_count, " objects.\n\n";

print "######\n###### Testing put methods\n######\n\n";

print "\nPrinting staden data in raw format:\n";
print $staden->put_raw;

print "\nPrinting staden data in embl format:\n";
print $staden->put_embl;

print "\nPrinting staden data in fasta format:\n";
print $staden->put_fasta;

print "\nPrinting staden data in gcg format:\n";
print $staden->put_gcg;

print "\nPrinting staden data in genbank format:\n";
print $staden->put_genbank;

print "\nPrinting staden data in PIR format:\n";
print $staden->put_pir;
```

The test program depends on certain files being present on the system; the contents of the files are clear from the program output, and the files can be downloaded from this book's web site, along with the rest of the programs for this book.

Results

Here is the output from `testSeqFileIO`:

```
The file name is file1.txt
The contents of the file are:
> sample dna  (This is a typical fasta header.)
agatggcggcgctgaggggtcttgggggctctaggccggccacctactgg
tttgcagcggagacgacgcatggggcctgcgcaataggagtacgctgcct
gggaggcgtgactagaagcggaagtagttgtgggcgcctttgcaaccgcc
tgggacgccgccgagtggtctgtgcaggttcgcgggtcgctggcgggggt
cgtgagggagtgcgccgggagcggagatatggagggagatggttcagacc
cagagcctccagatgccggggaggacagcaagtccgagaatggggagaat
acacctgagccactctcagatgaggaccta

The date of the file is Thu Dec  5 11:22:56 2002
The filetype of the file is _fasta
The reset date of the file is today
The write mode of the file is >

Resetting the data and filename
Writing a new file "file2.txt"
Appending to the new file "file2.txt"
Reading and printing the data from "file2.txt":
The file name is file2.txt
The contents of the file are:
line1
line2
line1
line2
The filetype of the file is _unknown

#########################################
#
# Test file format recognizing and reading
#
#########################################

The file name is record.gb

The date of the file is Sun Mar 30 14:30:09 2003
The filetype of the file is _genbank
The contents of the file are:
LOCUS       AB031069    2487 bp    mRNA            PRI       27-MAY-2000
DEFINITION  Sequence severely truncated for demonstration.
ACCESSION   AB031069
VERSION     AB031069.1  GI:8100074
```

```
KEYWORDS    .
SOURCE      Homo sapiens embryo male lung fibroblast cell_line:HuS-L12 cDNA to
            mRNA.
  ORGANISM  Homo sapiens
            Eukaryota; Metazoa; Chordata; Craniata; Vertebrata; Euteleostomi;
            Mammalia; Eutheria; Primates; Catarrhini; Hominidae; Homo.
REFERENCE   1  (sites)
  AUTHORS   Fujino,T., Hasegawa,M., Shibata,S., Kishimoto,T., Imai,Si. and
            Takano,T.
  TITLE     PCCX1, a novel DNA-binding protein with PHD finger and CXXC domain,
            is regulated by proteolysis
  JOURNAL   Biochem. Biophys. Res. Commun. 271 (2), 305-310 (2000)
  MEDLINE   20261256
REFERENCE   2  (bases 1 to 2487)
  AUTHORS   Fujino,T., Hasegawa,M., Shibata,S., Kishimoto,T., Imai,S. and
            Takano,T.
  TITLE     Direct Submission
  JOURNAL   Submitted (15-AUG-1999) to the DDBJ/EMBL/GenBank databases.
            Tadahiro Fujino, Keio University School of Medicine, Department of
            Microbiology; Shinanomachi 35, Shinjuku-ku, Tokyo 160-8582, Japan
            (E-mail:fujino@microb.med.keio.ac.jp,
            Tel:+81-3-3353-1211(ex.62692), Fax:+81-3-5360-1508)
FEATURES             Location/Qualifiers
     source          1..2487
                     /organism="Homo sapiens"
                     /db_xref="taxon:9606"
                     /sex="male"
                     /cell_line="HuS-L12"
                     /cell_type="lung fibroblast"
                     /dev_stage="embryo"
     gene            229..2199
                     /gene="PCCX1"
     CDS             229..2199
                     /gene="PCCX1"
                     /note="a nuclear protein carrying a PHD finger and a CXXC
                     domain"
                     /codon_start=1
                     /product="protein containing CXXC domain 1"
                     /protein_id="BAA96307.1"
                     /db_xref="GI:8100075"
                     /translation="MEGDGSDPEPPDAGEDSKSENGENAPIYCICRKPDINCFMIGCD
                     NCNEWFHGDCIRITEKMAKAIREWYCRECREKDPKLEIRYRHKKSRERDGNERDSSEP
                     RDEGGGRKRPVPDPDLQRRAGSGTGVGAMLARGSASPHKSSPQPLVATPSQHHQQQQQ
                     QIKRSARMCGECEACRRTEDCGHCDFCRDMKKFGGPNKIRQKCRLRQCQLRARESYKY
                     FPSSLSPVTPSESLPRPRRPLPTQQQPQPSQKLGRIREDEGAVASSTVKEPPEATATP
                     EPLSDEDLPLDPDLYQDFCAGAFDDHGLPWMSDTEESPFLDPALRKRAVKVKHVKRRE
                     KKSEKKKEERYKRHRQKQKHKDKWKHPERADAKDPASLPQCLGPGCVRPAQPSSKYCS
                     DDCGMKLAANRIYEILPQRIQQWQQSPCIAEEHGKKLLERIRREQQSARTRLQEMERR
                     FHELEAIILRAKQQAVREDEESNEGDSDDTDLQIFCVSCGHPINPRVALRHMERCYAK
                     YESQTSFGSMYPTRIEGATRLFCDVYNPQSKTYCKRLQVLCPEHSRDPKVPADEVCGC
                     PLVRDVFELTGDFCRLPKRQCNRHYCWEKLRRAEVDLERVRVWYKLDELFEQERNVRT
                     AMTNRAGLLALMLHQTIQHDPLTTDLRSSADR"
```

```
BASE COUNT      564 a    715 c    768 g    440 t
ORIGIN
        1 agatggcggc gctgaggggt cttgggggct ctaggccggc cacctactgg tttgcagcgg
       61 agacgacgca tggggcctgc gcaataggag tacgctgcct gggaggcgtg actagaagcg
      121 gaagtagttg tgggcgcctt tgcaaccgcc tgggacgccg ccgagtggtc tgtgcaggtt
      181 cgcgggtcgc tggcggggdt cgtgagggag tgcgccggga gcggagatat ggagggagat
      241 aaaaaaaaaa aaaaaaaaaa aaaaaaa
//


####################
####################
####################
The file name is record.raw

The date of the file is Sun Mar 30 14:30:39 2003
The filetype of the file is _raw
The contents of the file are:
AGATGGCGGCGCTGAGGGGTCTTGGGGGCTCTAGGCCGGCCACCTACTGGTTTGCAGCGGAGACGACGCATGGGGCCTGCGCAAT
AGGAGTACGCTGCCTGGGAGGCGTGACTAGAAGCGGAAGTAGTTGTGGGCGCCTTTGCAACCGCCTGGGACGCCGCCGAGTGGTC
TGTGCAGGTTCGCGGGTCGCTGGCGGGGGTCGTGAGGGAGTGCGCCGGGAGCGGAGATATGGAGGGAGATAAAAAAAAAAAAAAAA
AAAAAAAAAAAA
####################
####################
####################
The file name is record.embl

The date of the file is Sun Mar 30 14:31:23 2003
The filetype of the file is _embl
The contents of the file are:
ID    AB031069      2487 bp    mRNA            PRI        27-MAY-2000 Sequence severely
truncated for demonstration. AB031069 AB031069
XX
SQ    sequence 267 BP; 65 A; 54 C; 106 G; 42 T; 0 other;
AGATGGCGGC GCTGAGGGGT CTTGGGGGCT CTAGGCCGGC CACCTACTGG TTTGCAGCGG
AGACGACGCA TGGGGCCTGC GCAATAGGAG TACGCTGCCT GGGAGGCGTG ACTAGAAGCG
GAAGTAGTTG TGGGCGCCTT TGCAACCGCC TGGGACGCCG CCGAGTGGTC TGTGCAGGTT
CGCGGGTCGC TGGCGGGGGT CGTGAGGGAG TGCGCCGGGA GCGGAGATAT GGAGGGAGAT
AAAAAAAAAA AAAAAAAAAA AAAAAAA
//


####################
####################
####################
The file name is record.fasta

The date of the file is Sun Mar 30 14:31:40 2003
The filetype of the file is _fasta
The contents of the file are:
> AB031069      2487 bp    mRNA            PRI        27-MAY-2000 Sequence severely
truncated for demonstration. AB031069
AGATGGCGGCGCTGAGGGGTCTTGGGGGCTCTAGGCCGGCCACCTACTGG
TTTGCAGCGGAGACGACGCATGGGGCCTGCGCAATAGGAGTACGCTGCCT
GGGAGGCGTGACTAGAAGCGGAAGTAGTTGTGGGCGCCTTTGCAACCGCC
TGGGACGCCGCCGAGTGGTCTGTGCAGGTTCGCGGGTCGCTGGCGGGGGT
```

```
CGTGAGGGAGTGCGCCGGGAGCGGAGATATGGAGGGAGATAAAAAAAAAA
AAAAAAAAAAAAAAAAAA


####################
####################
####################
The file name is record.gcg

The date of the file is Sun Mar 30 14:31:47 2003
The filetype of the file is _gcg
The contents of the file are:
AB031069     2487 bp    mRNA              PRI       27-MAY-2000 Sequence severely
truncated for demonstration. AB031069
     AB031069 Length: 267 (today)  Check: 4285  ..
        1  AGATGGCGGC GCTGAGGGGT CTTGGGGGCT CTAGGCCGGC CACCTACTGG
       51  TTTGCAGCGG AGACGACGCA TGGGGCCTGC GCAATAGGAG TACGCTGCCT
      101  GGGAGGCGTG ACTAGAAGCG GAAGTAGTTG TGGGCGCCTT TGCAACCGCC
      151  TGGGACGCCG CCGAGTGGTC TGTGCAGGTT CGCGGGTCGC TGGCGGGGGT
      201  CGTGAGGGAG TGCGCCGGGA GCGGAGATAT GGAGGGAGAT AAAAAAAAAA
      251  AAAAAAAAAA AAAAAAA


####################
####################
####################
The file name is record.staden

The date of the file is Sun Mar 30 14:32:01 2003
The filetype of the file is _staden
The contents of the file are:
;<----AB031069------>
AGATGGCGGCGCTGAGGGGTCTTGGGGGCTCTAGGCCGGCCACCTACTGGTTTGCAGCGG
AGACGACGCATGGGGCCTGCGCAATAGGAGTACGCTGCCTGGGAGGCGTGACTAGAAGCG
GAAGTAGTTGTGGGCGCCTTTGCAACCGCCTGGGACGCCGCCGAGTGGTCTGTGCAGGTT
CGCGGGTCGCTGGCGGGGGTCGTGAGGGAGTGCGCCGGGAGCGGAGATATGGAGGGAGAT
AAAAAAAAAAAAAAAAAAAAAAAAAAAAAA


####################
####################
####################


###########################################
#
# Test file format reformatting and writing
#
###########################################


At this point there are 8 objects.

######
###### Testing put methods
######
```

Printing staden data in raw format:
```
AGATGGCGGCGCTGAGGGGTCTTGGGGGCTCTAGGCCGGCCACCTACTGGTTTGCAGCGGAGACGACGCATGGGGCCTGCGCAAT
AGGAGTACGCTGCCTGGGAGGCGTGACTAGAAGCGGAAGTAGTTGTGGGCGCCTTTGCAACCGCCTGGGACGCCGCCGAGTGGTC
TGTGCAGGTTCGCGGGTCGCTGGCGGGGGTCGTGAGGGAGTGCGCCGGGAGCGGAGATATGGAGGGAGATAAAAAAAAAAAAAAAA
AAAAAAAAAAAA
```
Printing staden data in embl format:
```
ID    AB031069 AB031069
XX
SQ    sequence 267 BP; 65 A; 54 C; 106 G; 42 T; 0 other;
AGATGGCGGC GCTGAGGGGT CTTGGGGGCT CTAGGCCGGC CACCTACTGG TTTGCAGCGG
AGACGACGCA TGGGGCCTGC GCAATAGGAG TACGCTGCCT GGGAGGCGTG ACTAGAAGCG
GAAGTAGTTG TGGGCGCCTT TGCAACCGCC TGGGACGCCG CCGAGTGGTC TGTGCAGGTT
CGCGGGTCGC TGGCGGGGGT CGTGAGGGAG TGCGCCGGGA GCGGAGATAT GGAGGGAGAT
AAAAAAAAAA AAAAAAAAAA AAAAAAA
//
```

Printing staden data in fasta format:
```
> AB031069
AGATGGCGGCGCTGAGGGGTCTTGGGGGCTCTAGGCCGGCCACCTACTGG
TTTGCAGCGGAGACGACGCATGGGGCCTGCGCAATAGGAGTACGCTGCCT
GGGAGGCGTGACTAGAAGCGGAAGTAGTTGTGGGCGCCTTTGCAACCGCC
TGGGACGCCGCCGAGTGGTCTGTGCAGGTTCGCGGGTCGCTGGCGGGGGT
CGTGAGGGAGTGCGCCGGGAGCGGAGATATGGAGGGAGATAAAAAAAAAA
AAAAAAAAAAAAAAAAAA
```

Printing staden data in gcg format:
```
AB031069
     AB031069 Length: 267 (today)  Check: 4285  ..
        1  AGATGGCGGC GCTGAGGGGT CTTGGGGGCT CTAGGCCGGC CACCTACTGG
       51  TTTGCAGCGG AGACGACGCA TGGGGCCTGC GCAATAGGAG TACGCTGCCT
      101  GGGAGGCGTG ACTAGAAGCG GAAGTAGTTG TGGGCGCCTT TGCAACCGCC
      151  TGGGACGCCG CCGAGTGGTC TGTGCAGGTT CGCGGGTCGC TGGCGGGGGT
      201  CGTGAGGGAG TGCGCCGGGA GCGGAGATAT GGAGGGAGAT AAAAAAAAAA
      251  AAAAAAAAAA AAAAAAA
```

Printing staden data in genbank format:
```
LOCUS       AB031069        267 bp
DEFINITION  AB031069 , 267 bases, 829 sum.
ACCESSION
ORIGIN
        1  agatggcggc gctgaggggt cttgggggct ctaggccggc cacctactgg tttgcagcgg
       61  agacgacgca tggggcctgc gcaataggag tacgctgcct gggaggcgtg actagaagcg
      121  gaagtagttg tgggcgcctt tgcaaccgcc tgggacgccg ccgagtggtc tgtgcaggtt
      181  cgcgggtcgc tggcggggggt cgtgagggag tgcgccggga gcggagatat ggagggagat
      241  aaaaaaaaaa aaaaaaaaaa aaaaaaa
//
```

Printing staden data in PIR format:
```
ENTRY           AB031069
TITLE           AB031069
DATE
REFERENCE
SUMMARY         #Molecular-weight 0  #Length 267  #Checksum 4285
```

```
SEQUENCE
            5        10       15       20       25       30
    1 A G A T G G C G G C G C T G A G G G G T C T T G G G G G C T
   31 C T A G G C C G G C C A C C T A C T G G T T T G C A G C G G
   61 A G A C G A C G C A T G G G G C C T G C G C A A T A G G A G
   91 T A C G C T G C C T G G G A G G C G T G A C T A G A A G C G
  121 G A A G T A G T T G T G G G C G C C T T T G C A A C C G C C
  151 T G G G A C G C C G C C G A G T G G T C T G T G C A G G T T
  181 C G C G G G T C G C T G G C G G G G G T C G T G A G G G A G
  211 T G C G C C G G G A G C G G A G A T A T G G A G G G A G A T
  241 A A A A A A A A A A A A A A A A A A A A A A A A A A A A A A
///
```

Resources

- Inheritance is a fundamental OO technique; see the Resources section in Chapter 3 for Perl OO reference material that includes discussion of inheritance.

- For programming with sequence data file formats, see the C program *readseq* by Don Gilbert (at *http://iobio.bio.indiana.edu/soft/molbio/readseq*).

- See the Bioperl project at *http://www.bioperl.org* for alternate ways to handle this programming task in Perl.

- For a more rigorous but slower approach to parsing sequence files (which is sometimes what you want) see the module Parse::RecDescent by Damien Conway at CPAN.

- Each sequence file format has documentation that describes it. These formats sometimes change to keep up with the changing nature of biological data. One of the following exercises challenges you to find the documentation for one of the formats and to improve the code in this chapter for that format.

Exercises

Exercise 4.1

Write an object-oriented module DNAsequence whose object has one attribute, a sequence of DNA, and two methods, get_dna and set_dna. Start with the code for Gene.pm, but see how far you can whittle it down to the minimum amount of code necessary to implement this new class.

Exercise 4.2

The FileIO.pm module implements objects that read and write file data. However, they can, depending on the program, deviate substantially from what are actually present in files on your computer. For instance, you can read in all the files in a folder, and then change the filenames and data of all the objects, without writing them out. Is this a good thing or a bad thing?

Exercise 4.3

In the text, you are asked why the new constructor for FileIO.pm has been whittled down to the bare bones. You can see that all it does is create an empty object. What functionality has been moved out of the new constructor and into the read and write methods? Does it make more sense to do without a new constructor entirely and instead have the read and write methods create objects? Try rewriting the code that way. Alternately, does it make sense to try rewriting the code so that both reading and writing are handled by the new constructor? Is creating an object sometimes logically distinct from initializing it?

Exercise 4.4

Use FileIO.pm as a base class for a new class that manages the annotation of a pipeline in your laboratory. For example, perhaps your lab gets sequence from your ABI machine, screens it for vectors, assesses the quality of the sequencing run, searches your local database to determine if you've seen it or something like it before, then searches GenBank to see what other known sequences it matches or resembles, and finally adds it to an assembly project. Each step has a person or persons, a timestamp for the beginning and ending of each phase, and data. You want to be able to track the work done on each sequence that emerges from your ABI. (This is just an example. Pick a set of jobs that you actually do in your lab.)

Exercise 4.5

For each sequence file format handled by the SeqFileIO.pm module, find the documentation that specifies the format. Compare the documentation with the is_, parse_, and put_ method to recognize, read, and write files in each format. How can you improve this code? Make it more complete? Faster?

Exercise 4.6

My parse_ methods are somewhat ad hoc. They don't really parse the whole file according to the definition of the format. They just extract the sequence and a small amount of annotation. Take one of the formats and write a more complete parser for it. What are the advantages and disadvantages of a simple versus a more complete parser in this code? How about for other applications you may want to develop in the future?

Exercise 4.7

Use the parser you developed in Exercise 4.6 to do a more complete job of identifying a file in the same format in the module's is_ method.

Exercise 4.8

Add a new sequence file format to SeqFileIO.

Exercise 4.9

In FileIO.pm, and in many other places in this book, the program calls croak and exits when a problem arises (such as when unsuccessfully attempting to open a file for reading). Such drastic measures are sometimes desirable; for example, you may want to kill the program if a security problem is discovered in which someone is attempting to read a forbidden file. Or, when developing software, you may like your program to print an informative message and die when a problem occurs, as that might help you develop the program faster.

However, very often what you really want is for the program to notice the error and take some appropriate steps, not simply die. If a file cannot be opened, it may be something as simple as the user of the program mistyping the filename, and what you'd like is to give the user another couple of chances to type the name in correctly. Rewrite FileIO.pm without calling croak. This may entail checking for the success or failure of certain operations and taking reasonable actions on failure. Should the class module take all such actions, or should the program that uses the class module be expected to behave appropriately when a failure is reported?

Exercise 4.10

The AUTOLOAD method in FileIO.pm tests for attributes that are scalars and references to arrays. The need for this comes from the list of attributes given in the %_ my_attribute_properties hash. Each attribute hash value is an anonymous array with two elements: default value and properties. From the default value you can see that a value is either a scalar (a string in this case) or an anonymous array (a reference to an array). The code that AUTOLOAD installs for accessor routines then checks if the attribute is either a scalar or a reference to an array.

This AUTOLOAD method is inherited by SeqFileIO.pm. One of the modifications that SeqFileIO.pm makes is defining its own %_my_attribute_properties to handle the new attributes that it defines, such as _sequence. In this case, all the attributes are either scalars or references to arrays, as before. What modifications are necessary if some other data type is needed for a new attribute by a class that inherited FileIO.pm? How can you rewrite FileIO.pm to make it easier to write classes that inherit it?

Exercise 4.11

The test program testSeqFileIO has certain shortcomings. For one thing, it repeats blocks of code that can be replaced with a short loop (with a little rewriting). Another problem is that it doesn't test everything in the class.

Rewrite testSeqFileIO so that it's clearer and more comprehensive. By default, make it just give a short summary of the number of tests performed and the number of tests passed, but add a verbose flag so that it prints out all its tests in detail when desired. The module SeqFileIO.pm is lacking POD documentation. Add POD documentation to the module that is fairly easily cut and pasted into a test program for the module.

Exercise 4.12

In SeqFileIO.pm, the hash %_all_attribute_properties changed from the base class and needed to be redefined. However, the code for the _all_attributes, _attribute_default, and _permissions helper methods didn't change. Why then did the new class SeqFileIO redefine these methods? (Hint: are these helper methods closures?) SeqFileIO.pm is also lacking POD documentation. Try adding POD documentation to the module soy that it can be easily cut and pasted into a test program for the module.

Exercise 4.13

The h2xs program that ships with Perl simplifies module creation, and even helps you create the Makefile.PL that you'll need to add your own module to CPAN or to your local installation (which helps you bypass the somewhat awkward use lib directive that appears in the programs in this book). See also the perlxstut, the ExtUtils::MakeMaker, and the AUTOLOAD manpages. In particular, see the -X option to h2xs. Write a module starting from the use of h2xs.

Exercise 4.14

The open calls in the read methods of the classes in this chapter specify a filehandle FileIOFH. Alternatives include using lexical scalars as filehandles or the IO::Handle package. Rewrite the read methods so files are opened with these alternative types of filehandles. What costs or benefits result from these rewritings? (See the perlopentut part of the Perl documentation.)

Exercise 4.15

In the AUTOLOAD method, a copy of the file data is returned from the get_filedata accessor; this will protect the actual file data in the object, but it makes a copy of a potentially very large amount of data, which can overtax your system. Discuss alternatives for this behavior, and implement one of them.

Exercise 4.16

Reading in a few hundred large files (as can easily happen with the modules in this chapter) can overtax your system, causing the system, or at least the program, to crash. Design two alternative methods that avoid this overuse of memory. For instance, you can avoid reading in a file until the sequence data is actually needed. You can also reread the data into the program each time needed but not save it in your object. Finally, you can reclaim memory from older files. Implement one of these methods or some other. What other parts of the code need to be altered?

## CHAPTER 5

A Class for Restriction Enzymes

In this chapter, you'll learn how to write an object-oriented class that handles restriction enzymes using the modules from the previous chapter as part of an interface to the Restriction Enzyme Database (Rebase). I'll develop a class that finds restriction sites in DNA sequence data. In my book *Beginning Perl for Bioinformatics*, I presented code that extracts information from Rebase and uses it to make restriction maps of DNA sequence data. In this chapter, I'll adapt and extend that software (or ideas from the accompanying exercises) in an object-oriented fashion. (All code is shown here and is available from this book's web site.)

Envisioning an Object

The Rebase project provides a set of files that specify restriction enzymes, their cut sites, and a great deal more information. Consider the problem of designing an object-oriented version of code that uses this data. What will be the objects and the methods?

Each restriction enzyme has a name; associated with its name are the definition of its recognition site (which I'll translate into a Perl regular expression), information about the chemistry of the restriction enzyme, vendors of the enzyme, and other annotation. This information is all part of the Rebase database.

Perhaps I should consider each restriction enzyme as a suitable candidate for my basic object. I can then read in the Rebase database, creating objects for each restriction enzyme that includes such attributes as the recognition site, the translation of the recognition site into a Perl regular expression, and whatever additional annotation I find useful.

With such objects, I can associate methods that take as their arguments sequence data and return the list of locations in which that particular enzyme has a recognition site in the sequence. Sounds good, let's start coding!

But wait. What happens if, as is often the case, you want to find multiple restriction enzymes in a sequence and display the resulting map. With my design, you'd have to find the object associated with each restriction enzyme, pass it to the sequence, collect the locations, and then combine the individual lists of locations in order to display the map. This can be slow (finding the right objects, one for each restriction enzyme) and inconvenient (combining the output of the various methods from the various objects).

You recognize this questioning as an essential step in program design—thinking about the problem and considering alternative ways to write code that solve it. I reprise the idea here because, so far, I've been simply seeing and discussing solutions. Although it's neat and tidy, it isn't really the way programming works. Programming often involves thinking of alternative program strategies, comparing them, coding the most promising alternatives as prototypes and testing them (i.e., benchmarking), and finally deciding on an approach to implement.

So, in that spirit, what alternatives come to mind to the one enzyme/one object approach just described? The Rebase database is essentially a key/value lookup database, in which the key is the enzyme name. The value is the recognition site or annotation: actually there are several datafiles provided in the database. But I'm most interested in getting the recognition site, translating it to a Perl regular expression, and reporting on the locations in some sequence data. A nice interface to display some of the annotation of the restriction enzyme would also be useful.

Any key/value type of data immediately brings the hash data structure to the mind of the Perl programmer. As you know from my introduction to object-oriented programming, the hash data structure is also the most useful way to implement an object.

So, perhaps instead of many objects, one for each restriction enzyme, you may want to consider one object that provides the fast lookup of a value (the recognition site and regular expression) for each key (the name of the restriction enzyme). Clearly, this can be implemented as a hash. Other attributes can hold the sequence and the map as an array of the positions in the sequence in which the recognition sites exist. Methods for the object could extract the site, the regular expression, and perhaps some annotation, for each enzyme. A method can also locate the recognition sites for an enzyme in the sequence.

If we go that way, how will we manage the actual restriction maps that are made? A restriction map has as input some sequence and a list of restriction enzymes, and has as output a list of the locations where the enzymes have recognition sites in the sequence. Should there be another kind of object, a Restriction object, that has attributes of sequence, enzyme names, and locations of recognition sites?

Perhaps we can use the SeqFileIO class from Chapter 4 as a base class for a new derived class that adds attributes for restriction maps on the sequence.

That might be possible, but it combines file manipulations with restriction mapping and seems, at best, a shotgun wedding.

So, after careful reflection, consultation with colleagues, a lab meeting, pressure from the PI, an opinion from an outside expert, and some quick and dirty Perl scripts to see some alternatives in action, a decision is reached. We'll make a big Rebase object to hold the enzyme/recognition site data, plus a new Restriction object that holds the sequence and the locations of the recognition sites (the "map"). The class will provide the methods needed to calculate a restriction map.

One of the considerations that led to this decision was that, at some point, it will be necessary to graphically display the restriction map; an object that contains the sequence and the map (the locations of the recognition sites in the sequence) will be well suited for adding some graphics capabilities.

Finally, in this chapter we'll use the Restriction class as a base class to develop a Restrictionmap class that does have some graphics capabilities.

For more discussion of how to design the component parts of this software development project, see the exercises at the end of the chapter.

Rebase.pm: A Class Module

Here is a very simple interface to the Rebase data contained in the bionet file that is part of its distribution:

```perl
package Rebase;

#
# A simple class to provide access to restriction enzyme data from Rebase
#  including regular expression translations of recognition sites
#

use strict;
use warnings;
use Carp;
use DB_File;

# Class data and methods
{
    # A hash of all attributes with default values
    my %_attributes = (
        _rebase      => { },
            #    key   = restriction enzyme name
            #    value = space-separated string of sites => regular expressions
        _bionetfile => '??',
        _dbmfile     => '??',
        _mode        => 0444,
    );
```

```
# Return a list of all attributes
sub _all_attributes {
    keys %_attributes;
}

# Return the value of an attribute
sub _attribute_value {
    my($self,$attribute) = @_;
    $_attributes{$attribute};
}
}
```

Notice that the opening block is considerably pared down, compared to earlier classes. For instance, I've tossed the code that keeps count of all objects. Why? Because it's unlikely that more than one of these objects will be necessary in a program: so why bother?

Attributes: Short and Sweet

Notice that the list of attributes is short:

_rebase
> A hash that will be populated to provide the lookup, with enzyme names for keys, and recognition sites (and their translation to regular expressions) for values. (Make sure you see how in the hash %_attributes the value of the key _rebase is itself an anonymous hash.)

_bionetfile
> The name of the datafile from the Rebase distribution. In my examples, I use the version numbered bionet.212, and by the time you read this book, more recent versions will be available (you can get bionet.212 from this book's web site).

_dbmfile
> The DBM filename that resides on disk and stores the data in the hash _rebase.*

_mode
> Contains the permissions with which you will create, or attempt to read, the DBM file. This is important for security purposes.

With so few attributes, the class methods can easily handle each attribute individually, without recourse to the use of AUTOLOAD to define various accessors and mutators, as seen in previous chapters.

---

* Recall that DBM files are tied to hashes in Perl and provide a simple, easy-to-program database for key/value pairs. They serve as a way to keep a hash on disk between invocations of a program, and so can help you avoid the cost of recalculating a hash each time a program is run. For more information, see O'Reilly's *Programming Perl*, the documentation for the DB_File module, and the documentation for the dbmopen and tie functions.

Creating a Rebase Object

Here's how a Rebase object is created and initialized:

```perl
# The constructor method
# Called from class, e.g. $obj = Rebase->new( dbmfile => 'DBMFILE' );
sub new {
    my ($class, %arg) = @_;

    # Create a new object
    my $self = bless { }, $class;

    # DBM file must be given as "dbmfile" argument
    unless($arg{dbmfile}) {
        croak("No dbm file specified");
    }

    # Set the attributes for the provided arguments
    foreach my $attribute ($self->_all_attributes()) {

        # E.g. attribute = "_name",  argument = "name"
        my($argument) = ($attribute =~ /^_(.*)/);

        # Initialize to defaults
        $self->{$attribute} = $self->_attribute_value($attribute);

        # Override defaults with arguments
        if (exists $arg{$argument}) {
            if($argument eq 'rebase') {
                croak "Cannot set attribute rebase";
            }
            $self->{$attribute} = $arg{$argument};
        }
    }

    # Open or create the DBM file
    unless(tie %{$self->{_rebase}}, 'DB_File', $arg{dbmfile}, O_RDWR|O_CREAT, $self->
{_mode}, $DB_HASH) {
        my $permissions = sprintf "%lo", $self->{_mode};
        croak "Cannot open DBM file $arg{dbmfile} with mode $permissions";
    }

    # If "bionetfile" argument given, calculate the hash from the bionet file
    if($arg{bionetfile}) {

        # Empty the hash
        %{$self->{_rebase}} = ( );

        # Recalculate the hash
        $self->parse_rebase;
    }

    return $self;
}
```

```
# For this simple class I have no AUTOLOAD or DESTROY

# No get_rebase method, I don't want to pass around a huge hash

# No "set" mutators: all initialization done by way of "new" constructor
```

The new constructor method is short. It requires a DBM database filename (existing or new), to which the hash data structure _rebase is tied. If the DBM file doesn't exist, the pathname of the bionet Rebase file is also required (that's where the data comes from that populates the DBM file). If a bionet datafile is given, the method calls the parse_rebase method that parses the bionet file to create the _rebase hash.

As the comments indicate, my class is so simple I've even decided to do away with AUTOLOAD and DESTROY, and I've dispensed with the _set mutators as well.

Methods for the Rebase Class

Now, let's continue by looking at the methods for the Rebase class. Given an enzyme, the following two methods, get_recognition_sites and get_regular_expressions, retrieve the enzyme's recognition sites and the translations of the recognition sites into regular expressions.

How do these two methods work? One method returns all recognition sites for an enzyme as given in the Rebase database; the other returns all the translations of the recognition sites into regular expressions. They both work very similarly. First, the enzyme is looked up in the _rebase hash. The value for each enzyme in the _rebase hash is a space-separated string that alternates recognition sites with their regular-expression translations. In both methods, the space-separated string is split to get a list of alternating recognition sites and regular expressions. This list is then assigned to the hash %sites to populate it with keys as recognition sites (the data that's actually in the Rebase bionet file) and values as regular expressions. The Perl operators keys and values are then used to generate the list of recognition sites (keys) or regular expressions (values).

The get_bionetfile, get_dbmfile, and get_mode methods just report on the arguments that are set to specific filenames or mode strings when the object was created:

```
sub get_regular_expressions {
    my($self, $enzyme) = @_;

    my(%sites) = split(' ', $self->{_rebase}{$enzyme});

    # May have duplicate values
    return values %sites;
}

sub get_recognition_sites {
    my($self, $enzyme) = @_;
```

```
    my(%sites) = split(' ', $self->{_rebase}{$enzyme});

    return keys %sites;
}

sub get_bionetfile {
    my($self) = @_;

    return $self->{_bionetfile};
}

sub get_dbmfile {
    my($self) = @_;

    return $self->{_dbmfile};
}

sub get_mode {
    my($self) = @_;

    return $self->{_mode};
}
```

parse_rebase

The workhorse method of the class is parse_rebase, which reads the bionet Rebase datafile (with a suffix that indicates the release version, such as bionet.212). The bionet input datafile begins like this:

```
REBASE version 212                                      bionet.212


    =-=-=-=-=-=-=-=-=-=-=-=-=-=-=-=-=-=-=-=-=-=-=-=-=-=-=-=-=-=-=-=-=
    REBASE, The Restriction Enzyme Database   http://rebase.neb.com
    Copyright (c) Dr. Richard J. Roberts, 2002.   All rights reserved.
    =-=-=-=-=-=-=-=-=-=-=-=-=-=-=-=-=-=-=-=-=-=-=-=-=-=-=-=-=-=-=-=

    Rich Roberts                                        Dec 01 2002

    AaaI (XmaIII)                   C^GGCCG
    AacI (BamHI)                    GGATCC
    AaeI (BamHI)                    GGATCC
    AagI (ClaI)                     AT^CGAT
    AaqI (ApaLI)                    GTGCAC
    AarI                            CACCTGCNNNN^
    AarI                            ^NNNNNNNNGCAGGTG
    AasI (DrdI)                     GACNNNN^NNGTC
    AatI (StuI)                     AGG^CCT
    AatII                           GACGT^C
    AauI (Bsp1407I)                 T^GTACA
```

As you can see, the header information ends with a line containing Rich Roberts. Apart from a blank line or two, the rest of the file contains records, one per line. Each record begins with a restriction enzyme name, optionally followed by another enzyme name in parentheses. The last field of each line is the recognition site. These are given using IUB codes for nucleotides. (For the IUB codes, see the comments in the program.)

They also contain cut sites, indicated by a caret symbol ^. *Cut sites* contribute very important information about a restriction enzyme; they show where the enzyme makes the break when it cuts the DNA. Among other things, they are needed to correctly perform restriction digests in the computer when determining if there are overhangs that will be useful when inserting vectors or otherwise reassembling the fragments. However, in the code here we'll ignore the cut sites taking as a goal the virtual fingerprinting of DNA by just locating the recognition sites. Cut sites are omitted to simplify the code. (See the exercises for more on handling cut sites.)

```perl
sub parse_rebase {
    my($self) = @_;

    # handles multiple definition lines for an enzyme name
    # also handles alternate enzyme names on a line

    # Read in the bionet(Rebase) file
    unless(open(BIONETFH, $self->{_bionetfile})) {
        croak("Cannot open bionet file $self->{_bionetfile}");
    }

    while(<BIONETFH>) {

        my @names = ( );

        # Discard header lines
        next if ( 1 .. /Rich Roberts/ );# discard all lines from the first line
                                        # to the first line containing "Rich Roberts"

        # Discard blank lines
        next unless /\S/; # discard a line unless it contains something not
                          # whitespace

        # Split the two (or three if includes parenthesized name) fields
        my @fields = split;

        # Get and store the recognition site
        my $site = pop @fields;
        # For the purposes of this exercise, I'll ignore cut sites (^).
        # This is not something you'd want to do in general, however!
        $site =~ s/\^//g;

        # Get and store the name and the recognition site.
        # Add alternate (parenthesized) names
        # from the middle field, if any
        foreach my $name (@fields) {
```

```
        $name =~ tr/)(//d;  # delete parentheses
        push @names, $name;
    }


    # Store the data into the hash, avoiding duplicates (ignoring ^ cut sites)
    # and ignoring reverse complements
    # Because these values are stored via DBM, I cannot use anything but
    #   a scalar string to store the site/regularexpression pairs, space-separated
    #   (but see the exercises)
    foreach my $name (@names) {

        # Add new enzyme definition
        unless(exists $self->{_rebase}{$name}) {
            $self->{_rebase}{$name} = "$site " . IUB_to_regexp($site);
            next;
        }

        my(%defined_sites) = split(' ', $self->{_rebase}{$name});

        # Omit already defined sites
        if(exists $defined_sites{$site}) {
            next;
        # Omit reverse complements of already defined sites
        }elsif(exists $defined_sites{revcomIUB($site)}) {
            next;
        # Add the additional site
        }else{
            $self->{_rebase}{$name}   .= " $site " . IUB_to_regexp($site);
        }
    }
  }
  return 1;
}
```

This subroutine is a bit complex, corresponding to the nature of the data that it's processing. For instance, because enzymes can appear on more than one line, it has to check if an enzyme was already entered as a key in the hash.

Let me remind you of the range operator that is used here to skip header lines:

```
# Discard header lines
next if ( 1 .. /Rich Roberts/ );  # discard all lines from the first line
                                  # to the first line containing "Rich Roberts"
```

The expression (1 .. /Rich Roberts/) returns true (and leads to the line being skipped) only when the line being read is included in the range bordered by the first line and the first line containing the regular expression /Rich Roberts/. (See the perlop section of the Perl manual for all the details on the range operator.)

The parse_rebase subroutine, after skipping the header and any blank lines, then processes each data line in a while loop. Each line is split into either two fields (name and recognition site) or three fields (name, parenthesized alternate name, and recognition site). The name or names are placed in the @names array and looped through.

In the last foreach loop, if the enzyme name hasn't yet been defined in the DBM-tied hash, it is added as a key. The value assigned to the key is a string with recognition site followed by a translation of the recognition site to a regular expression. The program passes to the next name.

If the enzyme name has previously been entered as a key, the previously entered recognition sites are examined, and if the new site is there, the program passes to the next name. Similarly, if the reverse complement of the site has been entered, the program passes to the next name. But otherwise (if the enzyme name was entered, but neither the site nor its reverse complement were in the list of sites for that enzyme), the recognition site is added with its translation to a regular expression.

This method has to handle reverse complements of recognition sites. Many restriction enzymes are palindromic in the sense that their reverse complements are the same. (For instance, the reverse complement of GAATTC is GAATTC.) These biological palindromes indicate that the enzyme can cut the site on both strands.

 Although the code presented here ignores cut sites, the exercises will ask you to reconsider them; note that if the cut site isn't exactly in the middle, there will be "sticky ends" of single stranded DNA that make it possible to anneal the fragment with a complementary sticky end. Refer to a standard molecular biology textbook for the essential biology of restriction enzymes. (The logic used here to handle reverse complements might not be ideal for all situations: see the exercises.)

Methods to Translate Nucleotides to Regular Expressions

Finally, the remaining methods translate IUB-coded nucleotide sequence data to Perl regular expressions. They also perform reverse complementation on IUB-coded sequence data.

```
sub revcomIUB {
    my($seq) = @_;

    my $revcom = reverse complementIUB($seq);

    return $revcom;
}

sub complementIUB {
    my($seq) = @_;

    (my $com = $seq) =~ tr [ACGTRYMKSWBDHVNacgtrymkswbdhvn]
                            [TGCAYRKMWSVHDBNtgcayrkmwsvhdbn];

    return $com;
}
```

```perl
# Translate IUB ambiguity codes to regular expressions
# IUB_to_regexp
#
# A subroutine that, given a sequence with IUB ambiguity codes,
# outputs a translation with IUB codes changed to regular expressions
#
# These are the IUB ambiguity codes
# (Eur. J. Biochem. 150: 1-5, 1985):
# R = G or A
# Y = C or T
# M = A or C
# K = G or T
# S = G or C
# W = A or T
# B = not A (C or G or T)
# D = not C (A or G or T)
# H = not G (A or C or T)
# V = not T (A or C or G)
# N = A or C or G or T

sub IUB_to_regexp {

    my($iub) = @_;

    my $regular_expression = '';

    my %iub2character_class = (

        A => 'A',
        C => 'C',
        G => 'G',
        T => 'T',
        R => '[GA]',
        Y => '[CT]',
        M => '[AC]',
        K => '[GT]',
        S => '[GC]',
        W => '[AT]',
        B => '[CGT]',
        D => '[AGT]',
        H => '[ACT]',
        V => '[ACG]',
        N => '[ACGT]',
    );

    # Remove the ^ signs from the recognition sites
    $iub =~ s/\^//g;

    # Translate each character in the iub sequence
    for ( my $i = 0 ; $i < length($iub) ; ++$i ) {
        $regular_expression
            .= $iub2character_class{substr($iub, $i, 1)};
    }
```

```perl
        return $regular_expression;
}

1;

=head1 Rebase

Rebase: A simple interface to recognition sites and translations of them into
        regular expressions, from the Restriction Enzyme Database (Rebase)

=head1 Synopsis

    use Rebase;

    # Use "bionetfile" to create and populate dbm file
    my $rebase = Rebase->new(
        dbmfile => 'BIONET',
        bionetfile => 'bionet.212',
        mode => 0644
    );

    # Use without "bionetfile" to attach to existing dbm file
    my $rebase = Rebase->new(
        dbmfile => 'BIONET',
        mode => 0444
    );

    my $enzyme = 'EcoRI';

    print "Looking up restriction enzyme $enzyme\n";

    my @sites = $rebase->get_recognition_sites($enzyme);
    print "Sites are @sites\n";

    my @res = $rebase->get_regular_expressions($enzyme);
    print "Regular expressions are @res\n";

    print "DBM file is ", $rebase->get_dbmfile, "\n";
    print "Rebase bionet file is ", $rebase->get_bionetfile, "\n";

=head1 AUTHOR

James Tisdall

=head1 COPYRIGHT

Copyright (c) 2003, James Tisdall

=cut
```

Testing the Module

Ending the module, as usual, is some POD documentation for the module. Recall that you can view the output of this documentation in various ways, as HTML on a web page, as PostScript, etc. However, the simplest way is to say the following at the command line:

```
perldoc Rebase.pm
```

Let's try running the sample code given in the documentation. Notice that the Rebase.pm module is available, as is the bionet.212 file from the Rebase distribution. Also, notice there are two alternate calls to Rebase->new, so you should comment out the first one, then the other, in tests. Save the sample code from the documentation in a file called testRebase, and when you run it with the command:

```
perl testRebase
```

you get the following output:

```
Looking up restriction enzyme EcoRI
Sites are GAATTC
Regular expressions are GAATTC
DBM file is BIONET
Rebase bionet file is bionet.212
```

Restriction.pm: Finding Recognition Sites

The time has now come to write the class that creates an object out of a sequence, enzyme name(s), and the map of the location(s) of the enzyme recognition sites in the sequence.

This module depends a great deal on the module Rebase developed in the previous section, but it is fairly short because it just tries to do a small job. This new Restriction class takes a Rebase object (which has the Rebase database translated to regular expressions), some sequence, and a list of enzymes, and uses the regular expressions to find the recognition sites in the sequence. (Note that it doesn't use inheritance; it simply creates a Rebase object to use.)

In this module, the restriction map (the list of locations where the enzymes have recognition sites in the sequence) is obtained through an auxiliary method map_enzyme that simply lists the locations. Clearly, a more graphical display would be easier and more useful. I'll consider that as the book progresses.

The Restriction.pm Module

Here is the Restriction.pm module:

```perl
package Restriction;

#
# A class to find locations of restriction enzyme recognition sites in
#  DNA sequence data.
#

use strict;
use warnings;
use Carp;

# Class data and methods
{
    # A list of all attributes with default values.
    # "enzyme" is given as an argument possibly multiple time, set as key to _map hash
    my %_attributes = (
        _rebase      => { },  # A Rebase.pm hash-based object
        # key    = restriction enzyme name
        # value = space-separated string of recognition sites => regular expressions
        _sequence    => '', # DNA sequence data in raw format (only bases)
        _map         => { },# a hash: keys are enzyme names,
                            # values are arrays of locations
        _enzyme      => '', # space- or comma-separated enzyme names,
                            # set as key to _map hash
    );

    # Global variable to keep count of existing objects
    my $_count = 0;

    # Return a list of all attributes
    sub _all_attributes {
        keys %_attributes;
    }

    # Manage the count of existing objects
    sub get_count {
        $_count;
    }
    sub _incr_count {
        ++$_count;
    }
    sub _decr_count {
        --$_count;
    }
}
```

This opening block shows that Restriction is also a class with a small and simple set of attributes. One is just the DNA sequence data, _sequence.

The attribute _map is a hash that stores the computed restriction map with a key for each restriction enzyme and a value consisting of an array of the positions in the sequence where recognition sites for that enzyme occur.

The attribute _enzyme is one or more enzyme names separated by spaces or commas.

The remaining attribute _rebase is an object of the class I developed in the last section, the class Rebase. Recall that a Rebase object gives you the ability to get regular expressions for recognition sites of restriction enzymes. When you call Restriction-> new you must include as one of its arguments a Rebase object, as is shown in the example given in the POD documentation later in this section.

Since a program can have many restriction maps, I also maintain the count of Restriction objects.

Initializing Restriction objects

Next, the new constructor method creates and initializes Restriction objects:

```
# The "new" constructor method, called from class, e.g.
sub new {
    my ($class, %args) = @_;
    # Create a new object
    my $self = bless { }, $class;

    # Set the attributes for the provided arguments
    foreach my $attribute ($self->_all_attributes()) {

        # E.g. attribute = "_name",  argument = "name"
        my($argument) = ($attribute =~ /^_(.*)/);

        if (exists $args{$argument}) {
            if($argument eq 'enzyme') {
                # permit space or comma separated enzyme names
                $args{$argument} =~ s/,/ /g;
            }
            $self->{$attribute} = $args{$argument};
        }
    }

    # Check that the correct arguments are given
    if( not defined $self->{_rebase} ) {
        croak "A Rebase object must be given as an argument";
    }elsif( ref($self->{_rebase}) ne 'Rebase' ) {
        croak "The argument to rebase is not a Rebase object";
    }elsif( not defined $self->{_sequence} ) {
        croak "A sequence must be given as an argument";
    }

    # Calculate the locations for each enzyme, store in _map hash attribute
    foreach my $enzyme (split(" ", $self->{_enzyme})) {
        $self->map_enzyme($enzyme);
    }
```

```
    $self->_incr_count;

    return $self;
}

# For this simple class I have no AUTOLOAD or DESTROY

# No get_rebase method, I don't want to pass around a huge hash

# No set mutators: all initialization done by way of "new" constructor

# No clone method.  Each sequence and set of enzymes can be easily calculated
#   by means of a "new" command.
```

The methods explained

The new constructor method checks that the proper and required arguments are provided: a sequence, enzyme(s), and a Rebase object.

Then the new constructor performs the required computation by calling the method map_enzyme for each enzyme to determine the (possibly empty) array of locations in which the enzyme can cut the sequence. These enzyme-array key/value pairs are stored in the _map attribute.

As you can see in the next segment of code from Restriction.pm, the method map_enzyme works by getting the regular expressions that have been calculated for the enzyme and then finding the positions where the regular expressions match the sequence.

The get_regular_expressions method accesses the Rebase object that was passed to the Restriction->new constructor method and appears as the $self->{_rebase} attribute. In that object, the attribute _rebase is the hash of the database, which looks for the value of the key $enzyme.

The match_positions method puts a match of a regular expression in a while loop, where it loops once for each location it finds. The offset of the matching sequence is available in the special variable $-[0] after a successful regular-expression match (see the perlvar section of the Perl documentation for more details).

```perl
sub map_enzyme {
    my($self, $enzyme) = @_;

    my(@positions) = ( );

    my(@res) = $self->get_regular_expressions($enzyme);

    foreach my $re (@res) {
        push @positions, $self->match_positions($re);
    }

    @{$self->{_map}{$enzyme}} = @positions;
    return @positions;
```

```perl
}

sub get_regular_expressions {
    my($self, $enzyme) = @_;

    my(%sites) = split(' ', $self->{_rebase}{_rebase}{$enzyme});

    # May have duplicate values
    return values %sites;
}

# Find positions of a regular expression in the sequence
sub match_positions {
    my($self, $regexp) = @_;

    my @positions = (  );

    # Determine positions of regular expression matches
    while ( $self->{_sequence} =~ /$regexp/ig ) {
        push @positions, ($-[0] + 1 );
    }

    return(@positions);
}
```

Finally, here are some helper methods that report on the attributes of sequence and of the calculated map for a given enzyme (or the entire hash that contains the map of all the enzymes). I didn't use AUTOLOAD here because there are only a handful of attributes that return a few different data types: array, scalar string, and hash.

```perl
sub get_enzyme_map {
    my($self, $enzyme) = @_;

    @{$self->{_map}{$enzyme}};
}

sub get_enzyme_names {
    my($self) = @_;

    keys %{$self->{_map}};
}
sub get_sequence {
    my($self) = @_;

    $self->{_sequence};
}

sub get_map {
    my($self) = @_;

    %{$self->{_map}};
}
```

Documentation

Here's the (bare bones) documentation for the class embedded right in the module using the POD documentation language:

```
=head1 Restriction

Restriction: Given a Rebase object, sequence, and list of restriction enzyme
    names, return the locations of the recognition sites in the sequence

=head1 Synopsis

    use Restriction;

    use Rebase;

    use strict;
    use warnings;

    my $rebase = Rebase->new(
        dbmfile => 'BIONET',
        bionetfile => 'bionet.212'
    );

    my $restrict = Restriction->new(
        rebase => $rebase,
        enzyme => 'EcoRI, HindIII',
        sequence => 'ACGAATTCCGGAATTCG',
    );

    print "Locations for EcoRI are ", join(' ',
                                 $restrict->get_enzyme_map('EcoRI')), "\n";

=head1 AUTHOR

James Tisdall

=head1 COPYRIGHT

Copyright (c) 2003, James Tisdall

=cut

1;
```

Saving the Synopsis example in a file and running it (making sure the required bionet.212 file is in place) gives the output:

```
EcoRI data in Rebase is GAATTC GAATTC
Sequence is ACGAATTCCGGAATTCG
Locations for EcoRI are 3 11
```

Drawing Restriction Maps

One of the most important lessons of scientific programming is the importance of a good display of a program's results.

In this section, I'm going to add the ability to output a restriction map by inheriting Restriction.pm and making a new derived class Restrictionmap.pm. The restriction map will be shown very simply as the sequence printed in lines of simple text. The locations of restriction sites are written over the lines of text, giving the names of the restriction enzymes at the restriction sites. In Chapter 8, this simple text-based graphic output is replaced by a real picture (with colors, different fonts, and whatever bells and whistles you choose to add). I designed my base class Restriction.pm to represent the restriction map as a simple list of recognition site locations because I wanted my software to be flexible enough to be extended to accommodate any of the many different graphic formats that might be desired.

The difference between an unreadable mass of data, and a good clean graphic display that leads the eye towards an interesting result, is profound. It's the difference between a successful program and a dud, between hours or days spent sorting through columns of data and a quick discovery of a region of interest. It's even the difference between a scientific discovery, and none at all.

Graphics programming is a bit of an advanced topic. (You'll get your feet wet in Chapter 8.) But even if you need a program that's restricted to text output, you still need to spend programming time displaying that output in a useful manner. So, in this section, I'll add a very simple map drawing capability to the software, drawn as simple text.

Storing Graphics Output in an Attribute

I want to display a graphic. Do I need to add _graphic and _graphictype attributes to my object? The question boils down to: shall I compute and display a graphic whenever needed, or shall I compute a graphic and store it in an attribute? If you're new to computer graphics, just think of a graphic as a mass of data, which can be stored in a variable, or in a file on disk, and can be used to generate a graphical display on the computer screen by the right software.

I do already compute the restriction map, by which I mean the actual locations of the recognition sites for each enzyme requested, and stored it in the _map attribute. I can also compute a graphic at the same time and store it in the proposed _graphic attribute.

Let's think about the pluses and minuses of storing graphics output in an attribute.

I'm not sure which graphics system I'll use in the future; for now, a simple text output may work as a stored attribute, but there are a lot of graphics outputs possible. Also, it seems likely that I'll be able to compute the graphics output very quickly, so the need for storing it is less compelling. And storing a large image for possibly hundreds or thousands of objects will be a strain on the computer system.

However, I may not be able to calculate quickly for fancier, full color, high resolution graphics that I might want in the future. And perhaps I'll need to flip between graphics very quickly, in which case having them precalculated would be a necessity!

Also, how about multiple digests? Should I just create one graphic for the entire set of enzymes in an object or add a single digest graphic for each enzyme?

Maybe I can't answer all these questions yet, either. At this point, I'm not sure of the kind of graphics I'll be producing, or of their size, or of the time to generate them. Perhaps I can decide to make just one graphic per object (the user can always make a new object with just one enzyme if desired).

Answering these questions is a judgment call. When the answers to such questions aren't known, you should at least try to make the code flexible enough to accommodate whatever decisions are eventually reached.

For now, let's add a graphics attribute and precalculate the graphics output. After all, if in the future I decide that, for instance, I can generate graphics quickly enough on the fly, but that they're a bit large, I'll just add a method that can generate the images when needed.

The Restrictionmap Class

Here's a simple extension of the `Restriction` class I'll call `Restrictionmap`, which adds a new `_mapgraphics` attribute. It doesn't compute the graphics output until the first time it's called; it then stores the result for future lookups:

```
package Restrictionmap;

use base ( "Restriction" );

#
# A class to find locations of restriction enzyme recognition sites in
#  DNA sequence data, and to display them.
#

use strict;
use warnings;
use Carp;

# Class data and methods
{
    # A list of all attributes with default values.
    my %_attributes = (
        #   key   = restriction enzyme name
        #   value = space-separated string of recognition sites => regular
expressions
```

```
          _rebase     => { },     # A Rebase.pm object
          _sequence   => '',      # DNA sequence data in raw format (only bases)
          _enzyme     => '',      # space separated string of one or more enzyme names
          _map        => { },     # hash: enzyme names => arrays of locations
          _graphictype => 'text', # one of 'text' or 'png' or some other
          _graphic    => '',      # a graphic display of the restriction map
      );

      # Return a list of all attributes
      sub _all_attributes {
          keys %_attributes;
      }
  }
```

Notice that I've declared a new class Restrictionmap using the base class Restriction. Notice also that no AUTOLOAD mechanism is provided.

Also, in the block containing the class data and methods, there's a new definition of the hash %_attributes that adds the new attribute _graphictype to indicate the type of graphic (at first, this will be "text"), and the new attribute _graphic as a simple scalar.

Why am I defining it as a scalar? As you'll see, the routines that make the text-based graphics that I'm adding here assemble the graphics output as an array. To store it as a scalar requires an extra call to the Perl join function.

The reason I'm storing the graphics display as a scalar is that image data comes in a variety of formats. If I plan on just saving an image as a scalar, it will perhaps cover the most common possibilities; it's always possible to read a file into a scalar in Perl. Hopefully, this decision to store the image data as a scalar gives the most flexibility for future development.

This opening block is similar to the opening block of the base class Restriction. Notice the only helper method I'm redefining is the _all_attributes method, which uses the redefined %_attributes data structure that appears in the same block with it. The other methods in this block in the base class count the number of objects in existence during the running of the program; those methods and the _count variable they depend on are inherited by this new derived class Restrictionmap and will work fine.

Adding graphics capability to the class

Next, come the methods that add the graphics capability to the class:

```
sub get_graphic {
    my($self) = @_;

    # If the graphic is not stored, calculate and store it
    unless($self->{_graphic}) {
```

```
        unless($self->{_graphictype}) {
            croak 'Attribute graphictype not set (default is "text")';
        }

        # if graphictype is "xyz", method that makes the graphic is "_drawmap_xyz"
        my $drawmapfunctionname = "_drawmap_" . $self->{_graphictype};

        # Calculate and store the graphic
        $self->{_graphic} = $self->$drawmapfunctionname;
    }

    # Return the stored graphic
    return $self->{_graphic};
}
```

This is the public method that is meant to be called from a program. Recall that I decided to only calculate the graphics for an object the first time the graphic is requested; it's then saved in the _mapgraphic attribute for subsequent calls.

Creation of the graphic

The first step in graphic creation is an initialization routine. This doesn't do much here, but other graphics I might create may well benefit from a separate initialization step, so I plan ahead and add it here as well.

Each enzyme is called in turn, and its matching positions are retrieved as you've seen before with the get_enzyme_map method. The appropriate annotation is added to the @annotation array. The resulting annotation is then formatted for output and returned:

```
#
# Methods to output graphics in text format
#

sub _drawmap_text {
    my($self) = @_;

    my @annotation = ();
    push(@annotation, _initialize_annotation_text($self->get_sequence));

    foreach my $enzyme ($self->get_enzyme_names) {
        _add_annotation_text(^annotation, $enzyme, $self->get_enzyme_map($enzyme));
    }

    # Format the restriction map as sequence and annotation
    my @output = _formatmaptext(50, $self->get_sequence, @annotation);

    # Return output as a string, not an array of lines
    return join('', @output);
}
```

```
  # Make a blank string of the same length as the given sequence string
sub _initialize_annotation_text {
    my($seq) = @_;

    return '' x length($seq);
```

The idea behind this text-based annotation is as follows. The lines of sequence output are separated by blank lines just for readability. Directly above the sequence lines are additional annotation lines containing the names of enzymes, which appear with their names starting exactly where the recognition site starts. Sometimes, enzyme names collide—two or more enzyme names might require the same space on an annotation line. In that case, an additional annotation line is created to print these overlapping enzyme names. There's an example of this in the program output following this discussion.

The code is fairly well commented. Check out the exercises: one will challenge you to improve it or to start from scratch and invent a better way to display this kind of text-based annotation. I'll omit a detailed commentary on exactly how this code accomplishes its job; as they say, it will be left as an exercise for the reader. Or, as one of my mathematics professors used to delight in saying, "A moment's reflection should clear the matter up for you."

```
  #   Add annotation to an annotation string
sub _add_annotation_text {

    my($array, $enz, @pos) = @_;

    # $array is a reference to an array of annotations

    # Put the labels for the enzyme name at the correct positions in the annotation
    foreach my $location (@pos) {

        # Loop through all the annotation strings as necessary
        for( my $i = 0 ; $i < @$array ; ++$i ) {

            # If the annotation contains only space characters at that position,
            # insert the annotation
            if(substr($$array[$i], $location-1, length($enz)) eq (' ' x
length($enz))){
                substr($$array[$i], $location-1, length($enz)) = $enz;
                last;

            # If the annotation collides, add it to the next annotation string on the
            # next iteration of the "for" loop.
            # But first, if there is not another annotation string, make one

            }elsif($i == (@$array - 1)) {
                push(@$array, _initialize_annotation_text($$array[0]));
            }
        }
    }
}
```

```
# Sequence with annotation lines formatted for the page with line breaks
sub _formatmaptext {

    my($line_length, $seq, @annotation) = @_;

    my(@output) = ();

    # Split strings into lines of $line_length
    for ( my $pos = 0 ; $pos < length($seq) ; $pos += $line_length ) {
        # Print annotation on top of sequence, using reverse
        foreach my $string ( reverse ($seq, @annotation) ) {
            # Discard blank lines?
            # if ( substr($string, $pos, $line_length) !~ /[^ \n]/ ) {
            #     next;
            # }

            # Add line to output
            push(@output, substr($string, $pos, $line_length) . "\n");
        }
        # separate the lines
        push(@output,"\n");
    }

    # Return the merged annotation and sequence
    return @output;
}

=head1 Restrictionmap

Restrictionmap: Given a Rebase object, sequence, and list of restriction enzyme
    names, return the locations of the recognition sites in the sequence

=head1 Synopsis

    use Restrictionmap;

    use Rebase;

    use strict;
    use warnings;

    my $rebase = Rebase->new(
        dbmfile => 'BIONET',
        bionetfile => 'bionet.212'
    );

    my $restrict = Restrictionmap->new(
        rebase => $rebase,
        enzyme => 'EcoRI',
        enzyme => 'HindIII',
        sequence => 'ACGAATTCCGGAATTCG',
        graphictype => 'text',
    );
```

```perl
    print "Locations are ", join ' ', $restrict->get_enzyme_map('EcoRI'), "\n";

    print $restrict->get_graphic;

=head1 AUTHOR

James Tisdall

=head1 COPYRIGHT

Copyright (c) 2003, James Tisdall

=cut

1;
```

Running the program

If you run the short program given in the Synopsis section of the documentation, you won't get very interesting output; the input data is too short. The following is a better example. There's some DNA sequence data that contains EcoRI and HindIII recognition sites, saved in a file called sampleecori.dna. The class SeqFileIO is used to read it in, and then Restrictionmap makes and displays a restriction map of that sequence.

Here's the program, an extension, really, of the short program that appears in the Synopsis section of the POD documentation. Let's use it to test this new Restrictionmap class:

```perl
use lib "/home/tisdall/MasteringPerlBio/development/lib";

use Restrictionmap;
use Rebase;
use SeqFileIO;

use strict;
use warnings;

my $rebase = Rebase->new(
    dbmfile => 'BIONET',
    bionetfile => 'bionet.212',
    mode => '0666',
);

my $restrict = Restrictionmap->new(
    rebase => $rebase,
    enzyme => 'EcoRI HindIII',  # GAATTC # AAGCTT
    sequence => 'ACGAATTCCGGAATTCG',
    graphictype => 'text',
);
```

```
print "Locations are ", join ' ', $restrict->get_enzyme_map('EcoRI'), "\n";

print $restrict->get_graphic;

## Some bigger sequence

my $biggerseq = SeqFileIO->new;
#$biggerseq->read(filename => 'map.fasta');
$biggerseq->read(filename => 'sampleecori.dna');

my $restrict2 = Restrictionmap->new(
    rebase => $rebase,
    enzyme => 'EcoRI HindIII',  # GAATTC # AAGCTT
    sequence => $biggerseq->get_sequence,
    graphictype => 'text',
);

print "\nHere is the map of the bigger sequence:\n\n";

print $restrict2->get_graphic;
```

Notice that a use lib directive is added to tell Perl where to find the modules; you can accomplish the same thing with the PERL5LIB environmental variable or with a command-line argument to Perl.

Here's is the output from the test program:

```
Locations are 3 11
  EcoRI   EcoRI
ACGAATTCCGGAATTCG

Here is the map of the bigger sequence:


AGATGGCGGCGCTGAGGGGTCTTGGGGGCTCTAGGCCGGCCACCTACTGG


TTTGCAGCGGAGACGACGCATGGGGCCTGCGCAATAGGAGTACGCTGCCT

                EcoRI
GGGAGGCGTGACTAGAAGCGGGAATTCAAGTAGTTGTGGGCGCCTTTGCA

ACCGCCTGGGACGCCGCCGAGTGGTCTGTGCAGGTTCGCGGGTCGCTGGC

        HindIII
GGGGGTCGTAAGCTTGAGGGAGTGCGCCGGGAGCGGAGATATGGAGGGAG

ATGGTTCAGACCCAGAGCCTCCAGATGCCGGGGAGGACAGCAAGTCCGAG

AATGGGGAGAATGCGCCCATCTACTGCATCTGCCGCAAACCGGACATCAA

                HindIII
CTGCTTCATGATCGGGTGTGACAAGCTTAACTGCAATGAGTGGTTCCATG
```

```
GGGACTGCATCCGGATCAGCGGGATGGCAATGAGCGGGACAGCAGTGAGC

CCCGGGATGAGGGTGGAGGGCGCAAGAGGCCTGTCCCTGATCCAGACCTG

CAGCGCCGGGCAGGGTCAGGGACAGGGGTTGGGGCCATGCTTGCTCGGGG

                                              EcoRI
CTCTGCTTCGCCCCACAAATCCTCTCCGCAGCCCTTGGTGGCCACGAATT

CACCCAGCCAGCATCACCAGCAGCAGCAGCAGCAGATCAAACGGTCAGCC

          EcoRI
HindIII
AAGCTTGAATTCCGCATGTGTGGTGAGTGTGAGGCACCAGTGACGCCCTC

AGAGTCCCTGCCAAGGCCCCGCCGGCCACTGCCCACCCAACAGCAGCCAC

                    EcoRI
AGCCATCACAGAAGTTAGGGAATTCGCGCATCCGTGAAGATGAGGGGGCA

                    EcoRI
GTGGCGTCATCAACAGTCAAGGAGCCTCCTGGAATTCAGGCTACAGCCAC

ACCTGAGCCACTCTCAGATGAGGACCTA
```

As you see, the sequence is printed out formatted for the page with the names of restriction enzymes appearing above their recognition sites.

Resources

- The primary resource for this section is the Restriction Enzyme Database web site found at *http://www.neb.com/rebase.*
- See the discussion of making restriction maps in O'Reilly's *Beginning Perl for Bioinformatics.*

Exercises

Exercise 5.1

Why use the object-oriented approach for the interface to the Rebase database at all? What are the benefits and detriments of going to the object-oriented style?

Exercise 5.2

The Restriction.pm module uses another module in a new way. Instead of inheriting the Rebase.pm class, it requires that a Rebase object be passed to the constructor Restriction->new to become one of the attributes of the Restriction object.

Consider alternative ways to write this code. Can Restriction inherit Rebase and achieve the same functionality? If so, write the code. Or, can the same functionality be achieved by some method that avoids having a Rebase object passed as an argument to a Restriction object? If so, write the code.

Exercise 5.3

Go to CPAN and read the documentation about the MLDBM module. It allows you to use a DBM file to store and retrieve complex data. Rewrite the Rebase.pm module to use MLDBM and replace my use of space-separated strings of recognition sites and regular expressions.

Exercise 5.4

As discussed in the text, there are some interesting considerations involved in parsing the data that relates to how the restriction enzymes actually work, such as handling reverse complements of recognition sites and cut sites. The logic used here to handle reverse complements might not be ideal for all situations. Review carefully the logic of the parse_rebase subroutine. Can you find any problems its logic might cause when you try to use the software to support a particular experiment?

Exercise 5.5

It would be nice to be able to ask some method in Restriction.pm if a particular restriction enzyme produces sticky ends at its cut site. It would also be useful to know what other enzymes create sticky ends that will anneal with the sticky ends of this enzyme. Check to see if this information appears in any of the datafiles of the Rebase database. Can you design a method that returns this information, given the name of a restriction enzyme? What changes do you have to make to your database; do you need any more datafiles from the Rebase distribution?

Exercise 5.6

Describe in detail how the logic for map_enzyme works. Can you devise a different way to accomplish the same thing?

Exercise 5.7

The code in this chapter uses the class Restriction as a base class for the class Restrictionmap which lets you make a graphic display of the restriction map. Would it be a better idea just to add the graphics capabilities to the Restriction class instead of inheriting it into a new class? Rewrite Restriction to add the graphics capability to it. What are the pros and cons of these two different ways of writing and organizing the code?

Exercise 5.8

In the method _formatrestrictionmap, some lines of code are commented out that shorten the output by not printing extra blank lines. Try it out both ways. (And may God have mercy on your souls.) Do you think it makes the output less lengthy at the expense of making it more difficult to read? What is the tradeoff here? Do you prefer the longer or shorter version? Defend your preference.

Exercise 5.9

Add position numbers to the output of Restrictionmap. Add the position of the first base in each line or the position of each restriction enzyme.

Exercise 5.10

The _drawmap_text method of the Restrictionmap class is a bit lengthy and involved. See if you can improve the method. Either alter the code in the book or start from scratch. Improve it by making it faster, simpler, or easier to read. Try making its output better or add options to make the output more flexible. Try any combination of the above.

Exercise 5.11

String copying is a great way to slow down a program. Consider the code I gave for the following subroutine:

```
sub complementIUB {
    my($seq) = @_;

    (my $com = $seq) =~ tr [ACGTRYMKSWBDHVNacgtrymkswbdhvn]
                           [TGCAYRKMWSVHDBNtgcayrkmwsvhdbn];

    return $com;
}
```

Explain why the subroutine is written in this somewhat slow way. Now, rewrite this subroutine to eliminate a string copy. (Extra challenge: there are actually two string copies here. Rewrite the subroutine another way to eliminate a string copy. Can you eliminate both string copies? Why or why not?) Also, what's with those square brackets around the arguments to the tr function?

Exercise 5.12

Consider the following lines from the subroutine IUB_to_regexp:

```
# Remove the ^ signs from the recognition sites
$iub =~ s/\^//g;
```

This operation is redundant because the caret ^ was removed from the recognition site in the subroutine parse_rebase. Why is it included here?

Exercise 5.13

Consider the following last two lines from the subroutine map_enzyme in Restriction.pm:

```
@{$self->{_map}{$enzyme}} = @positions;
return @positions;
```

How does the subroutine behave differently if the first line is changed to:

```
$self->{_map}{$enzyme} = \@positions;
```

Why does the subroutine return the array @positions since the return value isn't used in any of the code and the positions are saved in the object anyway?

Exercise 5.14

There is a difference in behavior and readability between the looping constructs for(;;) and for( ) or its synonym foreach( ). Try writing some small test programs that use these different loops and time them using the Perl modules Benchmark or Devel::DProf. Clearly, for and foreach are most useful when iterating through arrays, and for(;;) is most useful when iterating through numbers. However, there are places in the code presented in this chapter in which for(;;) iterates through an array using a scalar variable as a subscript counter (as $i in $array[$i].) Try finding and rewriting such loops using foreach; benchmark the two versions.

Perl and Bioinformatics

## CHAPTER 6

Perl and Relational Databases

Relational database systems are extremely important in all kinds of computing—commercial as well as scientific. The Perl programmer can perform most database manipulations from Perl programs using modules written for this purpose. I'll briefly review database lore and then concentrate on an introduction to the Perl modules that provide an interface to relational databases.

This and the remaining chapters of this book will continue to look at fundamental Perl topics but with this difference: these topics rely on Perl modules, not on new Perl syntax. The reason for this is a deliberate decision by the Perl language designers to keep the language itself fairly small and to move as much functionality as possible into modules. This decision is interesting and important, and it has the practical effect of making modules quite important in Perl.

First, I'll provide a quick explanation of database terminology and acronyms. Since I'll be discussing only relational databases, I sometimes say database to mean relational database. (They aren't synonymous in general, however.) I say DBMS (or database management system(s)) to refer to the software that provides database capabilities, such as MySQL or Oracle. Database or relational database refers to the definition and implementation of a particular collection of data in a DBMS, such as the examples I show later in the chapter. These terms, database for the data itself, and database management system for the software system that handles the data, are often used informally and interchangeably, and it's usually clear what is meant.

One Perl, Many Databases

There comes a time when disk files or the simple DBM hash database (that you've seen in previous chapters) just won't manage the data of a medium- or large-size project, and you must turn to relational databases. Although they take quite a bit more effort to set up and to program, they offer a standard and reliable way to store data and to ask questions about it.

There are two things that make relational databases standard. For one thing, they all follow a certain model of data structures, the *relational model*. These data structures have become a fixture in the computing world; they combine a level of constraint and flexibility that has proved its usefulness in many areas, including bioinformatics.

Almost all relational databases are programmed with a programming language called the Structured Query Language, or SQL. This is a fairly simple language that creates, populates, queries, and manages the kind of data structures relational databases provide. The combination of a standard data structure with a standard programming language is another reason relational databases have become so successful.

One thing that's not standard is the proliferation of relational database companies and their penchant for doing things their own way. This may sometimes be a marketing decision, but it's more often the natural process of evolution—of different sets of programmers having different ideas and making different implementations.*

This is important when you have some working database application that uses a particular DBMS such as Oracle, and you find that you have to port the application to work on another DBMS such as MySQL. Perhaps another database system has become significantly faster or cheaper, or your computer is replaced with a new one that supports a different database, or your computer center or CIO decrees that some new DBMS is now the mandatory standard. If your database application makes extensive use of a feature that is available only on your old DBMS, you'll have a lot of work ahead of you rewriting your software to make it work on the new DBMS.

Luckily, thanks to some expert Perl programming, there is a way to get around this proliferation of different DBMS with their special ways of doing things and their special extensions of SQL. In this chapter, I'll use the Perl DBI (DataBase Independent) module that provides a common interface to different relational database systems; it makes it possible to write SQL that will run on many different relational database systems with little or no change.

Still, unless you are subject to a decree, the problem that the Perl bioinformatics programmer faces at the beginning of a project is, "Which relational database system should I use?" It depends on the computer you're on and what DBMS is already in use, available, paid for, or known locally. There are very expensive systems, and there are free ones: we'll take a quick look at some of the alternatives and use one of the most popular free ones for the following examples.

The beginning programmer should be aware that relational databases are a large field of endeavor. Stop at any local bookstore with a good computer book section and

---

* When I first released software that used Perl for bioinformatics, I received a letter arguing that because C was available everywhere and Perl wasn't, Perl for bioinformatics was therefore a Bad Idea and I should use C instead. Of course, Perl is available everywhere now, including on the VMS systems that my correspondent was complaining about, and bioinformatics software is written in a variety of languages. He made the classic mistake of wanting to standardize a field long before it had settled down.

you'll see an impressive number of books dedicated to relational databases and SQL in general, and especially dedicated to working with specific relational database management systems such as Oracle, SQL Server (the database, not the language), Sybase, MySQL, etc. There are books devoted to specific tools for designing a database, managing a database system, and programming a database system. In the workplace, there are job titles and positions for people who specialize in these three areas, and more.

So, don't expect this one chapter to reveal all. Do expect it to explain the basic concepts, give you the lay of the land, and demonstrate a practical example you can use as a template as you begin to develop your own code. At the very least, you will want access to the documentation for the particular database system you will use in your own work.

Having given the obligatory warning, I'll also add that, unless you are tackling a fairly large project, relational databases aren't all that difficult to use. If they were, they wouldn't be so popular. You may well spend a lot of your programming time in the future dealing with databases, or you may just spend a little. If you expect it will be a lot, I recommend you do some further reading.

Relational databases are an important topic. Because they have their own software systems, language, and concepts, they are a bit of an additional challenge. Most bioinformaticians need to know the basics of how to use them; some specialize in them. This chapter will get you started.

Popular Relational Databases

Relational database management systems are big business. They account for a significant segment of the computer business. Large companies often use them to manage their internal affairs and their sales data. Universities manage their internal affairs, and their research projects with them. Various governments use them extensively, from the national to the local levels.

The industry leader at present for high-end systems is Oracle. Along with other DBMS vendors such as IBM, Microsoft, Sybase, Informix, and more, they provide large database systems that can handle large amounts of data, and many queries against that data, very quickly. They also provide design and management tools for the programming and support staff a large institution needs to maintain a database system.

Unfortunately, these very nice software systems are also very expensive. They have hefty price tags themselves, and they require high-end computer systems to run on.

From the top-of-the-line systems on down, there are many vendors and price ranges in the database marketplace.

The main contenders in the free DBMS marketplace are mSQL, MySQL, and Post-greSQL. These systems are all progressing steadily, even rapidly, in their abilities. I use MySQL in this book, but the reasons aren't terribly important. The code I write in Perl and SQL runs with little need for change on any of these systems. If you're in the position of actually having to decide on an DBMS to install on your computer, you can find the information you need on the home web pages for these systems.

MySQL is my DBMS of choice because it's free; suitable for small- to medium-size database projects; and runs on most operating systems found in the lab, such as Mac, Windows, and Unix/Linux. It lacks some features major systems have, but it has enough of them and is implemented well enough that many businesses and many research laboratories have found it quite suitable for their work. Approximately three million servers have it installed. On balance, it has very good performance.*

The details of MySQL are available, and you can get a free copy of it from *http:// www.mysql.org*.

Relational Database Definitions

A relational database is essentially a set of tables (*relations*) that are interrelated in certain ways. A table is a two-dimensional matrix with a name. Each table is composed of rows (*tuples*), and no two rows can have exactly the same values. Each row is composed of named fields (*attributes*); each field has a certain data type and a name, and a field can only contain one value.†

For instance, a table may be defined with the fields Name as a character string of at most 50 characters, an ID as an integer, and a Date as a special date datatype. Each row then has a Name, ID, and Date value. Tables 6-1 and 6-2 show a table called genename with three fields and three rows, and one called organism with two fields and five rows.

Table 6-1. genename

Name	ID	Date
aging	118	1984-07-13
wrinkle	9223	1987-08-15
hairy	273	1990-09-30

---

* MySQL's multithreading helps account for its good performance, but it lacks some of the more advanced features of other DBMS available. Competition between these DBMS is keen, however, and there has been a certain amount of jockeying for bragging rights as performance and feature sets are improved.

† As the name "relation" suggests to the mathematically inclined, each table represents a subset of the Cartesian product of the domains of the fields, in which each row is an element of the relation. However, the order of the fields in a table is not significant (because each field has a unique name), and that's an important departure from the standard set-theoretic definition of a relation.

Table 6-2. organism

Organism	Gene
human	118
human	9223
mouse	9223
mouse	273
worm	118

You'll notice that the tables each have a field with the same set of values as the other; ID in Table 6-1 and Gene in Table 6-2 use values from the same domain. (A typical domain is the set of positive integers, for example.) Such shared fields can be used to join information from two or more tables. For instance, given a gene Name from the Table 6-1, I can find its associated ID, and look for that value in the Gene field of the Table 6-2 to find what organism or organisms have a version of that gene.

In Table 6-1, the wrinkle gene has ID value 9223, and in Table 6-2, there are two entries in field Gene with value 9223, namely human and mouse.

Each row in a relation is unique and can therefore serve as its own unique identifier for the row. There may also be some smaller group of fields that, together, are unique for each row and for which removing any field destroys the uniqueness; such a group is a *candidate key*. Very often tables are defined so that each row has its own unique ID field (it may be called something besides ID) that alone may serve as a key; this usually is recommended.

In any event, some candidate key is designated as the *primary key* for the table.

If in another table there is a field with the same domain as the primary key, it can relate the information in the two tables. That field, in the other table, is called a *foreign key*, and the primary key's table is called the foreign key's *home relation*. In MySQL, foreign keys aren't specified as such; they are used only in joins, as you'll see.

In defining fields, you may also specify that no row has a null (undefined) entry in a field; this is required for primary key fields. Similarly, a foreign key is required to refer to an actually existing value in some field in its home relation. These constraints on the data are known as *entity integrity* and *referential integrity*.

Using some SQL statements, you can write a (very short) program that, given a gene name, returns the list of organisms in which a version of that gene is found (in this database). In fact, I'll do just that in the next section.

That's simple enough. However, there is a bit more to learn about designing tables that work well, implementing the tables in SQL, and writing the (Perl) programs that send SQL statements to the DBMS and that compute and display the results. These areas of database design, implementation, and application development, are often staffed by specialists in large projects. Each specialization has its own techniques and lore; each can be a full-time job, and there are even more areas of specialization than these. Most bioinformatics programmers know enough about each area to design and implement a web-based, database-driven interface to their laboratory, which is the basic skill set that I'm attempting to impart. Assuming you are a beginner interested in learning the ropes, the following sections and chapters will hopefully give you enough of a jump start to be able to tackle all these tasks for a small project and prepare you to attempt bigger jobs.

Structured Query Language

The Structured Query Language (SQL, pronounced "s q l" or "see quel") can be thought of as the working definition of a relational database. It provides the bioinformatics programmer with the wherewithal to create, populate, interrelate, query, and update a relational database on a computer system. Your DBMS comes with its own implementation of SQL, which will have all the basic commands plus some, or maybe all, the less-used commands and features in the standard definition of the language, perhaps even some special extensions to the standard.

SQL dates back to the 1970s when it was developed at IBM. The most widely used versions of SQL are based on the standard published in 1992 and commonly called SQL2. A newer standard called SQL3 is available and supports emerging database functionality such as object-oriented and object-relational data models. MySQL is based on a subset of the most commonly used parts of SQL2, with the goal of providing a very fast implementation of the key components of SQL. Some features of SQL3 are also being added.

SQL is actually a fairly simple language to learn. Most people find that getting an account established on their computer, reading through a quick tutorial, and then having example code to copy and modify with the SQL documentation close at hand, is enough to get started writing useful SQL code.

I'm not going to present an extensive SQL tutorial here, for three reasons. First, such tutorials are easily and widely available. Second, each DBMS has its own version of SQL, so the DBMS documentation (such as that which comes with MySQL, for example) is necessary and available to you anyway. Third, SQL is such a basically simple language that it's quite useful to learn the basics of it by simply seeing a few examples. That's the approach I'll take.

If you are new to SQL, the best way to get familiar with it is by using the interactive command-line interface to try out different commands. The following section demonstrates my Linux system running MySQL.

SQL Commands

First, I enter the interactive `mysql` program, providing my MySQL username ("tisdall") and interactively entering my MySQL account password:

```
[tisdall@coltrane tisdall]$ mysql -u tisdall -p
Enter password:
Welcome to the MySQL monitor.  Commands end with ; or \g.
Your MySQL connection id is 2 to server version: 3.23.41

Type 'help;' or '\h' for help. Type '\c' to clear the buffer.
```

Next, I ask for a list of all the databases that are defined in my MySQL DBMS:

```
mysql> show databases;
+----------+
| Database |
+----------+
| caudyfly |
| dicty    |
| gadfly   |
| master   |
| mysql    |
| poetry   |
| yeast    |
+----------+
7 rows in set (0.15 sec)
```

Creating a database

I want to create a database called "homologs". First, I create it, then I check that it's there, and finally I make it the active database with use `homologs;`:

```
mysql> create database homologs;
Query OK, 1 row affected (0.00 sec)

mysql> show databases;
+----------+
| Database |
+----------+
| caudyfly |
| dicty    |
| gadfly   |
| homologs |
| master   |
| mysql    |
| poetry   |
| yeast    |
+----------+
8 rows in set (0.01 sec)

mysql> use homologs;
Database changed
```

Creating tables

The next commands create the two tables for the homologs database. Initially they are empty. I ask to see the fields that have been defined with show fields (show full columns also works):

```
mysql> create table genename ( name char(20), id int, date date );
Query OK, 0 rows affected (0.00 sec)

mysql> create table organism ( organism char(20), gene char(20) );
Query OK, 0 rows affected (0.00 sec)

mysql> show tables;
+--------------------+
| Tables_in_homologs |
+--------------------+
| genename           |
| organism           |
+--------------------+
2 rows in set (0.00 sec)

mysql> show fields from genename;
+-------+----------+------+-----+---------+-------+
| Field | Type     | Null | Key | Default | Extra |
+-------+----------+------+-----+---------+-------+
| name  | char(20) | YES  |     | NULL    |       |
| id    | int(11)  | YES  |     | NULL    |       |
| date  | date     | YES  |     | NULL    |       |
+-------+----------+------+-----+---------+-------+
3 rows in set (0.00 sec)

mysql> show fields from organism;
+----------+----------+------+-----+---------+-------+
| Field    | Type     | Null | Key | Default | Extra |
+----------+----------+------+-----+---------+-------+
| organism | char(20) | YES  |     | NULL    |       |
| gene     | char(20) | YES  |     | NULL    |       |
+----------+----------+------+-----+---------+-------+
2 rows in set (0.00 sec)

mysql>
```

Populating the tables

Now, I've got a new database with two tables defined, and I'm ready to populate the tables. First, I verify that the genename table is empty by making a select command; then I issue three insert commands, one for each row that I want to insert in the table. After inserting the rows, I verify that the genename table now has the desired three rows by means of a select command:

```
mysql> select * from genename;
Empty set (0.00 sec)
```

```
mysql> insert into genename (name,id,date) values ('aging',118,'1984-07-13');
Query OK, 1 row affected (0.00 sec)

mysql> insert into genename (name,id,date) values ('wrinkle',9223,'1987-08-15');
Query OK, 1 row affected (0.00 sec)

mysql> insert into genename (name,id,date) values ('hairy',273,'1990-09-30');
Query OK, 1 row affected (0.01 sec)

mysql> select * from genename;
+---------+------+------------+
| name    | id   | date       |
+---------+------+------------+
| aging   |  118 | 1984-07-13 |
| wrinkle | 9223 | 1987-08-15 |
| hairy   |  273 | 1990-09-30 |
+---------+------+------------+
3 rows in set (0.00 sec)
```

Now, I repeat the same process to populate the other organism table:

```
mysql> show fields from organism;
+----------+----------+------+-----+---------+-------+
| Field    | Type     | Null | Key | Default | Extra |
+----------+----------+------+-----+---------+-------+
| organism | char(20) | YES  |     | NULL    |       |
| gene     | char(20) | YES  |     | NULL    |       |
+----------+----------+------+-----+---------+-------+
2 rows in set (0.00 sec)
mysql> insert into organism ( organism, gene ) values ( 'human', 118 );
Query OK, 1 row affected (0.00 sec)

mysql> insert into organism ( organism, gene ) values ( 'human', 9223 );
Query OK, 1 row affected (0.00 sec)

mysql> insert into organism ( organism, gene ) values ( 'mouse', 9223 );
Query OK, 1 row affected (0.01 sec)

mysql> insert into organism ( organism, gene ) values ( 'mouse', 273 );
Query OK, 1 row affected (0.00 sec)

mysql> insert into organism ( organism, gene ) values ( 'worm', 118 );
Query OK, 1 row affected (0.00 sec)

mysql> select * from organism;
+----------+------+
| organism | gene |
+----------+------+
| human    | 118  |
| human    | 9223 |
| mouse    | 9223 |
| mouse    | 273  |
| worm     | 118  |
+----------+------+
5 rows in set (0.00 sec)
```

Let's find out which organisms have a homolog of the wrinkle gene. My query has two stages. First, I get the ID of the gene and search for it in the ORGANISM table. Then I write it as a single SQL statement:

```
mysql> select id from genename where name = 'wrinkle';
+------+
| id   |
+------+
| 9223 |
+------+
1 row in set (0.00 sec)

mysql> select organism from organism where gene = 9223;
+----------+
| organism |
+----------+
| human    |
| mouse    |
+----------+
2 rows in set (0.00 sec)

mysql> select organism from organism, genename
    -> where genename.name = 'wrinkle' and genename.id = organism.gene;
+----------+
| organism |
+----------+
| human    |
| mouse    |
+----------+
2 rows in set (0.00 sec)

mysql>

mysql>
```

Notice how the last statement asks the same question as the two preceding statements combined.

Administering Your Database

Database administration encompasses such tasks as installing and configuring the DBMS, backing up the data, adding users and setting their various permissions, applying updates or new capabilities to the system, and similar tasks. If you just have yourself and a fairly small lab to deal with, it's not too bad. But organizations often hire one or more database administrators to do this work full time; even a smallish project, if it's critical and the budget exists, can benefit from the attention of a professional database administrator.

If you are a beginning programmer and need to install and maintain a database management system, you'll need to read the manuals and learn the tools. Even if you have some computer administration experience, there is a bit of learning involved. The best thing you can do is get help from an experienced database administrator.

Failing such expert help, it's necessary to get good documentation and follow it. This depends on the system you're using, of course. The following sections describe some of the basics.

Adding Users

One function a database administrator needs to know is how to add users and set their permissions, that is, what operations they're allowed to perform, and what resources they're allowed to view or change. In MySQL, for example, each user needs an account name and a password for access (these aren't tied to the rest of the account names and passwords on the computer system). Security can be important as well. You may use the database to manage your new data and results, which you don't want to release to the public just yet; at the same time, you may be providing the public, through a web site, access to your more established data and results. A system such as MySQL provides several tools to set up and manage accounts and security permissions.

Backup and Reloading

One essential task for any computer system's effort, including working with databases, is to back up your work. All computers will break; every disk drive will crash and become inoperable. If you don't have timely backups of your data, you will certainly lose it.

There are many ways to back up data; even MySQL has more than one method. However, even if you back up your data from the database to a backup file, it's still necessary to make a copy of the backup file in another location that's not on the same hard disk. For the small to medium project, it's possible to run a program that simply makes a text file containing MySQL commands that repopulates your database. This is often a convenient and workable method, but check the MySQL documentation if you wish for alternatives.

Here, then, is how you can make a backup, or dump, of a database, in this case to the disk file `homologs.dump`:

```
[tisdall@coltrane development]$ mysqldump homologs -u tisdall -p > homologs.dump
Enter password:
[tisdall@coltrane development]$
```

After that command, a dump file called `homologs.dump` is created. Here's what it looks like for my little two-table database:

```
[tisdall@coltrane development]$ cat homologs.dump
# MySQL dump 8.14
```

```
#
# Host: localhost    Database: homologs
#-----------------------------------------------------------
# Server version        3.23.41

#
# Table structure for table 'genename'
#

CREATE TABLE genename (
  name char(20) default NULL,
  id int(11) default NULL,
  date date default NULL
) TYPE=MyISAM;

#
# Dumping data for table 'genename'
#

INSERT INTO genename VALUES ('aging',118,'1984-07-13');
INSERT INTO genename VALUES ('wrinkle',9223,'1987-08-15');
INSERT INTO genename VALUES ('hairy',273,'1990-09-30');

#
# Table structure for table 'organism'
#

CREATE TABLE organism (
  organism char(20) default NULL,
  gene char(20) default NULL
) TYPE=MyISAM;

#
# Dumping data for table 'organism'
#

INSERT INTO organism VALUES ('human','118');
INSERT INTO organism VALUES ('human','9223');
INSERT INTO organism VALUES ('mouse','9223');
INSERT INTO organism VALUES ('mouse','273');
INSERT INTO organism VALUES ('worm','118');

[tisdall@coltrane development]$
```

Once you've backed up your data, you can drop the database (wiping out the data) and then create the (empty) database again. You can then use your dump file to redefine the tables and repopulate them with your saved rows of data.

Here's how you might delete a database and reload it from your dump backup file homologs.dump:

```
mysql> drop database homologs;
Query OK, 0 rows affected (0.00 sec)
```

```
mysql> show databases;
+----------+
| Database |
+----------+
| caudyfly |
| dicty    |
| gadfly   |
| master   |
| mysql    |
| poetry   |
| yeast    |
+----------+
7 rows in set (0.00 sec)

mysql> create database homologs;
Query OK, 1 row affected (0.00 sec)

mysql> use homologs;
Database changed
mysql> source homologs.dump;
Query OK, 0 rows affected (0.00 sec)

Query OK, 1 row affected (0.00 sec)

Query OK, 1 row affected (0.00 sec)

Query OK, 1 row affected (0.00 sec)

Query OK, 0 rows affected (0.00 sec)

Query OK, 1 row affected (0.00 sec)

Query OK, 1 row affected (0.00 sec)

Query OK, 1 row affected (0.00 sec)

Query OK, 1 row affected (0.00 sec)

Query OK, 1 row affected (0.00 sec)

mysql> show tables;
+--------------------+
| Tables_in_homologs |
+--------------------+
| genename           |
| organism           |
+--------------------+
2 rows in set (0.00 sec)

mysql> select * from genename;
```

```
+---------+------+------------+
| name    | id   | date       |
+---------+------+------------+
| aging   |  118 | 1984-07-13 |
| wrinkle | 9223 | 1987-08-15 |
| hairy   |  273 | 1990-09-30 |
+---------+------+------------+
3 rows in set (0.00 sec)

mysql> select * from organism;
+----------+------+
| organism | gene |
+----------+------+
| human    | 118  |
| human    | 9223 |
| mouse    | 9223 |
| mouse    | 273  |
| worm     | 118  |
+----------+------+
5 rows in set (0.00 sec)

mysql>
```

Relational Database Design

Database design is the process of effectively organizing data into tables in a relational database. When thinking about how to organize a database you need to ask, "What fields should I put together into tables, and how should I interrelate the tables?" In this section I will show you a short example that demonstrates some common and useful techniques for doing just that.

Relational database software projects are best broken down into separate stages. This list from *Database Systems: a Practical Approach to Design Implementation, and Management* (see the "Resources" section), shows the typical stages of database design and construction:

> Database planning
> System definition
> Requirements collection and analysis
> Database design
> DBMS selection
> Application design
> Prototyping
> Implementation
> Data conversion and loading
> Testing
> Operational maintenance

For the small biology lab in which database programming may be a one-person project, some of these stages may be brief and informal, but they still apply.

How should the tables be defined for a new database? The answer depends on the problems to be answered by the data, but it's also largely a matter of common sense and a feel for the data. The database beginner typically looks at the data, tries her hand at a few designs, and begins to get a sense of how tables can be used for a specific problem. Let yourself experiment and try a few alternatives, and you'll soon get the hang of it.

Tables are commonly interrelated by indexing and by joining fields from different tables. The SQL language implemented with your DBMS provides these abilities. Also, a group of techniques called *normalization* can help you produce a good design and avoid some problems. Simply putting data into tables doesn't guarantee a good design.

A set of rules called *normal forms* helps you arrange the data into tables in a way that avoids certain problems. One such problem is *data redundancy*, which is unnecessary duplication of data in different tables. A related problem is *update anomalies* caused by having the same data in more than one location. When such data is updated, copies may not be updated properly, and the database can become inaccurate.

Here are some simple rules to follow when designing your database:

- Each entry of each table has a single value. This is *first normal form*.
- Each table has a a unique identifier (called a primary key) for each row. This is *second normal form*.
- Names aren't used as identifiers because they can lead to data redundancy.

Third and other normal forms as well as other design considerations aren't covered in this book due to space limitations. See the "Resources" section at the end of the book for more information about relational database design. Consider Table 6-3, which shows this alternate, unnormalized version of my homologs database.

Table 6-3. Unnormalized homolog data

Name	Date	Organisms
aging	1984-07-13	human, worm
wrinkle	1987-08-15	human, mouse
hairy	1990-09-30	mouse

This table has multiple values in some of the locations in the table. To put the table into first normal form, I make new rows for each multiple entry (see Table 6-4).

Table 6-4. First normal form homolog data

Name	Date	Organisms
aging	1984-07-13	human
aging	1984-07-13	worm
wrinkle	1987-08-15	human
wrinkle	1987-08-15	mouse
hairy	1990-09-30	mouse

In relational databases, a functional dependency exists between fields for which the value of one field is always associated with no more than one value in a second field. In Table 6-4, the value "wrinkle" in the Name field is associated with Organism "mouse" in one row, and with Organism "human" in another row. This isn't a functional dependency. On the other hand, the value "wrinkle" in the Name field is associated only with the value "1987-08-15" in the Date field. This is a functional dependency. In a real database, you need to ascertain that the test for a functional dependency will hold even as the database is updated; it requires knowledge of the use of the database and the possible range of values of the fields. In Table 6-4, the functional dependencies are:

```
Name        ->      Date
Date        ->      Name
```

The *primary key* is a minimal group of fields that uniquely identifies each row. In Table 6-4, I can choose the pair of fields Organism/Name or Organism/Date as a primary key. Remember, a field is fully functionally dependent on a primary key if removing any field from the primary key destroys the functional dependency.

Practically speaking, you can ensure second normal form by making sure each table has a field that is a unique identifier: usually this field has integer values such as 1, 2, 3, etc; no row is missing an identifier integer, and no two rows have the same integer. More formally, a relation in first normal form for which every non-primary-key field is fully functionally dependent on the primary key, is in second normal form. The rule-of-thumb solution is to divvy up the fields into new tables, and possibly add some new unique identifier keys. But how exactly do you do that?

Looking over the data, I notice that Gene and Date are always associated with the same values (say they represent a gene name and the date it was first reported). I can make a new table Genes (Table 6-5) out of them, with Gene as the primary key. I can then make a second table Organism (Table 6-6) from the Organism field, adding an ID field OrgID. Finally, I can make a third table Variants (Table 6-7) with its own field VarID unique for each row, an OrgID field, and a GeneID field. Table 6-7 contains a row for each gene in each organism in the database. Tables 6-5 through 6-7 show my new design for the homologs database (in second normal form).

Table 6-5. homologs database design in second normal form: Genes

Gene	Date
aging	1984-07-13
wrinkle	1987-08-15
hairy	1990-09-30

Table 6-6. homologs database design in second normal form: Organism

OrgID	Organism
1	human
2	worm
3	mouse

Table 6-7. homologs database design in second normal form: Variants

VarID	OrgID	Gene
1	1	aging
2	2	aging
3	1	wrinkle
4	3	wrinkle
5	3	hairy

Each table contains a field that isn't null, that is unique for each row, and that I can use as a primary key. Such keys are called *unique identifiers*. These are Gene, OrgID, and VarID, in Tables 6-5, 6-6, and 6-7, respectively. Notice that in each table the other fields are functionally dependent on the unique identifier row. And, finally, it's clear that the definition of "fully functionally dependent," which involves removing fields from a primary key, is satisfied when the primary key has only one field.

My tables are now in second normal form and are much improved. You'll notice, however, that there is still a problem of data redundancy, which can lead to update anomalies. If, for instance, the name of the "aging" gene was changed to "fountain of youth," three changes would have to be made to this database to keep all the data in sync. Using names as unique identifiers is a problem. Sometimes it works, but you must consider the operation of your database over time. In this case, genetic nomenclature may (and does) change. If I use a numeric ID as a unique identifier for a gene name, I can handle a gene name change by making a single update in only one table in my database (see Tables 6-8, 6-9, and 6-10).

Table 6-8. homologs database design: Genes

GeneID	Gene	Date
118	aging	1984-07-13
9223	wrinkle	1987-08-15
273	hairy	1990-09-30

Table 6-9. homologs database design: Organism

OrgID	Organism
1	human
2	worm
3	mouse

Table 6-10. homologs database design: Variants

VarID	OrgID	GeneID
1	1	118
2	2	118
3	1	9223
4	3	9223
5	3	273

Here's an example from my Linux system in which I drop the previous definition of the homologs database in my MySQL RDMS and redefine it with the three tables as just shown. I just define the tables here, but I don't populate them, as that will be done in the section "Handling Tab-Delimited Input Files":

```
[tisdall@coltrane tisdall]$ mysql -u tisdall -p
Enter password:
Welcome to the MySQL monitor.  Commands end with ; or „.
Your MySQL connection id is 9 to server version: 3.23.41

Type 'help;' or '\h' for help. Type '\c' to clear the buffer.

mysql&gt; drop database homologs;
Query OK, 9 rows affected (0.13 sec)

mysql&gt; show databases;
+----------+
| Database |
+----------+
| caudyfly |
| dicty    |
| gadfly   |
| jkl      |
| master   |
| mysql    |
```

```
| poetry   |
| rebase   |
| test     |
| yeast    |
+----------+
10 rows in set (0.12 sec)

mysql&gt; create database homologs;
Query OK, 1 row affected (0.00 sec)

mysql&gt; use homologs;
Database changed
mysql&gt; CREATE TABLE organism (
        orgid int(11) default NULL,
        organism char(20) default NULL
    ) TYPE=MyISAM;
Query OK, 0 rows affected (0.00 sec)

mysql&gt; CREATE TABLE genes (
        geneid int(11) default NULL,
        gene char(20) default NULL,
        date date default NULL
    ) TYPE=MyISAM;
Query OK, 0 rows affected (0.01 sec)

mysql&gt; CREATE TABLE variants (
        varid int(11) default NULL,
        orgid int(11) default NULL,
        geneid int(11) default NULL
    ) TYPE=MyISAM;
Query OK, 0 rows affected (0.00 sec)

mysql&gt; show tables;
+--------------------+
| Tables_in_homologs |
+--------------------+
| genes              |
| organism           |
| variants           |
+--------------------+
3 rows in set (0.00 sec)

mysql&gt;
```

I have only briefly introduced some of the techniques useful in the design of a small database. There is, of course, training and skill involved in database design, as well as certain standard (and occasionally competing) methodologies; far more than I have the space to introduce here.

Perl DBI and DBD Interface Modules

SQL is a fairly simple and easy-to-learn language, considered by most to be well-tailored to its task. However, there are things available in most programming languages, such as control flow (while, for, foreach) and conditional branches (if-else) that aren't provided in most implementations of the language. The lack of these abilities severely restricts the use of SQL as a standalone language.

Most applications that use a relational database are written in another language such as Perl. Perl provides a link between the application, the programmer, the user, the files, the web server, and so on. Perl also provides the program logic. The interaction between the application and the database is typically to execute some database commands, such as fetching data from the database and processing it using Perl's capabilities. The logic of the program may depend on the data found in the database, but it is Perl, not SQL, that provides this logic (for the most part).

In Perl, a set of modules have been written that allow interaction with relational databases. The DataBase Independent (DBI) module handles most of the interaction from the program code; the DataBase Dependent (or DataBase Driver) (DBD) modules, different for each particular DBMS, handle communicating with the DBMS.

Installing and Configuring Perl DBI and DBD Modules

To use a MySQL database from Perl, you need first to have installed and properly configured MySQL. This is not a Perl job, but a database administration job; you have to get MySQL and install it on your system and set up the appropriate user accounts and permissions.

You have to then install the Perl DBI module (*http://www.symbolstone.org/technology/perl/DBI)* using CPAN from the command line:

```
perl -MCPAN -e shell;
```

Then type:

```
install DBI
```

You can also install it by downloading the module from CPAN, for example, via a web browser and following the QUICK START GUIDE instructions shown here:

```
QUICK START GUIDE:

    The DBI requires one or more 'driver' modules to talk to databases.

    Check that a DBD::* module exists for the database you wish to use.

    Read the DBI README then Build/test/install the DBI by doing
            perl Makefile.PL
            make
            make test
            make install
```

```
Then delete the source directory tree since it's no longer needed.

Use the 'perldoc DBI' command to read the DBI documentation.

Fetch the DBD::* driver module you wish to use and unpack it.
http://search.cpan.org/ (or www.activestate.com if on Windows)
It is often important to read the driver README file carefully.
Generally the build/test/install/delete sequence is the same
as for the DBI module.

The DBI.pm file contains the DBI specification and other documentation.
PLEASE READ IT. It'll save you asking questions on the mailing list
which you will be told are already answered in the documentation.

For more information and to keep informed about progress you can join
the a mailing list via mailto:dbi-users-help@perl.org

To help you make the best use of the dbi-users mailing list,
and any other lists or forums you may use, I strongly
recommend that you read "How To Ask Questions The Smart Way"
by Eric Raymond:

  http://www.tuxedo.org/~esr/faqs/smart-questions.html

Much useful information and online archives of the mailing lists can be
found at http://dbi.perl.org/

See also http://search.cpan.org/
```

Finally, you have to install the Perl DBD driver for MySQL, called `DBD::MySQL`. Look in CPAN at *http://cpan.org/modules/by-module/DBD/* for the latest version; at the time of writing, it's *http://cpan.org/modules/by-module/DBD/DBD-mysql-2.1026.tar.gz*.

The combination of MySQL (the DBMS), DBD (the particular driver for your DBMS), and DBI (the Perl interface to the DBI and DBMS), is what gives the actual connection from Perl to the database and enables you to send SQL statements to the database and retrieve results.

Getting these components installed is sometimes the most difficult part of getting involved with database programming. Installing and configuring MySQL has several steps, and if you are very new to computers, you may find some of the instructions difficult to follow, as they may assume that you know more about your computer system than you do. DBI and DBD are typically much easier to install, but you may run into snags with them as well. The help of experienced hands, either directly or by means of the type of mailing list mentioned in the QUICK START GUIDE, can make the difference between days of frustration and a successful installation.

Handling Tab-Delimited Input Files

Let's say you have the components installed (MySQL, Perl, DBD, DBI), and you want to write a program that talks to the database. I'll assume you've implemented a new version of the homologs database as shown. We'll now walk through a small Perl example that shows how to read data in from a file, populate a database, send queries, and retrieve results.

First, here is the data as you might find it in a file. All the whitespace between the words is the tab character in the file, not space characters:

```
TABLE       ORGANISM
OrgId       Organism
1           human
2           worm
3           mouse

TABLE       GENES
GeneId      Gene     Date
118         aging    1984-07-13
9223        wrinkle  1987-08-15
273         hairy    1990-09-30

TABLE       VARIANTS
VarId       OrgId    GeneId
1           1        118
2           2        118
3           1        9223
4           3        9223
5           3        273
```

There are several ways to find the data in a database. It's common to have it in a plain file that has tables represented by lines, one table row on each line, with the field values separated by tabs or some other character that doesn't appear in any of the values of any field.

You should bear in mind that this is just one of several possibilities for the source and format of your input data. See the interesting book *Data Munging with Perl*, by David Cross (Manning) for lots of useful lore about getting data in and out of various sources.

SQL itself provides a utility for this purpose, called load, which assumes that you have a file consisting of only rows of data. You can specify what columns to load, what delimiter the file uses (tab by default), and a few other options. Its performance is optimized, and it is much faster than executing several SQL insert statements. However, you still need to read data in from files in different formats: what better than your own program that you can alter to suit any occasion?

To start developing such a utility, here is a short program to populate the database. It reads the file and knows the table it's reading, the field names, and the data for each row:

```perl
#!/usr/bin/perl

use strict;
use warnings;

my $flag = 0;
my $table;
my @table;
my @fieldnames;
my @fields;

while(<>) {
    if(/^\s*$/) {
        # skip blank lines
        ;
    }elsif(/^TABLE\t(\w+)/) {
        # output previous table
        print(@table) if $flag;
        $flag = 1;
        # begin new table
        @table = ();
        $table = $1;
        push(@table, "\nTable is $table\n");
    } elsif($flag == 1) {
        @fieldnames = split;
        $flag = 2;
        push(@table, "Fields are ", join("|", @fieldnames), "\n");
    } elsif($flag == 2) {
        @fields = split;
        push(@table, join("|", @fields) . "\n");
    }
}

# output last table
print @table;
```

This program understands the file format I gave previously, reads it in, and then reformats it and prints it out. It's just an example of how you might read in data. In the following, I'll modify this program to read in the file, but instead of printing out the (reformatted) tables, it sends SQL commands to the MySQL database to insert the data into the appropriate tables.

As you see, this first version of the program uses the $flag variable to keep track of what it's reading. Every time the input line begins with TABLE\t (that \t is a tab that actually shows up as whitespace), the program outputs the previously read table (if $flag indicates there was one). It then saves the next word as the table's name, sets the $flag to 1, and prepares some output in the array @table.

Otherwise, if the $flag variable is set to 1, the program knows it's on the second line of a table (remember, this program is specially written for the input file format I gave previously). In this case, it saves the names of the fields in an array, and then reformats them and adds them to the @table output array.

Finally, if the $flag variable is set to 2, the program knows it's reading rows of the table; it reformats them and adds them to the @table output array.

When all the input is done, and the while loop finishes, there will be the last table's reformatted output ready to be printed from the @table output array.

If I call this program homologs.getdata and give it my data file homologs.tabs like so:

```
% perl homologs.getdata homologs.tabs
```

I get the following output:

```
Table is ORGANISM
Fields are OrgId|Organism
1|human
2|worm
3|mouse

Table is GENES
Fields are GeneId|Gene|Date
118|aging|1984-07-13
9223|wrinkle|1987-08-15
273|hairy|1990-09-30

Table is VARIANTS
Fields are VarId|OrgId|GeneId
1|1|118
2|2|118
3|1|9223
4|3|9223
5|3|273
```

Notice that all I've really done here is read in the data and print it out in a slightly different format; among other things, I've changed the delimiter between fields from a tab to a vertical bar, a common type of task with these database dumps. But now, let's see how to interact with an actual database.

DBI Examples

Let's take the homologs.getdata program from the previous section and add the DBI calls to the MySQL database that will populate the MySQL database with the read-in data.

homologs.tabs

For starters, let's just see a Perl program that connects to the database, asks a simple question ("What tables are in this database?"), displays the results, and disconnects:

```
#!/usr/bin/perl

use strict;
use warnings;
```

```
# Make connection with MySQL database

use DBI;

my $database = 'homologs';
my $server   = 'localhost';
my $user     = 'tisdall';
my $passwd   = 'NOTmyPASSWORD';

my $homologs = DBI->connect("dbi:mysql:$database:$server", $user, $passwd);

# prepare an SQL statement

my $query    = "show tables";
my $sql      = $homologs->prepare($query);

# execute an SQL statement

$sql->execute( );

# retrieve and print results

while (my $row = $sql->fetchrow_arrayref) {
    print join("\t", @$row), "\n";
}

# Break connection with MySQL database

$homologs->disconnect;

exit;
```

Here's the result of running this program:

```
GENES
ORGANISM
VARIANTS
```

This program does the basic tasks that all DBI programs have to do, so let's examine them in useful detail.

After the obligatory use DBI; that loads the DBI module, I declare some variables to hold the string that specifies to DBI who is connecting to what and where. The actual connection happens here:

```
my $homologs = DBI->connect("dbi:mysql:$database:$server", $user, $passwd);
```

The connect method is asked to connect to the particular database (in this case the homologs database) on the local computer (localhost; this can be replaced by a URL of another computer) as the user with the given password. mysql is specified; if you are using another DBMS, you should change this to reflect your database system. Other optional arguments, not used here, are possible (see the documentation). The connect method is the DBI new method that creates (and initializes) a DBI object.

The output of the connect call is saved as a new DBI object in the reference variable $homologs.

Next, the DBI object prepares an SQL statement, and the result is saved as a new statement object, which I call $sql here. This statement object $sql then calls its own execute method which actually does the job of sending the SQL to the database.

The actual SQL here is a very simple one. You've already seen that DBI->connect specifies the particular database on your MySQL (homologs in this case). This SQL statement show tables simply asks for a list of the names of the tables that are defined in that database.

After execute, the program retrieves the results of executing the SQL statement. There are several ways to retrieve results. Here, the statement object method fetchrow_arrayref is called in a loop to fetch all the rows of the result; at each pass through the loop, the return value in $row points to the array of fields in that row. Here, I simply separate the fields with tab characters with the help of the Perl join function on the dereferenced array @$row and print the row with a newline.

The last DBI call is to disconnect from the database. This is actually an important call to make; depending on your implementation and how you're running your program, it is sometimes possible to open a number of connections and eventually tax the MySQL DBMS to the point where it has to refuse any more connect requests. Especially if you have an active database with regular queries coming in, you want to disconnect as soon as possible from each connect.

The program you've just seen is the kind of sample program you should run when you first try to install and use the DBI module. If it works, you're in business. If not, you have to closely examine the error messages you get to identify where the problem is. One thing that can help is to add an additional argument to the connect call that asks for more error reporting, like so:

```
my $homologs = DBI->connect(
        "dbi:mysql:$database:$server", $user, $passwd, {RaiseError=>1}
);
```

This terminates the program with extra error messages if the connect call fails; this is usually where things go wrong when you first try to use this software. (See the documentation for other such options to connect.) Remember that you need a username and password for MySQL itself, and that these aren't related in any way to the username and password on your computer outside of MySQL. You also need to have the database defined (e.g., the SQL statement create database life creates a database called life), and you have to have your MySQL permissions set properly to allow you to do the things you want to do, such as create or modify databases, or see other databases on the system. If there's a problem, ask your database administrator, consult your MySQL documentation, or visit the MySQL web site.

homologs.load

This next program does a little more than the previous; it reads in the tab-delimited file `homologs.tabs`, extracts the data, and uses it to load the tables in a MySQL database. Read it over: most of it will be familiar from previous programs in this chapter.

```perl
#!/usr/bin/perl

use strict;
use warnings;

# Make connection with MySQL database

use DBI;

my $database = 'homologs';
my $server   = 'localhost';
my $user     = 'tisdall';
my $passwd   = 'NOTmyPASSWORD';

my $homologs = DBI->connect("dbi:mysql:$database:$server", $user, $passwd);
my $sqlinit  = $homologs->prepare("show tables");
$sqlinit->execute();
while (my $row = $sqlinit->fetchrow_arrayref) {
        print join("\t", @$row), "\n";
}

my $flag = 0;
my $table;
my @tables;
my $sql;

while(<>) {
    # skip blank lines
    if(/^\s*$/) {
        next;

    # begin new table
    }elsif(/^TABLE\t(\w+)/) {
        $flag = 1;
        $table = $1;
        push(@tables, $table);
        # Delete all rows in database table
        my $droprows = $homologs->prepare("delete from $table");
        $droprows->execute();

    # get fieldnames, prepare SQL statement
    } elsif($flag == 1) {
        $flag = 2;
        my @fieldnames = split;
        my $query = "insert into  $table ("
                    . join(",", @fieldnames)
                    . ") values ("
```

```
                              . "?, " x (@fieldnames-1)
                              . "?)";
            $sql = $homologs->prepare($query);

        # get row, execute SQL statement
        } elsif($flag == 2) {
            my @fields = split;
            $sql->execute( @fields);
        }
    }
}

# Check if tables were updated

foreach my $table (@tables) {
        my $query = "select * from $table";
        my $sql = $homologs->prepare($query);
        $sql->execute( );

        while (my $row = $sql->fetchrow_arrayref) {
            print join("\t", @$row), "\n";
        }
}

# Break connection with MySQL database

$homologs->disconnect;

exit;
```

This program is called by giving it the name of the tab-delimited file on the command line (the same file used previously with the `homologs.getdata` program):

```
% perl homologs.load homologs.tabs
```

This is the output of the program:

```
GENES
ORGANISM
VARIANTS

Table: ORGANISM

1       human
2       worm
3       mouse

Table: GENES

118     aging       1984-07-13
9223    wrinkle     1987-08-15
273     hairy       1990-09-30

Table: VARIANTS
```

1	1	118
2	2	118
3	1	9223
4	3	9223
5	3	273

This `homologs.load` program is very much like the previous `homologs.getdata` program. However, instead of building an output array `@tables` and printing the text to the screen, `homologs.load` puts the data into the MySQL database using SQL statements. When the database is loaded, it retrieves the data from the tables and prints it to the screen.

Notice that each time `homologs.load` finds a new table, it first empties all rows of that table in the database and then proceeds to read in the lines of data and insert new rows into the table.

Notice also that when the program reads the line of the input file that names the fields (when `$flag` equals 1), it prepares the SQL statement, saving the object in the `$sql` variable. Then, when the actual lines of data are read (when `$flag` equals 2), the values of the fields are passed to the execute command, which sends the SQL command by the `$sql` object to the database system.

An SQL query

The SQL statement that is the argument to the `prepare` method is built up from information that the program knows at that point. Here it is again:

```
my $query = "insert into  $table ("
          . join(",", @fieldnames)
          . ") values ("
          . "?, " x (@fieldnames-1)
          . "?)";
```

This is a bit hard to read at first sight. However, it is typical of what happens when you use one language (Perl) to make a statement in another language (SQL). So I'll explain this one carefully as a good example of the breed.

The SQL query is formed by five strings that are joined by the dot (.) string operator—recall that `"r"` . `"DNA"` has the value `"rDNA"`. Here are the five strings being joined:

```
"insert into  $table ("
join(",", @fieldnames)
") values ("
"?, " x (@fieldnames-1)
"?)"
```

The question marks in the SQL statement are *bind variables* that are passed the values from the `@fields` array when the execute statement is called with:

```
$sql->execute( @fields );
```

If the query is called with:

```
$table = EXONS
```

and:

```
@fieldnames = (Exon, Position)
```

the resulting SQL statement is:

```
"insert into  EXONS (Exon,Position) values (?, ?)"
```

How does this statement get constructed? Let's look at it in detail:

- The first string just interpolates the table name EXONS into the string.
- The second string joins the field names with commas.
- The third string appears as is.
- The fourth string uses the Perl x string operator to make a new string that has a certain number of copies of the original string "?, ". The desired number of copies is specified on the right side of the x operator. The string itself is on the left side of the x operator, "?, ".

  @fieldnames in a scalar context returns the number of elements of the @fieldnames array; I need one less "?, " than that plus an additional question mark without a comma (because no commas are allowed after the last item in the list in SQL). So, @fieldnames-1 is the desired number of copies of the string "?, ".

- The fifth string "?)" is just the last question mark and the closing parenthesis.

The final result is:

```
insert into EXONS (Exon,Position) values (?, ?)
```

As the Perl program reads in the data rows from the input file (when $flag equals 2), the values are placed in the array @fields and then passed as variables (to take the place of the question marks in the SQL statement that's been prepared) to the execute method, which sends the SQL statement to the database system. These question marks are the bind variables; here, I need one for each field, because I'll pass in the field values when execute is eventually called on this statement.

To check what actually happened to the database after the reading in and processing of the file is complete, the program sends an SQL query for each table to see what's in it. This is done with the SQL select command—a general-purpose command to get information out of a database that has a great many options.

Here, I'm asking to see all fields (*) from the database table, and because no restrictions are added, SQL shows us all the fields of all the rows. As before, the result of this SQL query is read using the fetchrow_arrayref DBI method in a while loop, and each resulting row is printed with tab-separated fields.

This last program homologs.load is a typical DBI program, interacting with the world through Perl (e.g., reading in files and displaying the results to the user) and also interacting with the database through the Perl DBI module and SQL statements.

A Rebase Database Implementation

In earlier chapters, I developed an object-oriented interface to Rebase that stores the data in a simple DBM hash database, and in this chapter I showed how to interact with a MySQL relational database management system.

Now, let's put the two things together.

In this section, I'll take the Rebase.pm module that implements the Rebase class and modify it to use a relational database instead of Perl's simple hash-based DBM database. I'll call the resulting class RebaseDB.

For a small problem like this, either approach works pretty well. In fact, on my computer, the DBM approach is considerably faster than the MySQL version.

The relational database implementation has a slower response due to the more complicated DBMS system involved and increased overhead in programming because a greater number of programming statements must be written. However, the reason for using it is probably clear: the relational database provides a lot more flexibility in making queries, organizing the data, and, especially, expanding the application to handle a greater variety of data.

This flexibility is very important. The Rebase database from *http://www.neb.com/rebase* includes several more datafiles, such as where to get the enzymes. It wouldn't be difficult to add a table or tables to store that information in the relational version of my Perl program; it would be a major pain to keep adding new DBM hashes for various complex relationships. So, I want a relational database because it has good *scalability* as the database application grows.

RebaseDB Class: Accessing Restriction Enzyme Data

Following is the code for a new class, RebaseDB, which aims to provide the same functionality as the previous class Rebase, but with a relational database instead of a DBM hash data storage.

In the interest of space, the code for the following subroutines isn't reproduced here; look for them in Chapter 5: revcomIUB, complementIUB, and IUB_to_regexp. They are, of course, included in the RebaseDB.pm module available for downloading from this book's web page.

```
package RebaseDB;

#
# A simple class to provide access to restriction enzyme data from Rebase
#   including regular expression translations of recognition sites
```

```perl
# Data is stored in a MySQL database
#

use strict;
use warnings;
use DBI;
use Carp;

# Class data and methods
{
    # A hash of all attributes with default values
    my %_attributes = (
        _rebase       => { },  # unused in this implementation
                        #   key   = restriction enzyme name
                        #   value = pairs of sites and regular expressions
        _mysql        => '??', #  e.g. mysql => 'rebase:localhost',
        _dbh          => '',   # database handle from DBI->connect
        _bionetfile   => '??', # source of data from e.g. "bionet.212" file
    );

    # Return a list of all attributes
    sub _all_attributes {
            keys %_attributes;
    }
}

# The constructor method
# Called from class, e.g. $obj = Rebase->new( mysql => 'localhost:rebase' );
sub new {
    my ($class, %arg) = @_;
    # Create a new object
    my $self = bless { }, $class;

    # Set the attributes for the provided arguments
    foreach my $attribute ($self->_all_attributes()) {

        # E.g. attribute = "_name",  argument = "name"
        my($argument) = ($attribute =~ /^_(.*)/);

        if (exists $arg{$argument}) {
            if($argument eq 'rebase') {
                croak "Cannot set attribute rebase";
            }
            $self->{$attribute} = $arg{$argument};
        }
    }

    # MySQL host:database string must be given as "mysql" argument
    unless($arg{mysql}) {
        croak("No MySQL host:database specified");
    }

    # Connect to the Rebase database
    my $user = 'tisdall';
    my $passwd = 'NOTmyPASSWORD';
```

```perl
    my $dbh;
    unless($dbh = DBI->connect("dbi:mysql:$arg{mysql}", $user, $passwd)) {
        carp "Cannot connect to MySQL database at $arg{dbmfile}";
        return;
    }
    $self->setDBhandle($dbh);

    # If "bionetfile" argument given, populate the database from the bionet file
    if($arg{bionetfile}) {

        $self->parse_rebase();
    }

    return $self;
}

# For this simple class I have no AUTOLOAD or DESTROY
# No "set" mutators: all initialization done by way of "new" constructor

sub get_regular_expressions {
    my($self, $enzyme) = @_;

    my $dbh = $self->getDBhandle;
    my $sth = $dbh->prepare(
        'select Regex from REGEXES, ENZYMES where
         ENZYMES.EnzId = REGEXES.EnzId and ENZYMES.Enzyme=?'
    );
    $sth->execute($enzyme);

    my @regexes;
    while( my $row = $sth->fetchrow_arrayref) {
            push(@regexes, $$row[0]);
    }
    return @regexes;
}

sub getDBhandle {
    my($self) = @_;

    return $self->{_dbh};
}

sub setDBhandle {
    my($self, $dbh) = @_;

    return $self->{_dbh} = $dbh;
}

sub get_recognition_sites {
    my($self, $enzyme) = @_;

    my $dbh = $self->getDBhandle;
    my $sth = $dbh->prepare(
        'select Site from SITES, ENZYMES
```

```perl
                 where ENZYMES.EnzId = SITES.EnzId and ENZYMES.Enzyme=?'
    );
    $sth->execute($enzyme);

    my @sites;
    while( my $row = $sth->fetchrow_arrayref) {
            push(@sites, $$row[0]);
    }
    return @sites;
}

sub get_bionetfile {
    my($self) = @_;

    return $self->{_bionetfile};
}

sub parse_rebase {
    my($self) = @_;

    # handles multiple definition lines for an enzyme name
    # also handles alternate enzyme names on a line

    # Get database handle
    my $dbh = $self->getDBhandle();

    # Delete existing tables, recreate them
    # Prepare statement handles with "bind" variables and autoincrement

    # ENZYMES table
    my $drop = $dbh->prepare('drop table if exists ENZYMES');
    $drop->execute();
    my $create = $dbh->prepare(
        "CREATE TABLE ENZYMES ( EnzId int(11) NOT NULL auto_increment default '0',
         Enzyme varchar(255) NOT NULL default '', PRIMARY KEY  (EnzId)) TYPE=MyISAM"
    );
    $create->execute();
    # Prepare filehandles outside of "while" loop
    my $enzymes_select = $dbh->prepare(
        'select EnzId from ENZYMES where Enzyme=?'
    );
    my $enzymes_insert =  $dbh->prepare(
        'insert ENZYMES ( EnzId, Enzyme ) values ( NULL, ? )'
    );

    # SITES table
    $drop = $dbh->prepare('drop table if exists SITES');
    $drop->execute();
    $create = $dbh->prepare(
        "CREATE TABLE SITES ( SiteId int(11) NOT NULL auto_increment default '0',
         EnzId int(11) NOT NULL default '0', Site varchar(255) NOT NULL default '',
         PRIMARY KEY  (SiteId)) TYPE=MyISAM"
    );
```

```perl
$create->execute( );
# Prepare filehandles outside of "while" loop
my $sites_insert = $dbh->prepare(
    'insert SITES ( SiteId, EnzId, Site ) values ( NULL, ?, ? )'
);
my $sites_select = $dbh->prepare(
    'select EnzId, Site from SITES where EnzId=? and Site=?'
);
my $sitesrevcom_select = $dbh->prepare(
    'select EnzId, Site from SITES where EnzId=? and Site=?'
);

# REGEXES table
$drop = $dbh->prepare('drop table if exists REGEXES');
$drop->execute( );
$create = $dbh->prepare(
    "CREATE TABLE REGEXES ( RegexId int(11) NOT NULL auto_increment default '0',
     EnzId int(11) NOT NULL default '0', Regex varchar(255) NOT NULL default '',
     PRIMARY KEY  (RegexId)) TYPE=MyISAM"
);
$create->execute( );
# Prepare filehandles outside of "while" loop
my $regexes_insert = $dbh->prepare(
    'insert REGEXES ( RegexId, EnzId, Regex ) values ( NULL, ?, ? )'
);

my $lastid =  $dbh->prepare('select LAST_INSERT_ID( ) as pk');

# Read in the bionet(Rebase) file
unless(open(BIONETFH, $self->get_bionetfile)) {
    croak("Cannot open bionet file " . $self->get_bionetfile);
}

while(<BIONETFH>) {

    my @names = ( );

    # Discard header lines
    ( 1 .. /Rich Roberts/ ) and next;

    # Discard blank lines
    /^\s*$/ and next;

    # Split the two (or three if includes parenthesized name) fields
    my @fields = split( " ", $_);

    # Get and store the recognition site
    my $site = pop @fields;
    # For the purposes of this exercise, I'll ignore cut sites (^).
    # This is not something you'd want to do in general, however!
    $site =~ s/\^//g;

    # Get and store the name and the recognition site.
    # Add alternate (parenthesized) names
```

```perl
            # from the middle field, if any
            foreach my $name (@fields) {

                if($name =~ /\(.*\)/) {
                    $name =~ s/\((.*)\)/$1/;
                }
                push @names, $name;
            }

            # Store the data, avoiding duplicates (ignoring ^ cut sites)
            # and ignoring reverse complements
            foreach my $name (@names) {

                my $pk;
                my $row;

                # if enzyme exists
                $enzymes_select->execute($name);
                if($row = $enzymes_select->fetchrow_arrayref) {
                        # get its "pk"
                    $pk = $$row[0];
                }else{
                    # Add new enzyme definition
                    $enzymes_insert->execute($name);

                    # Get last autoincremented primary id
                    $lastid->execute();
                    my $pkhash = $lastid->fetchrow_hashref;
                    $pk = $pkhash->{pk};
                }

                # if pk,site exist go to top of loop
                $sites_select->execute($pk, $site);
                if($row = $sites_select->fetchrow_arrayref) {
                    next;
                }
                # and if pk,revcomIUB(site) exist go to top of loop
                $sitesrevcom_select->execute($pk, revcomIUB($site));
                if($row = $sitesrevcom_select->fetchrow_arrayref) {
                    next;
                }

                # Add new site definition
                #   since neither pk,site nor
                #   pk,revcomIUB(site) exists.
                $sites_insert->execute($pk, $site);

                # Add new regex definition
                $regexes_insert->execute($pk, IUB_to_regexp($site));
            }
        }
    return 1;
}
```

```
1;

=head1 RebaseDB

Rebase: A simple interface to recognition sites and translations of them into
        regular expressions, from the Restriction Enzyme Database (Rebase)

=head1 Synopsis

    use RebaseDB;

    my $rebase = RebaseDB->new(
        mysql => 'rebase:localhost',
        bionetfile => 'bionet.212'
    );

    my $enzyme = 'EcoRI';

    print "Looking up restriction enzyme $enzyme\n";

    my @sites = $rebase->get_recognition_sites($enzyme);
    print "Sites are @sites\n";

    my @res = $rebase->get_regular_expressions($enzyme);
    print "Regular expressions are @res\n";

    my $enzyme = 'HindIII';

    print "Looking up restriction enzyme $enzyme\n";

    my @sites = $rebase->get_recognition_sites($enzyme);
    print "Sites are @sites\n";

    my @res = $rebase->get_regular_expressions($enzyme);
    print "Regular expressions are @res\n";

    print "Rebase bionet file is ", $rebase->get_bionetfile, "\n";

=head1 AUTHOR

James Tisdall

=head1 COPYRIGHT

Copyright (c) 2003, James Tisdall

=cut
```

testRebaseDB: A Testing Program

The following test program testRebaseDB is taken from the RebaseDB.pm documentation and slightly altered.

```
use lib "/home/tisdall/MasteringPerlBio/development/lib";

use RebaseDB;

my $rebase = RebaseDB->new(
    mysql => 'rebase:localhost',
    bionetfile => 'bionet.212'
);

my $enzyme = 'EcoRI';

print "Looking up restriction enzyme $enzyme\n";

my @sites = $rebase->get_recognition_sites($enzyme);
print "Sites are @sites\n";

my @res = $rebase->get_regular_expressions($enzyme);
print "Regular expressions are @res\n";

my $enzyme = 'HindIII';

print "Looking up restriction enzyme $enzyme\n";

my @sites = $rebase->get_recognition_sites($enzyme);
print "Sites are @sites\n";

my @res = $rebase->get_regular_expressions($enzyme);
print "Regular expressions are @res\n";

print "Rebase bionet file is ", $rebase->get_bionetfile, "\n";
```

Here's the output of testRebaseDB:

```
Looking up restriction enzyme EcoRI
Sites are GAATTC
Regular expressions are GAATTC
Looking up restriction enzyme HindIII
Sites are AAGCTT
Regular expressions are AAGCTT
Rebase bionet file is bionet.212
```

Analyzing RebaseDB

Let's take a walk through this RebaseDB.pm class module to see how it uses the DBI relational database interface.

For starters, the %_attributes hash has changed to reflect the new relational database method. The _rebase key is no longer needed, but the bionetfile is again used to load the database; in the absence of this argument, the program attempts to use a previously loaded database.

Two new argument keys are present. _mysql gives the database name (e.g., rebase) and the user's computer (localhost if the user is running the program on the same computer the database is served from). _dbh holds the DBI object returned from the DBI->connect call.

The new constructor method has changed in significant ways. It checks the arguments a little bit differently, of course, because this version of the class has different arguments coming in. It then actually connects to the MySQL database using the DBI calls seen previously in this chapter. In case of failure, it doesn't carp or die; it prints an error message and returns—a much better behavior than just dying. If this were a web script, for instance, you might want to keep running so you can return more input from the user in case of failure.

In case of success, the DBI->connect object reference is saved in the attribute reserved for this purpose, $self->{_dbh}. (dbh stands for "data base handle".) Elsewhere in the module two methods are defined: the accessor method, getDBhandle and the mutator method, setDBhandle. They get and set this MySQL database object handle in the class attribute _dbh.

The program then calls the parse_rebase program. Let's look closely at this method and the workhorse that reads Rebase data in from a file and populates the MySQL database with it.

After retrieving as $dbh the object that points to the database, the method sends several SQL statements to the DBMS. These statements delete each of the three tables in this MySQL database called rebase, tossing out all their data in the process. The calls then create the tables anew (and empty).

This section of the code also prepares SQL statements that insert new rows with the values being passed in as bind arguments and selects various sets of rows. These SQL statements are used repeatedly in the while loop that follows, and the program saves time by having the SQL statements prepared just once before the loop.

I won't examine the various SQL statements in detail here. However, I do want to point out the use of autoincrementing on the ID field of each table. This option, applicable only to single-field keys that serve as the primary key for a table, has the effect of always picking the next value for the field, and is perfect for the unique ID field I usually want in a table as the primary key. It's just one less thing to worry about in the module. An SQL statement is also prepared that uses an SQL function to return the value of the last autoincremented key.

Now that the new database tables are fresh and empty, the program opens the bionet file and prepares to read it within a while loop. The beginning of this loop is unchanged from the previous version Rebase.pm because it discards the file header and blank lines and extracts the names of the restriction enzymes and the associated recognition sites.

First, the program checks to see if there is already a definition for the enzyme entered in the database; if so, it just retrieves its unique ID, the primary key $pk. If the enzyme hasn't been entered, it is now, and the ID that is automatically created for it is saved.

Next, the program checks if that primary key ID and site are already paired in the SITES table; if so, it goes back to the top of the while loop.

Again, the program checks if that primary key ID and the reverse complement of the site are already paired in the SITES table; if so, it goes back to the top of the while loop.

However, if the ID and the site are still unknown, they are entered into the SITES table, and the ID and the regular expression generated from the site are entered into the REGEXES table.

That wraps it up for the parse_rebase method. Because of all the database interactions, this is a pretty slow bit of code (see the exercises).

The only parts of the RebaseDB.pm module code we haven't looked at are the two similar methods called get_recognition_sites and get_regular_expressions. They retrieve all recognition sites (or regular expressions) associated with a given enzyme. The SQL statement in each of these methods is an example of a join of two tables:

```
select Regex from REGEXES, ENZYMES
where ENZYMES.EnzId = REGEXES.EnzId and ENZYMES.Enzyme=?;
```

(This is one SQL statement.) The statement asks for the regular expressions from the REGEXES table that have the same EnzID as the enzyme given in argument has in the ENZYMES table.

That's the end of my discussion of the RebaseDB.pm class module. See the exercises for suggestions on how to improve this module.

Additional Topics

In this short chapter, I have not mentioned several topics that are of considerable importance in database work:

- SQL has only been demonstrated, not fully laid out. It's a fairly simple language; if you'll be doing much database work, you should read the language manual that comes with your DBMS carefully, and look at several examples. Tutorial books are also available for most popular DBMS.

- Transactions are loosely defined as a set of database queries and modifications that belong together. For example, you may enter a new gene into your database by updating several relevant tables. If your system should experience a failure in the middle of such a set of updates, it can leave your database in an ill-defined state. By defining transactions, it's possible to avoid such undesirable states, and many DBMS now provide support for this view of database updates.

- Entity-relationship modeling is a top-down design methodology with a fairly simple graphics representation that signifies relationships between the data in a system.

- Stored procedures are parts of a database application that are performed at the point of entry when a user is filling out a form for instance. MySQL is just now starting to support them; major DBMS such as Oracle have had them for a long time. They tend to improve performance of an application when used well; they also greatly increase the difficulty of migrating to a different DBMS if that becomes necessary in the future.

- Object-oriented and object-relational databases are new data models that are finding some acceptance. You may come across them on the job, although their use is much more limited than the standard relational model.

Resources

The literature on databases is very large, and so the documentation for your particular RDMS is essential. For this book, I use MySQL, but many others are suitable.

Here are a handful of basic textbooks:

- *Database Systems: A Practical Approach to Design, Implementation, and Management*, Thomas Connolly and Carolyn Begg (Pearson Addison Wesley)
- *A First Course in Database Systems,* Jeffrey Ullman (Prentice Hall)
- *An Introduction to Database Systems*, C.J. Date (Pearson Addison Wesley)
- *MySQL*, Paul DuBois (SAMS)
- *The MySQL Cookbook*, Paul DuBois (O'Reilly & Associates)
- *MySQL and Perl for the Web*, Paul DuBois (SAMS)
- *Programming the Perl DBI*, Alligator Descartes and Tim Bunce (O'Reilly)

Exercises

Exercise 6.1

What's the difference between a database and a database management system? What's the difference between MySQL and Oracle?

Exercise 6.2

What are the limitations of the simple built-in Perl hash database DBM compared to a relational database? Its strengths?

Exercise 6.3

Is my homologs database, which was placed into second normal form, also in third normal form?

Exercise 6.4

Write a program that checks if a relation is in second normal form.

Exercise 6.5

RebaseDB.pm is written to specify a MySQL database. Rewrite the module so it can specify another relational database supported by DBI.

Exercise 6.6

The parse_rebase method of the RebaseDB.pm module uses several database queries per input line as part of the logic of avoiding duplicate entries for palindromes and reverse complements. Compare it with the parse_rebase method in Rebase.pm. Make a new parse_rebase method that works for both DBM and DBI database storage and will improve the efficiency of the DBI method by minimizing database queries.

Exercise 6.7

RebaseDB.pm is a port of the earlier version Rebase.pm that used the DBM hash database. Make a version of this module that handles both DBM and MySQL databases depending on the arguments passed to the new method.

Exercise 6.8

Compare MySQL with some other relational database management system; include such management issues as cost of purchase, cost of maintenance, availability of skilled personnel, stability of vendor in the marketplace, and customer support.

Exercise 6.9

Given the many possible alternate forms of a small set of simple relations, would you say that the relational model is not specific enough? What constraints might you add to improve the quality and reduce the number of possible relational designs?

Exercise 6.10

Name two bioinformatics problems that are ill-served by the data structures of a relational database.

Exercise 6.11

Implement a relational database that supports a project in your wet lab.

## CHAPTER 7

Perl and the Web

One of the basic skills of a programmer is designing and putting up an interactive web site. This is as true for bioinformaticians as it is for other programmers.

Not every bioinformatician will need to implement a web site. Your work in bioinformatics may specialize early; perhaps you work in analyzing algorithms for representing gene cascades, while web programming is someone else's responsibility.

However, the Web has become the principal way to provide programs to users. This is certainly true in biology, where it is typical for laboratories to provide programs and access to data via the Web. Collaborations can be promoted between research groups, the need for publication of results can be addressed (witness the many peer-reviewed journal articles that invite readers to visit web sites for supporting information), and valuable research tools can be widely disseminated.

This chapter provides a quick introduction to the way web pages and the Internet work, followed by a closer look at some important parts of web programming. You'll see these techniques applied to create an interactive web page that accepts a sequence and enzyme names and returns a restriction map.

Along with the remarkable growth in use of the Web and the Internet have come an equal proliferation of languages, systems, and tools for web programming. There are now a variety of choices in how a programmer can create interactive web pages.

We will use one such system that employs the Perl language. To make the web pages interactive—to enable users to type in queries and get responses—we'll use the popular CGI.pm Perl module that's shipped with all recent versions of Perl. CGI stands for the Common Gateway Interface, a protocol that provides dynamic web content— web pages that change for various reasons (such as a user asking for a restriction map)—as opposed to static, unchanging web pages. Perl and CGI were an early success story in programming the Web and remain widely available as a standard web programming technique. They constitute a basic skill set in web programming, despite the many alternatives now available.

Because bioinformatics programmers need at least a basic working knowledge of web programming, I'll teach you the skills necessary to put an interactive web page on the Web; the example is based on a continuation of the restriction map example from previous chapters.

To begin, I'll give a brief run down of the chief components of web technology to give you the basic overview and terminology you'll need to do web programming and to read further in the field. If you're already familiar with servers, browsers, HTML, and the other components of web programming, feel free to skip ahead.

How the Web Works

The *Internet* is short for "interconnected networks." It is a set of conventions—protocols—with which computers and networks can intercommunicate. Its development from earlier work before 1980 allowed many different networks to join and users on many computers to communicate. This communication was originally done in several ways, such as by *email*, electronic mail, and by *FTP*, file transfer protocol. These methods remain very popular and widely used.

It wasn't until the early 1990s that the World Wide Web or Web was born as a new Internet service. The Web was based on the new hypertext transport protocol or HTTP, and the first software to use it was in the form of programs called web browsers and web servers. *Web browsers* are programs that handle user requests and display results to the user; the most widely known web browsers include Internet Explorer and Netscape. *Web servers* are programs that accept requests from web browsers and send results back to them for display; Apache is the most widely used web server. With the development of web browsers and their ability to handle images as well as text, these new protocols sparked intense popular interest in computers. At the same time, computer costs were falling steadily, and their capabilities were growing, which made the new web protocol even more widespread.

The Web has become critical to scientific programming; in fact, it started there. The Web and its associated protocols such as HTTP were originally developed at a high-energy physics laboratory in Switzerland, CERN, and they have been heavily used in the sciences ever since. In biology, as elsewhere, the Web has become one of the principal means of communication.

URLs

The Web is essentially a two-part system of browsers and servers, in which browsers get results from servers and display them for the user. This type of architecture is called a *client-server* design, in which the client (web browser) requests service from the server (web server). Web browsers and servers are just programs that run on computers. They may both be on the same computer, or, thanks to the Internet, they may be on opposite ends of the earth.

In order for this scheme to work, the web browser has to be able to send its request to the web server. For instance, say you want to see the *New York Times* from your Internet Explorer web browser (or your Netscape, Mozilla, or other web browser). You have to know the location of the *New York Times* on the Web and type it into the space provided in your browser screen.

So, you type `http://www.nytimes.com`, hit the Return or Enter key on your keyboard, and the next thing you know you're reading the latest articles about human cloning and double-stranded RNA. How does this work, exactly?

The answer is really very simple. The web browser sends your request to the Internet; the actual location of the desired computer is determined, and your request is sent to the web server program on that computer. The web server handles your request and sends back a *web page* your browser then displays. This web page may include other URLs of specific articles. You can click on one, and the whole process is repeated, but this time your request is for a specific article, which is then returned to your computer and displayed by your web browser.

Behind this simple overall architecture are several steps. A basic familiarity with some of these steps and the associated terminology is needed in order to learn the fundamentals of web programming.

The location you typed in, *http://www.nytimes.com*, is called a Uniform Resource Locator or URL. The Internet (to which you must be connected for this to work, of course) takes the URL you typed in and, with the help of a network of computers and their routing tables that are configured for this task, resolves the URL into an Internet address (IP address), which is numeric. The address you typed in has a vague resemblance to English; *www.nytimes.com* is translated by routing tables into the numeric IP address.

The details of this are not important; if you know it, you can also just type in the numeric Internet address instead of the domain name. The advantage of this design is that it allows the routing tables maintained by the Internet to take a domain name and translate it to the correct actual Internet address. Then, if the *New York Times* changes its main computer, or decides to move to Paris,* all that needs to be done is for the routing tables to be updated with the new actual Internet address. You can still type `www.nytimes.com` and get to the proper web server without worrying about where it actually lives on the Internet.

A URL can have several parts:

- It begins with a *scheme*, which is "http" in this case and specifies the protocol for the request. "http" is the most common scheme; others include "https" for increased security, "ftp" for file transfer protocol, and so on.

---

* The *Paris Review* moved from Paris to New York, after all.

- A colon and two forward slashes (://) separates the scheme from the hostname, which is *www.nytimes.com*. This is the part that's resolved by the routing tables on the Internet; it gives the address of the computer with which you actually want to communicate.

- Following the hostname, several other bits of information may optionally appear in the URL, such as a particular location on the server's computer, a port number, some parameters to pass to the server, and other details that tell the server exactly what the browser is requesting.

  For instance, say you want to use the web page the reporters for the *New York Times* use to organize their list of helpful web sites. You'd type in http://www.nytimes.com/navigator. Now, following the hostname is the additional information */navigator*. This is a *pathname* for the particular web page you're interested in. It's just like a pathname of a file or directory on your filesystem. Sometimes it is longer, such as *http://www.nytimes.com/library/tech/reference/cynavi.html*, and includes several directories and subdirectories, and finally a filename (in this case, it's *cynavi.html*).

  These path names are relative to the way the web server is installed and configured; they tell the web server exactly what resource is being requested by the browser.

- Following the pathname may come other information. If the pathname is the name of a CGI program (discussed later in this chapter), certain arguments may be sent to that program; of course, these vary depending on the particular CGI program involved. The arguments or queries are separated by question marks and give desired values to parameters. A typical example might be *http://www.mycomputer.com/cgi/rebase.cgi?enzyme=EcoRI?enzyme=HinDIII*. This requests a web page from the web server on the computer *www.mycomputer.com*. The web page to be returned is generated on the fly by the CGI script on that computer in the file *cgi/rebase.cgi*. The URL also passes that CGI script the names of two enzymes (which the script will presumably use to formulate its reply), EcoRI and HinDIII.

Other information may appear in a URL, and other variations are possible. As one more example, if you had a web page saved on your computer in the file */home/tisdall/arabidopsis.html,* you can display it by typing the following into a web browser running on the same computer: *file:/home/tisdall/arabidopsis.html*.

If you have to manipulate URLs in your program (and you very well may at some point), there is a collection of modules available on CPAN called URI::URL that will make your life a whole lot easier.

HTML

The Hypertext Markup Language (HTML) is the language that embellishes text so that it can be displayed in a web browser.

There are two important parts of HTML. It formats text, specifying such things as paragraphs, italics, numbered section headings, and the like. Although text is the most common type of information displayed, other types of information such as images and sound are also commonly incorporated into a document.

The other important part of HTML is that it incorporates *hypertext links*, which make a document interactive by providing the user viewing the document in a web browser the ability to click on links and go to other web pages.

The basic idea of HTML is to *embed* within a document directions for how to display the document. The directions are rather vague, compared to real typesetting tools such as FrameMaker or Quark. HTML commands may be interpreted differently by different web browsers so that your HTML document can look considerably different when viewed by different people. This limitation was a deliberate part of the design of HTML and web browsers. The disadvantage of not being able to exactly specify how a web page appears is offset by the advantages of the simplicity of HTML and the possibility to view HTML documents on a variety of computers and operating systems.

HTML web page example

To demonstrate, let's see a short example of an HTML web page:*

```
<html>
<head>
<title>Double stranded RNA can regulate genes</title>
</head>
<body>
<h2>Double stranded RNA can regulate genes</h2>
<p>A recent article in <b>Nature</b> describes the important
discovery of <i>RNA interference</i>, the action of snippets
of double-stranded RNA in suppressing gene expression.
</p>
<p>
The discovery has provided a powerful new tool in investigating
gene function, and has raised many questions about the
nature of gene regulation in a wide variety of organisms.
</p>
</body>
</html>
```

---

* The Rebase web page that I'll develop in this chapter will give you a more complete example. Most web browsers allow you to see the HTML for whatever web page you're viewing by clicking on the Page Source link in the View menu of the web browser. (Your browser may use slightly different names, but all the major web browsers enable you to look at the HTML source by selecting a menu item.)

This HTML, if contained in a file, can be displayed in a web browser. If the file is on the same computer as the web browser you're using, you can display it easily. If it's on a different computer, the file has to be in a place your computer's web server has been configured to look.

For instance, if a file on your computer */home/tisdall/htmlexample1.html* contained the previous HTML content, you can type the URL into your web browser as so:

```
file:/home/tisdall/htmlexample1.html
```

and the browser would display something like that in Figure 7-1.

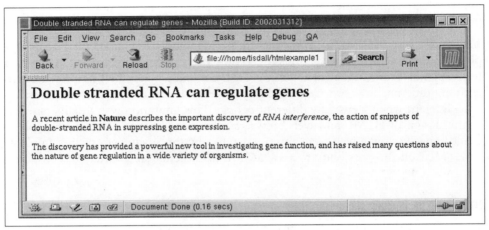

Figure 7-1. HTML example

I say "something like this" because many of the details of exactly how the text and layout appears are left to the browser program. The browser program may be set to use different font sizes or font types, break the lines at different places, display a different colored background, and, in general, specify locally several of the formatting options for the web page to be displayed. For example, the browser window may be very small, in which case the text will be reformatted to fit as well as possible into the available window size. Still, the basic content of the text should appear similarly to what is shown in Figure 7-1.

HTML directives

Let's take a look at how the HTML directives are embedded into the document.

HTML directives are mostly specified by enclosing them in angle brackets. The directives come in pairs, and the text between the opening and closing directive is affected. The second member of a pair has an added forward slash / before the tag name.

So, for example, to make a word italicized, you surround the word with the `<i>` and the `</i>` pair of tags. In the previous example, the term "RNA interference" is surrounded in this fashion, so it appears in italics in the browser.

The pair of tags `<html>` and `</html>` surrounds the entire document, and serves to delimit the HTML content for the web browser (or other HTML-reading program).

HTML documents have two major sections: the head and the body. The pair of tags `<head>` and `</head>` surrounds text that is related to the document as a whole. In Figure 7-1, there is only one item in the head section—a "title" that is displayed in the titlebar of the web browser. The title tags `<title>` and `</title>` surround the title "Double stranded RNA can regulate genes".

The head section can contain many different kinds of directives that influence the display of a document. It is followed by the "body" of the document which is surrounded by the tags `<body>` and `</body>` and comprises the rest of the document.

The body, in this simple example, has a header, paragraphs, and a few formatting directives, and it is surrounded by the tags `<body>` and `</body>`.

The headers can be of different levels, so you can make a document structure with primary headers and various subsections. This example specifies just a single header as follows:

```
<h2>Double stranded RNA can regulate genes</h2>
```

The first paragraph makes the journal name "Nature" appear in bold font, and the new term "RNA interference" appears in italics:

```
<p>A recent article in <b>Nature</b> describes the important
discovery of <i>RNA interference</i>, the action of snippets
of double-stranded RNA in suppressing gene expression.
</p>
```

Notice how the paragraph tags `<p>` and `</p>` surround a paragraph. (Actually, the closing paragraph tag can be omitted as a time-saving convenience; some very common tags have this feature, but most do not.)

The second paragraph contains only text:

```
<p>
The discovery has provided a powerful new tool in investigating
gene function, and has raised many questions about the
nature of gene regulation in a wide variety of organisms.
</p>
```

The following summary of the document highlights the major sections and omits the details within the head and the body:

```
<html>

<head>
  ... header information goes here
</head>
```

```
<body>
    ... the body of the document goes here
</body>

</html>
```

That's all there is to say about this simple example. Other features of HTML include embedded hyperlinks to web pages, email, and so forth. HTML has expanded in several ways over the last few years, and many more types of formatting are possible.

HTTP

The Web is based on a language called the Hypertext Transport Protocol, or HTTP. HTTP is the protocol that communicates between web browsers and servers.

Recall that in this chapter I'm using CGI to handle the communication between browsers and servers, and CGI can be thought of as a simplified interface to HTTP. So, it's necessary and useful to learn a few basic facts about HTTP before embarking on CGI programming.

HTTP works in a simple fashion. The browser sends a *request* which is made of a header and, often, a body. The server receives the request and sends a *response*, which is also made of a header and, sometimes, a body.

The first line of a request header is called the *request line* and contains the *request method*. The request method is usually GET. This is the most common request, and it asks for a specific resource from the web server, usually specified as a URL to be retrieved by a specific protocol such as HTTP.

The remaining lines of the request header are called *header fields* and consist of name-value pairs, which include such items as the hostname the request is being sent from.

The reply message also has a special first line called the *status line* which reports the protocol, a numeric code representing the specific response, and a text version of the response ("OK").

The remaining lines of the header contain name-value pairs of various other parameters. For instance, the name and version of the web server may be specified.

After the reply header may come the body of the response. This is always separated from the reply header by a blank line (actually a carriage return and line feed). In this case, the body of the reply is exactly the HTML code for the simple web page concerning RNA interference shown earlier.

There are many name-value pairs I have not mentioned and many other details that can have significance within this basically simple HTTP protocol scheme. However, this overview gives you the basic idea and the essential structure of the protocol that is exchanged between the web browser and the server.

Web Servers and Browsers

The whole architecture of the Web is based on the client-server, request-response protocol of HTTP. This colors everything that you do when you create interactive web pages.

Web browsers come in many flavors from many companies (or open source programming groups) and each has its own idiosyncrasies. Here, I'll stick to the basics, and the code should display okay on any standard web browser.

As you go forward, keep in mind the problem of incompatibility among web browsers and realize that at some point, it may become necessary for you to deal with the problem in the code you write for the Web.

The Common Gateway Interface

The preceding sections of this chapter have presented a brief overview of the design of the Web, the principal components of the programming environment such as HTTP, HTML, and URLs, and of the essential request-response nature of web interactions between web browsers and web servers. Now, it's time to look at CGI and a specific Perl module, CGI.pm, that is widely used to create interactive web pages on servers.

CGI, the Common Gateway Interface, is an interface between a web server and some other program that requests such web content as HTML documents or images.

A web browser may request from the web server the output from a *CGI program*. In this case, the web server finds the program or *script*, runs the program, and sends the output of the program back to the web browser. The output of the program may be HTML, just as it may be found in a static file, but it is created by the CGI script dynamically, so it may be different each time; for instance, it may include the time of day in its display.

In other words, a CGI script is just a program that produces web content that can be displayed in a web browser. It also can read information passed to it by the web server, usually parameters filled out by the user in a form displayed on a web browser that asks for the specifics of a query. For example, the parameters might be the name of a sequence file and the name of a restriction enzyme to map in the sequence. The CGI program takes the parameters, runs, and outputs a dynamically created web page to be returned to the user's web browser.

A CGI program can be written in just about any language, but the most common for CGI programs on the Web is Perl. Perl has a very nice module called CGI.pm that eases the task of writing CGI scripts; it's a popular way to create dynamic web sites with a minimum of bother.

Writing a CGI Program

So, how do you write a CGI Perl program? Basically, you write a Perl program that includes the line:

```
use CGI;
```

You then use the CGI.pm methods so that your Perl program outputs the code for the web page you want to return. After that, it's simply a matter of placing your new CGI script in the proper place in the web server's directory structure—namely, in a directory that the web server knows is supposed to contain CGI scripts. Finally, you type in the name of the CGI script to a web browser as a URL. The web browser sends the request to the web server, which executes the CGI script, collects its output, and returns it to your web browser to be displayed as a web page (or image, sound, or whatever).

You can actually write a Perl program that just prints out HTML code (without ever using the CGI.pm module) and install that as a CGI program. For instance, you can take the HTML page shown earlier and create a CGI Perl script that dynamically outputs that page. To prove it's dynamic, I'll add a little code that includes the time of day:

```perl
#!/usr/bin/perl

use strict;
use warnings;

my $time = localtime;

print "Content-type: text/html\n\n";

print <<EndOfHTML;
<html>
<head>
<title>Double stranded RNA can regulate genes</title>
</head>
<body>
<h2>Double stranded RNA can regulate genes</h2>
<p>A recent article in <b>Nature</b> describes the important
discovery of <i>RNA interference</i>, the action of snippets
of double-stranded RNA in suppressing gene expression.
</p>
<p>
The discovery has provided a powerful new tool in investigating
gene function, and has raised many questions about the
nature of gene regulation in a wide variety of organisms.
</p>
<p>
This page was created $time.
</p>
</body>
</html>
EndOfHTML
```

Notice that the program just prints out the HTML code. It also prints a header line: `print "Content-type: text/html\n\n";` before printing the HTML code as the body of the response. Notice the two \n's in that header line; these print a blank line between the header and the body of the response, as described earlier in this chapter.

Also, notice a new last paragraph that reports the time.

Installing a CGI Program

After writing the program, it is necessary to install it in the *cgi* script directory of your web server. Because of the multiplicity of web servers and operating systems, it is not possible for me to be comprehensive on this point. On my Linux system, using the Apache web server, I simply became superuser (root), copied the script (called cgiex1) into the directory */var/www/cgi-bin*, and then typed:

```
chmod 755 /var/www/cgi-bin/cgiex1
```

If you're working on a Mac OS X, the procedure is similar. If you're on a Microsoft Windows machine, the details are a little different; consult the documentation for your web server to see how to install a CGI script in the appropriate place.

Once I've installed the script, I simply entered the following URL into my web browser. Notice that the URL gives the hostname as `localhost`, which means the web server is on the same computer on which I'm using the web browser.

```
http://localhost/cgi-bin/cgiex1
```

I hit the Enter or Return key, and the web server returned the web page that's displayed in my web browser (see Figure 7-2).

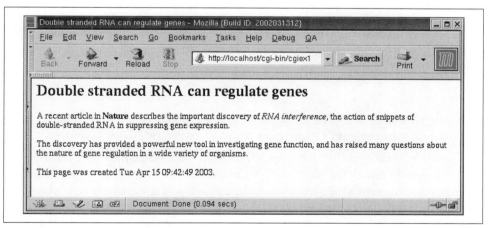

Figure 7-2. Web page for cgiex1

Notice that it's exactly the same as the previous version that just read a file, but this time, the current date on the web server is also being reported. So each time you run this program, you'll get a different output (as regards the date, that is). This qualifies the program as dynamic.

I'll go into more detail about CGI installation in the next section.

Using the CGI.pm Module

The following program was written using CGI.pm; it has the same output as the example in the previous section. Notice how almost the entire contents of this CGI script are a Perl print function with a list of arguments, ending with the argument end_html. The various arguments to print are either CGI.pm functions or text strings:

```perl
#!/usr/bin/perl

use strict;
use warnings;

use CGI qw/:standard/;

my $time = localtime;

print
header,
start_html('Double stranded RNA can regulate genes'),
h2('Double stranded RNA can regulate genes'),
start_form,
p,
"A recent article in <b>Nature</b> describes the important
discovery of <i>RNA interference</i>, the action of snippets
of double-stranded RNA in suppressing gene expression.",
p,
"The discovery has provided a powerful new tool in investigating
gene function, and has raised many questions about the
nature of gene regulation in a wide variety of organisms.",
p,
"This page was created $time.",
p,
end_form;
```

This program uses the most common routines defined in the CGI.pm module, as imported into the program's namespace by the directive use CGI qw/:standard/;.

The function header prints the header information discussed earlier in this chapter; it takes as an argument the document type and assumes the type is text/html by default. The function start_html starts the HTML and gives the title of the document (which most web browsers display in their titlebar above the document). The functions h1, h2, and so forth give the different levels of HTML headers in the document structure. The function p starts a new paragraph of text. Finally, the function end_form closes the HTML document.

Here is the body of the document the web browser receives for display from the CGI program cgiex1.cgi:

```html
<html>
<head>
<title>Double stranded RNA can regulate genes</title>
</head>
<body>
<h2>Double stranded RNA can regulate genes</h2>
<p>A recent article in <b>Nature</b> describes the important
discovery of <i>RNA interference</i>, the action of snippets
of double-stranded RNA in suppressing gene expression.
</p>
<p>
The discovery has provided a powerful new tool in investigating
gene function, and has raised many questions about the
nature of gene regulation in a wide variety of organisms.

</p>
<p>
This page was created Tue Apr 15 09:42:49 2003.
</p>
</body>
</html>
```

This simple web page is not much less complicated than the previous version cgiex1 that didn't use CGI.pm but simply output the HTML code. However, as you write more complicated web pages, with forms to be filled in by the user, choices to click on, and a button to push to submit a request, you'll see that using CGI.pm can significantly ease your programming work.

Testing a CGI Program

Let's assume the CGI scripts are where they should be, ownership and permissions have been assigned, and now your web server can find and attempt to execute them. So how do you test a CGI web program?

First, check the basic syntax by running:

```
perl -c cgiex1.cgi
```

and, hopefully, getting the message:

```
cgiex1.cgi syntax OK
```

If not, you can save a bit of trouble by at least fixing the syntax of your program before installing it in the web space, where you have to test it with the web browser and web logs and so forth, as I'll demonstrate in a moment.

Copy your CGI program cgiex1.cgi into your CGI directory (on my system, it's */var/www/cgi-bin*). I did this as the user root. Then, still as root, I made the program executable by typing:

```
chmod 755 /var/www/cgi-bin/cgiex1.cgi
```

Let's try the program out. Start up a web browser and type in the URL *http://ocalhost/cgi-bin/cgiex1.cgi* and hit the Enter key. Figure 7-3 shows what it looks like.

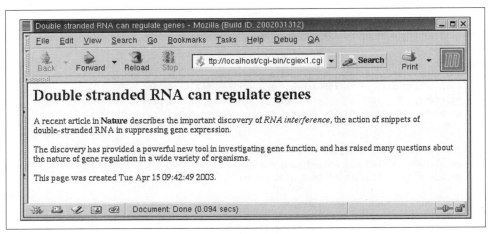

Figure 7-3. The results of a successful CGI program

It worked! But what would you do if it doesn't? Even though you check the syntax, the program may have had some other problem that caused it to fail. For this demonstration, I made another version of the program with a missing semicolon near the beginning of the program, called `cgiex1ouch.cgi`. When I ran it, I saw something like what's in Figure 7-4.

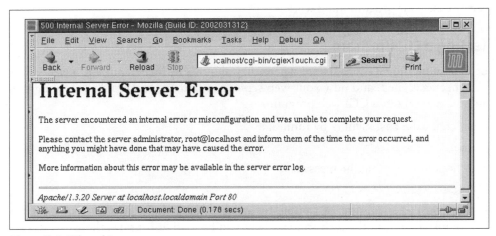

Figure 7-4. When things go wrong

The best way to proceed is to check the error logs for the web server to see if they give any useful hints as to why the program failed.

Again, this will be different on different systems. On Linux, Unix, and Mac OS X, some variation of the following will work. I determined where the error logs for the web server are kept on my system, which is in the directory */etc/httpd/logs*, and the most recent error log there is called error_log. I opened a new command window and typed the following command:

```
tail +0f /etc/httpd/logs/error_log
```

This prints out the error file, and then waits at the end. Whenever anything new is printed to the error file, it prints it out too. So, by hitting the Return key a few times to make space after what went before, and then trying to run the program again from the web browser, I can see clearly what new error messages resulted.

Here's what I saw in this example:

```
syntax error at /var/www/cgi-bin/cgiex1ouch.cgi line 6, near "use warnings

use CGI "
Execution of /var/www/cgi-bin/cgiex1ouch.cgi aborted due to compilation errors.
[Tue Apr 15 21:23:10 2003] [error] [client 127.0.0.1] Premature end of script
headers:
 /var/www/cgi-bin/cgiex1ouch.cgi
```

Sure enough, I'd removed the semicolon at the end of the use warnings statement.

For most web programming jobs, this is all you'll need, because the error log will show you the error output of the program. If it's a difficult problem, you can even put extra print statements in your CGI script—in the standard way they are used to debug a misbehaving program. For instance, you might see if a program ever gets to a certain line by placing directly after that line the statement:

```
print STDERR "Got to here!\n";
```

This message will appear in the error logs (if your program gets to that point before it dies).

Rebase: Building Dynamic Web Pages

The simple examples in the previous sections showed how to load and use the CGI.pm module to display a very simple web page and how to examine the error logs of the web server to help debug a CGI program that doesn't display properly.

The real power of CGI comes from its ability to provide dynamic content—web pages that may display different information depending on such factors as when they're called, such as the date and time in the previous example. Dynamic content also handles the requests of users that are entered by typing in text fields, clicking on so-called "radio" buttons, selecting from lists, or other ways of inputting.

In this section, I'll show you how to use some of the modules from previous chapters, combined with the use of the CGI.pm module, to make an interactive, dynamic web page for displaying restriction maps. In this web page, the user will select which restriction enzyme or enzymes to search for and specify the sequence to search either by entering the sequence data into a text window or by browsing for the file that contains the sequence.

Here is the short CGI program, webrebase1, that accomplishes this. The main reason that it's short is because I've already developed modules for reading sequence files, for accessing the Rebase database, for calculating restriction maps, and for displaying the maps with simple text graphics. I can just reuse those modules here to accomplish my task:

```perl
#!/usr/bin/perl

# webrebase1 - a web interface to the Rebase modules

# To install in web, make a directory to hold your Perl modules in web space
use lib "/var/www/html/re";

use Restrictionmap;
use Rebase;
use SeqFileIO;
use CGI qw/:standard/;

use strict;
use warnings;

    print header,
    start_html('Restriction Maps on the Web'),
    h1('<font color=orange>Restriction Maps on the Web</font>'),
    hr,
    start_multipart_form,
    '<font color=blue>',
    h3("1) Restriction enzyme(s)?  "),
    textfield('enzyme'), p,
    h3("2) Sequence filename (fasta or raw format): "),
    filefield(-name=>'fileseq',
        -default=>'starting value',
        -size=>50,
        -maxlength=>200,
    ), p,
    strong(em("or")),
    h3("Type sequence:  "),
    textarea(
        -name=>'typedseq',
        -rows=>10,
        -columns=>60,
        -maxlength=>1000,
    ), p,
    h3("3) Make restriction map:"),
    submit, p,
    '</font>',
```

```perl
    hr,
    end_form;

if (param( )) {

    my $sequence = '';

    # must have exactly one of the two sequence input methods specified

    if(param('typedseq') and param('fileseq')) {
        print "<font color=red>You have given a file AND typed in sequence: do only
one!</font>", hr;
                exit;
    }elsif(not param('typedseq') and not param('fileseq')) {
        print "<font color=red>You must give a sequence file OR type in sequence!</
font>", hr;
        exit;
    }elsif(param('typedseq')) {
        $sequence = param('typedseq');
    }elsif(param('fileseq')) {
        my $fh = upload('fileseq');
        while (<$fh>) {
            /^\s*>/ and next; # handles fasta file headers
            $sequence .= $_;
        }
    }

    # strip out non-sequence characters

    $sequence =~ s/\s//g;
    $sequence = uc $sequence;

    my $rebase = Rebase->new(
        #omit "bionetfile" attribute to avoid recalculating the DBM file
        dbmfile => 'BIONET',
        mode => '0444',
    );

    my $restrict = Restrictionmap->new(
        enzyme => param('enzyme'),
        rebase => $rebase,
        sequence => $sequence,
        graphictype => 'text',
    );

    print "Your requested enzyme(s): ",em(param('enzyme')),p,
    "<code><pre>\n";
    (my $paramenzyme = param('enzyme')) =~ s/,/ /g;
    foreach my $enzyme (split(" ", $paramenzyme)) {
        print "Locations for $enzyme: ",
        join(' ', $restrict->get_enzyme_map($enzyme)), "\n";
    }
    print "\n\n\n";
    print $restrict->get_graphic,
```

```
        "</pre></code>\n",
        hr;
    }

    print end_html;
```

Installing webrebase1

Installing `webrebase1` is almost exactly the same as installing the scripts seen earlier in this chapter, such as `cgiex1.cgi`. However, because this program depends on several modules, it is necessary to copy them into a directory that can be found by the web server. It's possible to configure a web server to look into any directory; you may prefer to leave your modules in one place and give the necessary permissions to your web server to look there. If your code lives in one place, there won't be any problem with out-of-sync duplicate copies.

However, there are security problems associated with letting the world execute programs from your own directories. Also, if you try out a change that doesn't work while you're tinkering with your code, any users on the web site will find the programs broken as well. So, often it does make sense to have a development area and a production area where you try to ensure that only working, tested, and secure programs are placed for public consumption.

On my Red Hat Linux system, I created a directory */var/www/html/re* and copied the modules `Restrictionmap.pm`, `Rebase.pm`, and `SeqFileIO.pm` there. On your system and web server, you may need to check that the existence, ownership, and permissions on that directory and those module files are suitable for your web server's configuration.

I then copied my CGI program `webrebase1` into my CGI directory (on my system, */var/www/cgi-bin*), and dealt with the same questions of ownership and file permissions as detailed in earlier sections of this chapter. (As they say down at the dealership, your mileage may vary depending on the operating system and web server that you are using.)

It's possible that the first line that invokes the Perl application, `#!/usr/bin/perl`, may have to be changed to run from your web space. Sometimes a web server is configured to restrict calling any programs from outside the web space, and a Perl application must be installed into the web space (usually with such extra security precautions as taint checks compiled into the application). If you plan to offer programs to the world from a computer that has sensitive information or is connected to other computers that have sensitive information, such precautions are often desirable. But just to get started, try using the same Perl application you've been using, and it's likely to work.

One consequence of running the `Restrict.pm` module is that the DBM file called bionet is created in your web server's CGI directory (*/var/www/cgi-bin* on my Linux system running an Apache web server). So, another thing to check is whether you have enough space for any files your programs may create in your web space.

Inside webrebase1

webrebase1 first loads the required modules: the ones you've written and the standard CGI.pm module.

The program has two parts. The first part is always executed, and displays the form that asks the user to enter the required information to run the program. The second part executes only when the program is called with parameters set, which happens after the user has filled out the form and hit the Submit Query button.

Let's look at the first part of the code that creates the form. Everything in this part of the form is one long print statement. The list of things to print is composed mostly of calls to various CGI.pm functions. For details on these functions, take a look at the CGI.pm documentation on *www.perldoc.org* or by typing perldoc CGI at a command prompt.

Here are the CGI functions called but not seen in the earlier programs:

h1('<font color=orange>Restriction Maps on the Web</font>')
> This is a header, as seen previously; however, it includes a color directive for the font.

start_multipart_form
> Makes the part of the form that handles file uploading work correctly.

hr Draws a horizontal line across the screen.

'<font color=blue>'
> Makes everything in the form blue, up to the closing directive '</font>'.

h3("1) Restriction enzyme(s)? ")
> This header, like similar headers in the form, labels the following textfield so the user knows what information is requested.

textfield('enzyme')
> textfield creates a place for the user to type in a line of text. The string the user types in is accessible by means of the parameter named enzyme when the form is submitted. The user can type in the names of enzymes such as EcoRI and HindIII to find more information.

p This starts a new paragraph in the form.

filefield(-name=>'fileseq', -default=>'starting value', -size=>50, -maxlength=>200,)
> filefield provides a way to give the name of a file that contains a sequence. When the form is submitted, that file is uploaded from the user's computer onto your computer where it can be used to find the restriction map. As you can see

in Figure 7-5, the user can type in the pathname of a sequence file or use a mouse to interactively browse until the desired sequence file is found.

The option *name* gives the name of the parameter that has the contents of the file; *size* and *maxlength* are the size of the field displayed and the maximum length of the filename.

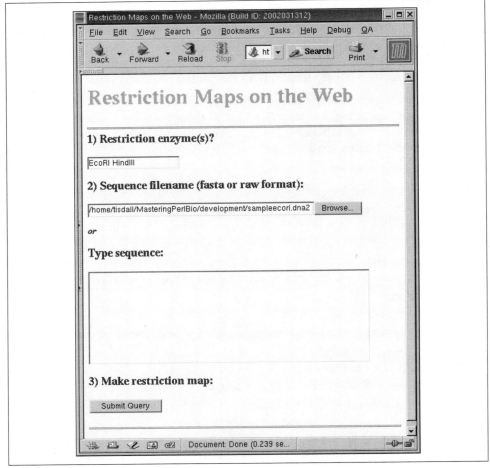

Figure 7-5. Rebase1 in a browser window

strong(em("or"))

This prints the word or in some strong fashion (usually in a bold font, but at the discretion of the user's web browser) and with some emphasis (usually in italics).

```
textarea( -name=>'typedseq', -rows=>10, -columns=>60, -maxlength=>1000,)
```
textarea provides a box in which the user can type or use the mouse to cut and paste the sequence directly, as opposed to giving the name of a file that contains the sequence.

submit

This button collects the values the user has given on the form into the named parameters and restarts the program by submitting the form to the web server, this time with the parameters set. webrebase1 has a section that uses the parameters to perform a computation, as you will see shortly.

end_form

This closes the start_multipart_form given earlier.

end_html

This CGI function is called at the end of the webrebase1 program, and it prints the final required HTML tags for the page before sending it back to the user's web browser.

When the user hits the Submit button, the parameters are assigned the values the user has indicated, and the program is called again. This time, after printing the form, the program gets to the conditional block beginning:

```
if (param()) {
```

The param() CGI function returns a true value if parameters have been sent to the program, so at this point the block is entered. The block does some error checking, extracts the information from the parameters, computes the restriction map, and displays the results.

The error checking ensures that all the data needed from the parameters for the computation to proceed is present.

Assuming the parameters have been set correctly, the program gets the sequence to be mapped from either the typed-in textbox field:

```
}elsif(param('typedseq')) {
    $sequence = param('typedseq');
```

or from the uploaded file:

```
}elsif(param('fileseq')) {
    my $fh = upload('fileseq');
    while (<$fh>) {
        /^\s*>/ and next; # handles fasta file headers
        $sequence .= $_;
    }
}
```

As you can see, the uploaded file is provided as an opened filehandle to your webrebase1 program. The while loop assumes that the file is in FASTA format (see the exercises for this chapter), skips the header, and collects the sequence.

After cleaning up the sequence by stripping out newlines and making it uppercase, the program then calls the Restrict and Restrictionmap modules to calculate the restriction map with the requested enzymes as available by means of the param('enzyme') CGI function call.

Finally, the program is ready to display the results. As you can see in Figure 7-6, the results appear after the form. First, webrebase1 prints out the names of the requested enzymes:

```
print "Your requested enzyme(s): ",em(param('enzyme')),p,
```

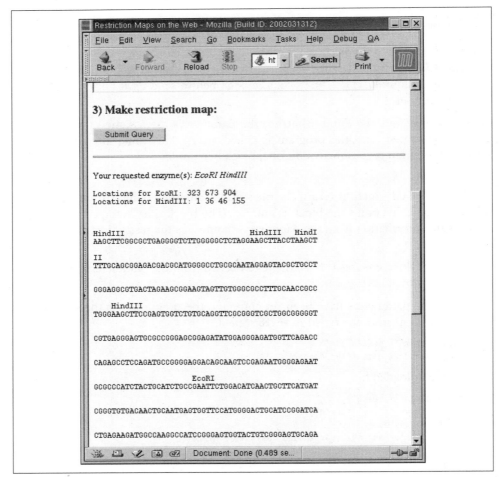

Figure 7-6. Results of the Rebase1 query

Recall that the trailing ,p, is a CGI directive to start a new paragraph; the em( ) CGI function asks the user's web browser to emphasis the text, probably by italics.

The next line is not part of CGI but is an HTML directive that ensures the following lines are printed in a fixed-width font. Every character will thus take the same amount of horizontal space, and all lines and spaces will line up just as they do when they're printed to your screen. Without this directive, the web browser could use a non-fixed font, and the map would improperly display:

```
"<code><pre>\n";
```

Of course, as you now know about HTML tags, they are almost always required to appear in pairs, so this directive has a closing tag after the map is displayed:

```
"</pre></code>\n",
```

The restriction map for each enzyme, by which I mean the simple list of locations for each enzyme in the sequence, is displayed by the following code:

```
(my $paramenzyme = param('enzyme')) =~ s/,/ /g;
foreach my $enzyme (split(" ", $paramenzyme)) {
    print "Locations for $enzyme: ",
    join(' ', $restrict->get_enzyme_map($enzyme)), "\n";
}
print "\n\n\n";
```

First the space- or comma-separated list of enzymes is collected from the parameter enzyme, and the commas, if present, are removed. The enzymes are then split (on whitespace) into a list, and for each such enzyme, the Restrictionmap method get_enzyme_map is called to display the list of locations.

Finally, the graphic map is displayed. This is accomplished, as before, by a simple call to the Restrictionmap method get_graphic, which returns a simple text version of the graphic (because graphictype => 'text' was specified when Restrictionmap object $restrict was created).

```
print $restrict->get_graphic,
```

Exercises

Exercise 7.1

Use your web browser to examine the actual HTML code for some of your favorite web pages. For example, on my Netscape browser, once a page is displayed, I can select the menu options View and then Page Source to see the HTML code.

Exercise 7.2

Identify the web server that is running on your computer. What version of the software is installed? Find the documentation for that web server. Are there good books available for that web server; free online tutorials, newsgroups, or FAQs; or local experts? Locate and examine the various logs for your web server. Where are the configuration files? How do you stop the web server, change a configuration file, and start the web server again? Is it a good idea to make a copy of a working configuration file before you change it?

Exercise 7.3

Is your computer located behind a firewall or a proxy server?

Exercise 7.4

Get the URL::URI module and read the documentation.

Exercise 7.5

Read the CGI module documentation. If available, look at a book about Perl and CGI.

Exercise 7.6

The sequence file uploaded by the CGI Perl script webrebase1 is assumed to be in FASTA format. Rewrite the program so that it uses the SeqFileIO.pm module and reports a problem back to the web page if that module can't determine the sequence file format.

Exercise 7.7

Write a new version of the CGI script webrebase1 that uses the RestrictDB.pm module instead of the Restrict.pm module; it will use a relational database store of Rebase information instead of a DBM hash-based store. Note that your DBMS will have to allow the web server to access its Rebase tables; this may occur as the user nobody or some other. Getting the permissions right is probably the hardest part of this exercise and is very much dependant on your operating system and web-server software.

Exercise 7.8

Write a web-based CGI Perl program that provides some information about your lab or an experiment that you've conducted. Include a means whereby users can send you email with questions.

## CHAPTER 8

Perl and Graphics

The importance of an attractive and useful graphical display of information is fundamental to scientific programming. Just imagine the difference between seeing a graph of this week's stock market activity, and seeing a list of several pages of numbers describing the same activity. The former can be surveyed in a glance; the latter requires considerable study. The same principle applies to the display of results in bioinformatics. Of course, sometimes you need the raw data; but very often what you need is the overview that a good graphic can provide.

Although there are many programming systems to produce graphics, the most popular are those that can be displayed via web browsers. This chapter builds on what you learned in Chapter 7 by showing you how to add graphics to your display of scientific results on a web page.

My vehicle of choice for displaying scientific data is the GD.pm module, which allows you to produce images in the standard graphics formats PNG (Portable Network Graphics) and JPEG (Joint Pictures Expert Group), among others. I'll also briefly mention the graphics packages ImageMagick and Gimp, two more full-featured graphics creation and manipulation packages.

GD.pm is an interface to the *gd* graphics library written in the C programming language by Thomas Boutell. The gd graphics library is fairly basic; it's fast, it handles text and various kinds of lines and space filling by means of its various functions, and it is easy to program elements such as graphs.

The main reason for its success, however, based on those important technical reasons, is that it makes it possible to produce nice-looking graphics from your web site on-the-fly, in immediate response to a request from a user submitting a form.

Computer Graphics

Computer graphics programming is a specialty within computer science, and it has its own journals and conferences and laboratories. It encompasses just about everything you can see on a computer, from the fonts with which letters are drawn (both on the screen, and when computer typeset and printed like this book), to elaborate images, animation, and the special effects in movies.

Computer graphics images are represented as data in the computer; they're usually organized in files, one per image, although they can also be stored in a computer program's memory, as I did when storing the graphics for the `Restrictionmap.pm` module in a scalar variable. Some kinds of animation store several images in one file, but I won't cover those kinds of image files here.

For the purposes of this chapter, we won't be digging into the details of how graphics files are designed; that level of detail isn't possible in a single chapter. Here, I'll just discuss the very basic information you need to get started generating and displaying images for your web site. I'm going to show you some easy (and inexpensive) ways to generate graphics, enough to set your feet on the right path. The modules I use have methods that handle the details of reading and writing the different file formats, so you can simply use the methods and ignore the details of the formats themselves.

Basic Graphics Concepts

There are two things you need for computer graphics: a program to create a graphics file and the correct software and hardware to display the image. These days, digital photography may be the source of digital images, or a printed image may be entered into digital format by a scanning device. As computer technology has developed, many graphics display devices and file formats have seen some use and then virtually disappeared as they are supplanted by other systems.* However, even though there are many file formats that are currently in use, a few standard formats are widely known and can be displayed by most graphics display programs. The PNG and JPEG files I use here are very commonly known.

Although I won't go into any detail about graphics file formats, there are a few basic facts you need to understand because you'll be asked to specify some of these parameters when you use a graphics library (such as `GD.pm`). For instance, in the Perl code that follows, you'll see a method `colorAllocate` that specifies and enters a color into a color table. The few short comments that follow in this section are meant to introduce these, and other common terms, and to give brief definitions.

---

* One of my first programming jobs was to write vector graphics for a Tektronix oscilloscope display. Vector graphics are specified by endpoints of lines. Although such graphic programs are still in use, they are almost always converted to raster graphics for display these days. The same year, I wrote a large graphics program to write and play computer music on a Blit terminal—a raster graphics display that was the first to have modern-style simultaneously updated windows. Both systems have faded away, but the software they were written in was ported to other display devices.

These days the standard graphics formats are mostly some variation of a *raster image*, in which a rectangular image is described by a two-dimensional matrix of pixel values. A *pixel* (short for "picture element") is one glowing dot on your computer screen. These values can be represented in different ways, from a simple 1 or 0 representing black or white (called a *bitmap*), to a number representing various shades of grey, to various color image schemes. A computer display may have different numbers of pixels overall; for instance, the one I'm working on now has 1024 horizontal and 768 vertical rows. Displays (or printers) are also rated by how closely packed the pixels are, usually by saying they have so many *DPI* or dots per inch.

Colors are typically represented in one of three ways:

RGB

> Colors might be represented in the RGB fashion by three numbers indicating the values for the primary colors red, green, and blue. All colors can be formed by mixing these values in different quantities. A typical standard is *24-bit color*, also called *truecolor*, in which each of the three primary colors is represented by an 8-bit value (256 possible values per primary color) for a total of over 16 million colors. This is well in excess of the 7 million colors most humans can distinguish, and as a result, a 24-bit color scheme is very popular, although many computer displays can handle only a smaller number of colors.

Color table

> Colors are also sometimes represented by a color table (also known as a palette), which uses 8 bits per color at each pixel, and uses the values as an index into a 256-slot table for a total of 256 colors. In this way, the image itself only needs to have 8 bits per color, instead of 24 bits, so the image can be much smaller as data. The drawback, of course, is that there are only 256 possible colors instead of 16 million; also, an image needs a color table in addition to the pixel values. Still, this scheme works quite well and is frequently used. Many computers give you the option of displaying using a color table or using truecolor.

CMYK

> The third popular way to represent colors is the CMYK color space, a subtractive color scheme used mainly in high-quality printing. The name CMYK comes from the colors cyan, magenta, yellow, and black, which can be combined to represent the range of colors, similar to the way that RGB does. I won't discuss this scheme further here.

Graphics and File Formats

I'm going to generate two kinds of graphics files in this chapter, PNG and JPEG. There are also many different file formats for computer graphics. Some of these different formats amount to little more than trivial variations in the header section of the files; others represent quite different ways of storing and displaying images on a computer screen.

PNG

Portable Network Graphic is a raster format that has become especially popular since the late 1990s when legal problems arose with the use of the very widely used GIF format. PNG can be used to create indexed color images (via the color table mentioned before) or to create 24-bit truecolor images. Because it does not perform compression on the image data, PNG is good for saving large images such as photographs because none of the photographic data is lost saving it in PNG format. But because images like photographs tend to be fairly large, and hence slow to display over the Web, PNG is best used for generating and displaying simpler graphics.

JPEG

Joint Photographic Experts Group is a popular format for displaying images, especially such large images as photographs. JPEG performs data compression, and although some of the picture quality is lost, the result is usually a good quality photographic image that is much smaller than the uncompressed original image. This has led to JPEG being widely adopted on the Web, where smaller picture sizes can dramatically improve the time it takes to download and display an image. (Displaying a JPEG image also requires decoding the compression, but that is a fairly fast operation on modern computers compared with the time it often takes to download a file.) However, the drawback to JPEG is exactly the same as its advantage: the compression. If you have a JPEG image, and want to do some editing of the digital image, you have to decode the image to perform the edits and then recompress it. But once an image is compressed, some of the original image data is lost. This compression/decompression will cause the loss of image data to become more apparent; several cycles of it can result in a noticeably poorer quality image. So it's best to save the original image in a noncompressed format, which can undergo editing without major loss of quality, and then create JPEG images directly from an uncompressed version.

GIF

An older file format which was standard on the Web and is still widespread, GIF (Graphic Interchange Format), has fallen afoul of some proprietary licensing issues; most Perl programmers have shifted to the similar PNG format which is in the public domain.

GD

GD is an excellent, relatively simple graphics toolkit for creating or modifying graphic images. You may create new images or read in images from several formats to edit or merge. GD contains a number of graphics *primitives*, objects such as lines and rectangles, which can be added to an image. It also includes support for TrueType fonts.

Installing GD

To install GD.pm on your computer, you should first test to see if the module is already there: try typing `perldoc GD` to see if the documentation that is installed with the module is running on your computer. If not, GD.pm is available from CPAN, which is the best way to get it (its real home is at *http://stein.cshl.org*).

The GD documentation explains which supporting libraries are necessary. In particular, you need to have Thomas Boutell's *gd* C library installed, and in the proper version, to work with the version of GD.pm you are installing. To work with different graphics file formats, the *gd* library is best compiled in the presence of additional libraries that handle PNG, JPEG, zlib compression, and the FreeType version of True-Type fonts. How to obtain and install these additional packages is all explained in the GD documentation. You may need extra time to get these various pieces into place before you can get GD to do everything it can do.

So, even if you use CPAN to install GD, the installation requires some information about those additional packages; it's a good idea to look at the documentation first, and to get those libraries in place, before installing GD. To install on my Linux system, I become root and issue the following commands:

```
perl -MCPAN -e shell;
cpan> install GD
```

Using GD

The following list is a partial overview of GD's capabilities:

- To create a new image, you call the new constructor with x and y values of the size in pixels of the desired image. You can also choose between a palette or a truecolor image. And you can either create a new image or open an existing image in a few common formats (such as PNG, JPEG, GD, and XPM).

- You can output images as PNG, JPEG, WBMP (a bitmap image format), or its own GD format and the compressed version GD2.

- The color table can be manipulated in several ways. A new color can be added or an old one deleted. The closest match in the color table to specified red, green, and blue values can be returned, and the RGB values of an existing color table entry can be determined. One color can be designated as transparent so that portions of an image drawn in that color are invisible.

- Lines can be drawn using defined "brushes," or in certain defined styles (like dotted lines, for example). Shapes may be filled with repeated copies of another image, or "tiled."

- You can draw individual pixels, lines, dashed lines, rectangles, polygons, and arcs. You can fill regions of the image (such as the interiors of rectangles) in various ways.

- You can copy regions of images, changing size if desired; you can also rotate and flip images.

- Text can be written in built-in or TrueType fonts, and rotated. Various methods return information about the fonts.

- A Perl module called GD::Graph adds some excellent graph drawing capabilities on top of the GD module.

In sum, GD.pm provides easy-to-program and attractive graphics capabilities for generating dynamic web pages (and for other uses as well). Now that you've had an introduction to the topic of graphics programming, and to the GD.pm module, I'll use GD.pm in a Perl script that generates images dynamically to display restriction maps.

Adding GD Graphics to Restrictionmap.pm

Now that you've seen an overview of the GD.pm Perl module, let's enhance the Restrictionmap.pm module that you've seen previously in Chapters 5, 6, and 7 so it can output PNG graphics files.

Reviewing how the Restrictionmap.pm module works, you can see that its get_ graphic method examines the _graphictype attribute to determine what graphics drawing method to call. Following is the get_graphic method again, along with the attributes the class defines. (Recall that this class inherits from the class Restriction.pm, so many things are defined there):

```
# Class data and methods
{
    # A list of all attributes with default values.
    my %_attributes = (
        #    key   = restriction enzyme name
        #    value = space-separated string of recognition sites => regular
expressions
        _rebase      => { },    # A Rebase.pm object
        _sequence    => '',     # DNA sequence data in raw format (only bases)
        _enzyme      => '',     # space separated string of one or more enzyme names
        _map         => { },    # a hash: enzyme names => arrays of locations
        _graphictype => 'text', # one of 'text' or 'png' or some other
        _graphic     => '',     # a graphic display of the restriction map
    );

    # Return a list of all attributes
    sub _all_attributes {
            keys %_attributes;
    }
}

sub get_graphic {
    my($self) = @_;
```

```
    # If the graphic is not stored, calculate and store it
    unless($self->{_graphic}) {

        unless($self->{_graphictype}) {
            croak 'Attribute graphictype not set (default is "text")';
        }

        # if graphictype is "xyz", method that makes the graphic is "_drawmap_xyz"
        my $drawmapfunctionname = "_drawmap_" . $self->{_graphictype};

        # Calculate and store the graphic
        $self->{_graphic} = $self->$drawmapfunctionname;
    }

    # Return the stored graphic
    return $self->{_graphic};
}
```

As you recall, the get_graphic method requires that some graphic type be defined in the _graphictype attribute. It then tries to call a method whose name incorporates the name of the graphic type; for instance, if the graphic type is "png", the get_graphic method tries to call a graphic drawing method called _drawmap_png.

How might you design such a get_graphic method?

Designing Graphics

There are several ways to construct a PNG graphic to draw a restriction map. You can extract the data necessary using _drawmap_text and its helper methods, _initialize_annotation_text, _add_annotation_text, and _formatmaptext. These methods use the methods of the Restriction class to get the locations of restriction sites for each enzyme and then make a text version of an annotated sequence string that shows the names of the restriction enzymes above their respective restriction sites in the sequence.

Having found the locations of the restriction sites in the sequence, there are many ways you can visually represent the map. You can incorporate a design of double-stranded DNA, for instance, to serve as a background to the actual sequence you can draw on top of the double helical design. You can use colors and different sizes and choices of fonts to make the restriction sites stand out. You can draw the annotation in various ways, perhaps giving the restriction enzyme and the location in some visually appealing way near the restriction site. You may or may not want to draw the entire sequence; perhaps you could truncate long stretches of sequence that have no restriction sites, for instance, to make the relevant information (the restriction site locations) fit better into a smaller, more easily grasped space, ideally on one screen.

The following _drawmap_png method uses the output of the _drawmap_text method and makes a PNG graphic out of it.

```
#
# Method to output graphics in PNG format
#

sub _drawmap_png {
    my($self) = @_;

    # Get text version of graphic
    my @maptext = split( /\n+/, $self->_drawmap_text);

    # Now make a PNG graphic from the text version

    use GD;

    #
    # Layout information: fonts, margins, image size
    #
    # Use built-in GD fixed-width font 'gdMediumBoldFont' (could use TrueType fonts)
    #
    # Font character size in pixels
    my ($fontwidth, $fontheight) = (gdMediumBoldFont->width,
        gdMediumBoldFont->height);

    # Margins top, bottom, right, left, and between lines
    my ($tmarg, $bmarg, $rmarg, $lmarg, $linemarg) = (10, 10, 10, 10, 5);

    # Image width is length of line times width of a character, plus margins
    my ($imagewidth) = (length($maptext[0]) * $fontwidth) + $lmarg + $rmarg;

    # Image height is height of font plus margin times number of lines, plus margins
    my ($imageheight) = (($fontheight + $linemarg) * (scalar @maptext)) + $tmarg
        + $bmarg;

    my $image = new GD::Image($imagewidth, $imageheight);

    # First one becomes background color
    my $white = $image->colorAllocate(255, 255, 255);
    my $black = $image->colorAllocate(0, 0, 0);
    my $red = $image->colorAllocate(255, 0, 0);

    # Origin at upper left hand corner
    my ($x, $y) = ($lmarg, $tmarg);

    #
    # Draw the lines on the image
    #
    foreach my $line (@maptext) {
        chomp $line;
        # Draw annotation in red
        if($line =~ / /) { #annotation has spaces
            $image->string(gdMediumBoldFont, $x, $y, $line, $red);
        # Draw sequence in black
        }else{ #sequence
```

```
            $image->string(gdMediumBoldFont, $x, $y, $line, $black);
        }
        $y += ($fontheight + $linemarg);
    }

    return $image->png;
}
```

_drawmap_png has a fairly straightforward logic, given that I just drew the same text as is formatted in the _drawmap_text method. So, it's no surprise that the first step of the _drawmap_png method is to get the formatted text. Recall that the lines of the text are joined into a string so the graphic can be stored in a scalar variable. So, the scalar string is split on newlines back into an array @maptext:

```
# Get text version of graphic
my @maptext = split( /\n+/, $self->_drawmap_text);
```

Now, the GD module is loaded:

```
# Now make a PNG graphic from the text version
use GD;
```

Next, various layout dimensions are calculated:

```
#
# Layout information: fonts, margins, image size
#
# Use built-in GD fixed-width font 'gdMediumBoldFont' (could use TrueType fonts)
#
# Font character size in pixels
my ($fontwidth, $fontheight) = (gdMediumBoldFont->width, gdMediumBoldFont->height);

# Margins top, bottom, right, left, and between lines
my ($tmarg, $bmarg, $rmarg, $lmarg, $linemarg) = (10, 10, 10, 10, 5);

# Image width is length of line times width of a character, plus margins
my ($imagewidth) = (length($maptext[0]) * $fontwidth) + $lmarg + $rmarg;

# Image height is height of font plus margin times number of lines, plus margins
my ($imageheight) = (($fontheight + $linemarg) * (scalar @maptext)) + $tmarg +
$bmarg;
```

GD includes a handful of built-in, fixed-width fonts. It also permits the use of True-Type fonts; however, although they are freely available, high quality, very extensive, and probably available on your system, they are nevertheless not available everywhere. As a result, I've decided to use a built-in font that's always available with GD.

However, as a result, the method has the font name hardcoded in a few places. (See the exercises at the end of the chapter.) For instance, GD built-in font names are objects with methods associated with them, in particular, methods that return the width and height of the font in pixels, which my _drawmap_png method saves in the variables $fontwidth and $fontheight.

Various margins are then set for the page as a whole and for the spacing between lines.

Finally, the overall dimensions of the image are calculated:

```
# Image width is length of line times width of a character, plus margins
my ($imagewidth) = (length($maptext[0]) * $fontwidth) + $lmarg + $rmarg;

# Image height is height of font plus margin times number of lines, plus margins
my ($imageheight) = (($fontheight + $linemarg) * (scalar @maptext)) + $tmarg +
$bmarg;
```

The comments explain the logic. Recall that @maptext is the array that contains the text to be formatted. $maptext[0] is the first line, which is either a full line and thus the maximum width, or it's less than a full line but is the only line, and thus the maximum width. (scalar @maptext) returns the number of lines in the @maptext array (because an array in scalar context returns the size of the array).

After those preliminary calculations, the constructor for the GD class can be called to create a new image object $image of the correct dimensions:

```
my $image = new GD::Image($imagewidth, $imageheight);
```

Applying color

The colors I use can now be allocated for the image object. In GD, the first call to the colorAllocate method determines the background color for the entire image. The triples of numbers are the red, blue, and green values that are combined to form the various possible colors:

```
# First one becomes background color
my $white = $image->colorAllocate(255, 255, 255);
my $black = $image->colorAllocate(0, 0, 0);
my $red = $image->colorAllocate(255, 0, 0);
```

Next, the x and y (horizontal and vertical) positions are initialized at the origin of the image to be drawn. In GD, the origin of the picture is 0,0 at the upper left corner. Increasing values of x move from left to right across the image; increasing values of y move from top to bottom down the image. Given that I want to have top and left margins, I set the image origin at the upper left corner, offset by the values of the margins:

```
# Origin at upper left corner
my ($x, $y) = ($lmarg, $tmarg);
```

Now, everything is set up, and it's time to draw the image. The text to be drawn is processed line-by-line; after each line is drawn, the vertical position $y is increased by the height of the font plus the interline margin.

There are two kinds of lines: sequence and annotation. I assume that each annotation line contains some spaces (this won't always be true; see the exercises).

Annotation lines are printed as strings in the color red, and sequence lines are printed in the color black.

```
#
# Draw the lines on the image
#
foreach my $line (@maptext) {
    chomp $line;
    # Draw annotation in red
    if($line =~ / /) { #annotation has spaces
        $image->string(gdMediumBoldFont, $x, $y, $line, $red);
        # Draw sequence in black
    }else{ #sequence
        $image->string(gdMediumBoldFont, $x, $y, $line, $black);
    }
    $y += ($fontheight + $linemarg);
}
```

Calling the method

Finally, after all the text lines have been formatted and added to the image, the png GD method is called on the image. This produces a PNG image, which is returned from my _drawmap_png method:

```
return $image->png;
```

Because that method was called by the method _getgraphic, the PNG graphic is both saved in the _graphic attribute and sent off to the user's browser, which knows how to display a PNG image.

In other circumstances you might want to save the image to a file, which you can do by opening a file, assigning it a filehandle (say IMG), and printing the $image->png output to the file:

```
print IMG $image->png;
```

Adding JPEG Output to Restrictionmap.pm

Let's consider how to add JPEG output to Restrictionmap.pm. I need a _drawmap_jpg method to handle the case when a JPEG image is requested by the programmer setting the _graphictype attribute to "jpg".

Looking over the GD documentation and the _drawmap_png method I've just written, I see that the last line of my _drawmap_png method:

```
return $image->png;
```

can be replaced by:

```
return $image->jpeg;
```

in order to output a JPEG format. So, here's my new _drawmap_jpg method, almost an exact duplicate of _drawmap_png (see the exercises at the end of the chapter).

```
#
# Method to output graphics in JPEG format
#

sub _drawmap_jpg {
    my($self) = @_;

    # Get text version of graphic
    my @maptext = split( /\n+/, $self->_drawmap_text);

    # Now make a JPEG graphic from the text version

    use GD;

    #
    # Layout information: fonts, margins, image size
    #
    # Use built-in GD fixed-width font 'gdMediumBoldFont' (could use TrueType fonts)
    #
    # Font character size in pixels
    my ($fontwidth, $fontheight) = (gdMediumBoldFont->width,
        gdMediumBoldFont->height);

    # Margins top, bottom, right, left, and between lines
    my ($tmarg, $bmarg, $rmarg, $lmarg, $linemarg) = (10, 10, 10, 10, 5);

    # Image width is length of line times width of a character, plus margins
    my ($imagewidth) = (length($maptext[0]) * $fontwidth) + $lmarg + $rmarg;

    # Image height is height of font plus margin times number of lines, plus margins
    my ($imageheight) =
                (($fontheight + $linemarg) * (scalar @maptext)) + $tmarg + $bmarg;

    my $image = new GD::Image($imagewidth, $imageheight);

    # First one becomes background color
    my $white = $image->colorAllocate(255, 255, 255);
    my $black = $image->colorAllocate(0, 0, 0);
    my $red = $image->colorAllocate(255, 0, 0);

    # Origin at upper left hand corner
    my ($x, $y) = ($lmarg, $tmarg);

    #
    # Draw the lines on the image
    #
    foreach my $line (@maptext) {
        chomp $line;
        # Draw annotation in red
        if($line =~ / /) { #annotation has spaces
            $image->string(gdMediumBoldFont, $x, $y, $line, $red);
        # Draw sequence in black
        }else{ #sequence
```

```
        $image->string(gdMediumBoldFont, $x, $y, $line, $black);
    }
    $y += ($fontheight + $linemarg);
}

return $image->jpeg;
}
```

To use this new method from the webrebase1 CGI Perl script, I'd have to change the requested graphictype attribute to jpeg; I'd also have to change the HTML header line that gets printed out just before printing the image data. Now, that line is set to:

```
print "Content-type: image/png\n\n";
```

but I'd have to change that to:

```
print "Content-type: image/jpeg\n\n";
```

You'll notice if you try that out, the JPEG graphic seems a bit blurry around the edges of the letters. This is a result of the compression algorithm that JPEGs use. They tend to work very well with photographic images, but the kind of text and line images that webrebase1 creates do not fare as well under JPEG compression.

Making Graphs

Displaying data graphically (graphs, bar graphs, pie charts, etc.) is the most common goal of image programming You've just seen how the GD Perl module helps you create graphics. It's great for quickly providing images from CGI web programs.

GD::Graph, another Perl module that uses GD as its underlying mechanism, does an excellent job of rendering all sorts of graphs. Programming graphs with GD::Graph is relatively easy, especially if you start with the example programs and modify them for your own purposes. The module is object oriented, and it provides many options for displaying the various graphs. Plan to take some time exploring the documentation and trying different options as you begin programming with GD::Graph. Its flexible yet relatively simple programming interface has made it a popular and powerful module. GD::Graph can be found on CPAN. It's simple to install once you have GD itself installed.

For more in-depth information on graphics programming in Perl, see *Perl Graphics Programming* by Shawn Wallace (O'Reilly). The book includes a chapter on GD::Graph that can serve as a fine tutorial. The documentation for GD::Graph (on CPAN, or type perldoc GD::Graph in a terminal window) is well-written and clearly organized. The software comes with several example programs that will help get you started.

The following short program, gd1.pl, uses GD::Graph to create a simple bar graph.

```perl
#!/usr/bin/perl

#
# gd1.pl -- create GD::Graph bar graph
#

use strict;
use warnings;
use Carp;
use GD::Graph::bars;

my %dataset = ( 1 => 3,
                2 => 17,
        3 => 34,
        4 => 23,
        5 => 25,
        6 => 20,
        7 => 12,
        8 => 3,
        9 => 1
);

# create new image
my $graph = new GD::Graph::bars(600, 300);

# discover maximum values of x and y for graph parameters
my( $xmax) = sort {$b <=> $a} keys %dataset;
my( $ymax) = sort {$b <=> $a} values %dataset;
# how many ticks to put on y axis
my $yticks = int($ymax / 5) + 1;

# define input arrays and enter 0 if undefined x value
my(@xsizes) = (0 .. $xmax);
my(@ycounts) = ();
foreach my $x (@xsizes) {
    if ( defined $dataset{$x}) {
        push @ycounts, $dataset{$x};
    }else{
        push @ycounts, 0;
    }
}

# set parameters for graph
$graph->set(
    transparent=> 0,
    title=> "Summary of mutation data",
    x_label=> 'Mutants per cluster',
    y_label=> 'Number of mutants',
    x_all_ticks=> 1,
    y_all_ticks=> 0,
    y_tick_number=> $yticks,
    zero_axis=> 0,
    zero_axis_only=> 0,
);
```

```
# plot the data on the graph
my $gd = $graph->plot(
    [ ^xsizes,
      ^ycounts
    ]
);

# output file
my $pngfile = "gdgraph1.png";
unless(open(PNG, ">$pngfile")) {
    croak "Cannot open $pngfile:$!\n";
}

# set output file handle PNG to binary stream
# (this is important sometimes, for example doing
# GCI programming on some operating systems
binmode PNG;

# print the image to the output file
print PNG $gd->png;
```

Figure 8-1 shows the image that is written to the file gdgraph1.png. On my system it's very small for an image, only 2028 bytes.

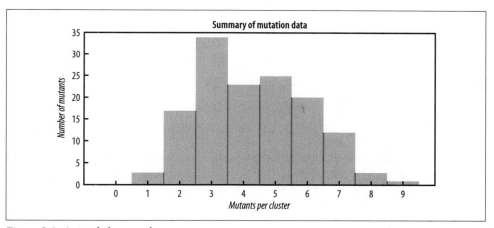

Figure 8-1. A simple bar graph

Here's how the code works. The new module is loaded like so:

```
use GD::Graph::bars;
```

The dataset is then defined as a hash. In reality, GD::Graph expects to see the data in arrays. However, since your program may first collect data in a hash, I've shown you how to incorporate hash data into a GD::Graph image and included the code that extracts the required x and y arrays from the hash.

Next, the module's new constructor method is called to initialize a graph of type bars and sized at 600 pixels horizontal and 300 pixels vertical.

```
# create new image
my $graph = new GD::Graph::bars(600, 300);
```

The next bit of code prepares some of the values needed to set parameters for the graph. The maximum x and y values are extracted from the hash %dataset. There is a way to specify how many ticks are desired along the y axis, but if you want one every five values, say, you have to figure out how many such values will just fit the data: hence the $yticks calculation.

```
# discover maximum values of x and y for graph parameters
my( $xmax) = sort {$b <=> $a} keys %dataset;
my( $ymax) = sort {$b <=> $a} values %dataset;

# how many ticks to put on y axis
my $yticks = int($ymax / 5) + 1;
```

Next, the actual arrays of x and y values are constructed from the data in %dataset:

```
# define input arrays and enter 0 if undefined x value
my(@xsizes) = (0 .. $xmax);
my(@ycounts) = ();
foreach my $x (@xsizes) {
    if ( defined $dataset{$x}) {
        push @ycounts, $dataset{$x};
    }else{
        push @ycounts, 0;
    }
}
```

Finally the various parameters are set (there are quite a few possible parameters, as you'll see in the documentation), the data is plotted in the graph, an output file handle is created and set to binary mode (important for CGI web programming), and the image data is written out.

Here is another version, gd2.pl, of the same program. This version creates "lines and points" graphs that have the values written over each datapoint. Instead of showing the data as a bar, this graph shows data points joined by lines. The data points have the value written next to them, except for the value at x=3, which is suppressed. Other than that, it's the same image from the same data as used in gd1.pl.

```
#!/usr/bin/perl

#
# gd2.pl -- create GD::Graph "linespoints" graph
#

use strict;
use warnings;
use Carp;
use GD::Graph::linespoints;

my %dataset = ( 1 => 3,
                2 => 17,
          3 => 34,
```

```perl
        4 => 23,
        5 => 25,
        6 => 20,
        7 => 12,
        8 => 3,
        9 => 1
);

# create new image
my $graph = new GD::Graph::linespoints(600, 300);

# discover maximum values of x and y for graph parameters
my( $xmax) = sort {$b <=> $a} keys %dataset;
my( $ymax) = sort {$b <=> $a} values %dataset;
# how many ticks to put on y axis
my $yticks = int($ymax / 5) + 1;

# define input arrays and enter 0 if undefined x value
my(@xsizes) = (0 .. $xmax);
my(@ycounts) = ();
foreach my $x (@xsizes) {
    if ( defined $dataset{$x}) {
        push @ycounts, $dataset{$x};
    }else{
        push @ycounts, 0;
    }
}

# define input data
# need to do separately so show_values will work
my $data = GD::Graph::Data->new(
    [ ^xsizes,
      ^ycounts
    ]
);

# use show_values to show values of data next to points
# use $values to suppress printing of value for x=3
my $values = $data->copy;
$values->set_y(1, 3, undef);

# set parameters for graph
$graph->set(
    transparent=> 0,
    title=> "Summary of mutation data",
    x_label=> 'Mutants per cluster',
    y_label=> 'Number of mutants',
    x_all_ticks=> 1,
    y_all_ticks=> 0,
    y_tick_number=> $yticks,
    zero_axis=> 0,
    zero_axis_only=> 0,
    show_values => $values,
);
```

```
# plot the data on the graph
my $gd = $graph->plot(
    [ ^xsizes,
      ^ycounts
    ]
);

# output file
my $pngfile = "gdgraph2.png";
unless(open(PNG, ">$pngfile")) {
    croak "Cannot open $pngfile:$!\n";
}

binmode PNG;

print PNG $gd->png;
```

Figure 8-2 shows the image that's written to the file gdgraph2.png.

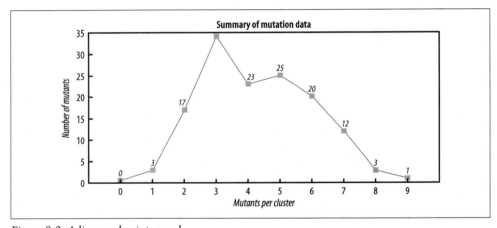

Figure 8-2. A lines and points graph

A variety of image viewing programs may be used to display your results while you're doing graphics programming. ImageMagick has a display program called display that runs on a Linux system and elsewhere. I often use xv, and while it usually works quite well, it seems to have trouble with PNG files. When programming, it's a good idea to pick an imaging program that can be set to automatically update the display when you overwrite the image file with new data. It's common for a system's user interface to allow you to click on the image file's name or thumbnail image in order to launch an image viewing program with the image loaded.

This section just gives you a taste of the capabilities of GD::Graph. The module provides many possibilities, all of which are easily incorporated into your Perl programs for output to files or sent to a web browser from your CGI program.

Resources

I recommend the book *The Visual Display of Quantitative Information* by Edward Tufte (Graphics Press).

Although I don't demonstrate their use in this book, I want to mention two more full-featured graphics software packages that are free, and very useful if you'll be doing graphics to any extent:

- ImageMagick and its Perl interface module Image::Magick is a valuable tool, especially for creating images. Over 60 different file formats are supported, compared to the much more limited number in GD. A wide range of image-manipulation techniques are supported, enabling you to create animation, thumbnails, and apply many image processing functions, for example.

- The Gimp (GNU Image Manipulation Program) is very much like the Photoshop program. It has an interface to Perl scripts that is built-in, and there are several modules, starting with the Gimp.pm module, that provide Perl programmers with access to its functionality.

Between GD, Gimp, and ImageMagick, the Perl programmer has ready access to a host of image creation and manipulation software, at no cost.

Exercises

Exercise 8.1

Add an argument "linelength=>50" to Restrictionmap to set the length of lines in the graphic output.

Exercise 8.2

What happens if you request a graphic type for which no corresponding method has been defined? Would there be a better way to handle this situation than the current behavior of the module?

Exercise 8.3

If more than one enzyme is present, draw each enzyme in a different color. You'll have to solve the problem of how to define the required number of colors and how to choose them so that they'll be easily distinguishable from each other. You'll also have to rework the annotation lines when more than one type of enzyme appears on an annotation line, drawing the different sections individually with different colors.

Exercise 8.4

Add header information such as filename, count of restriction sites for each enzyme, and date, to the text or PNG or JPEG graphic generated by _drawmap_ text or _drawmap_png or _drawmap_jpg.

Exercise 8.5

In _drawmap_text, add a number at the beginning of each line of sequence giving the position of the first base on that line. First figure out the number of digits needed for the last line, so you can make the appropriate amount of space before each line. Can you right-justify the numbers in the allotted space?

Exercise 8.6

In _drawmap_text, put a space between each group of 10 bases on a line to make it easier to find a particular base position.

Exercise 8.7

In _drawmap_png or _drawmap_jpg, instead of putting the enzyme names in annotation lines above the sequence lines, try simply printing the sequence lines, but highlight each restriction site with color and enclosing it in a box. Try giving each type of enzyme in the map a different color and type of box and add a key that shows which enzyme matches up with each color/box.

This works fine with a single enzyme. Does it work with two enzymes? With three or more? Do you need to change the output of _drawmap_text to accomplish this?

Exercise 8.8

Rewrite the webrebase1 CGI Perl script so that it is two programs: one that displays the opening screen form, and the other that calculates the PNG image. Say you call the image-generating CGI script rebase_png. Then use the CGI for an HTML tag such as:

```
print img({ -src => "/cgi-bin/rebase_png?enzyme=EcoRI;fileseq=
    sampleecori.dna2" });
```

In this way, you can embed a dynamically generated image into a larger HTML document; it's an alternative to the method shown in the text in which the image is shown by itself in the web browser.

Exercise 8.9

The _drawmap_jpg and _drawmap_png methods are almost identical. Add a third method that does most of the work of these methods, taking as an argument the file type desired for output. Then rewrite _drawmap_jpg and _drawmap_png so that they're much shorter. Now add a _drawmap_wbmp method.

Exercise 8.10

The _drawmap_png method assumes that annotation lines contain spaces while sequence lines do not. This is called an heuristic, a rule of thumb that is easy to compute and leads to a simplification of program logic. What if there is an annotation line that has no spaces because it annotates a line of sequence that is solid, wall-to-wall restriction sites? Invent another method of distinguishing between annotation and sequence lines.

Exercise 8.11

Use GD::Graph to make a different representation of a restriction map.

## CHAPTER 9

Introduction to Bioperl

Bioperl is a collection of more than 500 Perl modules for bioinformatics that have been written and maintained by an international group of volunteers. Bioperl is free (under a very unrestrictive copyright), and its home is *http://bioperl.org*.

One of the most difficult things about Bioperl is getting started using it. This is due to a scarcity of good documentation (which is being rectified) as well as the sheer size of the Bioperl module library. This chapter will help you get started using the Bioperl project software; it will guide you through the initial steps of getting the software, installing it, and exploring the tutorial and example material that it provides. After working through this chapter, you'll be well prepared to delve deeper into the riches of Bioperl, and, if you've also worked through the object-oriented chapters earlier in this book, you'll be in a good position to read the Bioperl code and contribute to the project yourself.

The modules in Bioperl are written in the object-oriented style. Perl programmers who do not know object-oriented programming can still use the Bioperl modules with just a bit of extra information, as outlined in Chapter 3.

The Bioperl modules cover various areas of bioinformatics, including some you've seen previously in this book. Although Bioperl includes some example programs, it is not meant to be a collection of complete user-ready programs. Rather, it's implemented as a toolkit you can dip into for help when writing your own programs. Its goal is to provide good working solutions to common bioinformatics tasks and to speed your program development.

One of the best things about Bioperl is that it's an open source project, meaning that interested developers are invited to contribute by writing code or in other ways, and the code is available to anyone interested. If you've learned enough about Perl for bioinformatics to have worked through a good portion of this book, you'll find plenty of opportunity to get involved in Bioperl if you have the time and inclination.

The Growth of Bioperl

The practice of freely distributing Perl software for bioinformatics over the Internet began around 1992. Gradually, Perl became more and more popular for biology applications.* The release of Perl Version 5 and its support for object-oriented programming accelerated the development of reusable modules for biology at many research centers around the world. The large-scale genome sequencing efforts, then underway, provided much of the impetus, as well as the talent and funding, for these efforts. The Bioperl project, officially organized in 1995, coalesced around one of these bioinformatics research groups that was doing a good job of organizing the collective volunteer effort such collaborative projects require. More information, including a short history and list of contributors, can be found at the Bioperl site *http:// bioperl.org*. The Bioperl web site is frequently being updated and improved, and is the primary source of Bioperl code and documentation.

Today, the Bioperl project has grown to a point where it is both useful enough, and well enough documented, that it is a must for Perl programming in bioinformatics. The documentation includes a program `bptutorial.pl` that comes with Bioperl, which explains and demonstrates several areas of the project (more on that later in this chapter).

Installing Bioperl

Installing Bioperl's large collection of modules isn't too difficult. It usually goes fairly painlessly, even though there are a few extra installation steps due to the additional outside programs and Perl modules on which Bioperl depends. You will probably want to use Perl's CPAN to fetch and install Bioperl.

`INSTALL` is a good document that covers Bioperl installation on Unix/Linux, Windows, and Mac operating systems. It's part of the Bioperl distribution and is located at *http://bioperl.org/Core/Latest/INSTALL*. This location may change, but it's easy to find from the Download link on the main Bioperl web page. If you're going to install Bioperl, I recommend you read this document first; here, I'll give an overview of what's available and add a few additional comments that may help with installation.

Here's how to get Bioperl on different platforms:

* On Unix/Linux, if you download the *tar* file from the web site, you merely need to untar it and go through the configure and make process by hand, as described in the `INSTALL` file that comes with the distribution.

---

* See, for example, the article "How Perl Saved the Human Genome Project" by Lincoln Stein at *http://bioperl. org/GetStarted/tpj_ls_bio.html*.

- If you have a Microsoft Windows machine with ActiveState's Perl (*http://www. activestate.com*), there's a PPM file available for Bioperl; at the time of this writing, it's at *http://bioperl.org/ftp/DIST/Bioperl-1.2.1.ppd.*
- There is also a CVS repository for Bioperl from which you can fetch the most current versions of the modules. But be careful: some newer versions of the modules are implementing new features and have more bugs than are found in some of the older, more stable releases. The details of how to install from CVS are also available at the Bioperl web page.

All these methods for installing Bioperl are fine, but probably the most common way for Perl programmers to install sets of modules is by way of CPAN. I discussed CPAN in Chapter 1, but it's worth discussing again as it relates to Bioperl.

To install Bioperl, you start by typing the following at the command line:

```
perl -MCPAN -e shell;
```

This gives the CPAN shell prompt:

```
cpan>
```

It's often the case that a module you want to install may require other modules for its proper operation, and perhaps one or more of these additional modules have not yet been installed. The CPAN system includes a way to check to see what other modules are required, and you can configure it to automatically follow and install missing prerequisites.

Especially with a large collection of modules like Bioperl, you may expect to see such prerequisites crop up. When I asked my CPAN session how it was configured:

```
cpan> o conf
```

one of the lines of output from that query was:

```
prerequisites_policy ask
```

I couldn't find a way to list the options within my CPAN session, so I took a look at the CPAN documentation in another window with `perldoc CPAN`, searched for the string `prerequisites_policy`, and read the following:

```
prerequisites_policy
              what to do if you are missing module prerequisites
              ('follow' automatically, 'ask' me, or 'ignore')
```

To handle the prerequisites automatically, I configured my CPAN session like so:

```
cpan> o conf prerequisites_policy follow
```

Now, if you have a slow Internet connection, setting the option this way can be a problem, because some prerequisites may take a long time to install, and you'll be stuck waiting for everything to finish. In that case, you may prefer to be asked about each prerequisite, so you can see if you have the needed time to do the installation. Plan on the process taking at least a couple of hours. My experience using both a dial-up modem and a cable modem from a home office is that the time involved was not too onerous.

As you probably know by now, you can see a summary of CPAN session commands by typing help:

```
cpan> help
```

```
Display Information
  command  argument         description
  a,b,d,m  WORD or /REGEXP/  about authors, bundles, distributions, modules
  i        WORD or /REGEXP/  about anything of above
  r        NONE             reinstall recommendations
  ls       AUTHOR           about files in the author's directory

Download, Test, Make, Install...
  get                       download
  make                      make (implies get)
  test     MODULES,         make test (implies make)
  install  DISTS, BUNDLES   make install (implies test)
  clean                     make clean
  look                      open subshell in these dists' directories
  readme                    display these dists' README files

Other
  h,?            display this menu    ! perl-code    eval a perl command
  o conf [opt]   set and query options  q            quit the cpan shell
  reload cpan    load CPAN.pm again    reload index  load newer indices
  autobundle     Snapshot             force cmd      unconditionally do cmd
cpan>
```

To find the Bioperl distribution, I typed:

```
cpan> i /bioperl/
```

and got the following output:

```
cpan> i /bioperl/
CPAN: Storable loaded ok
Going to read /root/.cpan/Metadata
  Database was generated on Sun, 27 Apr 2003 04:12:50 GMT
  Bundle          Bundle::BioPerl (C/CR/CRAFFI/Bundle-BioPerl-2.04.tar.gz)
  Distribution    B/BI/BIRNEY/bioperl-0.05.1.tar.gz
  Distribution    B/BI/BIRNEY/bioperl-0.6.2.tar.gz
  Distribution    B/BI/BIRNEY/bioperl-0.7.0.tar.gz
  Distribution    B/BI/BIRNEY/bioperl-1.0.2.tar.gz
  Distribution    B/BI/BIRNEY/bioperl-1.0.tar.gz
  Distribution    B/BI/BIRNEY/bioperl-1.2.1.tar.gz
  Distribution    B/BI/BIRNEY/bioperl-1.2.tar.gz
  Distribution    B/BI/BIRNEY/bioperl-db-0.1.tar.gz
  Distribution    B/BI/BIRNEY/bioperl-ext-0.6.tar.gz
  Distribution    B/BI/BIRNEY/bioperl-gui-0.7.tar.gz
  Distribution    C/CR/CRAFFI/Bundle-BioPerl-2.04.tar.gz
  Module          Bio::LiveSeq::IO::BioPerl (B/BI/BIRNEY/bioperl-1.2.1.tar.gz)
```

```
13 items found
```

```
cpan>
```

From looking at the Bioperl web page, I knew that the `Bundle::BioPerl` had extra useful modules in it that Bioperl uses.

I started the installation by first installing the `Bundle`:

```
cpan> install Bundle::BioPerl
```

This process fetched the module code from a CPAN repository, unpacked it, tested it, and installed it, including its prerequisites (without questions asked because I set the `follow` option as described earlier in this section).

Somewhat fortified by my success, I decided to go for broke and install the main Bioperl distribution.

From the search output from my CPAN query, `i /bioperl/`, just shown, I saw that the highest numbered release was 1.2.1. Just to be sure it was the latest release, I also spent some time at the Bioperl web site reading the news about the latest releases, so I was quite sure it was what I wanted.

I also spent some time reading the `INSTALL` file, and I knew that I was generally in good shape. I had a new-enough version of Perl (Version 5.8.0) and was on one of the standard supported platforms.

I installed it on a notebook computer with an Intel 686 processor that had the RedHat Linux 7.2 operating system. The computer and the operating system were about two years old, old enough that I did do some looking around on the Bioperl web site to see if there were any advisories about which versions of Linux were recommended or advised against.

In general, modern computer systems are complex, and they change rapidly. Operating systems and hardware have a replacement cycle of about two years. Some of this is planned obsolescence; some is legitimate technical progress. Whatever the cause, the result is that a system such as the one I'm describing needs several pieces to be in sync. The hardware, operating system software, Perl version, and Bioperl version have to coexist; other pieces such as the C compiler, web browser, web server, and so forth may also cause problems. Hence my interest in checking to see if there were any advisories on these topics.

However, I didn't see any warnings about my particular platform. And since I had recently installed the latest version of Perl with success, I felt I had performed due diligence and that I should go ahead and try to install the Bioperl modules.

To do so, I typed:

```
cpan> install B/BI/BIRNEY/bioperl-1.2.1.tar.gz
```

There followed a great amount of activity as CPAN got the distribution from the Internet and tested the various modules. After a time, the tests were complete; a few of them had failed, and CPAN decided not to install the modules. Since only a handful of module tests failed, I looked at the output on my screen and decided that the failures were only in peripheral parts of Bioperl I didn't have an immediate use for, and if I ever did need them, I could fix them later.

So, to finish the installation, I forced CPAN to do the installation despite the presence of some test failures:

```
cpan> force install B/BI/BIRNEY/bioperl-1.2.1.tar.gz
```

This resulted in the modules and the documentation being installed.

Testing Bioperl

To check that things were working okay with my new Bioperl installation, I first wrote a little test to see if a Perl program could find the Bio::Perl module:

```
use Bio::Perl;
```

I ran it by putting it in a file bp0.pl and giving it to the Perl interpreter:

```
[tisdall]# perl bp0.pl
[tisdall]#
```

As you see, it didn't complain, which means Perl found the Bio::Perl module. If it can't find it, it will complain. When I copied the bp0.pl program to a file called bp0.pl.broken and changed the module call of Bio::Perl to a call for the nonexistent module Bio::Perrl, I got the following (slightly truncated) error output:

```
[tisdall@coltrane development]$ perl bp0.pl.broken
Can't locate Bio/Perrl.pm in @INC
BEGIN failed--compilation aborted at bp0.pl.broken line 1.
```

Second Test

Now I knew that Bio::Perl could be found and loaded. I next tried a couple of test programs that are given in the bptutorial.pl document. I found a link to that tutorial document on the Web from the *http://bioperl.org* page. Alternately, I could have opened a window and typed at the command prompt:

```
perldoc bptutorial.pl
```

I went to the section near the beginning of the document called "I.2 Quick getting started scripts" and created a file tut1.pl on my computer by pasting in the text of the first tutorial script:

```
use Bio::Perl;

# this script will only work with an internet connection
# on the computer it is run on
$seq_object = get_sequence('swissprot',"ROA1_HUMAN");

write_sequence(">roa1.fasta",'fasta',$seq_object);
```

I then ran the program and looked at the output file:

```
[tisdall]$ perl tut1.pl
[tisdall]$ cat roa1.fasta
>ROA1_HUMAN Heterogeneous nuclear ribonucleoprotein A1 (Helix-destabilizing protein)
(Single-strand binding protein) (hnRNP core protein A1).
SKSESPKEPEQLRKLFIGGLSFETTDESLRSHFEQWGTLTDCVVMRDPNTKRSRGFGFVT
YATVEEVDAAMNARPHKVDGRVVEPKRAVSREDSQRPGAHLTVKKIFVGGIKEDTEEHHL
RDYFEQYGKIEVIEIMTDRGSGKKRGFAFVTFDDHDSVDKIVIQKYHTVNGHNCEVRKAL
SKQEMASASSSQRGRSGSGNFGGGRGGGFGGNDNFGRGGNFSGRGGFGGSRGGGGYGGSG
DGYNGFGNDGGYGGGGPGYSGGSRGYGSGGQGYGNQGSGYGGSGSYDSYNNGGGRGFGGG
SGSNFGGGGSYNDFGNYNNQSSNFGPMKGGNFGGRSSGPYGGGGQYFAKPRNQGGYGGSS
SSSSYGSGRRF
[tisdall]$
```

That seemed to work perfectly.

Third Test

I tried the next short script from the same section of the tutorial, pasting it into a file
called tut2.pl:

```
[tisdall]$ cat tut2.pl
use Bio::Perl;

# this script will only work with an internet connection
# on the computer it is run on

$seq_object = get_sequence('swissprot',"ROA1_HUMAN");

# uses the default database - nr in this case
$blast_result = blast_sequence($seq);

write_blast(">roa1.blast",$blast_report);
[tisdall]$ perl tut2.pl

-------------------- WARNING ---------------------
MSG: req was POST http://www.ncbi.nlm.nih.gov/blast/Blast.cgi
User-Agent: libwww-perl/5.69
Content-Length: 178
Content-Type: application/x-www-form-urlencoded

...
---------------------------------------------------
Submitted Blast for [blast-sequence-temp-id]
[tisdall]$ cat roa1.blast
[tisdall]$ ls -l roa1.blast
-rw-rw-r--    1 tisdall  tisdall         0 Apr 30 11:28 roa1.blast
[tisdall]$
```

Here, I experienced a problem. Running the program created a page of error output,
mostly formatted in HTML, which I've truncated in the output. When I tried to cat

the output file, there was nothing in it, which I verified (on Linux) by examining the file with ls -l, which showed that it had 0 bytes in it.

This wasn't very encouraging; the second of the two short example scripts was failing.

Looking at the two programs tut1.pl and tut2.pl, you can see that the second is an extension of the first; after getting the sequence, the second program also tries to blast it, and this is where it is failing. It's running (printing those ... dots took a while because the program was waiting for a reply from NCBI over the Internet), but it's not printing out the BLAST report to the file roa1.blast. What's going wrong?

I started my investigation by looking at the documentation for the Bio::Perl module by typing:

```
perldoc Bio::Perl
```

and searching for the function that is failing, blast_sequence. Here's what I found:

```
blast_sequence

   Title   : blast_sequence
   Usage   : $blast_result = blast_sequence($seq)
             $blast_result = blast_sequence('MFVEGGTFASEDDDSASAEDE');

  Function: If the computer has Internet accessibility, blasts
            the sequence using the NCBI BLAST server against nrdb.

            It choose the flavour of BLAST on the basis of the sequence.

            This function uses Bio::Tools::Run::RemoteBlast, which itself
            use Bio::SearchIO - as soon as you want to more, check out
            these modules
  Returns : Bio::Search::Result::GenericResult.pm

   Args    : Either a string of protein letters or nucleotides, or a
             Bio::Seq object
```

That last sentence about the Args gave me a clue. I went back and looked at the failing program, which I placed in a file called tut2.pl, and, sure enough, the argument for the blast_sequence function, $seq, is neither a string of sequence nor a Bio::Seq object. In fact, it's not even defined! Clearly, what the tutorial writer meant instead of $seq, was $seq_object, which is defined and populated by the earlier get_sequence method call.

I was visited by a brainwave, and I decided to put a use strict and a use warnings into the program and to declare variables with my to see what ensued:

```
[tisdall]$ cat tut2.pl
use Bio::Perl;
use strict;
use warnings;
```

```
# this script will only work with an internet connection
# on the computer it is run on

my $seq_object = get_sequence('swissprot',"ROA1_HUMAN");

# uses the default database - nr in this case
my $blast_result = blast_sequence($seq);

write_blast(">roa1.blast",$blast_report);
[tisdall]$ perl tut2.pl
Global symbol "$seq" requires explicit package name at tut2.pl line 11.
Global symbol "$blast_report" requires explicit package name at tut2.pl line 13.
Execution of tut2.pl aborted due to compilation errors.
[tisdall]$
```

Well, that's pretty clear. The variables $seq and $blast_report are wrong; apparently, the author intended to reuse the variables $seq_object and $blast_result instead. So, I edited the file and ran it again:

```
[tisdall]$ cat tut2.pl
use Bio::Perl;
use strict;
use warnings;

# this script will only work with an internet connection
# on the computer it is run on

my $seq_object = get_sequence('swissprot',"ROA1_HUMAN");

# uses the default database - nr in this case
my $blast_result = blast_sequence($seq_object);

write_blast(">roa1.blast",$blast_result);
[tisdall]$ perl tut2.pl
[tisdall]$ perl tut2.pl
Submitted Blast for [ROA1_HUMAN] ...................
[tisdall]$ ls -l roa1.blast
-rw-rw-r--    1 tisdall  tisdall      56888 May  5 15:05 roa1.blast
[tisdall]$
```

Examining the roa1.blast file convinced me that the program had successfully called blast. I decided that was a success, albeit a qualified one: this was a spot in the documentation that could use a little attention, clearly. By the time you're reading this, it may well have been fixed.

Fourth Test

Now, let me show you one more test of my new Bioperl installation.

Looking at the Bio::Perl documentation, I found the following example and discussion at the very beginning.

NAME
        Bio::Perl - Functional access to BioPerl for people who
        don't know objects

SYNOPSIS
        use Bio::Perl;

        # will guess file format from extension
        $seq_object = read_sequence($filename);

        # forces genbank format
        $seq_object = read_sequence($filename,'genbank');

        # reads an array of sequences
        @seq_object_array = read_all_sequences($filename,'fasta');

        # sequences are Bio::Seq objects, so the following methods work
        # for more info see L<Bio::Seq>, or do 'perldoc Bio/Seq.pm'

        print "Sequence name is ",$seq_object->display_id,"\n";
        print "Sequence acc is ",$seq_object->accession_number,"\n";
        print "First 5 bases is ",$seq_object->subseq(1,5),"\n";

        # get the whole sequence as a single string

        $sequence_as_a_string = $seq_object->seq();

        # writing sequences

        write_sequence(">$filename",'genbank',$seq_object);

        write_sequence(">$filename",'genbank',@seq_object_array);

        # making a new sequence from just strings you have
        # from something else

        $seq_object = new_sequence("ATTGGTTTGGGGACCCAATTTGTGTGTTATATGTA",
            "myname","AL12232");

        # getting a sequence from a database (assumes internet connection)

        $seq_object = get_sequence('swissprot',"ROA1_HUMAN");

        $seq_object = get_sequence('embl',"AI129902");

        $seq_object = get_sequence('genbank',"AI129902");

        # BLAST a sequence (assummes an internet connection)

        $blast_report = blast_sequence($seq_object);

```
            write_blast(">blast.out",$blast_report);

    DESCRIPTION
            Easy first time access to BioPerl via functions

    FEEDBACK
            Mailing Lists

            User feedback is an integral part of the evolution of this
            and other Bioperl modules. Send your comments and sugges-
            tions preferably to one of the Bioperl mailing lists.
            Your participation is much appreciated.

            bioperl-l@bio.perl.org

            Reporting Bugs

            Report bugs to the Bioperl bug tracking system to help us
            keep track the bugs and their resolution. Bug reports can
            be submitted via email or the web:

            bioperl-bugs@bio.perl.org
            http://bugzilla.bioperl.org/

    AUTHOR - Ewan Birney
            Email bioperl-l@bio.perl.org

            Describe contact details here

    APPENDIX
            The rest of the documentation details each of the object
            methods.  Internal methods are usually preceded with a _
    ...
```

I took the example code from the SYNOPSIS section and put it in a file called bp1.pl. I noticed that the code was not meant to be a running program. The variable $filename refers to some sequence file in the first line of code without being initialized, and then the same variable name is used in several other lines for different purposes. This is not an uncommon situation in such SYNOPSIS sections; the point is to show how individual calls can be made to methods in the class, not to demonstrate a complete working program (although sometimes the code can be run exactly as is).

I had to make some changes to make this code a working, runnable program. I declared the strict and warnings pragmas and declared each variable with my. I created variables for the different sequence filenames I needed as both input and output, and I made sure that the input sequence files were on disk and of the correct variety (for example, I created the array.fasta file with three FASTA headers and sequences one after the other). In the end I had this code:

```
use Bio::Perl;
use strict;
use warnings;
```

```perl
my $gbfilename = 'AI129902.genbank';

# will guess file format from extension
my $seq_object0 = read_sequence($gbfilename);

# forces genbank format
my $seq_object1 = read_sequence($gbfilename,'genbank');

my $fastafilename = 'array.fasta';

# reads an array of sequences
my @seq_object_array = read_all_sequences($fastafilename,'fasta');

# sequences are Bio::Seq objects, so the following methods work
# for more info see L<Bio::Seq>, or do 'perldoc Bio/Seq.pm'

print "Sequence name is ",$seq_object1->display_id,"\n";
print "Sequence acc  is ",$seq_object1->accession_number,"\n";
print "First 5 bases is ",$seq_object1->subseq(1,5),"\n";

# get the whole sequence as a single string

my $sequence_as_a_string = $seq_object1->seq( );

# writing sequences

my $gbfilenameout = 'bpout.genbank';

write_sequence(">$gbfilenameout",'genbank',$seq_object1);

write_sequence(">$gbfilenameout",'genbank',@seq_object_array);

# making a new sequence from just strings you have
# from something else

my $seq_object2 = new_sequence("ATTGGTTTGGGGACCCAATTTGTGTGTTATATGTA",
    "myname","AL12232");

# getting a sequence from a database (assumes internet connection)

my $seq_object3 = get_sequence('swissprot',"ROA1_HUMAN");

my $seq_object4 = get_sequence('embl',"AI129902");

my $seq_object5 = get_sequence('genbank',"AI129902");

# BLAST a sequence (assummes an internet connection)

my $blast_report = blast_sequence($seq_object3);

write_blast(">blast.out",$blast_report);
```

As you see, I didn't check on the output of all the method calls, but the real purpose of this test of my newly installed Bioperl modules was just to see if all the modules and methods could be found and would run when called.

As mentioned previously, I also added use strict; and use warnings; and declared all the variables with my. Often, you don't see that usage in this kind of documentation; it's not required in Perl, and it may distract some readers of the documentation from the main point of showing how the methods are called. This is not an unusual omission to find in Perl class documentation, but of course, it's recommended and often very helpful, as you saw in the last section.

So, I ran my slightly edited version of the example code from the beginning of the Bio::Perl manpage, with the following results:

```
[tisdall]$ perl bp1.pl
Sequence name is AI129902
Sequence acc  is AI129902
First 5 bases is CTCCG
Submitted Blast for [ROA1_HUMAN] ........
[tisdall]$
```

I looked at each of the input and output files and verified the expected contents. The following output from a listing of the files will give you an idea of what to expect (although you may get different results by running the program with different input files or database lookups):

```
-rw-rw-r--   1 tisdall  tisdall    2391 May  5 10:37 AI129902.genbank
-rw-rw-r--   1 tisdall  tisdall    2485 May  5 13:00 array.fasta
-rw-rw-r--   1 tisdall  tisdall    1513 May  5 13:02 bp1.pl
-rw-rw-r--   1 tisdall  tisdall    3653 May  5 13:02 bpout.genbank
-rw-rw-r--   1 tisdall  tisdall   56888 May  5 13:04 blast.out
```

Notice that at the end of the program I call the blast_sequence method on the protein sequence object $seq_object3. I discovered that trying to run the blast_sequence method on a nucleotide sequence object (such as $seq_object5) failed. Although the documentation for the method said that the sequence type would be examined and the appropriate BLAST program called (for example, blastp for protein sequence and blastx for nucleotide sequence, against the nr nonredundant protein database), it always seemed to call blastp no matter what the input sequence, and therefore it failed unless called with protein sequence as I had stored in $seq_object3. Perhaps this bug, a disconnect between the code and the documentation, has been fixed by the time you read this.

Bioperl Problems

Bioperl is still a work in progress, and it has some problems. I'd like to mention the two main problems now.

First, the Bioperl documentation is incomplete. In fact, until fairly recently, there was no document that provided a tutorial introduction to the project. This has changed; the bptutorial.pl document, which you've already seen and will see more of, is an excellent beginning, despite its occasional errors. This document cleverly combines a tutorial with quite a few example programs that you can run, as you'll soon see.

Other documentation for Bioperl is also available, including Internet-based tutorials, forthcoming books, example programs, and journal articles. So, the situation has recently improved.

Second, Bioperl is big (over 500 modules), written by volunteers, and gradually evolving. The size of the project is a sign that Bioperl addresses many interesting and useful problems, but it also means that, for the new user of Bioperl, an overview of the available resources is a task in itself.

The majority of the Bioperl code is quite good, especially the most-used parts of it. However, the volunteer and evolving nature of Bioperl development means that some of the code is unfinished and not as well integrated with other parts of the project as one would like. Newer or less used modules may still need some shaking out by users in real-world situations. This is where you can make an initial contribution to the project: as you find problems, report them (more on that later).

Many of the computing world's most successful programs are the result of the same kind of volunteer development as Bioperl (the Perl language itself and the Apache web server are two examples). Bioperl is well positioned to achieve a similarly central position in the field of bioinformatics.

Overview of Objects

Bioperl is a big project and a fairly large collection of modules. Some of these modules are standalone; others interact with each other in various ways.

Your first task in learning about Bioperl is to get an idea of the main subject areas the modules are designed to address. So to begin with, here is a brief overview of the main types of objects in Bioperl, collected in a few broadly defined groups.

Sequences
> Bio::Seq is the main sequence object in Bioperl.
> Bio::PrimarySeq is a sequence object without features.
> Bio::SeqIO provides sequence file input and output.
> Bio::Tools::SeqStats provides statistics on a sequence.
> Bio::LiveSeq::* handles changing sequences.
> Bio::Seq::LargeSeq provides support for very large sequences.

Databases
> Bio::DB::GenBank provides GenBank access. Similar modules are available for several biological databases.

`Bio::Index::*` indexing and accessing local databases.

`Bio::Tools::Run::StandAloneBlast` runs BLAST on your local computer.

`Bio::Tools::Run::RemoteBlast` runs BLAST remotely.

`Bio::Tools::BPlite` parses BLAST reports.

`Bio::Tools::BPpsilite` parses psiblast reports.

`Bio::Tools::HMMER::Results` parses HMMER hidden Markov model results.

Alignments

`Bio::SimpleAlign` manipulates and displays simple multiple sequence alignments.

`Bio::UnivAln` manipulates and displays multiple sequence alignments.

`Bio::LocatableSeq` are sequence objects with start and end points for locating relative to other sequences or alignments.

`Bio::Tools::pSW` aligns two sequences with the Smith-Waterman algorithm.

`Bio::Tools::BPbl2seq` is a lightweight BLAST parser for pairwise sequence alignment using the BLAST algorithm.

`Bio::AlignIO` also aligns two sequences with BLAST.

`Bio::Clustalw` is an interface to the Clustalw multiple sequence alignment package.

`Bio::TCoffee` is an interface to the TCoffee multiple sequence alignment package.

`Bio::Variation::Allele` handles sets of alleles.

`Bio::Variation::SeqDiff` handles sets of mutations and variants.

Features and genes on sequences

`Bio::SeqFeature` is the sequence feature object in Bioperl.

`Bio::Tools::RestrictionEnzyme` locates restriction sites in sequence.

`Bio::Tools::Sigcleave` finds amino acid cleavage sites.

`Bio::Tools::OddCodes` rewrites amino acid sequences in abbreviated codes for specific statistical analysis (e.g., a hydrophobic/hydrophilic two-letter alphabet).

`Bio::Tools::SeqPattern` provides support for regular expression descriptions of sequence patterns.

`Bio::LocationI` provides an interface to location information for a sequence.

`Bio::Location::Simple` handles simple location information for a sequence, both as a single location and as a range.

`Bio::Location::Split` provides location information where the location may encompass multiple ranges, and even multiple sequences.

`Bio::Location::Fuzzy` provides location information that may be inexact.

`Bio::Tools::Genscan` is an interface to the gene finding program.

`Bio::Tools::Sim4::Results` (and Exon) is an interface to the gene exon finding program.

`Bio::Tools::ESTScan` is an interface to the gene finding program.

`Bio::Tools::MZEF` is an interface to the gene finding program.

Bio::Tools::Grail is an interface to the gene finding program.

Bio::Tools::Genemark is an interface to the gene finding program.

Bio::Tools::EPCR parses the output of ePCR program.

bptutorial.pl

I've already shown you a little of the bptutorial.pl document. I ran and discussed a few of the short example programs in the preceding sections.

As you know, one of the easiest ways to get started with a programming system is to find some working and fairly generic programs in that system. You can read and run the programs, and then proceed to alter them using them as templates for your own programming development.

Bioperl comes with a directory of example programs, but the best place to begin looking for starting-off program code is right in the bptutorial.pl document itself. That .pl suffix on the name is the giveaway; the document is actually itself a program, cleverly designed so that you can read, and run, example programs that exercise the core parts of the Bioperl project.

The following explanation of the runnable programs that are part of bptutorial.pl appears at the end of the document (when you view it on the Web or as the output of perldoc bptutorial.pl).

```
V.2 Appendix: Tutorial demo scripts

The following scripts demonstrate many of the features of
bioperl. To run all the core demos, run:

 > perl -w  bptutorial.pl 0

To run a subset of the scripts do

 > perl -w  bptutorial.pl

and use the displayed help screen.

It may be best to start by just running one or two demos
at a time. For example, to run the basic sequence manipu-
lation demo, do:

 > perl -w  bptutorial.pl 1

Some of the later demos require that you have an internet
connection and/or that you have an auxilliary bioperl
library and/or external cpan module and/or external pro-
gram installed.  They may also fail if you are not running
under Linux or Unix.  In all of these cases, the script
should fail "gracefully" simply saying the demo is being
skipped.  However if the script "crashes", simply run the
```

```
other demos individually (and perhaps send an email to
bioperl-l@bioperl.org detailing the problem :-).
```

(Recall that the -w flag to Perl turns on warnings in almost the same manner as a use warnings; directive.)

To test my Bioperl installation, I started by running the basic sequence manipulation demo as suggested.

First, I thought I might copy the bptutorial.pl program file into my own working directory from the Bioperl distribution directory where I'd unpacked the source code. I wanted to put it in my own directory so as not to muddy up the Bioperl distribution directory with my own extraneous files. However, I discovered that the tutorial demo programs rely on a number of datafiles that are found in the *t/data/* subdirectory of the Bioperl distribution. Running the program in my own directory gave me an error because the program evidently requires a FASTA-formatted file called dna1.fa:

```
[tisdall]$ perl -w bptutorial.pl 1

Beginning sequence_manipulations and SeqIO example...

------------- EXCEPTION -------------
MSG: Could not open t/data/dna1.fa: No such file or directory
STACK Bio::Root::IO::_initialize_io /usr/local/lib/perl5/site_perl/5.8.0/Bio/Root/IO.
pm:264
STACK Bio::SeqIO::_initialize /usr/local/lib/perl5/site_perl/5.8.0/Bio/SeqIO.pm:437
STACK Bio::SeqIO::fasta::_initialize /usr/local/lib/perl5/site_perl/5.8.0/Bio/SeqIO/
fasta.pm:80
STACK Bio::SeqIO::new /usr/local/lib/perl5/site_perl/5.8.0/Bio/SeqIO.pm:355
STACK Bio::SeqIO::new /usr/local/lib/perl5/site_perl/5.8.0/Bio/SeqIO.pm:368
STACK main::__ANON__ bptutorial.pl:2758
STACK toplevel bptutorial.pl:3933

-------------------------------------
[tisdall]$
```

I decided it would be easier to run bptutorial.pl from the distribution directory. I entered that directory; on my Linux machine, I unpacked the Bioperl source code into */usr/local/src/bioperl-1.2.1.* I then tried to run the demo:

```
[tisdall]$ cd /usr/local/src/bioperl-1.2.1
[tisdall]$ perl -w bptutorial.pl 1

Beginning sequence_manipulations and SeqIO example...
First sequence in fasta format...
>Test1
AGCTTTTCATTCTGACTGCAACGGGCAATATGTCTCTGTGTGGATTAAAAAAAGAGTGTC
TGATAGCAGCTTCTGAACTGGTTACCTGCCGTGAGTAAATTAAAATTTTATTGACTTAGG
TCACTAAATACTTTAACCAATATAGGCATAGCGCACAGACAGATAAAAATTACAGAGTAC
ACAACATCCATGAAACGCATTAGCACCACC
Seq object display id is Test1
```

```
Sequence is
AGCTTTTCATTCTGACTGCAACGGGCAATATGTCTCTGTGTGGATTAAAAAAAGAGTGTCTGATAGCAGCTTCTGAACTGGTTAC
CTGCCGTGAGTAAATTAAAATTTTATTGACTTAGGTCACTAAATACTTTAACCAATATAGGCATAGCGCACAGACAGATAAAAAT
TACAGAGTACACAACATCCATGAAACGCATTAGCACCACC
Sequence from 5 to 10 is TTTCAT
Acc num is unknown
Moltype is dna
Primary id is Test1
Truncated Seq object sequence is TTTCAT
Reverse complemented sequence 5 to 10  is ATGAAA
Translated sequence 6 to 15 is LQRAICLCVD

Beginning 3-frame and alternate codon translation example...
ctgagaaaataa translated using method defaults     : LRK*
ctgagaaaataa translated as a coding region (CDS): MRK

Translating in all six frames:
 frame: 0 forward: LRK*
 frame: 0 reverse-complement: LFSQ
 frame: 1 forward: *EN
 frame: 1 reverse-complement: YFL
 frame: 2 forward: EKI
 frame: 2 reverse-complement: IFS
Translating with all codon tables using method defaults:
1 : LRK*
2 : L*K*
3 : TRK*
4 : LRK*
5 : LSK*
6 : LRKQ
9 : LSN*
10 : LRK*
11 : LRK*
12 : SRK*
13 : LGK*
14 : LSNY
15 : LRK*
16 : LRK*
21 : LSN*
[tisdall]$
```

That seemed to run without error. Now I wanted to see the Perl code that had run and produced that output.

Exploring a bit, I found that the POD documentation part of bptutorial.pl is roughly the first half of the file, and that the second half of the file contains the Perl code for the demos.

The author attributions and the libraries that are loaded are at the beginning of the Perl code section, somewhere near the middle of the bptutorial.pl file:

```
#!/usr/bin/perl

# PROGRAM  : bptutorial.pl
# PURPOSE  : Demonstrate various uses of the bioperl package
```

```
# AUTHOR    : Peter Schattner schattner@alum.mit.edu
# CREATED   : Dec 15 2000
# REVISION : $Id: ch09,v 1.30 2003/09/08 05:49:27 free8 Exp mam $

use strict;
use Bio::SimpleAlign;
use Bio::AlignIO;
use Bio::SeqIO;
use Bio::Seq;
```

That seems like a good bet for a list of the most important Bioperl modules. Actually, some other modules are loaded for individual demos; at various points, the following come into play:

```
use Bio::SearchIO;
use Bio::Root::IO;
use Bio::MapIO;
use Bio::TreeIO;
use Bio::Perl
```

Following those use Module directives comes the following:

```
# subroutine references

my ($access_remote_db, $index_local_db, $fetch_local_db,
    $sequence_manipulations, $seqstats_and_seqwords,
    $restriction_and_sigcleave, $other_seq_utilities, $run_remoteblast,
    $run_standaloneblast,  $blast_parser, $bplite_parsing, $hmmer_parsing,
    $run_clustalw_tcoffee, $run_psw_bl2seq, $simplealign,
    $gene_prediction_parsing, $sequence_annotation, $largeseqs,
    $run_tree, $run_map, $run_struct, $run_perl, $searchio_parsing,
    $liveseqs, $demo_variations, $demo_xml, $display_help, $bpinspect1 );

# global variable file names.  Edit these if you want to try
#out a tutorial script on a different file

 Bio::Root::IO->catfile("t","data","ecolitst.fa");

# used in $sequence_manipulations
my $dna_seq_file = Bio::Root::IO->catfile("t","data","dna1.fa");

# used in $other_seq_utilities and in $run_perl and $sequence_annotation
my $amino_seq_file = Bio::Root::IO->catfile("t","data","cysprot1.fa");

# used in $blast_parser
my $blast_report_file = Bio::Root::IO->catfile("t","data","blast.report");

# used in $bplite_parsing
my $bp_parse_file1 = Bio::Root::IO->catfile("t","data","blast.report");

# used in $bplite_parsing
my $bp_parse_file2 = Bio::Root::IO->catfile("t","data","psiblastreport.out");

# used in $bplite_parsing
my $bp_parse_file3 = Bio::Root::IO->catfile("t","data","bl2seq.out");
```

```
# used in $run_clustalw_tcoffee
my $unaligned_amino_file = Bio::Root::IO->catfile("t","data","cysprot1a.fa");

# used in $simplealign
my $aligned_amino_file = Bio::Root::IO->catfile("t","data","testaln.pfam");

# other global variables
my (@runlist, $n );
```

A look at the documentation (perldoc Bio::Root::IO) shows that the catfile method returns the pathname of a file, which is being saved in a scalar variable such as $dna_seq_file. This method is there for portability between operating systems, because operating systems each have their own syntax for specifying pathnames.

After that comes the code for the help screen, the output of which you've already seen; next comes the individual demo subroutines; and finally the code for the main subroutine, which you saw in the last section.

At the very end of the bptutorial.pl file, I found the part of the code that launches all the demos:

```
## "main" program follows
#no strict 'refs';

    @runlist = @ARGV;
    # display help if no option
    if (scalar(@runlist)==0) {&$display_help;};
    # argument = 0 means run tests 1 thru 22
    if ($runlist[0] == 0) {@runlist = (1..22); };
    foreach $n (@runlist) {
        if ($n ==100) {my $object = $runlist[1]; &$bpinspect1($object); last;}
        if ($n ==1) {&$sequence_manipulations; next;}
        if ($n ==2) {&$seqstats_and_seqwords; next;}
        if ($n ==3) {&$restriction_and_sigcleave; next;}
        if ($n ==4) {&$other_seq_utilities; next;}
        if ($n ==5) {&$run_perl; next;}
        if ($n ==6) {&$searchio_parsing; next;}
        if ($n ==7) {&$bplite_parsing; next;}
        if ($n ==8) {&$hmmer_parsing; next;}
        if ($n ==9) {&$simplealign ; next;}
        if ($n ==10) {&$gene_prediction_parsing; next;}
        if ($n ==11) {&$access_remote_db; next;}
        if ($n ==12) {&$index_local_db; next;}
        if ($n ==13) {&$fetch_local_db; next;}
        if ($n ==14) {&$sequence_annotation; next;}
        if ($n ==15) {&$largeseqs; next;}
        if ($n ==16) {&$liveseqs; next;}
        if ($n ==17) {&$run_struct; next;}
        if ($n ==18) {&$demo_variations; next;}
        if ($n ==19) {&$demo_xml; next;}
        if ($n ==20) {&$run_tree; next;}
        if ($n ==21) {&$run_map; next;}
        if ($n ==22) {&$run_remoteblast; next;}
        if ($n ==23) {&$run_standaloneblast; next;}
```

```
        if ($n ==24) {&$run_clustalw_tcoffee; next;}
        if ($n ==25) {&$run_psw_bl2seq; next;}
         &$display_help;
    }

    ## End of "main"
```

So, I searched for sequence_manipulation and found the following code for this, the
first of the bptutorial.pl demos:

```
####################################################
# sequence_manipulations  ():
#

$sequence_manipulations = sub {

    my ($infile, $in, $out, $seqobj);
    $infile = $dna_seq_file;

    print "\nBeginning sequence_manipulations and SeqIO example... \n";


    # III.3.1 Transforming sequence files (SeqIO)

    $in  = Bio::SeqIO->new('-file' => $infile ,
                           '-format' => 'Fasta');
    $seqobj = $in->next_seq();

    # perl "tied filehandle" syntax is available to SeqIO,
    # allowing you to use the standard <> and print operations
    # to read and write sequence objects, eg:
    #$out = Bio::SeqIO->newFh('-format' => 'EMBL');

    $out = Bio::SeqIO->newFh('-format' => 'fasta');

    print "First sequence in fasta format... \n";
    print $out $seqobj;

    # III.4 Manipulating individual sequences

    # The following methods return strings

    print "Seq object display id is ",
    $seqobj->display_id(), "\n"; # the human read-able id of the sequence
    print "Sequence is ",
    $seqobj->seq()," \n";        # string of sequence
    print "Sequence from 5 to 10 is ",
    $seqobj->subseq(5,10)," \n"; # part of the sequence as a string
    print "Acc num is ",
    $seqobj->accession_number(), " \n"; # when there, the accession number
    print "Moltype is ",
    $seqobj->alphabet(), " \n";  # one of 'dna','rna','protein'
    print "Primary id is ", $seqobj->primary_seq->primary_id()," \n";
    # a unique id for this sequence irregardless
    #print "Primary id is ", $seqobj->primary_id(), " \n";
```

```
    # a unique id for this sequence irregardless
    # of its display_id or accession number

    # The following methods return an array of  Bio::SeqFeature objects
    $seqobj->top_SeqFeatures; # The 'top level' sequence features
    $seqobj->all_SeqFeatures; # All sequence features, including sub
    # seq features

    # The following methods returns new sequence objects,
    # but do not transfer features across
    # truncation from 5 to 10 as new object
    print "Truncated Seq object sequence is ",
    $seqobj->trunc(5,10)->seq(), " \n";
    # reverse complements sequence
    print "Reverse complemented sequence 5 to 10  is ",
    $seqobj->trunc(5,10)->revcom->seq, "  \n";
    # translation of the sequence
    print "Translated sequence 6 to 15 is ",
    $seqobj->translate->subseq(6,15), " \n";

    my $c = shift;
    $c ||= 'ctgagaaaataa';

    print "\nBeginning 3-frame and alternate codon translation example... \n";

    my $seq = new Bio::PrimarySeq('-SEQ' => $c,
                                  '-ID' => 'no.One');
    print "$c translated using method defaults    : ",
    $seq->translate->seq, "\n";

    # Bio::Seq uses same sequence methods as PrimarySeq
    my $seq2 = new Bio::Seq('-SEQ' => $c, '-ID' => 'no.Two');
    print "$c translated as a coding region (CDS): ",
    $seq2->translate(undef, undef, undef, undef, 1)->seq, "\n";

    print "\nTranslating in all six frames:\n";
    my @frames = (0, 1, 2);
    foreach my $frame (@frames) {
        print " frame: ", $frame, " forward: ",
        $seq->translate(undef, undef, $frame)->seq, "\n";
        print " frame: ", $frame, " reverse-complement: ",
        $seq->revcom->translate(undef, undef, $frame)->seq, "\n";
    }

    print "Translating with all codon tables using method defaults:\n";
    my @codontables = qw( 1 2 3 4 5 6 9 10 11 12 13 14 15 16 21 );
    foreach my $ct (@codontables) {
        print $ct, " : ",
        $seq->translate(undef, undef, undef, $ct)->seq, "\n";
    }

    return 1;
} ;


#################################################
```

bptutorial.pl: sequence_manipulation Demo

In this section, I'll go through the code for the demo subroutine sequence_manipulation that was shown in the last section.

The subroutine is actually an anonymous subroutine; a reference to the subroutine is saved in the scalar reference variable $sequence_manipulation:

```
$sequence_manipulations = sub {
...
}
```

The first few lines of code declare some variables with my. Notice that these are not being passed in as arguments; this method uses no arguments but does occasionally use global variables such as $dna_seq_file, which, as you've just seen, contain the pathname of the input sequence file the demo will use:

```
my ($infile, $in, $out, $seqobj);
$infile = $dna_seq_file;

print "\nBeginning sequence_manipulations and SeqIO example... \n";
```

The code is cross-referenced to the tutorial sections of the file. The next comment line refers to the part of the document:

```
# III.3.1 Transforming sequence files (SeqIO)
```

which can be looked up in the table of contents to the document for further reading:

```
III.3 Manipulating sequences
III.3.1 Manipulating sequence data with Seq methods (Seq)
```

Now, I'll take a look at the first section of example code in the sequence_manipulations method:

```
# III.3.1 Transforming sequence files (SeqIO)

$in  = Bio::SeqIO->new('-file' => $infile ,'-format' => 'Fasta');
$seqobj = $in->next_seq();

# perl "tied filehandle" syntax is available to SeqIO,
# allowing you to use the standard <> and print operations
# to read and write sequence objects, eg:
#$out = Bio::SeqIO->newFh('-format' => 'EMBL');

$out = Bio::SeqIO->newFh('-format' => 'fasta');

print "First sequence in fasta format... \n";
print $out $seqobj;
```

The code starts with a call to the new object constructor of the Bio::SeqIO class. The new method is being passed the pathname to a FASTA file in $infile, and told that the format is FASTA.

A quick look at the Bio::SeqIO documentation explains that the call to Bio::SeqIO-> new returns a stream object for the specified format. So, $out is a stream object (a stream is input or output of data) for FASTA-formatted data, and $in is a stream object for FASTA-formatted input from the file named in the $infile variable. These $in and $out objects are also filehandles.

After the $in object is initialized on the FASTA file named in $infile, it calls the next_seq method, which gets the next (in this case, the first and perhaps only) FASTA record from the file, and it creates a sequence object $seqobj. The output $out object is created. The Perl print statement is then called, using $out as a filehandle, and printing $seqobj. This prints the first FASTA record from that file, as shown in the demo output in the last section and repeated here:

```
First sequence in fasta format...
>Test1
AGCTTTTCATTCTGACTGCAACGGGCAATATGTCTCTGTGTGGATTAAAAAAAGAGTGTC
TGATAGCAGCTTCTGAACTGGTTACCTGCCGTGAGTAAATTAAAATTTTATTGACTTAGG
TCACTAAATACTTTAACCAATATAGGCATAGCGCACAGACAGATAAAAATTACAGAGTAC
ACAACATCCATGAAACGCATTAGCACCACC
```

The next part of the sequence_manipulation demo code shows many of the methods for extracting information from a sequence object:

```
# III.4 Manipulating individual sequences

# The following methods return strings

print "Seq object display id is ",
$seqobj->display_id(), "\n"; # the human read-able id of the sequence
print "Sequence is ",
$seqobj->seq()," \n";        # string of sequence
print "Sequence from 5 to 10 is ",
$seqobj->subseq(5,10)," \n"; # part of the sequence as a string
print "Acc num is ",
$seqobj->accession_number(), " \n"; # when there, the accession number
print "Moltype is ",
$seqobj->alphabet(), " \n";    # one of 'dna','rna','protein'
print "Primary id is ", $seqobj->primary_seq->primary_id()," \n";
# a unique id for this sequence irregardless
#print "Primary id is ", $seqobj->primary_id(), " \n";
# a unique id for this sequence irregardless
# of its display_id or accession number

# The following methods return an array of  Bio::SeqFeature objects
$seqobj->top_SeqFeatures; # The 'top level' sequence features
$seqobj->all_SeqFeatures; # All sequence features, including sub
# seq features

# The following methods returns new sequence objects,
# but do not transfer features across
# truncation from 5 to 10 as new object
print "Truncated Seq object sequence is ",
```

```
$seqobj->trunc(5,10)->seq( ), " \n";
# reverse complements sequence
print "Reverse complemented sequence 5 to 10  is ",
$seqobj->trunc(5,10)->revcom->seq, "  \n";
# translation of the sequence
print "Translated sequence 6 to 15 is ",
$seqobj->translate->subseq(6,15), " \n";
```

This section of the tutorial produced the following output (slightly reformatted to fit the pages of this book):

```
Seq object display id is Test1
Sequence is AGCTTTTCATTCTGACTGCAACGGGCAATATGTCTCTGTGTGGATTAAAAAAAGAGTGTCTGA
TAGCAGCTTCTGAACTGGTTACCTGCCGTGAGTAAATTAAAATTTTATTGACTTAGGTCACTAAATACTTTAACC
AATATAGGCATAGCGCACAGACAGATAAAAATTACAGAGTACACAACATCCATGAAACGCATTAGCACCACC
Sequence from 5 to 10 is TTTCAT
Acc num is unknown
Moltype is dna
Primary id is Test1
Truncated Seq object sequence is TTTCAT
Reverse complemented sequence 5 to 10  is ATGAAA
Translated sequence 6 to 15 is LQRAICLCVD
```

This part of the demo code is self-explanatory. As you can see, the methods return:

- The FASTA ID (the part immediately following the > sign in the first line)
- The sequence alone as a string (reformatted with line breaks to fit this book)
- The accession number if it is known (FASTA format won't have this, but Genbank format will, for instance)
- The type of molecule (dna, rna, or protein)
- A unique ID compared to other IDs in the running program but drawn from the file itself if possible
- The sequence of a new truncated sequence object defined from the original sequence object; a reverse complement
- The peptide resulting from a translation of a specified part of a sequence

The final section of the sequence_manipulation demo demonstrates the ability to translate nucleotides into all six reading frames using alternate codon translation tables if desired:

```
my $c = shift;
$c ||= 'ctgagaaataa';

print "\nBeginning 3-frame and alternate codon translation example... \n";

my $seq = new Bio::PrimarySeq('-SEQ' => $c, '-ID' => 'no.One');
print "$c translated using method defaults   : ",
$seq->translate->seq, "\n";

# Bio::Seq uses same sequence methods as PrimarySeq
my $seq2 = new Bio::Seq('-SEQ' => $c, '-ID' => 'no.Two');
```

```
print "$c translated as a coding region (CDS): ",
$seq2->translate(undef, undef, undef, undef, 1)->seq, "\n";

print "\nTranslating in all six frames:\n";
my @frames = (0, 1, 2);
foreach my $frame (@frames) {
    print " frame: ", $frame, " forward: ",
    $seq->translate(undef, undef, $frame)->seq, "\n";
    print " frame: ", $frame, " reverse-complement: ",
    $seq->revcom->translate(undef, undef, $frame)->seq, "\n";
}

print "Translating with all codon tables using method defaults:\n";
my @codontables = qw( 1 2 3 4 5 6 9 10 11 12 13 14 15 16 21 );
foreach my $ct (@codontables) {
    print $ct, " : ",
    $seq->translate(undef, undef, undef, $ct)->seq, "\n";
}
```

This produces the output:

```
Beginning 3-frame and alternate codon translation example...
ctgagaaaataa translated using method defaults    : LRK*
ctgagaaaataa translated as a coding region (CDS): MRK

Translating in all six frames:
 frame: 0 forward: LRK*
 frame: 0 reverse-complement: LFSQ
 frame: 1 forward: *EN
 frame: 1 reverse-complement: YFL
 frame: 2 forward: EKI
 frame: 2 reverse-complement: IFS
Translating with all codon tables using method defaults:
1 : LRK*
2 : L*K*
3 : TRK*
4 : LRK*
5 : LSK*
6 : LRKQ
9 : LSN*
10 : LRK*
11 : LRK*
12 : SRK*
13 : LGK*
14 : LSNY
15 : LRK*
16 : LRK*
21 : LSN*
```

Again, this code is fairly easy to follow, although you may find yourself turning to the documentation for some of the finer points when you try to use these objects and methods in your own code.

This part of the code starts by getting an argument of sequence data if one is available to be shifted off of the @_ argument array and into the variable $c; otherwise, it sets the variable $c to a preset sequence:

```
my $c = shift;
$c ||= 'ctgagaaaataa';
```

Briefly, the methods that follow in this part of the sequence_manipulation demo do the following:

- Call the PrimarySeq::new constructor to create a lightweight sequence object from $c that doesn't have the extra annotation often present in a standard sequence file (see perldoc Bio::PrimarySeq for the whole story)

- Translate the sequence (from $c)

- Call the Bio::Seq constructor to create the $seq2 sequence object (from the same sequence data in $seq)

- Translate the CDS in the sequence object $seq2

- Translate the sequence in all six reading frames

- Translate the sequence using all 21 defined codon tables

The translate method seems to have lots of interesting options. However, if you try to look up the documentation for this method, you may have difficulty finding it. The problem is that Bioperl classes often make considerable use of inheritance. Say that the code is calling a method on a Bio::PrimarySeq object, as do the following lines from the demo (somewhat separated in the original):

```
my $seq = new Bio::PrimarySeq('-SEQ' => $c, '-ID' => 'no.One');
$seq->translate(undef, undef, $frame)->seq, "\n";
```

You may try perldoc Bio::PrimarySeq and not find a discussion of the translate method because it is being inherited from some other class. And since multiple inheritance is possible, it can take considerable effort to track down this method documentation by figuring out the parent classes and searching the documentation.

There's a very convenient way to find the documentation for a method, even if it's only inherited—it's built into the bptutorial.pl script. In the example just mentioned, you ask for the list of methods used by the Bio::PrimarySeq method.

```
[tisdall]$ perl bptutorial.pl 100 Bio::PrimarySeq

***Methods for Object Bio::PrimarySeq ********

Methods taken from package Bio::DescribableI
description    display_name

Methods taken from package Bio::IdentifiableI
authority   lsid_string   namespace   namespace_string   object_id   version

Methods taken from package Bio::PrimarySeq
accession   direct_seq_set   validate_seq
```

```
Methods taken from package Bio::PrimarySeqI
accession_number   alphabet   can_call_new   desc   display_id   id
is_circular   length   moltype   primary_id   revcom   seq
subseq   translate   trunc

Methods taken from package Bio::Root::Root
DESTROY   debug   verbose

Methods taken from package Bio::Root::RootI
carp   confess   deprecated   new   stack_trace   stack_trace_dump
throw   throw_not_implemented   warn   warn_not_implemented
[tisdall]$
```

Sure enough, there under the heading "Methods taken from package Bio::Primary-SeqI" appears the method translate. You should then look at the Bio::PrimarySeqI documentation and find the following method description:

```
              translate

Title    : translate
Usage    : $protein_seq_obj = $dna_seq_obj->translate
           #if full CDS expected:
           $protein_seq_obj = $cds_seq_obj->translate(undef,undef,undef,undef,1);
Function :

           Provides the translation of the DNA sequence using full
           IUPAC ambiguities in DNA/RNA and amino acid codes.

           The full CDS translation is identical to EMBL/TREMBL
           database translation. Note that the trailing terminator
           character is removed before returning the translation
           object.

           Note: if you set $dna_seq_obj->verbose(1) you will get a
           warning if the first codon is not a valid initiator.

Returns  : A Bio::PrimarySeqI implementing object
Args     : character for terminator (optional) defaults to '*'
           character for unknown amino acid (optional) defaults to 'X'
           frame (optional) valid values 0, 1, 2, defaults to 0
           codon table id (optional) defaults to 1
           complete coding sequence expected, defaults to 0 (false)
           boolean, throw exception if not complete CDS (true) or
           defaults to warning (false)
```

You will want to explore at least a few more of the tutorials embedded in bptutorial.pl, as we've done here with the first of the tutorials.

Using Bioperl Modules

I've reached my stated goal: to get you started using Bioperl. Needless to say, there is a great deal more to explore than will fit into the confines of this chapter.

For those who wish to continue, here is a short list of some of the interesting and useful parts of Bioperl that will repay your efforts to learn them with considerably increased programming power:

- Overview of Bioperl objects
- Seq objects
- Gbrowse and gff files
- BLAST parsing
- Automated database searching

## PART III

Appendixes

Perl Summary

This appendix summarizes those parts of the Perl programming language that will be most useful to you as you read this book. It is not a comprehensive summary of the Perl language. Remember that Perl is designed so that you don't need to know everything in order to use it. Source material for this appendix came from *Programming Perl* (O'Reilly).

Command Interpretation

The Perl programs in this book start with a line something like:

```
#!/usr/bin/perl
```

On Unix (or Linux) systems, the first line of a file can include the name of a program and some flags, which are optional. The line must start with #!, followed by the full pathname of the program (in this case, the Perl interpreter), followed optionally by a single group of one or more flags. It's common in Perl programs to see the -w flag on this first command interpreter line, like so:

```
#!/usr/bin/perl -w
```

The -w flag turns on extra warnings. I prefer to do that with the line:

```
use warnings;
```

because it's more portable to different operating systems.

If the Perl program file is called myprogram and has executable permissions, you can type myprogram (or possibly ./myprogram or the full or relative pathname for the program) to start the program running.

The Unix operating system starts the program specified in the command interpretation line and gives it as input the rest of the file after the first line. So, in this case, it starts the Perl interpreter and gives it the program in the file to run.

This is just a shortcut for typing the following at the command line:

```
/usr/bin/perl myprogram
```

Comments

A comment begins with a # sign and continues from there to the end of the same line. It is ignored by the Perl interpreter and is only there for programmers to read. A comment can include any text.

Scalar Values and Scalar Variables

A scalar value is a single item of data, such as a string, a number, or a reference.

Strings

Strings are scalar values and are written as text enclosed within single quotes, like so:

```
'This is a string in single quotes.'
```

or double quotes, such as:

```
"This is a string in double quotes."
```

A single-quoted string prints out exactly as written. With double quotes, you can include a variable in the string, and its value will be inserted or "interpolated." You can also include commands such as \n to represent a newline (see Table A-3):

```
$aside = '(or so they say)';
$declaration = "Misery\n $aside \nloves company.";
print $declaration;
```

This snippet prints out:

```
Misery
 (or so they say)
loves company.
```

Numbers

Numbers are scalar values that can be:

- Integers:

    ```
    3
    -4
    0
    ```

- Floating-point (decimal):

    ```
    4.5326
    ```

- Scientific (exponential) notation (3.13×10^{23} or 313000000000000000000000):

    ```
    3.13E23
    ```

- Hexadecimal (base 16):

    0x12bc3

- Octal (base 8):

    05777

- Binary (base 2):

    0b10101011

Complex (or imaginary) numbers, such as 3 + i, and fractions (or ratios, or rational numbers), such as 1/3, can be a little tricky. Perl can handle fractions but converts them internally to floating-point numbers, which can make certain operations go wrong (Perl is not alone among computer languages in this regard):

```
if ( 10/3  == ( (1/3) * 10 ) {
    print "Success!";
}else {
    print "Failure!";
}
```

This prints:

    Failure!

To properly handle rational arithmetic with fractions, complex numbers, or many other mathematical constructs, there are mathematics modules available, which aren't covered here.

References

Perl *references* are scalar values that contain a location in memory where some other Perl data can be found. Think of references as scalar values that point to other data, such as scalars like strings or numbers, or arrays, hashes, or subroutines.

References are mainly used to:

- Pass diverse types of arguments into a Perl subroutine
- Avoid copying large amounts of data
- Define the objects of object-oriented programming
- Build complex data structures

To create a reference, prepend a Perl value, variable, or subroutine with a backslash.

To save a reference, assign it to a scalar variable.

You can refer to a string by preceding it with a backslash:

    \'A referenced string'

and you make a reference to a number similarly:

    \3.1415925

These references may be saved in scalar variables, discussed next.

Scalar Variables

Scalar values can be stored in scalar variables. A scalar variable is indicated with a $ before the variable's name. The name begins with a letter or underscore and can have any number of letters, underscores, or digits. A digit, however, can't be the first character in a variable name. Here are some examples of legal names of scalar variables:

```
$Var
$var_1
```

Here are some improper names for scalar variables:

```
$1var
$var!iable
```

Names are case-sensitive: $dna is different from $DNA.

These rules for making proper variable names (apart from the beginning $) also hold for the names of array and hash variables and for subroutine names.

A scalar variable may hold any type of scalar value mentioned previously, such as strings or the different types of numbers.

Assignment

Scalar variables are assigned scalar values with an assignment operator (the equals sign) in an assignment statement:

```
$thousand = 1000;
```

assigns the integer 1000, a scalar value, to the scalar variable $thousand.

The assignment statement looks like an equal sign from elementary mathematics, but its meaning is different. The assignment statement is an instruction, not an assertion. It doesn't mean "$thousand equals 1000." It means "store the scalar value 1000 into the scalar variable $thousand". However, after the statement, the value of the scalar variable $thousand is, indeed, equal to 1000.

References are usually saved in scalar variables. For example:

```
$pi = \3.14159265;
```

If you try to print $pi after this assignment, you get an indication that it's a reference to a scalar value at a memory location represented in hexadecimal digits. To print the value of a variable that's a reference to a scalar, precede its name with an additional dollar sign:

```
print $pi,"\n";
print $$pi, "\n";
```

This gives the output:

```
SCALAR(0x811d1bc)
3.14159265
```

You can assign values to several scalar variables by surrounding variables and values in parentheses and separating them by commas, thus making lists:

```
($one, $two, $three) = ( 1, 2, 3);
```

There are several assignment operators besides = that are shorthand for longer expressions. For instance, $a += $b is equivalent to $a = $a + $b. Table A-1 is a complete list.

Table A-1. Assignment operator shorthands

Example of operator	Equivalent	
$a += $b	$a = $a + $b	(addition)
$a -= $b	$a = $a - $b	(subtraction)
$a *= $b	$a = $a * $b	(multiplication)
$a /= $b	$a = $a / $b	(division)
$a **= $b	$a = $a ** $b	(exponentiation)
$a %= $b	$a = $a % $b	(remainder of $a / $b)
$a x= $b	$a = $a x $b	(string $a repeated $b times)
$a &= $b	$a = $a & $b	(bitwise AND)
$a |= $b	$a = $a | $b	(bitwise OR)
$a ^= $b	$a = $a ^ $b	(bitwise XOR)
$a >>= $b	$a = $a >> $b	($a shift $b bits)
$a <<= $b	$a = $a >> $b	($a shift $b bits to left)
$a &&= $b	$a = $a && $b	(logical AND)
$a ||= $b	$a = $a || $b	(logical OR)
$a .= $b	$a = $a . $b	(append string $b to $a)

Statements and Blocks

Programs are composed of statements often grouped together into blocks.

A statement ends with a semicolon (;), which is optional for the last statement in a block.

A block is one or more statements usually surrounded by curly braces:

```
{
  $thousand = 1000;
  print $thousand;
}
```

Blocks may stand by themselves but are often associated with such constructs as loops or if statements.

Arrays

Arrays are ordered collections of zero or more scalar values, indexed by position. An array variable begins with the @ sign followed by a legal variable name. For instance, here are two possible array variable names:

```
@array1
@dna_fragments
```

You can assign scalar values to an array by placing the scalar values in a list separated by commas and surrounded by a pair of parentheses. For instance, you can assign an array the empty list:

```
@array = ();
```

or one or more scalar values:

```
@dna_fragments = ('ACGT', $fragment2, 'GGCGGA');
```

Notice that it's okay to specify a scalar variable such as $fragment2 in a list. Its current value, not the variable name, is placed into the array.

The individual scalar values of an array (the elements) are indexed by their position in the array. The index numbers begin at 0. You can specify the individual elements of an array by preceding the array name by a $ and following it with the index number of the element within square brackets, like so:

```
$dna_fragments[2]
```

This equals the value of 'GGCGGA', given the values previously set for this array. Notice that the array has three scalar values indexed by numbers 0, 1, and 2. The third and last element is indexed 2, one less than the total number of elements 3, because the first element is indexed number 0.

You can make a copy of an array using an assignment operator =, as in this example that makes a copy @output of an existing array @input:

```
@output = @input;
```

If you evaluate an array in scalar context, the value is the number of elements in the array. So if array @input has five elements, the following example assigns the value 5 to $count:

```
$count = @input;
```

Figure A-1 shows an array @myarray with three elements, which demonstrates the ordered nature of an array by which each element appears and can be found by its position in the array.

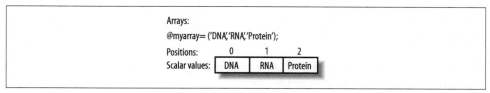

Figure A-1. Schematic of an array

You can make a reference to an array by preceding it with a backslash; you dereference it by preceding the reference with an at sign @ for the entire array or with an extra dollar sign $ for an individual element of the array:

```
@a = ( 'one', 'two', 'three');
$aref = ^a;
print $aref, "\n";
print $$aref[0], "\n";
print "@$aref", "\n";
```

gives the output:

```
ARRAY(0x811d1e0)
one
one two three
```

You can also define an array as an anonymous array. An anonymous array isn't saved in a named array variable; it's a reference to array data and can only be saved in a reference. It's initialized within square brackets:

```
$anonarray = [ 'one', 'two', 'three'];
print "@$anonarray", "\n";
```

gives the output:

```
one two three
```

Hashes

A hash (also called an associative array) is a collection of zero or more pairs of scalar values, called keys and values. The values are indexed by the keys. An array variable begins with the % sign followed by a legal variable name. For instance, possible hash variable names are:

```
%hash1
%genes_by_name
```

You can assign a value to a key with a simple assignment statement. For example, say you have a hash called %baseball_stadiums and a key Phillies to which you want to assign the value Citizens Bank Park. This statement accomplishes the assignment:

```
$baseball_stadiums{'Phillies'} = 'Citizens State Bank';
```

Note that a single hash value is referenced by a $ instead of a % at the beginning of the hash name; this is similar to the way you reference individual array values using a $ instead of a @.

You can assign several keys and values to a hash by placing their scalar values in a list separated by commas and surrounded by a pair of parentheses. Each successive pair of scalars becomes a key and a value in the hash. For instance, you can assign a hash the empty list:

```
%hash = ( );
```

You can also assign one or more scalar key/value pairs:

```
%genes_by_name = ('gene1', 'AACCCGGTTGGTT', 'gene2', 'CCTTTCGGAAGGTC');
```

There is an another way to do the same thing, which makes the key/value pairs more readily apparent. This accomplishes the same thing as the preceding example:

```
%genes_by_name = (
    'gene1' => 'AACCCGGTTGGTT',
    'gene2' => 'CCTTTCGGAAGGTC'
);
```

To get the value associated with a particular key, precede the hash name with a $ and follow it with a pair of curly braces containing the scalar value of the key:

```
$genes_by_name{'gene1'}
```

This returns the value 'AACCCGGTTGGTT', given the value previously assigned to the key 'gene1' in the hash %genes_by_name. Figure A-2 shows a hash with three keys.

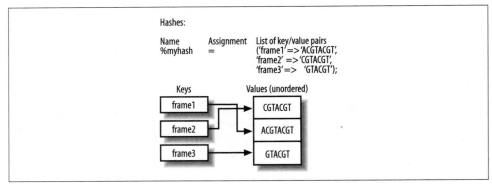

Figure A-2. Schematic of a hash

You can get an array of all the keys in a hash with the operator "keys", and you can get an array of all the values in a hash with the operator "values".

The arrays you get won't be sorted. Here's an example:

```
%h = ( 'one'      => 'for the money',
        'two'      => 'for the show',
        'three'    => 'to get ready'
```

```
);
@keys = keys %h;
@values = values %h;
print "@keys\n@values\n";
```

gives the output:

```
three one two
```

to get ready for the money for the show.

You can make a reference to a hash by preceding it with a backslash; you dereference it by preceding the reference with a percent sign % for the entire hash or with an
extra dollar sign $ for an individual value of some hash key:

```
%h = ( 'one'        => 'for the money',
       'two'        => 'for the show',
       'three'      => 'to get ready'
);
$href = %h;
print $href, "\n";
print $$href{'two'}, "\n";
foreach $key ( keys %$href ) {
    print "key = $key value = $$href{$key}\n";
}
```

gives the output:

```
HASH(0x811d1e0)
for the show
key = three      value = to get ready
key = one        value = for the money
key = two        value = for the show
```

You can also define a hash as an anonymous hash. An anonymous hash isn't saved in
a named hash variable; it's a reference to hash data, and can only be saved in a reference. It is initialized within curly brackets:

```
$anonhash = { 'one' => 'first',
              'two' => 'second',
              'three' => 'third'
            };
foreach $key ( keys %$anonhash ) {
    print "key = $key value = $$anonhash{$key}\n";
}
```

gives the (unsorted) output:

```
key = three    value = third
key = one       value = first
key = two       value = second
```

Complex Data Structures

The standard Perl data types, scalar, array, and hash, can be combined into more complex data structures using references. The construction of complex data structures is summarized in Chapter 2.

As an example, you can define a two-dimensional matrix as an array of anonymous arrays (recall that an anonymous array is a reference to array data):

```
@microarray = (
    [ 10, 2, 14 ],
    [ 15, 4, 54 ],
    [ 51, 0, 99 ]
);
```

Operators

Operators are functions that represent basic operations on values: addition, subtraction, etc. They are frequently used and are core parts of the Perl programming language. They are really just functions that take arguments. For instance, + is the operator that adds two numbers, like so:

```
3 + 4;
```

Operators typically have one, two, or three operands; in the example just given, there are two operands 3 and 4.

Operators can appear before, between, or after their operands. For example, the plus operator + appears between its operands.

Operator Precedence

Operator precedence determines the order in which the operations are applied. For instance, in Perl, the expression:

```
3 + 3 * 4
```

isn't evaluated left to right, which calculates 3 + 3 equals 6, and 6 times 4 results in a value of 24; the precedence rules cause the multiplication to be applied first, for a final result of 15. The precedence rules are available in the perlop manpage and in most Perl books. However, I recommend you use parentheses to make your code more readable and to avoid bugs. They make the following expressions unambiguous; the first:

```
(3 + 3) * 4
```

evaluates to 24, and the second:

```
3 + (3 * 4)
```

evaluates to 15.

Basic Operators

For more information on how operators work, consult the `perlop` documentation bundled with Perl.

Arithmetic Operators

Perl has the basic five arithmetic operators:

+   Addition

−   Subtraction

*   Multiplication

/   Division

** Exponentiation

These operators work on both integers and floating-point values (and if you're not careful, strings as well).

Perl also has a `modulus` operator, which computes the remainder of two integers:

```
% modulus
```

For example, 17 % 3 is 2, because 2 is left over when you divide 3 into 17.

Perl also has autoincrement and autodecrement operators:

```
++ add one
-- subtract one
```

Unlike the previous six operators, these change a variable's value. $x++ adds one to $x, changing 4 to 5 (or a to b).

Bitwise Operators

All scalars, whether numbers or strings, are represented as sequences of individual bits "under the hood." Every once in a while, you need to manipulate those bits, and Perl provides five operators to help:

&   Bitwise and

| Bitwise or

^   Bitwise xor

>> Right shift

<< Left shift

String Operators

Two strings may be concatenated, i.e., joined end to end, with the dot operator:

```
'This is a ' . 'joined string'
```

This results in the value 'This is a joined string'.

A string may be repeated with the x operator:

```
print "Hear ye! " x 3;
```

This prints:

```
Hear ye! Hear ye! Hear ye!
```

File Test Operators

File test operators are unary operators that test files for certain characteristics, such as -e $file, which returns true if the file $file exists. Table A-2 lists some available file test operators.

Table A-2. File test operators

Operator	Meaning
−r	File is readable
−w	File is writable
−x	File is executable
−o	File is owned by "you"
−e	File exists
−z	File has zero size in bytes
−s	File has nonzero size (returns size in bytes)
−f	File is a plain file
−d	File is a directory (a.k.a. folder)
−l	File is a symbolic link
−t	Filehandle is opened to a terminal
−T	File is a text file
−B	File is a binary file
−M	Age of file (at startup of program) in days since modification
−A	Age of file (at startup of program) in days since last access
−C	Age of file (at startup of program) in days since last inode change

Conditionals and Logical Operators

This section covers conditional statements and logical operators.

true and false

In a conditional test, an expression evaluates to true or false, and based on the result, a statement or block may or may not be executed.

A scalar value can be true or false in a conditional. A string is false if it's the empty string (represented as "" or ' '). A string is true if it's not the empty string.

Similarly, an array or a hash is false if empty and true if nonempty.

A number is false if it's 0; a number is true if it's not 0.

Most things you evaluate in Perl return some value (such as a number from an arithmetic expression or an array returned from a subroutine), so you can use most things in Perl in conditional tests. Sometimes you may get an undefined value, for example, if you try to add a number to a variable that has not been assigned a value. Things might then fail to work as expected. For instance, the following:

```
use strict;
use warnings;
my $a;
my $b;
$b = $a + 2;
```

produces the warning output:

```
Use of uninitialized value in addition (+) at - line 5.
```

You can test for defined and undefined values with the Perl function defined.

Logical Operators

There are four logical operators:

```
not
and
or
xor
```

not turns true values into false and false values into true. Its use is best illustrated in code:

```
if(not $done) {...}
```

This executes the code only if $done is false.

and is a binary operator that returns true if both its operands are true. If one or both of the operands are false, the operator returns false:

```
1   and 1    returns true
'a' and ''   returns false
''  and 0    returns false
```

or is a binary operator that returns true if one or both of the operands are true. If both operands are false, it returns false:

```
1   or  1     returns true
'a' or  ''    returns true
''  or  0     returns false
```

xor, or exclusive-OR, returns true if one operand is true and the other operand is false; xor returns false if both operands are true or if both operands are false:

```
1 xor 0    returns true
0 xor 1    returns true
1 xor 1    returns false
0 xor 0    returns false
```

There are also variants on most of these:

```
! for not
&& for and
|| for or
```

These have different precedence but otherwise behave the same. Some older versions of Perl may only have:

```
!
||
&&
```

instead of not or and.

Using Logical Operators for Control Flow

A quick and popular way to take an action, depending on the results of a previous action, is to chain the statements together with logical operators. For instance, it's common in Perl programs to see the following statement to open a file:

```
open(FH, $filename) or die "Cannot open file $filename: $!";
```

The use of or in this statement shows another important thing about the binary logical operators: they evaluate their arguments left to right. In this case, if the open succeeds, the or operator never bothers to check the value of the second operand (die, which exits the program with the message in the string, plus additional messages if $! is included). The or never bothers, because if one operand is true, the or is true, so it doesn't need to check the second operand. However, if the open fails, the or needs to check that the second operand is true or false, so it goes ahead and executes the die statement.

You can use the and statement similarly to test the second operand only if the first operand succeeds.

xor doesn't work for control flow, because both its arguments have to be evaluated each time.

I haven't used this chaining of logical operators much; instead, I've used `if` statements. This is because I often find that I want to add more statements following a test, and it's easier if the original is written as an `if` statement with a block, and it's harder if the original is written as a logical operator.

The if Statement

Conditional tests are commonly found in `if` statements and in their variants and loops. Here's an example of an `if` statement:

```
if (open (FH, $filename) {
    print "Hurray, I opened the file.";
}
```

The `if` statement is followed by a conditional expression enclosed in parentheses, which is followed by a block enclosed in curly braces. When the conditional expression evaluates as `true`, the statements in the block are executed.

The `if` statement may optionally be followed by an `else`, which is executed when the conditional evaluates to `false`:

```
if ( open(FH, $filename) {
    print "Hurray, I opened the file.";
} else {
    print "Rats. The file did not open.";
}
```

The `if` statement may also optionally include any number of `elsif` clauses, which check additional conditional statements if none of the preceding conditional statements are true:

```
if ( open(FH, $file1) {
    print "Hurray, I opened file 1.";
} elsif ( open(FH, $file2) {
    print "Hurray, I opened file 2.";
} elsif ( open(FH, $file3) {
    print "Hurray, I opened file 3.";
} else {
    print "None of the dadblasted files would open.";
}
```

In the preceding example, if file 1 opened successfully, the `if` statement doesn't try to open additional files.

There is also an `unless` statement, which is the same as an `if` statement with the conditional negated. So these two statements are equivalent:

```
unless ( open(FH, $filename) {
    print "Rats. The file did not open.";
}
```

```
if ( not open(FH, $filename) {
    print "Rats. The file did not open.";
}
```

Binding Operators

Binding operators are used for pattern matching, substitution, and transliteration on strings. They are used with regular expressions that specify the patterns:

```
'ACGTACGTACGTACGT' =~ /CTA/
```

The pattern is the string CTA, enclosed by forward slashes. The string binding operator is =~; it tells the program which string to search, returning true if the pattern appears in the string.

!~ is another string binding operator; it returns true if the pattern isn't in the string:

```
'ACGTACGTACGTACGT' !~ /CTA/
```

This is equivalent to:

```
not 'ACGTACGTACGTACGT' =~ /CTA/
```

You can substitute one pattern for another using the string binding operator. In the next example, s/thine/nine/ is the substitution command, which substitutes the first occurrence of thine with the string nine:

```
$poor_richard = 'A stitch in time saves thine.';
$poor_richard =~ s/thine/nine/;
print $poor_richard;
```

This produces the output:

```
A stitch in time saves nine.
```

Finally, the transliteration (or translate) operator tr substitutes characters in a string. It has several uses, but the two uses I've covered are first, to change bases to their complements A → T, C → G, G → C, and T → A:

```
$DNA = 'ACGTTTAA';
$DNA =~ tr/ACGT/TGCA/;
```

This produces the value:

```
TGCAAATT
```

Second, the tr operator counts the number of a particular character in a string, as in this example which counts the number of Gs in a string of DNA sequence data:

```
$DNA = 'ACGTTTAA';
$count = ($DNA =~ tr/A//);
print $count;
```

This produces the value 3; it shows that a pattern match can return a count of the number of translations made in a string, which is then assigned to the variable $count.

Loops

Loops repeatedly execute the statements in a block until a conditional test changes value. There are several forms of loops in Perl:

```
while(CONDITION) {BLOCK}
until(CONDITION) {BLOCK}
for(INITIALIZATION ; CONDITION ; RE-INITIALIZATION ) {BLOCK}
foreach VAR (LIST) {BLOCK}
for VAR (LIST) {BLOCK}
do {BLOCK} while (CONDITION)
do {BLOCK} until (CONDITION)
```

The while loop first tests if the conditional is true; if so, it executes the block and then returns to the conditional to repeat the process. If false, it does nothing, and the loop is over:

```
$i = 3;
while ( $i ) {
    print "$i\n";
    $i--;
}
```

This produces the output:

```
3
2
1
```

Here's how the loop works. The scalar variable $i is first initialized to 3 (this isn't part of the loop). The loop is then entered, and $i is tested to see if it has a true (nonzero) value. It does, so the number 3 is printed, and the decrement operator is applied to $i, which reduces its value to 2. The block is now over, and the loop starts again with the conditional test. It succeeds with the true value 2, which is printed and decremented. The loop restarts with a test of $i, which is now the true value 1; 1 is printed and decremented to 0. The loop starts again; 0 is tested to see if it's true, and it's not, so the loop is now finished.

Loops often follow the same pattern, in which a variable is set, and a loop is called, which tests the variable's value and then executes a block, which includes changing the value of the variable.

The for loop makes this easy by including the variable initialization and the variable change in the loop statement. The following is exactly equivalent to the preceding example and produces the same output:

```
for ( $i = 3 ; $i ; $i-- ) {
    print "$i\n";
}
```

The foreach loop is a convenient way to iterate through the elements in an array. Here's an example:

```
@array = ('one', 'two', 'three');

foreach $element (@array) {
    print $element\n";
}
```

This prints the output:

```
one
two
three
```

The foreach loop specifies a scalar variable $element to be set to each element of the array. (You may use any variable name or none, in which case the special variable $_ is used automatically.) The array to be iterated over is then placed in parentheses, followed by the block. You can use for instead of foreach as the name of this loop, with identical behavior.

The first time through the loop, the value of the first element of the array is assigned to the foreach variable $element. On each succeeding pass through the loop, the value of the next element of the array is assigned to the foreach variable $element. The loop exits after it has reached the end of the array.

There is one important point to make, however. If, in the block, you change the value of the loop variable $element, the array is changed, and the change stays in effect after you've left the foreach loop. For example the following:

```
@array = ('one', 'two', 'three');

foreach $element (@array) {
    $element = 'four';
}

foreach $element (@array) {
    print $element,"\n";
}
```

produces the output:

```
four
four
four
```

In the do-until loop, the block is executed before the conditional test, and the test succeeds until the condition is true:

```
$i = 3;
do {
    print $i,"\n";
    $i--;
} until ( $i );
```

This prints:

```
3
```

In the do-while loop, the block is executed before the conditional test, and the test succeeds while the condition is true:

```
$i = 3;
do {
    print $i,"\n";
    $i--;
} while ( $i );
```

This prints:

```
3
2
1
```

Input/Output

This section covers getting information into programs and receiving data back from them.

Input from Files

Perl has several convenient ways to get information into a program. The non-CGI programs in this book usually get input by opening and reading files. I've emphasized this way of getting input because it behaves very much the same way on any computer you may be using. You've observed the open and close system calls and how to associate a filehandle with a file when you open it, which then is used to read in the data. As an example:

```
open(FILEHANDLE, "informationfile");
@data_from_informationfile = <FILEHANDLE>;
close(FILEHANDLE);
```

This code opens the file informationfile and associates the filehandle FILEHAN-DLE with it. The filehandle is then used within angle brackets to actually read in the contents of the file and store the contents in the array @data_from_informationfile. Finally, the file is closed by referring once again to the opened filehandle.

Input from STDIN

Perl allows you to read in any input that is automatically sent to your program via standard input (STDIN). STDIN is a filehandle that by default is always open. Your program may be expecting some input that way. For instance, on a Mac, you can drag and drop a file icon onto the Perl applet for your program to make the file's contents appear in STDIN. On Unix systems, you can pipe the output of some other program into the STDIN of your program with shell commands such as:

```
somprog | my_perl_program
```

You can also pipe the contents of a file into your program with:

```
cat file | my_perl_program
```

or with:

```
my_perl_program < file.
```

Your program can then read in the data (from program or file) that comes as STDIN just as if it came from a file that you've opened:

```
@data_from_stdin = <STDIN>;
```

Input from Files Named on the Command Line

You can name your input files on the command line. <> is shorthand for <ARGV>. The ARGV filehandle treats the array @ARGV as a list of filenames and returns the contents of all those files, one line at a time. Perl places all command-line arguments into the array @ARGV. Some of these may be special flags, which should be read and removed from @ARGV if there will also be data files named. Perl assumes that anything in @ARGV refers to an input filename when it reaches a <> command. The contents of the file or files are then available to the program using the angle brackets without a filehandle, like so:

```
@data_from_files = <>;
```

For example, on Microsoft, Unix, or on the Mac OS X, you specify input files at the command line, like so:

```
% my_program file1 file2 file3
```

Output Commands

The print statement is the most common way to output data from a Perl program. The print statement takes as arguments a list of scalars separated by commas. An array can be an argument, in which case, the elements of the array are all printed one after the other:

```
@array = ('DNA', 'RNA', 'Protein');
print @array;
```

This prints:

```
DNARNAProtein
```

If you want to put spaces between the elements of an array, place it between double quotes in the print statement, like this:

```
@array = ('DNA', 'RNA', 'Protein');
print "@array";
```

This prints:

```
DNA RNA Protein
```

The print statement can specify a filehandle as an optional indirect object between the print statement and the arguments, like so:

```
print FH "@array";
```

The printf function gives more control over the formatting of the output of numbers. For instance, you can specify field widths; the precision, or number of places after the decimal point; and whether the value is right- or left-justified in the field. Check the Perl documentation that comes with your copy of Perl for all the details.

The sprintf function is related to the printf function; it formats a string instead of printing it out.

The format and write commands are a way to format a multiline output, as when generating reports. format can be a useful command, but in practice it isn't used much. The full details are available in your Perl documentation, and O'Reilly's *Programming Perl* contains an entire chapter on format.

Output to STDOUT, STDERR, and files

Standard output, with the filehandle STDOUT, is the default destination for output from a Perl program, so it doesn't have to be named. The following two statements are equivalent unless you used select to change the default output filehandle:

```
print "Hello biology world!\n";
print STDOUT "Hello biology world!\n";
```

Note that the STDOUT isn't followed by a comma. STDOUT is usually directed to the computer screen, but it may be redirected at the command line to other programs or files. This Unix command pipes the STDOUT of my_program to the STDIN of your_program:

```
my_program | your_program
```

This Unix command directs the output of my_program to the file outputfile:

```
my_program > outputfile
```

It's also common to direct certain error messages to the predefined standard error filehandle STDERR or to a file you've opened for input and named with a particular filehandle. Here are examples of these two tasks:

```
print STDERR "If you reached this part of the program, something is terribly wrong!";

open(OUTPUTFD, ">output_file");
print OUTPUTFD "Here is the first line in the output file output_file\n";
```

STDERR is also usually directed to the computer screen by default, but it can be directed into a file from the command line. This is done differently for different systems, for example, as follows (on Unix with the *sh* or *bash* shells):

```
myprogram 2>myprogram.error
```

You can also direct STDERR to a file from within your Perl program by including code such as the following before the first output to STDERR. This is the most portable way to redirect STDERR:

```
open (STDERR, ">myprogram.error") or die "Cannot open error file
    myprogram.error:$!\n";
```

The problem with this is that the original STDERR is lost. This method, taken from *Programming Perl*, saves and restores the original STDERR:

```
open ERRORFILE, ">myprogram.error"
    or die "Can't open myprogram.error";
open SAVEERR, ">&STDERR";
open STDERR, ">&ERRORFILE";

print STDERR "This will appear in error file myprogram.error\n";

# now, restore STDERR
close STDERR;
open STDERR, ">&SAVEERR";

print STDERR "This will appear on the computer screen\n";
```

There are a lot of details concerning filehandles not covered in this book, and redirecting one of the predefined filehandles such as STDERR can cause problems, especially as your programs get bigger and rely more on modules and libraries of subroutines. One safe way is to define a new filehandle associated with an error file and to send all your error messages to it:

```
open (ERRORMESSAGES, ">myprogram.error")
    or die "Cannot open myprogram.error:$!\n";

print ERRORMESSAGES "This is an error message\n";
```

Note that the die function, and the closely related warn function, print their error messages to STDERR.

Regular Expressions

Regular expressions are, in effect, an extra language that lives inside the Perl language. In Perl, they have quite a lot of features. First, I'll summarize how regular expressions work in Perl; then, I'll present some of their many features.

Overview

Regular expressions describe patterns in strings. The pattern described by a single regular expression may match many different strings.

Regular expressions are used in pattern matching, that is, when you look to see if a certain pattern exists in a string. They can also change strings, as with the s/// operator that substitutes the pattern, if found, for a replacement. Additionally, they are used in the tr function that can transliterate several characters into replacement characters throughout a string. Regular expressions are case-sensitive, unless explicitly told otherwise.

The simplest pattern match is a string that matches itself. For instance, to see if the pattern 'abc' appears in the string 'abcdefghijklmnopqrstuvwxyz', write the following in Perl:

```
$alphabet = 'abcdefghijklmnopqrstuvwxyz';
if( $alphabet =~ /abc/ ) {
    print $&;
}
```

The =~ operator binds a pattern match to a string. /abc/ is the pattern abc, enclosed in forward slashes to indicate that it's a regular-expression pattern. $& is set to the matched pattern, if any. In this case, the match succeeds, since 'abc' appears in the string $alphabet, and the code just given prints out abc.

Regular expressions are made from two kinds of characters. Many characters, such as 'a' or 'Z', match themselves. Metacharacters have a special meaning in the regular-expression language. For instance, parentheses are used to group other characters and don't match themselves. If you want to match a metacharacter such as (in a string, you have to precede it with the backslash metacharacter \(in the pattern.

There are three basic ideas behind regular expressions. The first is concatenation: two items next to each other in a regular-expression pattern (that's the string between the forward slashes in the examples) must match two items next to each other in the string being matched (the $alphabet in the examples). So, to match 'abc' followed by 'def', concatenate them in the regular expression:

```
$alphabet = 'abcdefghijklmnopqrstuvwxyz';
if( $alphabet =~ /abcdef/ ) {
        print $&;
}
```

This prints:

```
abcdef
```

The second major idea is alternation. Items separated by the | metacharacter match any one of the items. For example, the following:

```
$alphabet = 'abcdefghijklmnopqrstuvwxyz';
if( $alphabet =~ /a(b|c|d)c/ ) {
```

```
        print $&;
    }
```

prints as:

```
abc.
```

The example also shows how parentheses group things in a regular expression. The parentheses are metacharacters that aren't matched in the string; rather, they group the alternation, given as b|c|d, meaning any one of b, c, or d at that position in the pattern. Since b is actually in $alphabet at that position, the alternation, and indeed the entire pattern a(b|c|d)c, matches in the $alphabet. (One additional point: ab|cd means (ab)|(cd), not a(b|c)d.)

The third major idea of regular expressions is repetition (or closure). This is indicated in a pattern with the quantifier metacharacter *, sometimes called the Kleene star after one of the inventors of regular expressions. When * appears after an item, it means that the item may appear 0, 1, or any number of times at that place in the string. So, for example, all of the following pattern matches will succeed:

```
'AC' =~ /AB*C/;
'ABC' =~ /AB*C/;
'ABBBBBBBBBBBC' =~ /AB*C/;
```

Metacharacters

The following are metacharacters:

```
\ | ( ) [ { ^ $ * + ? .
```

Escaping with \

A backslash \ before a metacharacter causes it to match itself; for instance, \\ matches a single \ in the string.

Alternation with |

The pipe | indicates alternation, as described previously.

Grouping with ( )

The parentheses ( ) provide grouping, as described previously.

Character classes

Square brackets [ ] specify a character class. A character class matches one character, which can be any character specified. For instance, [abc] matches either a, or b, or c at that position (so it's the same as a|b|c). A-Z is a range that matches any uppercase letter, a-z matches any lowercase letter, and 0-9 matches any digit. For instance, [A-Za-z0-9] matches any single letter or digit at that position. If the first

---

character in a character class is ^, any character except those specified match; for instance, [^0-9] matches any character that isn't a digit.

Matching any character with a dot

The period or dot . represents any character except a newline. (The pattern modifier /s makes it also match a newline.) So, . is like a character class that specifies every character.

Beginning and end of strings with ^ and $

The ^ metacharacter doesn't match a character; rather, it asserts that the item that follows must be at the beginning of the string. Similarly, the $ metacharacter doesn't match a character but asserts that the item that precedes it must be at the end of the string (or before the final newline). For example: /^Watson and Crick/ matches if the string starts with Watson and Crick; and /Watson and Crick$/ matches if the string ends with Watson and Crick or Watson and Crick\n.

Quantifiers

These metacharacters indicate the repetition of an item. The * metacharacter indicates zero, one, or more of the preceding item. The + metacharacter indicates one or more of the preceding item. The brace {} metacharacters let you specify exactly the number of previous items, or a range. For instance, {3} means exactly three of the preceding item; {3,7} means three, four, five, six, or seven of the preceding item; and {3,} means three or more of the preceding item. The ? matches none or one of the preceding item.

Making quantifiers match minimally with ?

The quantifiers just shown are greedy (or maximal) by default, meaning that they match as many items as possible. Sometimes, you want a minimal match that will match as few items as possible. You get that by following each of * + {} ? with a ?. So, for instance, *? tries to match as few as possible, perhaps even none, of the preceding item before it tries to match one or more of the preceding item. Here's a maximal match:

```
'hear ye hear ye hear ye' =~ /hear.*ye/;
print $&;
```

This matches 'hear' followed by .* (as many characters as possible), followed by 'ye', and prints:

```
hear ye hear ye hear ye
```

Here is a minimal match:

```
'hear ye hear ye hear ye' =~ /hear.*?ye/;
print $&;
```

This matches 'hear' followed by .*? (the fewest number of characters possible), followed by 'ye', and prints:

```
hear ye
```

Capturing Matched Patterns

You can place parentheses around parts of the pattern for which you want to know the matched string. Take, for example, the following:

```
$alphabet = 'abcdefghijklmnopqrstuvwxyz';
$alphabet =~ /k(lmnop)q/;
print $1;
```

This prints:

```
lmnop
```

You can place as many pairs of parentheses in a regular expression as you like; Perl automatically stores their matched substrings in special variables named $1, $2, and so on. The matches are numbered in order of the left-to-right appearance of their opening parenthesis.

Here's a more intricate example of capturing parts of a matched pattern in a string:

```
$alphabet = 'abcdefghijklmnopqrstuvwxyz';
$alphabet =~ /(((a)b)c)/;
print "First pattern = ", $1,"\n";
print "Second pattern = ", $2,"\n";
print "Third pattern = ", $3,"\n";
```

This prints:

```
First pattern = abc
Second pattern = ab
Third pattern = a
```

Metasymbols

Metasymbols are sequences of two or more characters consisting of backslashes before normal characters. These metasymbols have special meanings in Perl regular expressions (and in double-quoted strings for most of them). There are quite a few of them, but that's because they're so useful. Table A-3 lists most of these metasymbols. The column "Atomic" indicates Yes if the metasymbol matches an item, No if the metasymbol just makes an assertion, and – if it takes some other action.

Table A-3. Alphanumeric metasymbols

Symbol	Atomic	Meaning
\0	Yes	Match the null character (ASCII NULL)
\NNN	Yes	Match the character given in octal, up to 377

Table A-3. Alphanumeric metasymbols (continued)

Symbol	Atomic	Meaning
\n	Yes	Match *n*th previously captured string (decimal)
\a	Yes	Match the alarm character (BEL)
\A	No	True at the beginning of a string
\b	Yes	Match the backspace character (BS)
\b	No	True at word boundary
\B	No	True when not at word boundary
\cX	Yes	Match the control character Control-*X*
\d	Yes	Match any digit character
\D	Yes	Match any nondigit character
\e	Yes	Match the escape character (ASCII ESC, not backslash)
\E	–	End case (\L, \U) or metaquote (\Q) translation
\f	Yes	Match the formfeed character (FF)
\G	No	True at end-of-match position of prior m//g
\l	–	Lowercase the next character only
\L	–	Lowercase till \E
\n	Yes	Match the newline character (usually NL, but CR on Macs)
\Q	–	Quote (do-meta) metacharacters till \E
\r	Yes	Match the return character (usually CR, but NL on Macs)
\s	Yes	Match any whitespace character
\S	Yes	Match any nonwhitespace character
\t	Yes	Match the tab character (HT)
\u	–	Titlecase the next character only
\U	–	Uppercase (not titlecase) till \E
\w	Yes	Match any "word" character (alphanumerics plus _)
\W	Yes	Match any nonword character
\x{abcd}	Yes	Match the character given in hexadecimal
\z	No	True at end of string only
\Z	No	True at end of string or before optional newline

Extending Regular-Expression Sequences

Table A-4 includes several useful features that have been added to Perl's regular-expression capabilities.

Table A-4. Extended regular-expression sequences

Extension	Atomic	Meaning
(?#...)	No	Comment, discard
(?:...)	Yes	Cluster-only parentheses, no capturing
(?imsx-imsx)	No	Enable/disable pattern modifiers
(?imsx-imsx:...)	Yes	Cluster-only parentheses plus modifiers
(?=...)	No	True if lookahead assertion succeeds
(?!...)	No	True if lookahead assertion fails
(?<=...)	No	True if lookbehind assertion succeeds
(?<!...)	No	True if lookbehind assertion fails
(?>...)	Yes	Match nonbacktracking subpattern
(?{...})	No	Execute embedded Perl code
(??{...})	Yes	Match regex from embedded Perl code
(?(...)...|...)	Yes	Match with if-then-else pattern
(?(...)...)	Yes	Match with if-then pattern

Pattern Modifiers

Pattern modifiers are single-letter commands placed after the forward slashes. They delimit a regular expression or a substitution and change the behavior of some regular-expression features. Table A-5 lists the most common pattern modifiers, followed by an example.

Table A-5. Pattern modifiers

Modifier	Meaning
/i	Ignore upper- or lowercase distinctions
/s	Let . match newline
/m	Let ^ and $ match next to embedded \n
/x	Ignore (most) whitespace and permit comments in patterns
/o	Compile pattern once only
/g	Find all matches, not just the first one

As an example, say you were looking for a name in text, but you didn't know if the name had an initial capital letter or was all capitalized. You can use the /i modifier, like so:

```
$text = "WATSON and CRICK won the Nobel Prize";
$text =~ /Watson/i;
print $&;
```

This matches (since /i causes upper- and lowercase distinctions to be ignored) and prints out the matched string WATSON.

Scalar and List Context

Every operation in Perl is evaluated in either scalar or list context. Many operators behave differently depending on the context they are in, returning a list in list context and a scalar in scalar context.

The simplest example of scalar and list contexts is the assignment statement. If the left side (the variable being assigned a value) is a scalar variable, the right side (the values being assigned) are evaluated in scalar context. In the following examples, the right side is an array @array of two elements. When the left side is a scalar variable, it causes @array to be evaluated in scalar context. In scalar context, an array returns the number of elements in an array:

```
@array = ('one', 'two');
$a = @array;
print $a;
```

This prints:

```
2
```

If you put parentheses around the $a, you make it a list with one element, which causes @array to be evaluated in list context:

```
@array = ('one', 'two');
($a) = @array;
print $a;
```

This prints:

```
one
```

Notice that when assigning to a list, if there are not enough variables for all the values, the extra values are simply discarded. To capture all the variables, you'd do this:

```
@array = ('one', 'two');
($a, $b) = @array;
print "$a $b";
```

This prints:

```
one two
```

Similarly, if you have too many variables on the left for the number of right variables, the extra variables are assigned the undefined value undef.

When reading about Perl functions and operations, notice what the documentation has to say about scalar and list context. Very often, if your program is behaving strangely, it's because it is evaluating in a different context than you had thought.

Here are some general guidelines on when to expect scalar or list context:

- You get list context from function calls (anything in the argument position is evaluated in list context) and from list assignments.
- You get scalar context from string and number operators (arguments to such operators as . and + are assumed to be scalars); from boolean tests such as the conditional of an if () statement or the arguments to the || logical operator; and from scalar assignment.

Subroutines

Subroutines are defined by the keyword sub, followed by the name of the subroutine, followed by a block enclosed by curly braces containing the body of the subroutine. The following is a simple example.

```
sub a_subroutine {
    print "I'm in a subroutine\n";
}
```

In general, you can call subroutines using the name of the subroutine followed by a parenthesized list of arguments:

```
a_subroutine();
```

Arguments can be passed into subroutines as a list of scalars. If any arrays are given as arguments, their elements are interpolated into the list of scalars. The subroutine receives all scalar values as a list in the special variable @_. This example illustrates a subroutine definition and the calling of the subroutine with some arguments:

```
sub concatenate_dna {
    my($dna1, $dna2) = @_;

    my($concatenation);

    $concatenation = "$dna1$dna2";

    return $concatenation;
}

print concatenate_dna('AAA', 'CGC');
```

This prints:

```
AAACGC
```

The arguments 'AAA' and 'CGC' are passed into the subroutine as a list of scalars. The first statement in the subroutine's block:

```
my($dna1, $dna2) = @_;
```

assigns this list, available in the special variable @_, to the variables $dna1 and $dna2.

The variables $dna1 and $dna2 are declared as my variables to keep them local to the subroutine's block. In general, you declare all variables as my variables; this can be enforced by adding the statement use strict; near the beginning of your program. However, it is possible to use global variables that are not declared with my, which can be used anywhere in a program, including within subroutines.

The statement:

```
my($concatenation);
```

declares another variable for use by the subroutine.

After the statement:

```
$concatenation = "$dna1$dna2";
```

performs the work of the subroutine, the subroutine defines its value with the return statement:

```
return $concatenation;
```

The value returned from a call to a subroutine can be used however you wish; in this example, it is given as the argument to the print function.

If any arrays are given as arguments, their elements are interpolated into the @_ list, as in the following example:

```
sub example_sub {
    my(@arguments) = @_;

    print "@arguments\n";
}

my @array = ('two', 'three', 'four');

example_sub('one', @array, 'five');
```

This prints:

```
one two three four five
```

Note that the following attempt to mix arrays and scalars in the arguments to a subroutine won't work:

```
# This won't work!!
sub bad_sub {
    my(@array, $scalar) = @_;

    print $scalar;
}

my @arr = ('DNA', 'RNA');
my $string = 'Protein';

bad_sub(@arr, $string);
```

In this example, the subroutine's variable @array on the left side in the assignment statement consumes the entire list on the right side in @_, namely ('DNA', 'RNA', 'Protein'). The subroutine's variable $scalar won't be set, so the subroutine won't print 'Protein' as intended. To pass separate arrays and hashes to a subroutine, you need to use references. Here's a brief example:

```perl
sub good_sub {
    my($arrayref, $hashref) = @_;

    print "@$arrayref", "\n";

    my @keys = keys %$hashref;

    print "@keys", "\n";
}

my @arr = ('DNA', 'RNA');
my %nums = ( 'one' => 1, 'two' => 2);

good_sub(\@arr, \%nums);
```

This prints:

```
DNA RNA
one two
```

Modules and Packages

Chapter 1 summarizes the basic concepts of namespaces, packages, and modules.

A namespace is a table containing the names and values of variables and subroutines. Namespaces are excellent ways to protect one part of your code from unintentionally using the same variable or subroutine name as appears in another part of your code, causing a namespace collision and often leading to incorrect (but hard to identify) program behavior.

By default, a Perl program uses the namespace called main.

The package declaration enables you to declare and use different namespaces for different parts of your program. For instance, to declare a new namespace called Outer, use the following statement:

```perl
package Outer;
```

Package declarations usually occur at or near the top of a file and are in effect throughout the file, but they can appear several times within a file, causing the active namespace to switch each time they are called.

When a file has one package declaration at the top of the file and it's named with the package name followed by the .pm suffix (e.g, Outer.pm), the file is called a Perl module. (The module also needs to end with the statement "1;" to load correctly when called.)

The code for a Perl module can be used in a Perl program by referencing the file defining the module with a use statement, as in the following example:

```
use Outer;
```

The Perl interpreter will then try to find a file called Outer.pm.

Chapter 1 gives the basic details on how to manage modules so that the Perl interpreter can find them.

Object-Oriented Programming

Object-oriented Perl programming is introduced in Chapters 3 and 4, and used in all the remaining chapters of the book.

There are three main concepts:

- A class is a Perl module with a package declaration. The name of the class is the same as the name of the package; the module file also has the same name but with ".pm" (for Perl module) appended.
- An object is a reference to a collection of data used by a Perl class, usually but not necessarily, implemented as a hash. An object is marked with the name of its class using bless.
- A method is a subroutine in the class.

Arrow notation -> is used in a special way in object-oriented Perl code and has an effect on what arguments are passed to the class methods.

You use a class in your code by saying, for example:

```
use Goodclass;
```

You create an object by calling a constructor method in the class, which is usually (but not necessarily) called new, for example:

```
$goodobject = Goodclass->new( parameter1 => 1, parameter2 => 2);
```

Note that arguments are usually (but not necessarily) specified using the hash notation key => value, and therefore can be given in any order.

You call other methods in the class by invoking them from a class object. For example you call the method stuff in class Goodclass on a Goodclass object $goodobject, with argument type initialized to the value 'good', and save its output in the array @goodstuff, like so:

```
@goodstuff = $goodobject->stuff(type => 'good');
```

The arrow notation causes the called method to insert an additional argument. (In the examples just shown, the methods are the subroutines new and stuff).

The additional argument is the class information that appears to the left of the arrow. So, in these examples, the method new has the argument list:

```
('Goodclass', parameter1=1, parameter2=2)
```

The method stuff has the argument list:

```
($goodobject, type='good')
```

The details of how arguments are passed to methods are important to know only if you are writing a class, not if you are using one. If you simply use a class, you only have to know how to call the class methods using the arrow notation as just shown.

Inheritance is a technique with which you can write a new class that uses definitions from an already existing class.

AUTOLOAD is a subroutine that handles calls to undefined methods, and DESTROY is a subroutine that handles cleanup when a class object goes out of scope.

In addition to object methods that operate on individual class objects, you can also define class methods that have access to information about multiple class objects—for example, a count of how many objects have been created.

A great deal of the utility of existing Perl code is available only in class modules. In this book I use some of the important and well-known modules including DBI, CGI, GD and GD::Graph, and the Bioperl collection of modules. Almost all modules are available at *http://www.CPAN.org*.

Built-in Functions

Perl has many built-in functions. Table A-6 is a partial list with short descriptions.

Table A-6. Perl built-in functions

Function	Summary
abs VALUE	Return the absolute value of its numeric argument
atan2 Y, X	Return the principal value of the arc tangent of Y/X from $-\pi$ to π
chdir EXPR	Change the working directory to EXPR (or home directory by default)
chmod MODE LIST	Change the file permissions of the LIST of files to MODE
chomp (VARIABLE or LIST)	Remove ending newline from string(s), if present
chop (VARIABLE or LIST)	Remove ending character from string(s)
chown UID, GID, LIST	Change owner and group of LIST of files to numeric UID and GID
close FILEHANDLE	Close the file, socket, or pipe associated with FILEHANDLE
closedir DIRHANDLE	Close the directory associated with DIRHANDLE
cos EXPR	Return the cosine of the radian number EXPR
dbmclose HASH	Break the binding between a DBM file and a hash
dbmopen HASH, DBNAME, MODE	Bind a DBM file to a HASH with permissions given in MODE

Table A-6. Perl built-in functions (continued)

Function	Summary
defined EXPR	Return true or false if EXPR has a defined value or not
delete EXPR	Delete an element (or slice) from a hash or an array
die LIST	Exit the program with an error message that includes LIST
each HASH	Step through a hash with one key, or key/value pair, at a time
exec PATHNAME LIST	Terminate the program and execute the program PATHNAME with arguments LIST
exists EXPR	Return true if hash key or array index exists
exit EXPR	Exit the program with the return value of EXPR
exp EXPR	Return the value of e raised to the exponent EXPR
format	Declare a format for use by the write function
grep EXPR, LIST	Return list of elements of LIST for which EXPR is true
gmtime	Get Greenwich mean time; Sunday is day 0, January is month 0, year is number of years since 1900—example: ($sec,$min,$hour,$mday,$mon,$year,$wday,$yday, $isdaylightsavingstime) = gmtime;
goto LABEL	Program control goes to statement marked with LABEL
hex EXPR	Return decimal value of hexadecimal EXPR
index STR, SUBSTR	Give the position of the first occurrence of SUBSTR in STR
int EXPR	Give the integer portion of the number in EXPR
join EXPR, LIST	Join the strings in LIST into a single string, separated by EXPR
keys HASH	Return a list of all the keys in HASH
last LABEL	Exit the immediately enclosing loop by default, or loop with LABEL
lc EXPR	Return a lowercased copy of string in EXPR
lcfirst EXPR	Return a copy of EXPR with first character lowercased
length EXPR	Return the length in characters of EXPR
localtime	Get local time in same format as in gmtime function
log EXPR	Return natural logarithm of number EXPR
m/PATTERN/	The match operator for the regular-expression PATTERN, often abbreviated as /PATTERN/
map BLOCK LIST (or map EXPR, LIST)	Evaluate BLOCK or EXPR for each element of LIST, return list of return values
mkdir FILENAME	Create the directory *FILENAME*
my EXPR	Localize the variables in EXPR to the enclosing block
next LABEL	Go to next iteration of enclosing loop by default or to loop marked with LABEL
oct EXPR	Return decimal value of octal value in EXPR
open FILEHANDLE, EXPR	Open a file by associating FILEHANDLE with the file and options given in EXPR
opendir DIRHANDLE, EXPR	Open the directory EXPR and assign handle DIRHANDLE
pop ARRAY	Remove and return the last element of ARRAY

Table A-6. Perl built-in functions (continued)

Function	Summary
pos SCALAR	Give location in string SCALAR where last m//g search left off
print FILEHANDLE LIST	Print LIST of strings to FILEHANDLE (default STDOUT)
printf FILEHANDLE FORMAT, LIST	Print string specified by FORMAT and variables LIST to FILEHANDLE
push ARRAY, LIST	Place the elements of LIST at the end of ARRAY
rand EXPR	Give pseudorandom decimal number from 0 to less than EXPR (default 1)
readdir DIRHANDLE	Return list of entries of directory DIRHANDLE
redo LABEL	Restart a loop block without reevaluating the conditional
ref EXPR	Return true or false if EXPR is a reference or not: if true, returned value indicates type of reference
rename OLDNAME, NEWNAME	Change the name of a file
return EXPR	Return from the current subroutine with value EXPR
reverse LIST	Give LIST in reverse order, or reverse strings in scalar context
rindex STR, SUBSTR	Like the index function but returns last occurrence of SUBSTR in STR
rmdir FILENAME	Delete the directory FILENAME
s/PATTERN/REPLACEMENT/	Replace the match of regular-expression PATTERN with string REPLACEMENT
scalar EXPR	Force EXPR to be evaluated in scalar context
seek FILEHANDLE, OFFSET, WHENCE	Position the file pointer for FILEHANDLE to OFFSET bytes (if WHENCE is 0, current position plus OFFSET if WHENCE is 1, or OFFSET bytes from the end if WHENCE is 2)
shift ARRAY	Remove and return the first element of ARRAY
sin EXPR	Return the sine of the radian number EXPR
sleep EXPR	Cause the program to sleep for EXPR seconds
sort USERSUB LIST (or sort BLOCK LIST)	Sort the LIST according to the order in USERSUB or BLOCK (default standard string order)
splice ARRAY, OFFSET, LENGTH, LIST	Remove LENGTH elements at OFFSET in ARRAY and replace with LIST, if present
split /PATTERN/, EXPR	Split the string EXPR at occurrences of /PATTERN/, return list
sprintf FORMAT, LIST	Return a string formatted as in the printf function
sqrt EXPR	Return the square root of the number EXPR.
srand EXPR	Set random number seed for rand operator; only needed in versions of Perl before 5.004
stat (FILEHANDLE or EXPR)	Return statistics on file EXPR or its FILEHANDLE—example: ($dev,$inode,$mode,$num_of_links,$uid,$gid,$rdev,$size,$accesstime, $modifiedtime,$changetime,$blksize,$blocks) = stat $filename;
study SCALAR	Try to optimize subsequent pattern matches on string SCALAR
sub NAME BLOCK	Define a subroutine named NAME with program code in BLOCK
substr EXPR, OFFSET, LENGTH, REPLACEMENT	Return substring of string EXPR at position OFFSET and length LENGTH; the substring is replaced with REPLACEMENT if used

Function	Summary
system PATHNAME LIST	Execute any program PATHNAME with arguments LIST; returns exit status of program, not its output; to capture ouput, use backticks—example: @output = '/bin/who';
tell FILEHANDLE	Return current file position in bytes in FILEHANDLE
tr/ORIGINAL/REPLACEMENT/	Transliterates each character in ORIGINAL with corresponding character in REPLACEMENT
truncate (FILEHANDLE or EXPR), LENGTH	Shorten file EXPR or opened with FILEHANDLE to LENGTH bytes
uc EXPR	Return uppercased version of string EXPR
ucfirst EXPR	Return string EXPR with first character capitalized
undef EXPR	Return the undefined value; if a defined variable or subroutine EXPR is given, it's no longer defined; it can be assigned a value when you don't need to save the value
unlink LIST	Delete the LIST of files
unshift ARRAY, LIST	Add LIST elements to the beginning of ARRAY
use MODULE	Load the MODULE
values HASH	Return a list of all values of the HASH
wantarray	In a subroutine, return true if calling program expects a list return value
warn LIST	Print error message including LIST
write FILEHANDLE	Write formatted record to FILEHANDLE (default STDOUT) as defined by the format function

APPENDIX B
Installing Perl

Perl is a popular programming language that is extensively used in areas such as bioinformatics and web programming. It's become popular with biologists because it is so well suited to several bioinformatics tasks. This appendix is geared to those who are attempting the language for the first time.

Perl is also an application and is available (at no cost) to run on all operating systems found in the average biology lab (Unix and Linux, Macintosh, Windows, VMS, and more). The Perl application on your computer takes a Perl language program (such as one of the programs in this book), translates it into instructions the computer can understand, and runs (or executes) it.

The word Perl, then, refers both to the language in which you write programs and to the application on your computer that runs those programs. You can always tell from context which of these two meanings is being used.

Every computer language such as Perl needs to have a translator application (an interpreter or compiler) that can turn programs into instructions the computer can actually run. The Perl application is often referred to as the Perl interpreter, and it includes a Perl compiler as well. You will also see Perl programs referred to as Perl scripts or Perl code.

Installing Perl on Your Computer

Here are the basic steps for installing Perl on your computer:

1. Check to see if Perl is already installed; if so, check the version.
2. Get Internet access and go to the Perl home page at *http://www.perl.com.*
3. Go to the Downloads page and determine which Perl distribution to download.
4. Download the Perl distribution.
5. Install the distribution on your computer.

Perl May Already Be Installed

Many computers—especially Unix and Linux computers—come with Perl already installed. (Note that Unix and Linux are essentially the same thing, as far as the operating system is concerned; Linux is a clone, or functional copy, of a Unix system.) So, first check to see if Perl is already there. On Unix and Linux, type the following at a command prompt:

```
$ perl -v
```

If Perl is already installed, you'll see a message something like this:

```
This is perl, v5.8.0 built for i686-linux

Copyright 1987-2002, Larry Wall

Perl may be copied only under the terms of either the Artistic License or the
GNU General Public License, which may be found in the Perl 5 source kit.

Complete documentation for Perl, including FAQ lists, should be found on
this system using 'man perl' or 'perldoc perl'.  If you have access to the
Internet, point your browser at http://www.perl.com/, the Perl Home Page.
```

If Perl isn't installed, you'll get a message something like this:

```
perl: command not found
```

If you're on a shared Unix system, at a university or business, check with the system administrator if this fails, because although Perl may be installed, your environment may not be set to find it. (Or, the system administrator may say, "You need Perl? Okay, I'll install it for you!")

On Windows or Macintosh, look at the program menus, or use the find program to search for perl. You can also try typing perl -v at an MS-DOS command window or at a shell window on the Mac OS X. (Note that the Mac OS X is a Unix system!)

Versions of Perl

Perl, like almost all popular software, has gone through much growth and change over the course of its 15-year life. The authors, Larry Wall and a large group of cohorts, publish new versions periodically. These new versions have been carefully designed to support most programs written under old versions, but occasionally some major new features are added that simply won't work with older versions of Perl.

This book assumes you have Perl Version 5 or higher installed. It's likely that if you have Perl already installed on your computer, it's Perl 5. But it's best to check. On a Unix or Linux system, or from an MS-DOS or Mac OS X command window, the perl -v command just shown displays the version number, in my case Version 5.8.0. The number 5.8.0 is "bigger" than 5, so I'm okay. If you get a smaller number (very likely 4.036), you'll have to install a recent version of Perl to enable the majority of programs in this book to run as shown.

What about future versions? Perl is always evolving, and Perl Version 6 is on the horizon. Will the code in this book still work in Perl 6? The answer is yes. Although Perl 6 is going to add some new things to the language, it should have no trouble with the Perl 5 code in this book.

Internet Access

To install Perl, you will need to download it from the Internet, as shown in the next few pages.

If you don't have Internet access, you can try taking your computer to a friend who does have such access, and connecting long enough to install Perl. You can also use a Zip drive or burn a CD from a friend's computer to bring the Perl software to your computer. There are also commercial shrink-wrapped CDs of Perl available from several sources (ask at your local software store), and several books include CDs with Perl.

Downloading

Following are some directions for getting Perl to work on your Unix or Linux, Macintosh, and Windows computers. (It is also available for several other less common operating systems from the Perl web site.)

There is one web site that serves as a central jumping off point for all things Perl: *http://www.perl.com*. This web page has a Downloads clickable button that guides you to everything you need to install Perl on your computer.

The more specific directions that follow are up-to-date as of this writing, but you should be aware that the web pages they refer to may change their design. So, basically, go to *http://www.perl.com*, and look for the Downloads link to click on. The system should tell you everything you need to know after that. There will be a HELP link and other helpful links besides. So even if the information in this section becomes outdated, you will certainly be able to visit the main Perl web site and find all you need to install Perl.

Downloading and installing Perl is usually quite easy; in fact, the majority of the time it's perfectly painless, but sometimes you may have to put some effort into getting it to work. If you're new at programming, and you run into difficulties, the best thing to do is to ask for help from someone who is a professional computer programmer and/or administrator, teacher, or someone in the lab who already programs in Perl. But the chances are that you won't need any help: keep reading!

Binary Versus Source Code

One choice you will find when downloading is the choice between binary or source code distributions of Perl. The chances are very good that a binary version will be available for your computer. Get that if it's available for your particular system.

Recall that a binary (or executable or compiled program) is a program that has been translated into machine language and is ready to run. Source code is a program written in a language such as C or Perl, which can then be compiled or interpreted to become a binary. The Perl application is actually written in the C programming language, so it's also possible to get the C source code for the Perl application and compile it to create the Perl application binary.

The best choice for installing Perl on your computer is usually to get an already made binary version of the program, because nothing else needs to be done. However, if no binary is available, or if you want to control the various options of your Perl installation, you can get the source code for Perl, which is itself written in the C programming language. You then compile it using a C compiler. But I repeat: see if you can find a binary for your particular computer operating system; compiling from source code is more complicated for beginners! Details are available at the Perl web site.

Perl for Unix and Linux

Recall that Unix and Linux are essentially the same kind of operating system—Linux is a clone of Unix. Both Unix and Linux come in several variants offered by various companies.

Perl was originally developed on Unix and for quite some time now it has come already installed on most such systems. Open a window and type `perl -v`. If you get version information, Perl is there.

If Perl isn't installed on your Unix or Linux machine, first try to find a binary to install. Go to the Downloads page of *http://www.perl.com*. You'll see the subheading Binary Distributions. Select Unix or Linux, and then see if your particular flavor of system has a binary available. Several versions of Unix and Linux are available here, and the instructions available at the web site should be enough for you to get Perl installed once you've downloaded the binary. Most versions of Linux maintain up-to-date Perl binaries on their web sites. For instance, if you have a Redhat Linux system, you need to identify which version of the system you have (by typing `uname -a`); then get the appropriate `rpm` file to download and install. Redhat has an `rpm` for Perl that Redhat Linux users can install by typing:

```
rpm -Uvh perl.rpm
```

Note that the actual name of the `perl.rpm` file varies.

If no binary version of Perl is available for your flavor of Unix or Linux, it is necessary to compile Perl from its source code. In this case, starting from the main web page *http://www.perl.com*, you click on the Downloads button and then select Source Code Distribution. The source code has an INSTALL file that has instructions that will guide you through downloading the source code, installing it on your system, compiling the source code into a binary, and finally installing the binary.

Compiling from source code is a considerably more lengthy process than installing an already made binary and requires a bit more reading of instructions, but it usually works quite well. Occasionally, however, a problem does arise, and if you are a beginner, I strongly suggest that you search out an experienced programmer or system administrator who knows Unix, Linux, or Perl, as it's an easy task for the experienced, but can be a bit confusing the first time around for the beginner. You need a C compiler on your computer to install Perl from the source code. Nowadays, some Unix systems ship without a complete C compiler! Linux will always have the free C compiler called gcc installed, and you can also install gcc on any Unix (or Windows, or Mac) system that lacks a C compiler.

Perl for Macintosh

The MacOS X is a Unix-based system. It ships with Perl installed. But you may be able to find more recent versions by looking at the Downloads page, then at Binary Distributions, then at Unix or Linux, and go to the Mac OS X link.

MacPerl is a port of Perl to pre-OS X Macintosh operating systems. The MacPerl installation steps are clearly explained on the MacPerl web page, *http://www.macperl. com* (which you can also find from the Perl web page *http://www.perl.com* and its Downloads button). I'll give a brief overview of the process here.

From the MacPerl page, click on Get MacPerl, and follow the directions to download the application. It will appear on your desktop. Double-click it to unstuff it. If you don't have Alladin Stuffit Expander (most Macs already do) this won't work, and you'll first have to go to *http://www.alladinsys.com* to download and install Stuffit.

MacPerl can be installed as a standalone application under the Mac OS Finder or as a tool under the Macintosh Programmer's Workbench; most users will want the standalone application. Perl Version 5 is available for Mac OS 7.0 and later. More details about which Perl version is available for your particular hardware and Mac OS version are available at the MacPerl web page.

Perl for Windows

Several binaries for different Windows versions are available. Since Windows is closely coupled with Intel 32-bit chips, these binaries are often called Wintel or Win32 binaries. The standard Perl distribution now is ActivePerl from ActiveState, at the web address *http://www.activestate.com/ActivePerl/* and the complete installation directions are there on the web page. You can also get to that web page via the Downloads button from the Perl web site *http://www.perl.com*. You'll then see the subheading Binary Distributions. Under that, click on Win32. Then, click on the ActivePerl site.

From the ActiveState web site's ActivePerl page, click the Downloads button. Then you can download the Windows-Intel binary. Note that installing it requires a program called Windows Installer which is available at that same web page if it's not already on your computer.

How to Run Perl Programs

The details of how to run Perl vary depending on the operating system of your computer. The instructions that come with the version of Perl you install on your computer contain all you need to know. I'll just give a short summary here that will point you in the right direction.

There is a part of the Perl documentation called perlrun. You can find it at *http:// www.perl.com/pub/doc/manual/html/pod/perlrun.html*. It gives all the options of running Perl, especially on Unix and Linux; it's complete but not for the beginner.

Running Perl Programs on Unix or Linux

On Unix or Linux, you usually run Perl programs from the command line. You can run a Perl program in a file called this_program by typing:

```
perl this_program
```

if you're in the same directory as the program. If you're not in the same directory, you may have to give the pathname of the program:

```
perl /usr/local/bin/this_program
```

Usually, you set the first line of this_program to have the correct pathname for Perl on your system, since different machines may have installed Perl in different directories. On my computer, I use the following as the first line of my Perl programs:

```
#!/usr/bin/perl
```

You can type which perl to find the pathname where Perl is installed on your system.

You also usually make the program executable, using the chmod program:

```
chmod 755 this_program
```

If you've set the first line correctly and used chmod, you can just type the name of the Perl program to run it. So, if you're in the same directory as the program, you can type ./this_program or, if the program is in a directory that's included in your $PATH or $path variable, you can type this_program.*

---

* $PATH is the variable used for the shells sh, bash, and ksh; $path is the variable used for *csh, tcsh,* and so on.

If your Perl program won't run, the error messages you get from the shell in the command window may be a little confusing. For instance, the *bash* shell on my Linux system gives the error message:

```
bash: ./my_program: No such file or directory
```

in two cases: if there really is no program called my_program in the current directory, or if the first line of my_program has incorrectly given the location of Perl. So watch for that, especially when running programs from CPAN that may have different pathnames for Perl embedded in their first lines. Also, if you type my_program, you may get the error message:

```
bash: my_program: command not found
```

which means that the operating system can't find the program. But it's right there in your directory! The problem is probably that your $PATH or $path variable doesn't include the current directory, so that the system isn't even looking in the current directory for the program. In this case, change the $PATH or $path variable (depending on which shell you're using); or just type ./my_program instead of my_program.

Running Perl Programs on the Macintosh

On Macs, the recommended way to save Perl programs is as "droplets." The MacPerl documentation gives the simple instructions. Basically, you open the Perl program with the MacPerl application and then choose Save As and select the Type option Droplet.

You can drag and drop a file onto a droplet in order to use the file as input (via the @ARGV array).

The new Mac OS X is a Unix system, and on those systems, you have the option of running Perl programs from the command line as just described for Unix and Linux systems.

Running Perl Programs on Windows

On Windows computers, it's usual to associate the filename extension .pl with Perl programs. This is usually done as part of the installation process, which modifies the registry settings to include this file association. You can then launch this_program.pl by typing this_program or perl this_program.pl in an MS-DOS command window. Windows also has a PATH variable specifying folders in which the system looks for programs; this is modified by the Perl installation process to include the path to the folder for the Perl application, usually c:\perl. If you're trying to run a Perl program that isn't installed in a folder known to the PATH variable, you can type the complete pathname to the program, e.g., perl c:\windows\desktop\my_program.pl.

Finding Help

Make sure you have any available documentation. If you install Perl as outlined earlier, this is already done as part of the general Perl installation, and the instructions that come with your Perl distribution will explain how to get at the documentation on your system. There is also excellent online Internet documentation, which can be found at *http://www.perl.com*.

First, point your web browser at the main Perl web site, bookmark it, and look around a little, especially at the available documentation. This is an essential resource. Also, point your browser at *http://ncbi.nlm.nih.gov* (the National Center for Biotechnology Information) and *http://www.ebi.ac.uk/* (the European Bioinformatics Institute) for two of the biggest government-sponsored bioinformatics resources. These are among the most important web sites for Perl and bioinformatics.

Also very useful is the standard book *Programming Perl* (now in its third edition). You can do fine with the (free) online documentation, but if you end up doing a lot of Perl programming, *Programming Perl* (and perhaps a few others) will probably end up on your bookshelf.

Most languages have a standard document set that includes the whole story about the language definition and use. In Perl, this is included with the program as the on-line manual. Although programming manuals often suffer from poor writing, it is best to be prepared to dig into them. A well-honed ability to skim is a great asset. The Perl manual isn't bad; its main problem, that it shares with most manuals, is that all the details are in there, so it can be a bit overwhelming at first. However, the Perl documentation does a decent job of helping the beginner navigate, by means of tutorial documents.

Index

Symbols

& (ampersand)
  && (logical and) operator, 336
  (bitwise and) operator, 333
< and > (angle brackets)
  << left shift operator, 333
  <> line input operator, 342
  > (arrow operator), 38
  >> right shift operator, 333
* (asterisk) quantifier, 347
@ (at sign), 33
@INC array, 9
-- (autodecrement operator), 333
\ (backslash)
  escaping metacharacters, 346
  metasymbols, use in, 348
\@ (backslash-at), 37
! (bang)
  ! (logical negation) operator, 336
  !~ (binding) operator, 338
  #! (shebang) notation, 323
!~ (binding operators), 338
^ (caret), 180
  metacharacter in regular expressions, 347
  bitwise xor operator, 333
/i (case-insensitive) matching, 350
:// (colon-slashes), 250
{} (curly braces), 6, 41
  dereferencing and, 36
{} (curly braces) quantifier, 347
-w flag, 323
$flag variable, 227

$ (dollar sign), 33
  $_ variables, 340
  metacharacter, 347
. (dot)
  character wildcard, 347
  current directory), 10
  string operator, 233
:: (double colons) in module names, 11
= (equal sign)
  =~ (pattern binding) operator, 338
  => (syntactic sugar symbol), 90
/ (forward slash), 252
() (parentheses), 348
%genetic_code hash, 14
% (percent sign), 34
+ (plus sign) quantifier, 347
++ (autoincrement) operator, 333
? (question mark), in quantifiers, 347
" (quotes, double) in strings, 324
' (quotes, single) in strings, 324
; (semicolon), ending Perl statements, 327
#! (shebang notation), 323
[ ] (square brackets), 39
| (vertical bar)
  (bitwise OR) operator, 333
  || (logical or) operator, 336
  alternation, 346

Numbers

24-bit color, 273

We'd like to hear your suggestions for improving our indexes. Send email to *index@oreilly.com*.

A

abstraction, 4
accessor methods, 92
    Gene2.pm, 101
algorithms
    border conditions and, 66
    data structures and, 74
    references, 69
    (see also string algorithms)
alternation, 346
and operator
    bitwise and (&) operator, 333
    logical and, 335
        control flow, using for, 336
angle operator, 342
anonymous arrays, 39
anonymous data, 36
anonymous hashes, 41
anonymous referents, 37
approximate string matching, 60–68
arguments, 352
@ARGV arrays, 342
arithmetic operators, 333
arrays, 33, 328
    anonymous arrays, 39
    @ARGV, 342
    of arrays, 47
    elements, specifying, 328
    matrices, 47
    references to, 37
    sparse arrays, 50
    as subroutine arguments, 353
    two-dimensional arrays, 53
arrow notation, 81
arrow operator (>), 38
assignment, 326
    scalar and list context, 351
assignment operators, 327
at sign (@), 33
attributes, 74, 81
    graphics output, storing in, 191
    key/value pairs, 81
attributes (databases), 208
autoincrement and autodecrement
        operators, 333
AUTOLOAD subroutine, 107–112
    accessors, 111
    arguments, 109
    FileIO.pm, 139–141
    get_ and set_, 109
    mutators, 111
    speeding up the code, 112
    writing methods using, 108

B

backslash-at (\@), 37
base 16 (hexadecimal) numbers, 325
base 8 (octal) numbers, 325
base class, 132
bases, changing to reverse complements, 338
binary (base 2) numbers, 325
bind variables, 233
binding operators, 338
    !~, 338
bioinformatics, xi
Bioperl, xv, 291–319
    bptutorial.pl, 306–318
    documentation, 291, 303
    history, 292
    installing, 292–296
    modules, 304
    object-oriented style, 291
    objects, 304
    problems, 303
    testing, 296–303
    test 1, 296
    test 2, 296
    test 3, 297–299
    test 4, 299–303
Bioperl modules, 76–80, 129
bitmaps, 273
bitwise operators, 333
    & (bitwise and), 333
bless function, 89
blocks, 327
body tags, 253
border conditions, 66
Boutell, Thomas, 271
bptutorial.pl, 306–318
browsers, 248
built-in functions, Perl, 356–359

C

candidate keys, 209
capturing in patterns, 348
caret (^), 180
Carp module, 76, 86
case-insensitive matching, 350
CERN, 248
CGI (Common Gateway Interface), 247,
        255–261

strings, 324
    binding operators, 338
    capturing matched patterns in, 348
    formatting (sprintf function), 343
    matching, 58
        genetic variability and, 59
    operators, 334
    substituting characters in (tr/// operator), 338
subroutines, 4, 352
    passing data to
        by reference, 354
    passing references to, 44
    references to, 41
    returning references from, 46
substitution (s///) operator, 338
SUPER class, 133
superclass, 132
symbol tables, 5
symbolic references, 46
syntactic sugar symbol (=>), 90
system calls, open and close, 341

T

tab-delimited input files, 226
    SQL load utility and, 226
tables, 208
    creating, 212
    populating, 212
tags, 253
testRebaseDB program, 241
title tags, 253
tr/// (transliteration) operator, 338
transactions, 244
transliteration (tr///) operator, 338
true or false value, evaluating with conditionals, 335
truecolor, 273
tuples, 208
two-dimensional arrays, 53
two-dimensional matrices, 47

U

undefined values, 335, 351
unique identifiers, 221
Unix
    compiling Perl from source, 363
    installing Perl binaries on, 363

Perl programs, running on, 365
    specifying input files on command line, 342
unless statements, 337
update anomalies, 219
URI::URL modules, 250
URLs (Uniform Resource Locators), 248
use lib directive, 10, 198
use strict, 6
    AUTOLOAD, bypassing with, 109
use strict directive, 43

V

variables
    scalar, 326
        assigning scalar values to, 326
    testing and changing value in loops, 339–341
vector graphics, 272

W

warn function, 344
warnings flag, 323
Web, 248
web browsers, 248
web pages, 249
    building, 261–269
    directory locations, 264
    example, 251–252
web programming, xiv
web servers, 248
webrebase1, 262–269
    analysis, 265–269
    installing, 264
while loops, 339
Windows
    Perl programs, running on, 366
Windows systems
    specifying input files on command line, 342
World Wide Web (see Web)
write function, 343
write method
    FileIO.pm, 138

X

x operator, 334
x string operator, 234
xor operator, 335

About the Author

James D. Tisdall has worked as a musician, a programmer at Bell Labs (where he programmed for speech research and discovered a formal language for musical rhythm), and as a bioinformaticist at Mercator Genetics in Menlo Park, California, and at Fox Chase Cancer Center in Philadelphia. He has a B.A. in mathematics from the City College of New York and an M.S. in computer science from Columbia University; he is working towards a Ph.D. in computer science at the University of Pennsylvania. In his spare time, Jim teaches computer music at the Settlement Music School in Philadelphia. He is also the author of O'Reilly's *Beginning Perl for Bioinformatics*.

Colophon

Our look is the result of reader comments, our own experimentation, and feedback from distribution channels. Distinctive covers complement our distinctive approach to technical topics, breathing personality and life into potentially dry subjects.

The animal on the cover of *Mastering Perl for Bioinformatics* is a North American bullfrog (*Rana catesbeiana*). It is native to the central and eastern United States, as well as southern portions of Canada. However, this bullfrog has since been introduced as far away from its native habitat as Asia, Europe, and Hawaii.

The North American bullfrog is the largest true frog in North America and can weigh over a pound. It can grow up to eight inches in length, although the norm is four to five inches. The gender of the bullfrog is ascertained by comparing the size of the external ear (the tympanum) relative to the size of the eye.

Bullfrogs are predators and also are cannibalistic. Their role in the environment is to control the population of insect pests as well as snakes and mice. In fact, the zeal of the North American bullfrog threatens to drive other frog species to extinction.

The generic name (*rana*) comes from the Latin for frog, while the species name (*catesbeiana*) honors an English naturalist. In the 18th century, Mark Catesby (1683–1749) produced the authoritative and exhaustive record of the flora and fauna found in the New World. Wealthy patrons in England eagerly received Catesby's regular shipments of specimens, including plants, birds, reptiles, insects, and frogs.

Mary Anne Weeks Mayo was the production editor and copyeditor, and Marlowe Shaeffer was the proofreader, for *Mastering Perl for Bioinformatics*. Jane Ellin and Colleen Gorman provided quality control. Marlowe Shaeffer, Mary Agner, and James Quill provided production assistance. John Bickelhaupt wrote the index.

Ellie Volckhausen designed the cover of this book, based on a series design by Edie Freedman. The cover image is a 19th-century engraving from the Dover Pictorial Archive. Emma Colby produced the cover layout with QuarkXPress 4.1 using Adobe's ITC Garamond font.

David Futato designed the interior layout. This book was converted by Andrew Savikas to FrameMaker 5.5.6 with a format conversion tool created by Erik Ray, Jason McIntosh, Neil Walls, and Mike Sierra that uses Perl and XML technologies. The text font is Linotype Birka; the heading font is Adobe Myriad Condensed; and the code font is LucasFont's TheSans Mono Condensed. The illustrations that appear in the book were produced by Robert Romano and Jessamyn Read using Macromedia FreeHand 9 and Adobe Photoshop 6. The tip and warning icons were drawn by Christopher Bing. This colophon was written by Reg Aubry.

Other Titles Available from O'Reilly

Bioinformatics

Beginning Perl for Bioinformatics

By James Tisdall
1st Edition October 2001
384 pages, 0-596-00080-4

This book shows biologists with little or no programming experience how to use Perl, the ideal language for biological data analysis. Each chapter focuses on solving a particular problem or class of problems, so you'll finish the book with a solid understanding of Perl basics, a collection of programs for such tasks as parsing BLAST and GenBank, and the skills to tackle more advanced bioinformatics programming.

Developing Bioinformatics Computer Skills

By Cynthia Gibas & Per Jambeck
1st Edition April 2001
446 pages, 1-56592-664-1

Developing Bioinformatics Computer Skills will help biologists, researchers, and students develop a structured approach to biological data and the computer tools they'll need to analyze it. The book covers the Unix file system, building tools and databases for bioinformatics, computational approaches to biological problems, an introduction to Perl for bioinformatics, data mining, data visualization, and tips for tailoring data analysis software to individual research needs.

Sequence Analysis in a Nutshell

By Scott Markel & Darryl León
1st Edition January 2003
302 pages, ISBN 0-596-00494-X

Sequence Analysis in a Nutshell: A Guide to Common Tools and Databases pulls together all of the vital information about the most commonly used databases, analytical tools, and tables used in sequence analysis. The book contains details and examples of the common database formats (GenBank, EMBL, SWISS-PROT) and the GenBank/EMBL/DDBJ Feature Table Definitions. It also provides the command line syntax for popular analysis applications such as Readseq and MEME/MAST, BLAST, ClustalW, and the EMBOSS suite, as well as tables of nucleotide, genetic, and amino acid codes.

UNIX in a Nutshell: System V Edition, 3rd Edition

By Arnold Robbins
3rd Edition September 1999
616 pages, ISBN 1-56592-427-4

The bestselling, most informative Unix reference book is now more complete and up-to-date. Not a scaled-down quick reference of common commands, *UNIX in a Nutshell* is a complete reference containing all commands and options, with descriptions and examples that put the commands in context. For all but the thorniest Unix problems, this one reference should be all you need. Covers System V Release 4 and Solaris 7.

Learning Perl, 3rd Edition

By Randal Schwartz & Tom Phoenix
3rd Edition July 2001
330 pages, ISBN 0-596-00132-0

Learning Perl is the quintessential tutorial for the Perl programming language. The third edition has not only been updated to Perl Version 5.6, but has also been rewritten from the ground up to reflect the needs of programmers learning Perl today. Other books may teach you to program in Perl, but this book will turn you into a Perl programmer.

Web Database Applications with PHP & MySQL

By Hugh E. Williams & David Lane
1st Edition March 2002
582 pages, ISBN 0-596-00041-3

This book offers both theoretical and practical guidance for creating web database applications. The detailed information on designing relational databases and the web application architectures that interact with them will be especially useful to readers who have worked with or built database-backed web sites before. The book implements a sample web application using PHP and MySQL on the Apache platform.

O'REILLY®

To order: *800-998-9938* • *order@oreilly.com* • *www.oreilly.com*
Online editions of most O'Reilly titles are available by subscription at *safari.oreilly.com*
Also available at most retail and online bookstores.

How to stay in touch with O'Reilly

1. Visit our award-winning web site

http://www.oreilly.com/

★ "Top 100 Sites on the Web"—PC Magazine
★ CIO Magazine's Web Business 50 Awards

Our web site contains a library of comprehensive product information (including book excerpts and tables of contents), downloadable software, background articles, interviews with technology leaders, links to relevant sites, book cover art, and more. File us in your bookmarks or favorites!

2. Join our email mailing lists

Sign up to get email announcements of new books and conferences, special offers, and O'Reilly Network technology newsletters at:

http://elists.oreilly.com

It's easy to customize your free elists subscription so you'll get exactly the O'Reilly news you want.

3. Get examples from our books

To find example files for a book, go to:

http://www.oreilly.com/catalog

select the book, and follow the "Examples" link.

4. Work with us

Check out our web site for current employment opportunities:

http://jobs.oreilly.com/

5. Register your book

Register your book at:
http://register.oreilly.com

6. Contact us

O'Reilly & Associates, Inc.
1005 Gravenstein Hwy North
Sebastopol, CA 95472 USA
TEL: 707-827-7000 or 800-998-9938
      (6am to 5pm PST)
FAX: 707-829-0104

order@oreilly.com
For answers to problems regarding your order or our products. To place a book order online visit:

http://www.oreilly.com/order_new/

catalog@oreilly.com
To request a copy of our latest catalog.

booktech@oreilly.com
For book content technical questions or corrections.

corporate@oreilly.com
For educational, library, government, and corporate sales.

proposals@oreilly.com
To submit new book proposals to our editors and product managers.

international@oreilly.com
For information about our international distributors or translation queries. For a list of our distributors outside of North America check out:

http://international.oreilly.com/distributors.html

adoption@oreilly.com
For information about academic use of O'Reilly books, visit:

http://academic.oreilly.com

O'REILLY®

To order: *800-998-9938* • *order@oreilly.com* • *www.oreilly.com*
Online editions of most O'Reilly titles are available by subscription at *safari.oreilly.com*
Also available at most retail and online bookstores.